THE
GREATEST

THE
GREATEST

The players, the moments, the matches

1993–2008

MALCOLM KNOX

hardie grant books
MELBOURNE · LONDON

To SPK – Round arm, round the wicket

This edition published in 2010

First published in 2009 by
Hardie Grant Books (Australia)
85 High Street
Prahran, Victoria 3181
www.hardiegrant.com.au

Hardie Grant Books (UK)
Second Floor, North Suite
Dudley House
Southampton Street
London WC2E 7HF
www.hardiegrant.co.uk

National Library of Australia Cataloguing-in-Publication Data:
Knox, Malcolm, 1966-
The greatest   / Malcolm Knox.
2nd ed.
9781740669986 (pbk.)
Cricket–Australia–History–20th century.
Cricket players–Australia.
796.3580994

Cover design by Dominic Hofstede/Hofstede Design
Text design by Design by Committee
Typesetting by Prowling Tiger Press
Photographs by Getty Images
Additional Photographs on page 17 courtesy of Channel Nine and Cricket Australia
Statistics by Ross Dundas
Printed and bound by C & C Offset Printing Co. Ltd. in China.

10 9 8 7 6 5 4 3 2 1

CONTENTS

INTRODUCTION

This is a book about cricket. Specifically, it is a book about cricket matches involving Australia since the early 1990s. Most are Test matches, but there have also been occasions in the past fifteen or sixteen years when a limited-overs international has risen out of the amnesic swamp to live in the open air of memory, as fresh as yesterday. There are no Twenty20 matches in this account. Like pulp fiction or Chinese food, the shorter forms of cricket can absorb and satisfy us while they have our attention, but afterwards tend to leave us hungry.

Six of the Test matches Australia played between 1993 and 2000 were included in *Wisden*'s 100 Matches of the Twentieth Century. Several more they played between 2000 and 2008 will no doubt be in *Wisden*'s 100 Matches of the Twenty-first. The Australian team, in this period, aroused many conflicting moods among cricket followers but indifference was not one of them. Whatever else they were, these Australian teams were constantly magnetic. In the physical sense if not always the aesthetic, they exerted an irresistible power of attraction.

Those who remember the 1980s will recall that Test cricket was quite often a dull spectacle. Scoring rates were low, bowling was attritional, and many Test matches did not just peter out to dull draws, but even petered out to dull wins and losses. By the early 1990s there was little to promise the new decade wouldn't provide more of the same. In fact, Australian Test cricket since Bradman's time was more often than not a drab affair, punctuated by periodic flurries of excitement – 1958 to 1961, 1972 to 1977 – that were all the more memorable for their rarity. If Australian cricket followers had been told in 1991 or 1992 that we were about to be gripped by the revival of leg-spin bowling, a new variety of dynamic seam, swing and pace, at times unthinkable acts of athleticism in the field, and scoring rates regularly exceeding four runs an over, we would not have believed it until we had seen it. If told that this new era would feature Test matches won with a six off the last ball, World Cup finals won with run rates of seven an over, series decided by margins of one run, two runs and one wicket, not to mention pot-boilers involving bookmakers, strikes, chucking, drugs, organised crime and 'sext' messages, we would have rolled our eyes and said we were not interested in the exaggerations of escapist fiction.

The timespan of this book, 1993 to 2008, has been chosen not because fifteen years is a nice round figure. The primary reason is that Australia did not lose a Test series at home between 1993, when the West Indies won the last of its five straight undefeated series in Australia (Australia managed a draw in 1981–82), and 2008, when Graeme Smith's South Africans sealed a two-Test lead at the Melbourne Cricket Ground. During that time, Australia was seldom beaten overseas either: 1994 in Pakistan; 1996, 1998 and 2001 in India; 1999 in Sri Lanka and 2005 in England were the only lost series. It is some record.

The secondary reason to choose 1993 and 2008 as bookends is that those years coincided more or less with the Test careers of the two most influential players of the era. Shane Warne played for Australia from January 1992 to January 2007, Glenn McGrath from December 1993 to April 2007. 'Coincidence' is of course the wrong word. The Australian golden era *was* Warne and McGrath. Their personalities, and those of a host of other players both major and minor, Australian and foreign, combine with the contests on the field to provide the strokes of colour between the hard outlines of events themselves.

In Gideon Haigh's view, trying to pick and weigh up Great Test Matches is 'the ultimate cricket fogey topic'. This book, then, is for, and possibly by, the ultimate cricket fogey. This is nothing to be embarrassed about. We have increasing cause to remember, and talk about, and reconstruct the drama of, great Test matches. When I was a touring cricket newspaper journalist in the 1990s, print media had long renounced the first task of traditional journalism. We were no longer writing the first draft of history. We were writing about injuries, forecasts, threats, scandals and politics. Why? The orthodox belief was that television and radio were doing such a good job of bringing audiences the drama of the game itself that there was little space left for the printed word to revisit what had happened on the field. We had to do more. Instead of recounting what had happened in the game, we had to give readers 'extra value' on top of what they already knew of innings, scores, wickets and results. So the accent for print media became 'throwing forward', or producing stories that would be relevant the next day. This was how an interview in which Mark Taylor or Shane Warne said they were looking forward to pushing home their psychological edge over an opponent came to take precedence over the hundred runs Taylor may have scored, or the six wickets Warne had taken, that very day. This was how the worries about Glenn McGrath's groin or Steve Waugh's hamstring affecting their availability for the next Test match pushed aside a written prose record of what they had done in the present one.

I always found this an unnecessary evil of the coverage. Instead of giving more, I sensed that paradoxically we were giving less. By writing for tomorrow and skating over today, we were actually increasing the ephemerality of what we were providing. Nothing obsolesces as quickly as a forecast. Once the game has started, who cares whether Warne had been in doubt with a stiff bowling finger? I was far from the most skilful practitioner of modern sports journalism, because what happened off the field never interested me half as much as what happened on it. Speculating on tomorrow's play never held my interest half as much as ruminating on today's.

As a child, I had loved nothing more after going out to the SCG to watch a day's international cricket than to stay up late that night to watch the highlights replayed on television. The next morning, I lunged for the newspaper reports. If they rehashed everything

I had seen, all the better. Just because I had lived through it once didn't mean I didn't want to live through it again. And again.

The selection of matches in this book is not a trainspotting exercise for us fogeys to dispute over our thumbed copies of *Wisden*. Some of Australia's great Test matches receive only passing mention here: against Sri Lanka in Galle in 2004, against Bangladesh in Fatullah in 2006, against New Zealand in Wellington in 2005, for instance. Conversely, there are some matches recounted in detail, such as that against England at The Oval in 2001, which were not among the great Tests in themselves. Rather, the guiding principle is to serve the dramatic needs of the story of Australian cricket through those years. The Test matches included in this book are the plot points around which that story pivots. Many of them, inevitably, also happen to be the greatest cricket contests of the time.

Richie Benaud has said that cricket is the most controversial game, but that doesn't mean cricket's controversies are the most important thing about it. Controversies are a by-product of our interest in the great game itself. Benaud might as well have said that cricket is the most fascinating game, and being so fascinating, it cannot help being controversial as well. The controversies cannot be swept to one side, because cricket is not played in a vacuum. Indeed, the boyish wish that it were, that the game is the only thing that matters, has generated a tension that has proven central to the cricketing drama. For instance, the ferocious desire to force the world outside cricket to the periphery of consciousness, a desire that drove the greatest Australian batsman and bowler of the era, inflamed the off-field controversies out of proportion and then fed back into the epic qualities of what occurred on the field. Allan Border and Shane Warne only wanted to play cricket. By wishing this so fervently, they set themselves up as magnets for controversy. Mark Taylor and, in his captaincy years, Steve Waugh, both welcomed the outside world and understood how it interlocked with cricket; as a result, they became leaders with skins of Teflon.

The view expressed in this book is that while the controversies are unignorable, they are subplot rather than main plot. They add texture, but are not the foreground narrative. The best and most memorable thing about cricket is cricket.

So, the aim of this book is to do for readers what those long-ago late-night replays did for me: immerse us back into the on-field dramas of the great modern era of Australian cricket by selecting and telling the stories of the most influential matches. We might know how these games ended up, or we might have forgotten. Does it really matter? Re-reading a favourite book can be equally riveting even though, and in some ways because, we know what is going to happen. There is an exquisite pleasure in suspending disbelief once again, even to wonder, as I once did, if *this time* it will end differently.

Asked what he missed most when he was under suspension for his positive drug test in 2003–04, Shane Warne said that he missed waking up each day to the feeling of not knowing what was going to happen on the field. 'You don't know whether you're going to knock them over or you're going to get slogged, whether you'll have a bad day or take a couple of screamers.' It is that spirit of the unknown that this book hopes to recapture: those clammy-handed moments of the cricketing past when we could not bear to look away.

THE WORRY BALL

Adelaide, January 1993

TO BORDER, HIS LAST THIRTEEN YEARS COULD HAVE SEEMED LIKE AN ENDLESS NIGHTMARE OF CARIBBEAN GIANTS HURLING BALLS AT HIS RIBS, AT HIS THROAT, AT HIS FACE. GENERATION AFTER GENERATION OF STORMS ROLLING IN LIKE A PERMANENT CYCLONE SEASON.

After all he had done, it came down to this: he was a spectator, sitting on his seat in the changing room, with no more influence than anyone else in the stands or in front of their television. Powerless. He tossed a cricket ball from hand to hand. Nothing he could do but watch, and feel his nerves burn, and pound that ball from hand to hand. Had he been Greek, he might have used beads; Catholic, a crucifix. Instead, Allan Border was a cricketer, and what he had was his worry ball.

It could seem that he had been worrying as long as he'd been playing. When he entered Test cricket, he came into the remnants of a team physically and mentally battered in the Caribbean in 1978. He'd lost to the West Indians in Australia in 1979–80, snared a drawn series in 1981–82. Lost to them away in 1984, left in the lurch by Chappell, Lillee and Marsh. Lost to them, drowned in Kim Hughes's tears, at home in 1984–85. Lost to them at home again in 1988–89. Marched onto their patch with high hopes in 1991, the last chance to beat a jaded Richards, Greenidge and Marshall – and lost again.

Never won once. Nobody else had beaten them either, barring a New Zealand fluke in 1980, but that was no consolation.

WIN THIS MATCH, THIS ONE MATCH, AND FIFTEEN YEARS OF LOSS COULD BE WIPED OUT

Border was *Australian*, and he had never beaten them. Even in the home one-day series over all those years, Australia had never beaten the West Indies in the finals. For everything else Border had achieved in cricket, he had done nothing but lose to these blokes.

Until now. Australia was one-up thanks to two draws and a Melbourne win spun from the right hand of the new boy. Two Tests to go. Win *this* match, this one match, and thirteen years of loss could be wiped out. Just this once: a win. Please.

Adelaide had played out like one of those matches both teams were too desperate to take, each freezing up when they held the advantage. Or, put another way: neither would let the other take it. In the first innings, Merv Hughes got five wickets and Australia bowled out the West Indies for 252. But they couldn't press it home. Border's 19 runs, eked out in an hour and a quarter, typified Australia's limping 213. Hughes, whose gift with bat and ball was always magnified by the when and the where of his contributions, whacked 43 to give the score some ballast.

But the West Indies couldn't grasp the initiative either, losing 6/22 and being dismissed for 146. The destroyers: Craig

LEFT: Merv Hughes, one of the most appealing characters of the Border years.

THE GREATEST 9

McDermott with three at the top of the innings, and Tim May, re-called to the team after four years, on his home pitch, tweezering out five batsmen in seven overs. May's previous Test match had been on this field against this opponent in 1989, when he'd taken two wickets in thirty-nine overs.

So: 186 to get in the last innings. One innings, one small target, and a poultice for thirteen years of Allan Border's pain.

But on the fourth day, it went wrong. Boon, Taylor, the Waughs, Border himself hadn't been able to do it. A very young debutant, Justin Langer, had almost died for his runs. Langer had only come into the team when Bob Simpson had accidentally poked Damien Martyn in the eye at training. Martyn was a prodigy; Langer, his state and junior teammate, all thick skin and thick edges. Before he'd scored a Test run, even before he'd laid bat on ball, Langer had got one from Ian Bishop that would have killed him but for his helmet. He made twenty in the first innings and was now on his way to fifty. But at the other end, Healy went, Hughes went, Warne went. Langer put on forty-two with May, but then Langer went too for 54, fine-edging a pull shot off Bishop. At 9/144, it seemed, they were all gone.

All except May and McDermott. As batsmen.

Doing the damage were the usual suspects, the merchants of battery and assault. Two wickets had gone to Courtney Walsh, who had seemed nothing more than a useful number three bowler for many years, yet now, now that they needed him, he had gone to another level and become one of the best. He jogged in, year after year, opened his chest and flung the ball from wide on the crease: there was nothing much to him except accuracy, brains and a light-ness of step that resisted injury. And another four wickets had gone to Curtly Ambrose, who'd looked unpleasant from the moment he emerged out of Antigua in 1988, a frowning giant, twitching his shoulders, impatient and arrogant and mercilessly accurate. They said basketball was stealing the best young Caribbeans, but every batsman who faced him regretted the day the game of hoop and key hadn't stolen Ambrose.

Australia had owned this summer, until Dean Jones got Ambrose angry a week before the Adelaide Test. Border's men would have won the First Test but for some umpiring decisions that saved a draw for the West Indies. The new kid had taken 7/52 in Melbourne, where Mark Waugh had backed off to square leg and helped Ambrose's bouncers on their way over slips for a one-of-a-kind century. A big win. Rain had ruined Sydney. Then Australia dominated the one-dayers – until in the first final in Sydney, Jones did one of those things that embodied his whole career: a little victory for bravado, a grand failure for commonsense.

Australia had been chasing a modest West Indian total. Jones, at number three in the one-dayers but still churlish about his omission from Test cricket, was in a pugnacious mood. Ambrose was rumbling in from the Randwick end. Jones ran down the wicket and smashed him back over his six-foot-eight head, one bounce into the straight boundary. Total courage and skill, the type of feat only Jones could pull off. And then, the stupidity to match: Jones complained to the umpires about Ambrose's wrist bands distracting him. Ambrose couldn't believe it. He flew off the handle, took five wickets that night and another three in the second final. One minute Australia were in command; the next they were out in straight sets. Border had lost a finals series to the West Indies. Again.

Still simmering, Ambrose had come to Adelaide and taken ten wickets.

Border gripped the worry ball, just an old practice ball from the kit bag, pounded it, watched McDermott and May. It's impossible to know what he was thinking – or even if he was thinking, as opposed to stewing – but at some level lurked those great tumours of pent-up frustration. Lost, lost, lost, lost, lost: thirteen years of losing.

And yet, somehow, McDermott and May were still there. Word got about. Locals were rushing from the city to the Adelaide Oval. Sections of the crowd were striking up *Waltzing Matilda* in anticipation of a great Australian theft. It was a murky summer afternoon, but the last pair were still in the middle and Border was still sitting here with the worry ball, only pausing from pounding it hand to hand to shine it on his pants. Now he wasn't daring to change his seat. Nor was anyone else. In front of Border was twelfth man Tony Dodemaide. Beside Dodemaide, Langer. Next to Border, Stephen

Waugh. In front of Waugh, Healy. Nobody move! At Lord's in the 1989 Ashes series, Border had been trapped in the shower while Steve Waugh and Boon set up the match-winning partnership – for an hour, Border had stayed under the nozzle, scared to tempt fate.

The target seemed to erode by itself, like the fourth-day pitch. It almost seemed a cruel joke that Border's fate lay in the hands of May and McDermott as batsmen.

May: class clown in a side-of-the-mouth kind of way, a drollness in his heart, as if all of this didn't mean so much in the greater scheme of things. Today was his thirty-first birthday. As a batsman, against this kind of bowling, May's pinched-up, nervous stance betrayed the battle between techniques learnt from a textbook and the human instinct to run for the hills. His Test average to that point was 13; he'd scored a total of 96 runs. You could never in a million years imagine him hitting Ambrose past mid-on. But he didn't need to. May's mainstay was the tuck behind square leg, and that's where the West Indians were bowling it, into his ribs, and, as they grew tired, onto his hip.

And McDermott. What could you say about Craig McDermott? He would take 291 Test wickets, more than Jeff Thomson, more than Merv Hughes, more than Richie Benaud, many more than Ray Lindwall and Keith Miller and Garth McKenzie and Jack Gregory, more, when he retired, than any Australian except Dennis Lillee, and yet Craig McDermott had somehow risen without trace. He was probably the strongest athlete to have played cricket for Australia, and yet in a way, that's what he was: an athlete, a body. He was said to regularly consume a whole roast chicken and three giant chocolate milkshakes per lunch break. He had the flowing run-up and side-on action, he had the outswinger, he had the stamina, he had the essential chip on the shoulder, but in some indefinable way he didn't have the last thing, the X-factor of a Test match winner against the highest quality. Hughes, an

TOO MUCH PUNISHMENT AND EVEN THE BEST OF THEM GOT PUNCH-DRUNK

inferior bowler in most ways, had it. The new kid, the leg-spinner, certainly had it. McDermott had it against England, or against India or New Zealand, but not against these blokes.

As for his batting, McDermott was a travesty of his potential. For most of his career he had looked like he should have been better than he was, almost all-rounder quality, but then he'd been hit in the face by the West Indians and his back foot had begun to twitch towards backward square. Some uncontrollable firing mechanism, or yip, had taken hold of his feet. He could barely bat now, against these blokes anyway. Too much punishment and even the best of them got punch-drunk. Except for Border; but with a bat in his hands McDermott was no Allan Border.

Yet today was different. The end of another over came up, and May and McDermott were improbably there, a few runs closer. A nick through slips for three, a tuck off the hip for a single. This is the thing about cricket: the match is always, ultimately, in the hands of the batsmen. The bowlers can apply their skill and hope, but they cannot control destiny in the way a batsman can. If only Australia had a real batsman at the crease.

The real batsmen, though, hadn't been able to finish the job. On a pitch separating into baked plates of bone-dry turf, wobbly around their crusty edges, Mark Waugh was the only one who had looked as if he could handle it. With his eye and his technique, he'd got to 26 in apparent comfort before nicking Walsh to slip. Little Langer, nine-tenths heart and stomach, unscarred by the past, battled on to 54. Border himself: a throat ball from Ambrose, a pop-up to short leg.

To Border, his last thirteen years could have seemed like an endless nightmare of Caribbean behemoths hurling balls at his ribs, at his throat, at his face. He'd survived Roberts and Holding, only to have Garner, Clarke and Croft. He'd survived them, only to have Marshall and Patterson. He'd survived them, only to have Ambrose, Walsh and Bishop. They never let up. Generation after generation of storms rolling in like a permanent cyclone season.

For all those thirteen years, he was the one who had stood up to them. In the Caribbean in 1984, the worst series, the most dismal of the drubbings, he had scored 521 runs at 74. In Trinidad, he made 100 and 98. Both not out. How many of those runs would he have traded for another two today? He'd taken all the punishment, year after year, and he'd never flinched. He'd got out of the way of the nastiest and punched the hittable ones through mid-wicket or point. He was nature's bantamweight counter-puncher, crouched, nimble, ducking, ducking, ducking, then – smack! His career Test average in the Caribbean was 53. The West Indians thought he was the best. They would say he was, in fact, the best Australian to hold a bat after Bradman. And they were right.

But not today. Today it was down to McDermott and May.

Of all people.

He sat there and pounded the worry ball and refused to move. He would estimate he threw it from hand to hand 60,000 times in the eighty-eight minutes May and McDermott batted together. May had trodden on his right thumb while fielding – a very Tim May kind of injury – and it was further pulped by the balls spitting up and squashing it against the bat handle. Bishop, who'd got Warne and Langer, grew tired. May kept tucking him away. Kenny Benjamin tired. Back to Walsh and Ambrose, but they looked tired too. Richie Richardson was trying to stay cool under his umbrella-sized maroon hat, but Border allowed himself a moment of grim hope, to see a West Indies captain moving his fieldsmen around not to set up the kill but to stop the leaking.

And the target came down: ten, nine, eight. May kept playing straight. Seven, six, five. McDermott scooped an off-drive off Ambrose, and Richardson couldn't hang onto it at wide mid-off. Three runs. *Please!*

It was down to Walsh. Walsh against McDermott. Walsh, his armament an injury-proof body, a Jamaican poor boy's spirit and a bouncer with a suspect kink, the second-stringer who would take 519 Test wickets and retire with the world record. McDermott, who ran like Bernborough but couldn't quite finish his races. Walsh, running in. A smiler, a grimacer, one of those fellows whose face always looked like it was about to break into a laugh. McDermott's, into a sneer. Walsh, nothing much to look at as a bowler, but the template for a Narromine stringbean who at that moment was living in a caravan and hoping for a scholarship to the Academy. Keep it simple, be accurate, just short of a length, don't give the batsman any free runs. Walsh, not McDermott, would be the model for the Australian fast bowler who would change things for good.

After Border.

Walsh's nineteenth over, the seventy-ninth of the innings, starts with Australia needing three to win, two to tie. Border has played in a tied Test before, at Madras in 1986. As everyone on that ground learnt, to the bowling side a tie feels like a win, to the batting side a loss. The game is in the batsmen's hands.

Off the third ball, May glances one between Desmond Haynes at short square and Ambrose at fine-leg. Two to tie? The batsmen settle for one.

Two runs to win, the last hope. Ball four: Walsh in to McDermott. A push to mid-off, the run turned down. Ball five: a loose one on the pads. McDermott turns it away, middle of the bat – yes! No. The ball takes a freakish right-angled spin out of the rough and smacks Haynes in the shin pad. No run. In the changing room, the Australian team goes up – then down.

Richardson notices Walsh looking at him as if to say something. Richardson wanders over, but Walsh changes his mind: keeps his thoughts to himself. Ball six is a bouncer that follows McDermott in from the off side. McDermott's right foot doesn't back away. It doesn't move at all, aside from a little hop. He stays in line as the ball leaps at his face. Pure animal reflexes: even with a helmet on, a human cannot help but protect his face. His hands and bat come up, he twists away to leave the ball, but the ball won't leave him. Like a heat-seeking missile it keeps following him in from Walsh's wide delivery angle.

McDermott grunts, the ball deflects, keeper Junior Murray catches it, they're all up. What did it hit? Peak of the helmet? Glove? Handle? Glove when it had come off the handle? Doesn't matter: Darrell Hair's finger points to heaven.

Reactions stagger through time. The human instinct is to linger in the immediate past, to refuse to acknowledge the present. To live in hope. Even as Walsh has taken off like a water bird towards third man, ten other West Indians chasing him, even as

ABOVE: Walsh moving to a higher plane.

McDermott trudges without protest, there is no immediate movement around Border. Steve Waugh's expression hasn't changed. Healy hasn't moved. The mouth of Ian McDonald, the team manager, opens silently.

The first to move is Border. Thirteen years of losing to these blokes. Thirteen years of losing, a whole lifetime of losing, all go into that wretched old red ball he's been gripping.

He's always had a good arm. A great left arm, a baseballer's flat bullet throw.

He turns his back on the field and down he flings his worry ball, into the wooden floor. It ricochets into the wall, the ceiling. Thirteen long years into that throw. None of the Australian team will say a word for the next fifteen minutes. Not a word. The brave or unwary will catch Border's eye, and shy away from the empty devastation in there. He will ask McDermott if the decision was all right. Then both will sit on their own. Border will confront a press conference. McDermott won't, instead sending a message: 'Tell them I didn't back away.' He didn't. If he had backed away, been a little less courageous, the ball wouldn't have hit him.

One run: this day has been chosen for the closest winning margin in 1210 matches and 116 years of Test cricket.

Three days later, Ambrose – still angry! – will take 7/1 in Perth, and that's that. Border will make his first pair in Tests. Another series lost.

Border's reputation as a batsman will, in his retirement, grow and grow. The more we think about Border, the greater he is, because of all the thousands of runs he scored in losing teams. If batting had a degree of difficulty, it would rise exponentially in situations where the team is behind in the match. The Australian greats – Bradman, Trumper, the Chappells, the Waughs, Morris, Simpson, Lawry, Ponting, Harvey, Ponsford – all played in teams that mostly won. None played under the pressure of chasing and losing, defending and failing, as much as Allan Robert Border. He is a one of a kind. But there is no reconciliation for him, this day. Those blokes have beaten him again.

26 January 1993: Australia Day.

OPPOSITE: Border always had a good arm.

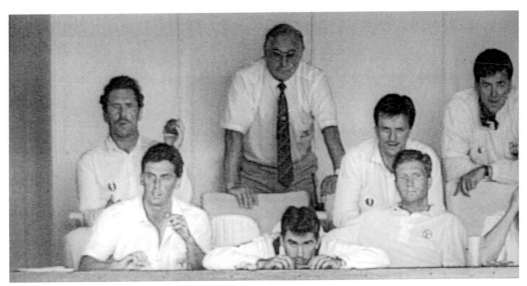

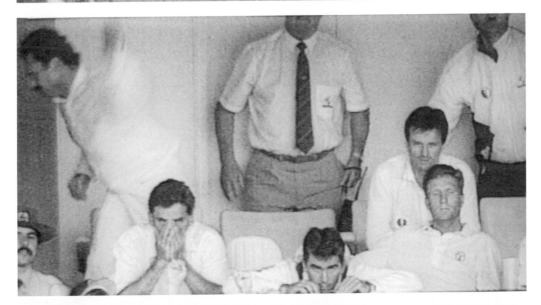

'BLOODY HELL, WARNEY, WHAT HAPPENED?'

Manchester, June 1993

HE MIGHT HAVE LOOKED LIKE A MIDDLESEX BRICKLAYER, OR A SEA CAPTAIN WHO PLAYED RUGBY (IN THE FORWARDS), BUT HE HAD THE QUICKNESS IN HIS FEET AND THE TOUCH IN HIS HANDS OF AN INDIAN GRANDMASTER.

T he other worry ball – the ball that triggered an English neurosis that lasted fourteen years – was called the 'ball of the century', but it wasn't unique, not as a piece of bowling. Shane Warne bowled hundreds of balls as good as this in Test cricket. Sometimes it resulted in a nick, a catch, a dropped chance. Sometimes the batsman came forward far enough to cover it. Sometimes it hit the pad and failed to yield a leg-before-wicket because it pitched too wide and spun too far. Sometimes it did what it did to Gatting, plucking the bail from the off-stump as precisely as William Tell shooting an apple from his son's head.

The ball was Warne's stock ball: the plain leg-spinner. Plain? All it did was start up the pitch in an innocent loop, then veer radically to the leg side and pitch in the area, around leg stump but beyond the batsman's leading left shoulder, known as the 'blind spot'. Then, all it did was grip the pitch and turn away sharply to the off side. Simple! If all went to plan, the batsman would adjust to the curvature in flight and close the face of his bat to turn the ball off his legs; because he was not presenting the bat's full face to the ball, it had more potential to beat his outside edge. If all went to plan, the ball would hit the off stump.

BUT THE BALL ITSELF – AS ALWAYS WITH WARNE – WAS ONLY ONE PART OF THE MAGIC

This is the textbook leg-spinner, and Warne was not the first to bowl it, even if he often seemed like he was. But the ball itself – as always with Warne – was only one part of the magic.

After that gruesome, unforgettable Australia Day in Adelaide, the Australians had rebounded with a fair result in New Zealand in the autumn of 1993, squaring the Test series and winning the one-dayers. Warne, entering his second year of Test cricket, topped the wicket-taking with 17 in the three Tests, winning supporters with his 1.6-run-an-over economy rate, so unusual for a wrist spinner. But he never ripped through the New Zealanders the way he had through the West Indies in Melbourne.

Two footnotes to the New Zealand tour: in the First Test, at Lancaster Park, Christchurch, Border passed Sunil Gavaskar's world record of 10,122 runs. He did it off the anonymous spin of Dipak Patel, miscuing a sweep shot and nearly being caught in front of a few thousand polite Cantabrians. His batting partner, Healy, didn't know Border had passed the mark. 'Why are they all clapping?' he asked. The captain celebrated with a slice of ice-cream cake. Pure Border.

LEFT: The perfect combination of technique and a sense of theatre.

Footnote two: in the Third Test, at Auckland, when they needed five wickets for less than thirty-three runs on the last day to win, the Australians made a pact to wear their baggy green caps. The tradition would be associated with later captains, who turned it into a regular ritual. But Border was the one who revived the practice, which had been initiated by Bradman in 1948. Usually these rituals grow out of superstition, but there was nothing lucky about the caps that morning in Auckland. Australia didn't take a wicket and New Zealand won easily.

The Australian squad to tour England in the northern summer was an appealing blend of three generations: the old guard represented by Border, Boon, Hughes, May, Steve Waugh, Tim Zoehrer and McDermott; the next wave of Mark Waugh, Healy, Taylor and Paul Reiffel; and the youngbloods Martyn, Brendon Julian, Wayne Holdsworth, Warne and two new openers, Michael Slater and Matthew Hayden, batting off to partner Taylor. Having just played their second Sheffield Shield seasons, Slater and Hayden were part of a rising generation that also included Adam Gilchrist, Justin Langer, Greg Blewett, Michael Kasprowicz, Stuart Law, Michael Bevan and a pubescent Tasmanian named Ricky Ponting.

The trauma inflicted by the West Indies was quarantined to matches against that opponent. Since 1989, Border's team had beaten all others, and came to England full of vim. Warne's start to the tour was typically quiet. Against the England Amateur XI, now aged twenty-three (his lucky number), he nabbed only numbers X and XI. Against the Duchess of Norfolk's men, he took no wickets. Against Worcestershire he took 1/122. Graeme Hick smashed him into the crowd six times, correctly picking the standard small-spinning leg-breaks Border had asked Warne to restrict himself to bowling. He took five against Somerset but was hidden away for the one-day internationals, which Australia won 3-0. He got among the wickets against Surrey and Leicestershire, but it's fair to say that his selection for the First Test aroused interest of a mildness that would never be repeated.

For the series which would start at Old Trafford, England's curators took some heavy hints to prepare turning wickets, which might negate Australia's strong suit of McDermott and Hughes.

Accordingly, on the first day of the series, spin did the damage – in the predictable-looking off breaks of the Scotsman Peter Such, who had the best day of his eleven-Test career. Australia was strong at the top, Taylor making a century and the vivacious Slater, chosen ahead of Hayden, notching 58 on debut. Steve Waugh likened Slater to 'a balloon that had just escaped before being tied up'. Better imagery for the opening batsman would never be found. But from 0/128 they folded for 289, having aimed for a decisive opening knockout but landing only a jab before taking a solid counter-blow.

England were well into the second day, cruising at 1/80, when Border gave Warne the ball. Mike Atherton had fallen to Hughes for a struggling 19; the buccaneering, huge-appetited Victorian pantomime villain took special glee in dismissing the correct university graduate, every caricature of Australian and English sport contained in one head-to-head.

Now Graham Gooch, the indomitable captain, was batting with his predecessor, Mike Gatting. Gatting had scored four runs in eleven balls.

Gatting was a great example of the cruel law of reputation: it takes a lifetime to build and just one act to destroy. Gatting was a much better batsman than his Test average of 35 suggests: strong, straight and a delightful surprise against spin. He might have looked like a Middlesex bricklayer, or a sea captain who played rugby (in the forwards), but he had the quickness in his feet and the touch in his hands of an Indian grandmaster. He had been chosen for England as a twenty-year-old, a rare accolade attesting to his natural talent, and in 1986–87 was captain of the team that Martin Johnson famously said had only three problems – couldn't bat, couldn't bowl, couldn't field – yet came to Australia and won the Ashes.

Actually, it took more than one act to diminish Gatting's reputation. He'd played the silliest of shots – not the reverse sweep per se, but the reverse sweep that got him out – in the 1987 World Cup final. As captain he took the blame for England's loss. Then he forgot who he was and openly abused the Pakistani umpire Shakoor Rana on England's 1988 tour, doing what every cricketer would have liked to do but which a captain of England was not permitted. Then he was involved in the English tabloid media's favourite noun – a romp – with a barmaid, was stripped of the captaincy, and stormed off with a rebel team to South Africa.

Each of those disasters was in some way of Gatting's own making. The act that would guarantee his place in cricket folklore, on 4 June 1993, wasn't. Gatting did nothing wrong. Warne bowled the ball, and Gatting was merely the wrong person in the wrong place at the wrong time.

Border had told Warne to warm up an over before. Warne didn't do much: swung the shoulders, loosened the fingers. Nothing complicated. He thought most non-cricket exercise was pointless. Later in his career, he would praise Adam Gilchrist for making a century after arriving late at the ground because it 'proves warm-ups are a waste of time'.

Warne aimed to bowl a leg-break with plenty of spin. 'For some reason,' he would write with uncharacteristic understatement, 'I've always been able to land my first few balls fairly accurately.'

The ball: the drive with the back leg, the rip from the right wrist, the snap in the fingers, the float up the pitch, the late, late curve into Gatting's blind spot; the grip and hum of it, seam biting the pitch, ball turning away. Gatting watching it all like a hawk, a presentable forward defence from one of the accredited guildsmen, yet he was still unable to get anywhere near it. One of the reasons the moment was so unforgettable was Gatting's face. Ian Botham said Gatting hadn't shown such wide-eyed horror since the day someone had stolen his lunch, but that wasn't quite it. Very often batsmen put on a show of shock and puzzlement when they get out; it helps their self-respect if the world shares their belief that they were beaten by an unplayable ball. But Gatting's wide eyes, his round mouth, were spontaneous. He covered them with a frown, but too late. He'd looked like a poker player who'd peeked at a handful of rubbish he'd been dealt, and been momentarily unable to stay in countenance. Nonplussed, he stared at the point on the wicket where the ball had pitched. He looked to the square-leg umpire, Ken Palmer, for confirmation that Ian Healy hadn't bumped the stumps by mistake. And then he turned around and looked at his barely disturbed castle. The leg bail was still there. The dismissal was, aside from everything else, neat.

Healy's arms went up and around in twin windmills ending with a clap. Beaming, he was on the leg-side of the stumps – a sign that he had been deceived as thoroughly as Gatting. Warne smiled, right arm in the air. No need for Healy to give him a 'Bowled, Warney'. If he'd been offered retirement at that moment, Warne might have been tempted to take it: life had to be all down-hill from there. Compared with the theatrics of big dismissals later in his career, Warne took this one in his stride. He looked, simply, happy. He wasn't putting on a show. He hadn't become *Shane Warne* yet. But he would now.

Between Shane Warne and the English cricket public, that ball was like eyes meeting across a crowded room. England would always love him more forgivingly than Australia, and the love was mutual. He would come to prefer living there. Everything about him that embarrassed his countrymen would endear him to the English. Not only was he a genius on the field, but off the field he was everything England wanted an Australian to be.

That ball was only the beginning. Just one perfect leg-spinner in a lifetime of perfect leg-spinners; but Warne happened to do it with his first Test delivery in England. He did it to Gatting, the number three, the best player of spin they could muster up. With the way he did it, the timing and the panache, he was waving a wand and cast-ing a magic spell. In his opponents' minds, and more crucially in his own, Warne would with this ball transform himself into a man who could turn the course of history, who could control events with his will. This, every bit as much as the ability to drift the ball to leg and turn it away out of the blind spot, would be his weapon.

Gatting would approach Warne after that day's play on 4 June. He said, 'Bloody hell, Warney, what happened?'

Warne didn't know. He still felt that a ball in his next over, when he out-thought Robin Smith and pulled off a specific plan to get the batsman nicking to slip, was better than the Gatting ball. 'Sorry mate. Bad luck.'

And then they had a laugh, as if both had been witnesses to some marvel in a Las Vegas showroom.

That 1993 Ashes tour would be one of the happiest for Border, notwithstanding some grumpy moments in the nervous lead-up to the First Test. He was fined for smashing his stumps after getting out against Middlesex, and a microphone picked up his on-field argument with McDermott during the Somerset game. Victory, life's own Pine-O-Cleen, would wash all that away.

In 1989 Border had climbed the mountain and won the urn back, in 1990–91 he'd kept it, but 1993, after the hell of Adelaide and the West Indies, was pure gravy.

IT WAS THE GREATEST DRUBBING OF ALL THE AUSTRALIA–ENGLAND DRUBBINGS

Australia dismissed England for 210 on that second day at Old Trafford, Warne taking another two wickets after Gatting and Smith. Healy would score his first Test century in Australia's 5/432, and then Warne and his drinking buddy Hughes would rumble the English in the second innings, the main threat defused when Gooch, on 133, couldn't help punching a deflected ball away from his stumps, and was out handled ball. Hughes was ropable when he learnt that he wouldn't be credited with the wicket.

At the end of the fourth day, Hughes gave Gatting his second memorable dismissal of the game. When Warne had bowled his 'ball of the century' in the first innings, Hughes, at backward square leg, hadn't seen how much it turned. When he asked Healy what the ball had done and why Gatting was taking so long to leave, Healy said, 'Pitched off, hit off.' Only after Hughes saw the replay did he go back to Healy, who said, 'Pitched off the wicket, hit off stump.'

In their second innings, England were 1/133 when Hughes started the last over of the fourth day. Gatting, on 23, kept out the first five balls and took strike for the last, certain that Hughes would bowl a bouncer. Hughes was thought to be predictable and none too bright. As Gatting lingered on his heels, Hughes speared a full ball into his pads. Gatting jammed down late and was bowled. More Victorian theatre.

Australia would have the series wrapped up by the Fourth Test; in a thirty-match tour they only lost two county games and the dead Sixth Test. It was the greatest drubbing of all the Australia–England drubbings between 1989 and 2005. At Lord's in the Second Test, Australia lost only four wickets and won by an innings, despite only being able to use three bowlers, McDermott having succumbed to complications from a twisted bowel. It didn't matter. In the series, England used twenty-four players, many of whose careers were either ended or beaten-up by that series: names like Emburey, McCague, Lathwell, Foster, Maynard, Watkin and Ilott would see little or no Test cricket after the 1993 Australians had done with them. Not to mention Mike Gatting, traumatised and dropped after the Second Test. Gooch's four-year captaincy wouldn't survive the series. Atherton would become the eighth England captain in the period during which Border was Australia's only one. Gooch would, however, bat on until he was forty-one and become the highest run scorer from any country in all forms of top-line cricket, without ever giving much sign that he enjoyed a minute of it.

Victory can be as exhausting as defeat, and that series also effectively finished off Merv Hughes. In McDermott's absence, Hughes carried the new-ball attack and bowled 296 overs, more than anyone on either team apart from Warne, who bowled more overs than anyone in any Ashes series to that point. Hughes took 31 wickets, all of them important. For someone who had been a laughing stock when he'd started in Test cricket, he had turned into a match-winning force, his uncouthness and sledging usually mitigated by its grotesque exaggerations. He was credited with the 'mental disintegration' of Graeme Hick, the Zimbabwean prodigy, during the first two Tests of the series. Although Hick said Hughes's sledging only consisted of three or four words, which Hick was easily able to memorise, observers couldn't help but note Hick's timidity when Hughes came on, and even Border, who knew Hick well from playing with him for Queensland, would murmur from close in, 'Make runs now Hicky, second new ball is soon and you know who'll be coming back ...'

For everyone except, perhaps, batsmen, Hughes added great life to the game. But for every Test day of the 1993 tour, he was suffering such pain in his left knee that he popped painkilling Digesic pills before and during play. An operation after the tour would show that he had no cartilage left in the knee, just a dead piece of bone the size of a fifty-cent piece; over a twelve-week period he had bowled nearly 1800 balls, each time thundering down on a knee reduced to bone grinding against bone. His career would last another year, but in terminal decline.

At the end of his fourth and last Ashes tour, Border had many causes for satisfaction. Australia only used thirteen players, and would have used twelve if McDermott hadn't gone home. Slater had come into the team and blazed like the kid too good for his age group, which was what he had always been. Everyone had piled up runs, including Border himself who'd made his first double-century since 1987. Boon, who had never scored a hundred in England, scored three in the series. The Australians seemed to make 600 each time they batted and six of them scored more than 400 runs for the series. Then Warne and Hughes mopped up, aided and abetted by Reiffel and May. Warne took 34 wickets, more than any other Australian spinner in an Ashes series except for Arthur Mailey three-quarters of a century earlier.

It was no consolation for what had happened in Adelaide, and the West Indies remained the untied loose end of Border's cricket life, but there was something about his character that would never sit squarely with the titles 'world champion' or 'all-conquering'. As the circumstances of his retirement would show, Border was too much the common man to stage-manage his moves or finesse his image. Warne, who came into the team when it was Border's, would openly idolise his first captain. Despite their success, the captains who followed would never quite match Border in Warne's eyes. That idol worship says a lot about Warne's loyalty, and his nostalgia for those uninhibited first years. It also says something about the curious attraction of opposites.

OPPOSITE: By 1993 the strain on his knee was showing on Hughes's face.

28 MALCOLM KNOX

THE CONTENDERS

Sydney, January 1994
Johannesburg, February 1994

TWENTY-ONE YEARS OF EXCLUSION HAD BEEN LIFTED IN 1991, AND SOUTH AFRICAN CRICKET HAD COME BACK TO THE WORLD LIKE A MYSTERY GIFT. WHO KNEW WHAT LAY INSIDE THE WRAPPING?

By the end of 1993, Border's team had all but one of their known opponents well covered. England was half-dead and rotting in the sun, sustained only by the mirages of its win in another dead rubber at The Oval. New Zealand, who would need to wait for another Hadlee or Martin Crowe, was dealt with in Australia in late 1993. Pakistan and India had all the talent in the world but their Drs Jekyll turned into Messrs Hyde the moment they got onto a plane. The minnows were still minnows. Only the West Indians remained undefeated.

So much for the knowns. What remained unknown was South Africa. Twenty-one years of exclusion had been lifted in 1991, and South African cricket had come back to the world like a mystery gift. Who knew what lay inside the wrapping? During the apartheid-ban years, the South Africans had routinely demolished visiting rebel teams. Great names had endured – Barry Richards, Graeme Pollock, Mike Procter, Eddie Barlow, Garth Le Roux – and as they faded, new names emerged. But how good was Allan Donald? How reliable were the Currie Cup stats for Jimmy Cook, Peter Kirsten and Darryl Cullinan? Had Brian McMillan and Hansie Cronje been

ENGLAND WAS HALF-DEAD AND ROTTING IN THE SUN

tested against real top quality, or just a motley of mercenary visitors? And Kepler Wessels – surely he couldn't step back into Test cricket after nearly a decade?

The South Africans had surprised by getting to the World Cup semifinals in 1992, and had then gone to the West Indies for a one-off Test only to be dismembered, chasing a small total, by Ambrose and Walsh. They beat the touring Indians, but everyone beat the Indians when they were touring. They beat Sri Lanka on the road. But not until they came to Australia in the summer of 1993–94 would they undergo their thorough inspection. The box would be fully unwrapped and we would see what was inside.

From the start they had a refreshing naivety about them, as if they were a team of Rip Van Winkles returning with the customs of a bygone era. They were jumping out of their skins to prove themselves against Australia and sometimes, like overexcited children, got carried away, notably Cullinan, who talked on the field as if he had twenty-one years of sledging to catch up on. Unfortunately he was so busy sledging, he dropped his first four catches and never really recovered. Several of their cricketers were also gifted rugby players, just

LEFT: White Lightning: they knew he was good, but how good?

as, up to the 1970s, in Australia it was possible to play multiple sports up to an elite level. It wasn't that the South Africans weren't hard; but there was something about their hardness that was eager-beaver rather than world-weary.

They placed a high premium on team spirit, as would be expected from a group that grew into adulthood under siege, and they did things together. Eventually this would become a problem for them. They were up together, and they were down together. They arrived in Australia in late 1993 carrying a flu virus together.

After two pre-Christmas one-day matches were split, the First Test in Melbourne was a washout, memorably forgettable for Mark Taylor scoring a century stretched over four sodden days. The teams went to Sydney like veterans of a phony war, all wound up but unexercised.

This changed on the first day at the Sydney Cricket Ground. South Africa won the toss and batted, and in the second over Andrew Hudson was leg-before-wicket to a strange specimen called Glenn McGrath, in for the injured Hughes. McGrath, as the saying had it, could have run around in a shower and not got wet. Built along Bruce Reid lines, he had made his debut against New Zealand earlier that summer without having achieved a great deal in domestic cricket. Whatever the selectors saw in him was apparent to few in the general public. He had moved to Sydney from Narromine, on the western plains of New South Wales, having taken up fast bowling a few years earlier, and lived in a Millard caravan at the Ramsgate Beach Caravan Park on Botany Bay. Because of his height and raw talent, he appealed to the State selectors and was sent to the Australian Cricket Academy in Adelaide. But there didn't seem much more to him. He was quite fast, but not express. He moved the ball a little, but had no natural swing. He was a little surly on the field, but not aggressive when McDermott and Hughes were setting the standard. He was hard to hit, but so was Paul Reiffel. He ran through the crease in one smooth movement, rather than leaping and hurling the ball, reminding many of Angus Fraser: a fair prospect for a good State career, maybe a few Tests and one-day internationals, but not much more.

After McGrath removed Hudson for a duck, Gary Kirsten and

Hansie Cronje put on 90. Kirsten was notable for being the younger brother of the highly credentialled Peter. Cronje was a classic school-captain type, handsome, upstanding and dark-browed, a forceful batsman, a fitness fanatic and a natural leader. A devout Christian, he carried his moral rectitude like a sword and shield.

McDermott ended the partnership after lunch, and then Warne put on a clinic, taking 7/56. The huge hauls would later elude Warne, but in his early years he had a number of days when he simply ran through entire teams. He'd done it against the West Indies in Melbourne, and would do it against England in Brisbane a year later and against Pakistan, also in Brisbane, in 1995. He unleashed the full repertoire of leg-spinners, flippers, top-spinners and zooters, over and around the wicket, bowling Cullinan – whom he had already publicly targeted – with the flipper. That day the flipper alone took three wickets, Jonty Rhodes and Gary Kirsten as well as Cullinan. He also bowled Pat Symcox around his legs after the bolshie South African spinner loudly declared that Warne couldn't get one behind him. By the end of the day the only South African to make double figures after Cronje was Fanie de Villiers in the tail.

Australia made 292 in response to the visitors' 169. Martyn, recalled for the injured Steve Waugh, composed a solid three-hour 59 and Slater made 92, the first of his nine Test scores truncated between 90 and 100. Why did Slater get so nervous in the nineties? It went hand-in-glove with his irrepressible enthusiasm and attacking instincts, his ability to get to 90 in the first place. Test cricketers try to train themselves to treat every ball on its merits, but even as a commentator Slater cannot hold back, audibly slavering as he urges a batsman to smash a four or a six to get to three figures.

The match was a slow grind, a typical response to how the Sydney Cricket Ground wicket was playing. Once a green, fast, typical Australian deck, it had turned grey-black and puddingy under the curatorial skills of Peter Leroy. It produced dour cricket but gripping matches, if you had the patience: Test cricket for the purists. The run rate in that 1994 New Year Test was two an over. By stumps on the third day South Africa was 2/94, with Cronje and Wessels in, still 29 behind Australia.

In the second innings Warne and McDermott had to work harder for their wickets, but they popped out like triplets on the fourth morning. McDermott bowled Cronje. The South African captain-in-waiting had scored 41 and 38 for the match, pretty close to what would be his Test average. Warne bowled Wessels, then trapped the swiftly-becoming-hapless Cullinan with the flipper, a ball as frightful as a squeaking door in a haunted house. The South African golden boy had balance and timing and a prodigious domestic scoring record, but in that week he was given his first push down a slippery psychiatric slope that would end on the couch. Just as the West Indies used to do, Australia made a practice of wrecking batsmen's otherwise productive Test careers, and none embodied this better than Cullinan: in 63 Tests against other nations, he would make 4401 runs at 48.4; in seven Tests against Australia, he would be a rabbit, making 153 at fewer than 13 an innings.

Jonty Rhodes, a sparky right-hander who already had a reputation as the best fieldsman on the planet, staged a recovery with the wicketkeeper Dave Richardson. A careful, slim type with sleepy eyes and a good defence, Richardson would be a steady down-the-order batsman and later a steady down-the-order administrator for cricket's governing body.

Warne wheeled away for forty-two overs. Border was merciless in the two years he had the leg-spinner. It was characteristic of Warne's loyalty to Border that he never held him responsible for the injuries that began to afflict him from that series; but they were a direct result of Border's orders. Not that Warne was complaining of wage slavery. By the end of the innings he had another five wickets. But thanks to a crucial last-wicket thirty-six from Rhodes and Donald, South Africa had crept up to 239, setting Australia 117 to win.

The hardest step in any victory is the last. The most mentally demanding sports, like golf and cricket, make wonderful theatre for the self-destruction humans are capable of wreaking on themselves when they are about to win something precious. Greg Norman is not the only golfer who choked; but he is the only one to pick himself up and have the courage and talent to go out there and choke again, and again. Likewise Australia, in this era, in cricket. They had failed to make 186 to win the Frank Worrell Trophy in Adelaide. Before that, in 'Botham's Ashes' in 1981, Australia had choked repeatedly when chasing small fourth-innings targets. After 1994, they would do it over and over, even when indisputable world champions. Indeed, it can be theorised that Australia became such ruthless frontrunners during the Taylor and Waugh captaincies, closing out matches in three or four days, precisely because they wanted to avoid leaving themselves with a small target to chase in the fourth innings.

But why? To a non-sportsperson, a choke is the most bizarre and tragic, sometimes tragi-comic, sight. To a participant, it needs no explaining. To choke is to be human. Golfers call it 'throwing up', and it can feel, physically, like nausea. When the batting brain starts to recalibrate its thoughts from 'How do I treat this ball?' to 'How many more runs do we need now?', the mind moves from process to result, and the result, once grasped for, slithers away. The batsman loses the components of concentration that have made him a Test-grade practitioner in the first place. He is thinking desperately of how to get the ball through the field, or off the square, and reducing the target. Or he is thinking about how crucial it is for him not to get out. He is thinking about all the things he is not meant to be thinking about. He is in an altered state. Once in that state, he is liable to panic.

Australia began the chase in the last session of the fourth day, on a pitch that was crumbling and variable in bounce, bursting into powder as balls broke the surface. Slater was out for 1, but Boon and Taylor were closing in on a half-century stand as stumps approached. Easy does it. Australia could start the fifth day with about sixty to get and nine wickets in hand.

Donald and de Villiers were bowling. Donald was every bit as fast and rhythmic as his reputation had promised, with a beautiful athletic run-up and a flowing side-on action somehow reminiscent of both Michael Holding and Craig McDermott. He had taken hundreds of wickets in county and South African domestic cricket, and was lucky enough to be entering his physical prime as South Africa returned from isolation. De Villiers, two years older, looked like an army reservist and ran in from a wide angle, with a shuffling kind of gait, bringing his arm over in a quick, low action. Nowhere near Donald's pace, he was thought to be an accurate foil rather than a strike bowler.

Suddenly, in the last minutes before stumps, Fanie had three wickets. Boon was caught in close, and Tim May entered as night-watchman. First ball, May played back and was leg-before: 3/51. Mark Waugh, who might have been looking around for a second nightwatchman, came in. In de Villiers's next over, Taylor was caught behind and Border replaced him. Australia went to stumps at 4/63. Momentum, as a boxer knows, is everything. Land a few good punches at the end of a round and, whatever has gone before, you sit down in your corner feeling you are on top. That night, even though Australia still only needed 54 with six wickets in hand the South Africans had their dinner feeling like favourites.

Momentum would also be confirmed, one way or the other, first thing on the fifth morning. There was no time for starting cold and working your way into the game. Obviously South Africa could not afford a mistake. Australia could afford a few, but not as many as they made.

As play resumed, so did the collapse. Border, shouldering arms, was bowled by Donald before most spectators were in their seats; then went Waugh, leg-before to Donald; Healy, bowled by de Villiers; and Warne, run out by a direct hit from Cronje.

His partner in the run out was Martyn. Poor Martyn. History reserves its strongest condemnation for great talent frittered away. But only the supremely talented are so lumbered. Allan Border, Mark Taylor, Gary Kirsten, Justin Langer – these were unpretty batsmen who, because of their perceived pugnacity and lack of style, never seemed to give their wicket away cheaply. Then there were others who made batting look too easy – Mark Waugh, Steve Waugh in his early days (prior to the transformation that was taking place in this very 1993–94 season), Slater, Michael Bevan, Damien Martyn. Because they had such elegance and timing and apparent ease, their mistakes could look careless. It was only perception, not reality, but it was powerful enough to dog Mark Waugh through-out his career and it cost Damien Martyn six years of his.

On the final morning in Sydney, it was Martyn who stood firm. Martyn batted the way his mate Langer had in Adelaide a year before. The youngest in the team, he batted like the toughest. He watched four wickets fall at the other end. He endured. He scored 6 runs in nearly two hours. At the other end, the batting McDermott – again! – held the spotlight. He was at number ten now. It wasn't that he'd become a better batsman. But McGrath had a lock on number eleven, as he would for a decade and a half. On this day, McDermott was the fluent strokeplayer in the partnership with Martyn, clipping Donald and de Villiers off his pads and slashing the loose ones, leading a thirty-five-run partnership in an hour that took Australia once again to the brink of victory.

But sometimes the brink is a precipice. Poor Martyn! Australia needed seven to win, and McDermott was batting as if he would win it as soon as he got back on strike. Donald bowled Martyn what looked like a half-volley. A fast-scoring, flowing child prodigy, Martyn had reined himself in this day. It didn't matter that he was only 6 after 106 minutes. He was Australia's sheet anchor. He only had to stay there. But when he saw that half-volley, he relaxed; he played his natural game.

It wasn't a half-volley. Martyn wasn't quite to the pitch of it, but he was through the shot as the ball stopped on him. It lobbed to Hudson at extra cover. Martyn's misfortune wasn't that he played the shot; it was that his style made the shot look airy, carefree. And it was that the shot came at that moment, when so few runs were needed. He had held the fort while Border, Waugh, Healy and Warne

HISTORY RESERVES ITS STRONGEST CONDEMNATION FOR GREAT TALENT FRITTERED AWAY

had fallen, he had done more than any of them to ensure the target was reached, but few would remember that; after this shot he would be the one to go to the gallows.

McGrath, who must have lain awake in his caravan at nights dreading this scenario, came in with six to win and popped de Villiers a return catch. It was over. McGrath stayed at the wicket, distraught, as if it were all his fault.

A year after the West Indies had beaten Australia by the narrowest margin in Test cricket, South Africa had beaten Australia by the fourth-narrowest. The circumstances were so similar as to raise the question of whether Border's team had a complex, a mental block – a 'small-target syndrome', as the sport's legion of amateur psychologists put it. The South Africans went nuts on the field, pouring two decades of exclusion into their screams and hugs – this was their moment of triumphal return to Test cricket. De Villiers had his fifteen minutes of fame. The Australians in their rooms were a shoal of stunned mullet. McDermott, by the way, ended up 29 not out. He hadn't backed away today either.

Australia's Test performances were being judged against a long-term narrative. In the mid-1980s, they had been poor. Fragmented, dispirited, suffering from a loss of world-class talent, they had lost at home to the West Indies, New Zealand and England. Then, the first green shoots of recovery: by the end of 1987 they had won the World Cup in India, scored a courageous tie in Madras, and held out the New Zealanders in Melbourne. But these were rearguard actions, and in 1988–89 they had been thumped again, put in their place, by the West Indies.

The improvement was never steady, but two steps forward, one step back. They won back the Ashes in 1989, retained them in 1990–91, but then suffered a miserable loss to the West Indies in 1991 and failed as favourites in the 1992 World Cup.

Even when there were failures, though, there was a long-term anticipation that this Australian team was destined to be the world's best. By early 1994, the key pieces were in place: the new generation of batsmen in Taylor, Slater and the Waughs; the rock-steady keeper in Healy; and the spearhead in Warne. The foundation was still provided by the old guard of Boon, Border, McDermott and, when fit, Hughes. The question-mark, really, was how many of the old guard would survive until Australia claimed the crown, and – much more contentious and potentially painful – how many of that old guard were actually standing in the way.

During the South African series, those questions grew more rather than less insistent. Was the collapse in Sydney somehow a product of Border's own mentality: was there a fear of winning in the team that emanated from the captain himself? Was the negative batting that mired the Australians in Sydney an example of a team growing in its captain's image? Was the narkiness and the sledging, which had reached a zenith, or a nadir, that summer, and was nurtured by Border's own grizzled combativeness, blocking the team's development?

Even the team's comeback, after Sydney, belonged to the Border era – that is, the old era. Border was nothing if not a fighter. If he had been a racehorse, he would never have led a race until the final stride. Comfortable as the underdog, he led his men to a come-from-behind win in the one-day series and then a series-equalling Test victory in Adelaide, marred by more sledging and contention over umpiring.

Three Tests did not settle the issue between Australia and South Africa, and the teams flew across the Indian Ocean steaming with unresolved hostilities. The New Year was turning into a marathon of intense one-day and Test rivalry. It was all very well to extol the Australia–South Africa competitiveness while one team was absent, but now that they were back, it was downright vicious. You can't have it both ways.

Australia had counter-punched in Adelaide, but in South Africa the home side comfortably won the four-match one-day series that preceded Australia's first official Test tour since 1970. It was a momentous time: weeks away, the African National Congress would be voted into power, and the election campaign was in full swing. The Australian team was attracting almost as much attention, with hundreds of fans turning up at six o'clock in the morning to see them arrive at Johannesburg's airport. Sensitive to omens, however, the Australians were unnerved to see six dead bodies lying on the roadside on their bus trip to their hotel, the aftermath of a terrible multi-vehicle accident. As Warne said grimly, 'Welcome to South Africa.'

After the one-dayers, the Test battle was resumed, in steamy late-summer Johannesburg. The Wanderers Ground is known as the Bullring thanks to its small size and steeply raked grandstands. The players really did feel as though they were in a *plaza de toros*, especially given the enthusiasms of a South African audience who hadn't seen Australian Test cricketers for so long and harboured strong opinions about what had happened in Adelaide. The roar the crowds generated was far in excess of the ground's official capacity, which was only about 20,000. In addition, a unique feature of the Wanderers was the race linking the changing rooms to the field. The changing rooms themselves were attractive, with white picketed balconies overlooking the field from square of the wicket. But the race was 30 metres long and spectators would line it to shout abuse at visiting players, pull at their clothes, even knocking their hats off. Part of the race was shielded by a clear perspex screen. Rather than signalling to the crowd that they should respect the players, the screen seemed to give fresh license for verbal and physical abuse. Behind the plastic, players were seen as fair game, rather like, when Tony Greig first wore his crash helmet during World Series Cricket, all bowlers wanted to do was aim at it. Steve Waugh said he had never felt so angry during a match, and the Australian team started every session in a rage.

The first two days saw some uncharacteristically breezy cricket, as if simmering tempers prevented sustained concentration. Batting first, all of the South Africans made a start but only Rhodes passed fifty, and their 251 didn't seem enough when Australia went to stumps at 0/34. A year after losing his bat-off against Slater in England, Matthew Hayden was making his debut, replacing the ill Taylor. He lasted that final half-hour, watching Slater smack the ball around with the bright confidence of a twelve-Test veteran.

The next morning, both young openers were soon out and Australia's innings was a carbon copy of South Africa's, a long list of two-digit scores and a moderate 248. The turning point came when Mark Waugh and Border both managed to get run out within a few minutes, careless cricket that couldn't be dissociated from the brewing unhappiness off the field.

Warne, for the first time in his Test career but not the last, had had enough. Fielding on the boundary in South Africa's second innings, he tried to have fun with the crowd but was pelted in the back with an orange. He looked around to see the security guards laughing at him. He wasn't getting enough sleep. He was enjoying the nightlife of a superstar, and when he got to his hotel room he would be woken through the night by South African phone callers telling him how they would get him the next day. Few of his team-mates knew what was building up inside him, but externally his fatigue was obvious. His Ashes performance in 1993 had required the highest number of balls from any bowler in 116 years. He had bowled further stints of forty-plus overs in many Test innings since then, as well as his full complement in one-day internationals. He had looked tired in Adelaide, when tendonitis started to flare in his bowling shoulder, but kept pressing on. Always he was anaesthe-tised by the wickets he took.

The South African public and media smothered him with a double-edged, peculiarly South African, kind of admiration: they put him on a very high pedestal, giving him nicknames like Flipperman and Sultan of Spin and Wizard of Oz, partly so as to increase the pleasure in ripping him down. He soon found him-self in a fractious relationship with the public. Warne was always a willing signer of autographs, but after being treated rudely by parents who would demand an autograph for their child and not bother thanking him, Warne tried to be more selective. He was duly pilloried for being 'stuck up'.

In South Africa's second innings at the Wanderers, he would not bowl until the forty-fourth over. It was inexplicable, as if Border was playing mind games to work him up into an aggressive bowl-ing state; or perhaps there was some domestic team issue at play, and Border was punishing Warne for some private misdemeanour. Finally, Border walked up to him and, with the Test match slip-ping away, told Warne how desperate he was for a wicket. Warne would bowl another 45 overs in the innings. Border squeezed ev-erything he could get out of the (always willing) Warne, but now they were about to register the cost.

Andrew Hudson, as inoffensive a man as ever played Test crick-et, had batted three hours for his 60. The game was edging out of Australia's reach as, on an easy-paced wicket, Hudson and Cronje took the lead to 126. Cronje, who had smashed the Australians for 251 in a warm-up game and a hundred in a one-dayer, now hurtling towards a Test century, was in the best form of his career. Warne, wound tight by the crowd, ignored by Border, *angry*, came in to Hudson and, with his third ball, bowled him around his legs. Then, Warne lost his sense of where he was and who was watching. He gave Hudson an overblown, undeserved send-off, snarling and chasing him and gesticulating towards the changing room. 'Fuck off, go on, Hudson, fuck off out of here!'

It wasn't Hudson he was seeing from behind the red veil: it was South Africa, it was life in the fishbowl, it was his own weariness. But it looked like a petulant eruption from a young man who was meant to have the world at his feet, a spoilt brat throwing his toys out of the cot the moment everything had stopped going his way.

Healy restrained him; later, Warne was stricken with remorse, saying he looked at the film and concluded: 'It's pretty awful and the guy in the footage is not the real me.'

Hughes had come back in for McGrath, but was also at the end of his tether. His recuperation from the Ashes tour had involved surgery, and he had been selected on a light preparation at home. In South Africa he hadn't bowled well, but now he was asked to send down nearly as many overs as Warne in a hostile place. Hughes must also have been frustrated by the soreness in his knee and the feeling that the match was ebbing out of reach. He let fly with a tirade at Gary Kirsten which had none of the Hughes pantomime-villain humour. It was a cranky old dog biting the nearest hand. Again, like Hudson, Gary Kirsten was no provocateur. 'You're a weak little prick, Kirsten,' Hughes roared. 'Why don't you play a shot?'

Although the usually avuncular David Shepherd wagged his finger in redress at Border, bringing the Australian leader to heel like a naughty class captain, neither umpire placed Hughes or Warne on report. Yet that evening both players were fined $400 by the ICC match referee, Donald Carr. It might have ended with that, but there was such an outcry at home that the Australian Cricket Board fined the players a further $4000 each. There was no hearing, no right of appeal, no consultation with the players. The players' tour contracts stated that all disciplinary matters would be handled by

ABOVE: Dog bites self: Hughes letting fly at Gary Kirsten.

tour management, not the ACB. But the ACB would argue that it had held a meeting before the Adelaide Test specifically to address the Test players' worsening behaviour. At that meeting, they had promised to come down hard on pre-meditated and persistent sledging, dissent at umpiring decisions, and send-offs, which were seen as particularly egregious because of the batsman's inability to respond. The Board chairman, Alan Crompton, described send-offs as 'cowardly, un-Australian and un-any other country you care to name'. By way of exonerating itself, the Board stated that the $4000 fines for Hughes and Warne had not been specifically for the Johannesburg transgressions, but for 'a series of incidents involving the same two players ... over a lengthy period of time.'

The identification of these issues, preconceived sledging, dissent and send-offs, says much about how the Australian players were perceived. The Board said it had given them fair warning. The players felt that this warning hadn't been clearly communicated. Whatever the specifics, a cultural change was underway, and change was hardest to handle for the likes of Hughes and Border, who had been playing for so many years while the tide of public opinion on player behaviour was turning behind their backs. Expectations had risen; the behaviour of some players had not. As Hughes would reason, he had not changed in South Africa; he was playing just the way he'd always played. Which was, precisely, the problem.

South Africa batted well enough to set Australia a target of 454 in the fourth innings, in nine sessions. There was no swift collapse, but a steady fall of wickets leaving Hughes and May, the final pair, with three hours to survive on the fifth afternoon.

They lasted more than an hour before a shower forced the teams from the field. The South Africans must have been beside themselves with worry. As Hughes and May went up the Wanderers race, a spectator leaned in and spat at Hughes, swearing as he and May walked past. Hughes, tired of the constant abuse in social situations on the tour and riled up by the fines from day three, stopped and thought about replying to the spectator. He told himself not to; but then he snapped. He smacked his bat against the wall, leaned over the fence and said, 'Mate, if you've got something to say, let's hear it.' When the man backed away, Hughes said, 'You're like every prick I've met here, you're as weak as piss.'

May, noticing film cameras at the top of the race, went back and beckoned Hughes to follow.

The game was soon lost – Hughes remaining 26 not out – but the footage of the incident in the race, on the heels of the day three incidents, turned into controversy in both South Africa and Australia. It caused barely a mention within the Australian team, which was disconsolate at the loss on the field. The tour manager, Cam Battersby, said Hughes had been provoked and left it at that. Border, who seemed at times to delegate the entire outside world to coach Bob Simpson, appeared to be sealed off from any consciousness of the cultural context in which he was playing. Border only wanted to play, and at times like these he could be trapped within his own blinkers. Senior journalist Mike Coward was one of those on the tour who was able to separate the wood from the trees and register the central issue, which was that, 'given the historic nature of the tour, this was a terrible wasted opportunity. After twenty-four years, Australia had the chance to show South Africans how they played; the shame of it was, Australia did show South Africans the way they played.'

HEALY PUT THE CAPTAIN'S BAT IN ICE, TO PUT OUT THE 'FIRE'

The gap between how the incidents were perceived inside and outside the team was now an abyss. Hughes wore an extra $2000 suspended fine for the incident with the spectator. Border circled the wagons and threatened to boycott the next tour game. Throughout the tour, burdened by his uncertainty over whether or not to retire, he had erupted periodically at the team. In one match, when Border was batting particularly slowly, Healy put the captain's bat in ice, to put out the 'fire'. Instead of laughing Border blew up, not only at Healy but at the rest of the 'party boys' he said he was leading.

When under siege from the public and the Board, Border characteristically took his players' side. He felt that the Board had caved in to remarks from commentators such as David Hookes, who said Hughes and Warne should have been sent home, and a widespread pressure to levy greater punishments. Border asked what was the point in having an ICC referee and tour contracts if they were then to be ignored by extra-judicial actions by a Board that was blown around by every new gust of media talk?

Hughes would never repent. He said his only regret about the incident in the race, over time, was that he'd had the chance to hit the spectator's fingers with his bat but had slapped the wall instead.

Neither players nor Board covered themselves in glory. The players' actions would entrench an ongoing perception of the 'ugly Australians'. When things were not going their way, particularly when opposing batsmen were frustrating them with a long partnership, the Australians resorted to sledging and abuse. It seemed all too calculated. The Johannesburg eruption was out of character for Warne, but over the years the sledging would begin to look like a tactic, a last resort. The Australian public could forgive excessive passion, but not cynical mock outrage. For the Board's part, their response was craven and disloyal, showing that they were prepared to put public image above justice and due process. Hughes and Warne were denied a fair hearing, and weren't allowed to explain the events behind their actions. It mightn't have changed the final result, but they should have been given their chance.

Ugliness from the Australian players; cravenness from the ACB. Two themes were set that would play out to their full denouement over the next fifteen years.

As in Adelaide, the Australians showed their resilience by rebounding in Cape Town. Hughes played his last Test match. He had ceased working on his fitness hard enough; as it turned out, the 1993 Ashes series had finished him off. Not knowing that this would be the end of his long road, his parents had flown from Victoria to Cape Town to watch him play. He made a duck and took no wickets. 'Mum thought I fielded very well,' he commented.

With the scores at 1-1 in this series and 2-2 over the whole summer, the teams prepared for a showdown at Kingsmead, Durban, on the wicket known as the 'green mamba' due to the high water table that sometimes softened the pitch and produced a fast bowler's dream.

Not this time. Steve Waugh would describe the match as 'a waste of time for five days'. Australia plodded to 269 in its first innings, and South Africa then batted for two days and a session to make 422 – an effort that led the Australians to believe their opponents were playing for a draw. It was perplexingly negative cricket. Australia defended for the last day and a half, losing only four wickets as neither side dared press for victory. Border, coming in at 4/157, prodded and jabbed in the humidity, his back to the wall for one last time. Beside him was Mark Waugh, the treble and bass of whose batting had been tamped down, slouching along towards Border's retirement. They batted for four hours and added 140 runs, of which Border made 42.

Amid the gloomy coastal humidity, such an anticlimactic end was a tribute, in its way, to the captaincy of Wessels and Border. They were battle weary. The defining episodes of their careers had involved conflict. For Border it was the traumatic years of loss at home to the West Indies, England and New Zealand, and having the captaincy thrust upon him. He had led Australia for ninety-three Tests, but even though the team had evolved into an exciting attacking outfit he did not fully evolve with it. Early in his captaincy Wessels had been one of Border's henchmen, but when Wessels quit to return to his native South Africa, he lost Border's trust. They were both warriors from a more defensive time, and their tactics in Durban were those of men who dreaded loss more than they craved victory. Border went moodily into the night, treating the bowling of Jonty Rhodes as respectfully as if facing Derek Underwood back in the 1970s. He told Mark Waugh, 'This might be my last innings, I'm not going to let them get me out.' To the end he was true to his nature.

THE YEAR OF THE RAT

Karachi, September/October 1994

WITH OCEANS OF MONEY SWILLING THROUGH ILLEGAL BETTING HOUSES IN THE SUBCONTINENT AND MIDDLE EAST, IT WAS INEVITABLE THAT PLAYERS FROM LOW-WAGE COUNTRIES WOULD BE DRAWN IN.

The weaknesses of the late Border era glared in the two South African series: the vulnerability when chasing small targets, the petulant behaviour, and a tendency under high heat to curl into a defensive shell. All of it reflected Border's personality. He was a worrier, and anxious when on top. While not a vicious sledger himself, he turned a blind eye when it served the team cause. The reflexive retreat into negativity, the moodiness, was the meeting place of his history and his temperament.

Border's retirement was spontaneous, yet it couldn't have been more fitting if he had planned it. Mismanaged, passionate, let loose in a fit of pique on a golf course, it was perfectly Border. One thing Border was never about was polish or choreography. It would have been wrong for him to take a bow and a stage-managed exit. And he didn't.

He had been considering retirement since the South African tour, but understood that the ACB was giving him as much time as he needed. But there were those inside and outside the cricket community who saw him as an obstacle to progress. The selection of the Australian team for its next tour, of Pakistan in September 1994, was postponed twice while the

ONE THING BORDER WAS NEVER ABOUT WAS POLISH OR CHOREOGRAPHY

ACB waited for Border to make his decision. ACB chairman Alan Crompton and chief executive Graham Halbish held a press conference in May implying that Border was 'gumming up the works'. Then, after learning that the Board had met with the next rank of players – Taylor, Healy, Steve Waugh, Boon – in apparent 'job interviews' for the captaincy, Border called up a friend, the television journalist Pat Welsh, invited him for a game of golf, and announced he was quitting Test cricket. He *kvetched* about the Board not giving him more time to make up his mind. He made not one positive statement about his time in cricket or his achievements. It was, in the matter-of-fact Border style, a temper tantrum. 'A part of me,' he concluded, 'has died.'

Exit Captain Cranky. Over time, Border would be seen as authentic, down-to-earth, the most human of the greats. When he introduced himself to strangers, Border would never assume they knew who he was. He'd hold out his hand, very modestly, and say, just like a normal person, 'Hello, I'm Allan Border.' Placed into relief by history, the rancorous mood has passed, and Border's reputation continues to grow.

Enter Captain Chirpy. For all Border's stature, Taylor's ascent to the captaincy had the effect of a blood transfusion.

LEFT: One for the road: Border enters Kingsmead for his last Test innings.

Where Border carried the problems of the world in his face, Taylor shrugged them off. Where Border was susceptible to mood swings, Taylor was impervious, his temperament dial fluctuating on a narrow spectrum between cheerful and cheerfully pensive. As the staff of any organisation know, the best bosses are those who absorb the pressure from above and without, and make themselves a buffer, protecting those below them. This was Taylor. Like any good boss, he was decisive and brisk. It was easy to imagine him as a sporty high school headmaster, bustling about, well organised, in control. Taylor was a diplomat and a politician, at home with administrators, media and sponsors as well as players, whereas Border was more like a platoon sergeant, most comfortable in the trenches with his men. Most importantly, Taylor was openly *happy*. This was what most distinguished him from Border. He was an optimist.

What Taylor didn't have was Border's monumental standing among the team. Even to Boon, the longest-serving of Border's deputies, Border was as unquestionable as Uluru. The man hadn't missed a Test since 1978. Whatever they thought of Border's outbursts and moods, there was no second-guessing the man's fundamental authority: he was beyond disrespect.

Taylor, on the other hand, was among equals. Boon, May and McDermott were his seniors. The Waughs and Healy had played with him in junior representative teams. Warne was a superstar with a deep loyalty to Border. So, while the public and the ACB and the media and the cricket world in general welcomed Taylor as a breath of fresh air, he still had to earn changing-room fealty.

The gap in the team's record was its performance overseas. This could be said of all teams of the time except the West Indies, who won everywhere; but if Australia was going to challenge it had to start winning away from home and the cushiony turf of England. What better venue for Taylor to litmus-test his team, then, than Pakistan?

An Australian side had not won a Test series in Pakistan since Richie Benaud's in 1959–60, a fact which merits some examination. Pakistan was not India (where Australia hadn't won a series since 1969). Whereas India had been a wild ride of mayhem, with chaotic streets, uncontrolled crowds, often dreadful cricket facilities and hotels, and food that tended to disagree violently with the

Australian sportsman's digestion, Pakistan was a much more orderly tour. Military rule made the streets quieter, the cities better planned. It was a nation of moustached men and not so many women: everywhere the players looked, there were uniformed men openly carrying guns, and plainclothed men not openly carrying guns. Hotels and grounds were less variable than India. Hygiene and food preparation were closer to western standards. For young Australian cricketers it could seem a somewhat strange place, with little by way of bars or nightlife or – gulp – golf courses, but the public's enthusiasm for cricket was devout and their hospitality second to none.

So why had Australia been unable to win there? There was the obvious reason: Pakistan produced some of the world's best cricketers. This was the land of Javed Miandad, Imran Khan, Zaheer Abbas, Abdul Qadir, Hanif and Mushtaq Mohammad, and Fazal Mahmood. By the early 1990s they had a new crop: Wasim Akram, Waqar Younis, Salim Malik, Inzamam-ul-Haq. There was no dishonour in losing to this kind of quality. But it was also true that Pakistan had enjoyed the favours of local umpires. Miandad, it was said, was never leg-before-wicket in his hometown of Karachi. Greg Chappell was once dismissed lbw in Faisalabad to a ball that pitched the length of a bat outside his leg stump. The stories were legion, and the legend immeasurable. Indeed, the Miandad myth was just a part of that legend: the fact was that in sixteen Tests he had thrice been given out lbw in Karachi. Yet you could never tell an Australian cricketer that. They simply wouldn't have believed you. Miandad's supposed impunity at home was integral to the myth of playing in Pakistan.

Cricketers can cope, mentally, with all kinds of adversity, but when they think the umpires are cheating them they soon descend into despondency. If the umpires are going to decide a match, what is the point? Australia's 1988 tour had imploded over the team's unshakeable conviction that they were being cheated. Yet, with international pressure and the raising of umpiring standards following the Gatting–Shakoor Rana confrontation in 1988, things were said to be on the mend.

Australia flew over with a kind of willed optimism. Their theme was 'To lose patience is to lose the battle' (a slogan observed by the leg-spinner and would-be selector Jim Higgs from a housefront sign in Madras in 1979). Not for the first or last time, Item One in their code of behaviour was 'No whingeing'. They were even issued with 'media training', including comments they were meant to memorise:

'Harsh conditions are part of international cricket.'

'Conditions in Pakistan are comfortable: five-star accommodation, hotel-prepared food at the grounds, and bottled water.'

This was before they left Australia.

The Australians were looking at the tour as part of their long drive to the top, their first step post-Border. If they were going to become world champions, they needed to find a new gear. Perhaps Taylor's captaincy would provide it.

The tour started not in Pakistan but Sri Lanka, for a quadrangular one-day tournament. It was one of those brief and unremembered jamborees that would become increasingly common, like asthma. There was little for the Australians to do but practise, play and go to the hotel casino. Australia beat Pakistan but lost to Sri Lanka and India, missing the final. Nevertheless, Taylor's imprint on the captaincy was immediately visible in the changed role of Bob Simpson.

Simpson's part in the revival of Australian cricket will long be debated. He became coach soon after Border became captain, and they formed a complementary duumvirate. Simpson loved power and influence. Border wanted anything but. Simpson loved to communicate. Border loved to bat. Border, wishing to minimise the leadership demands, at first delegated some duties to Simpson. Instead of just advising players on technical issues and running practices, Simpson was soon the motivator, guide, chief tactician and counsel. He became a national selector too, sparking questions of propriety. How are players expected to be candid about their problems and fears with their coach, when the coach was also their hirer or firer? No doubt Simpson believed he could compartmentalise, and never hold a player's fears against him – but the players didn't necessarily know that.

Had Simpson been a conciliatory kind of person, the

ABOVE: Warne and May: days later, their Pakistan tour would be no laughing matter.

arguments about his role would never have generated much heat. But Simpson was a political player, a behind-the-scenes wheeler-dealer. He would alienate the press corps by giving scoops to his favourites. He would traffic in patronage. He had the autocrat's essential belief in his rightness. He was a perfect partner for Border, because he did all the dirty work. But as many critics, including Ian Chappell, would say, Border had allowed a coach to take control of an international cricket team, to assume duties that a captain should never abdicate.

From day one of this tour, the hyper-alert Simpson must have sniffed his end in the way Taylor was taking charge. In Sri Lanka and Pakistan, Taylor ran the fielding drills and team meetings himself, took charge of media briefings, liaised directly with his employers, and reduced the amount of training. When the team met before taking the field, Taylor took the ten other players into the changing rooms and left Simpson outside drilling the 'benchies'. Simpson would claim that more of his suggestions were put into place by Taylor than by Border. Perhaps that describes the shift best: he had become the person making suggestions, not decisions.

As much as Taylor wanted and loved the job, his first performances with the bat were an evil omen: scores of 8, 4 and 41 in Sri Lanka, then 4 and 1 in the warm-up match against a Pakistan Board President's XI. In his first Test innings as Australian captain, after winning the toss and batting, on what must surely have been the proudest day of his life, he made a fourth-ball duck, chipping a return catch to Wasim Akram. Taylor's batting would recover over the next two years, before its career-threatening trough in 1996–97 when he would sail very close to the 'English' or 'Mike Brearley' model of captaincy, which would be an affront to Australian pride even if it had been successful for England. But at this stage he was a consistent and at times attractive left-handed driver, glider and puller. His batting was overshadowed, in time, by his teammates and the high quality of his own captaincy, but to put him in the Brearley category as a batsman is to do him a gross disservice. He scored more runs than Bradman, including nineteen Test centuries, and was actually, some days, quite pretty to watch.

The First Test took place at Karachi's National Stadium, where Pakistan had not lost one of its thirty Tests. Australia scored 7/325 by stumps, meeting one of Taylor's most pleasing ambitions as captain, which was to score at least 300 a day. What a change this would make from the South African series, where sub-250-run days were routine. Half-centuries in the middle order came from Steve Waugh, Healy and Michael Bevan, the replacement for Border. Bevan, though from New South Wales, had amassed a David Hookes–like record for South Australia, for whom he played while at the Academy. He was a slim left-hander with subcontinental wrists and hands; unfortunately, his mind and personality would play devilish tricks on him and he would never realise

HE WAS ACTUALLY, SOME DAYS, QUITE PRETTY TO WATCH

his potential in Test cricket. That first day, he fell for a bubbly three-hour 82. If he had gone on to make a century … well, the what-ifs of cricket would fill another roomful of *Wisdens*.

Pakistan's bowling mainstays were Wasim, Waqar and the leg-spinner Mushtaq Ahmed. Wasim was the most gifted international bowler of the era. A tall, well-built left-armer with coathanger shoulders, he shuffled in off a short run and was able to deliver off-cutters, leg-cutters, bouncers, outswingers and inswingers with no apparent change to his busy and slightly arrhythmic action. If any bowler was the heir to Richard Hadlee, it was Akram. As a batsman, he was elegant and powerful and could have averaged in the forties in Test cricket if he had restrained his big-hitting instincts. He looked like a handsome movie star villain, all aquiline nose, pocked skin and sly charm. Full of fire, he was a typical Pakistani cricket leader, flying into terrible tempers and seemingly suffering from bipolar disorder most of the time he was on the field.

His partner, Waqar, had fewer tricks but was just as potent. Waqar was a stocky right-armer with a low slinging action. Most round-arm bowlers were thought to be incapable of swinging the ball into right-handed batsmen, and this gave Waqar his weapon: he would pelt in at high pace, sling the ball round-arm and full, and the batsman anticipating an outswinging full toss got instead an inswinging yorker that crushed his toe or uprooted his middle stump. Waqar, who like most seasoned Pakistani Test players would be his country's captain at some point, was probably the fastest bowler in the world in 1994.

Mushtaq bowled leg-spinners with the action of a Max Walker, if that can be imagined. He bounded up and looped both arms over at the same time. With a higher arm action than Warne, he imparted more top-spin and dip, and had a deadlier wrong'un. He had just enough flamboyance to raise the question of what he was hiding.

At some point in their careers, each of Mushtaq, Wasim and Waqar would be tainted by allegations of corruption.

But not yet. On the second morning they completed their work, skittling the Australian tail for 337.

Pakistan's dashing cackhanded opening combination of Saeed Anwar and Aamir Sohail put on 90 runs in even time, seeing off Australia's green new-ball pairing of McGrath and West Australian Jo Angel. McDermott was down again, this time with an infected ingrown toenail, and Angel's selection was just reward after five five-wicket bags for his State the previous season. But it must have felt like a poisoned chalice as the Pakistani left-handers went after him. A huge deficit threatened, until Warne and May took advantage of the deteriorating wicket and set off a collapse from 1/153 to the stumps score of 7/209.

On the ground where Pakistani captains were meant never to get lbw decisions against them, Salim Malik received a poor one, inside-edging onto his pads, given out by local Khizer Hayat, nicknamed 'The German Hotel' (say his name out loud a few times). So much for hometown bias: perhaps the world really was turning.

Pakistan reached 256 the next morning, and Australia built on its 81-run lead after losing Taylor. The bright new spirit was affecting everyone positively except the captain, who had become the first man ever to record a pair on his captaincy debut. But Boon hit one of the best centuries of his career and with Mark Waugh took the score to 2/171, effectively 2/252.

Australia had victory within sight, then fluffed it. At the very end of the day, just as the Australians were thinking about curries and an early night, Waqar bowled Mark Waugh and Wasim rolled Bevan and Steve Waugh, both first ball, to leave Australia at a nervous 5/183. Boon carried his bat the next day, but Wasim and Waqar were otherwise irresistible, mowing through the Australian tail for an innings total of 232, the last eight wickets falling for 61. The teams went to the Karachi Pearl Intercontinental on the fourth evening with Pakistan at 3/155, needing a further 159 to win. Either way, 2 October had the potential to be a history-making day.

And here is where it got interesting.

Salim Malik had got out late on the fourth day for 43. With his dismissal, caught at first slip by Taylor off Angel, much of Pakistan's hope evaporated. The Australians nicknamed Salim 'The Rat', although at this point it was more a reference to his facial features than his actions. That would soon change.

At around 10.30 pm, Malik phoned the room occupied by May and Warne. May answered. Malik invited the two spinners to come and see him. May refused, saying he was tired, but Warne agreed to go.

To understand why the Pakistan captain would suddenly phone two opponents late on the last night of a Test match, it is necessary to backtrack a few weeks to that one-day tournament in Colombo, the one everyone had forgotten until they were asked to remember it again.

ABOVE: The Rat: smashing centuries off Australia wasn't enough for Salim Malik.

One night during that series, Mark Waugh was approached in the Australians' hotel by a man, presumably Sri Lankan or Indian, who introduced himself as John. Oozing flattery, like many admiring businessmen around the world, John ingratiated himself with Waugh. Usually off-hand with such fans, Waugh pricked up his ears when John offered him money: $US4000 for 'general information about weather and pitch conditions' over the next six months. He also asked Waugh if he would tell him about team selections and tactics. A deal was struck. Waugh would say that he took it as 'the same thing you do in a radio interview'. He didn't know much about John except that he was a man 'who bets on cricket', and he didn't ask any questions. Hey, money fell out of the sky for a professional cricketer; all Junior had to do was catch it.

John then asked another favour: he wanted to meet Shane Warne. They were in a casino near the team's hotel. 'Casino' is a grand name for these establishments, little more than the lounges of hotel bars with a couple of roulette wheels and card tables. That night, Warne had lost $US5000 playing roulette. Waugh introduced John. Warne later drew a distinction between 'a man who bets on cricket' and a bookmaker. Yet, given that betting on cricket was illegal, the distinction was self-serving and disingenuous. There was little misunderstanding what John was about, and when he pulled out an envelope with $US5000 in it – 'a gift to make up for your gambling losses' – initially Warne refused.

As luck would have it, John was staying at the same hotel as the Australians. The next day, he pressed the cash on Warne again, and this time Warne (who had not made good his losses on the night) accepted. John described his gift as a thankyou for the times Warne had helped John win bets he had placed on Australia winning. Warne would give John 'pitch and weather information' on the three occasions John called him through the following Australian summer.

In Sri Lanka, Warne and Waugh kept the news of John's gifts to themselves. They knew that betting on cricket was illegal, but did not think to form a link between corruption and what John was asking of them. But they couldn't have felt all that innocent about it, because they didn't tell Simpson or Taylor. Waugh informed Sue Porter, his then partner, who agreed with him that it was no different from giving radio interviews for money. He also spoke to another player, whose identity he couldn't or wouldn't divulge, who told him it was an unwise thing to do and might come back and haunt him later in his career.

Another incident during that Sri Lankan leg would later be reviewed in a more sinister light. In their game against Pakistan, Australia scored a paltry 179 but were able to defend it when the Pakistanis, after a bright start, lost their urgency. Malik scored 22 runs in eighty-four minutes off fifty-one balls, enough to prompt surprise among the Australians. Steve Waugh, noting that Malik was 'particularly watchful of my non-deviating medium pacers', wondered: 'Why are these guys blocking everything?' Other

Pakistan batsmen also lost their wickets meekly and they were out for 151. Inzamam, having crawled to 29 off sixty-nine balls, ran a long way down the wicket to Warne and missed the ball by almost as far. Saeed Anwar would later tell a Pakistani court that he believed certain players had thrown the match. A bookmaker, Salim Pervez, told the same court that he had offered Salim Malik and Mushtaq Ahmed $US100,000 to throw a one-day match against Australia, though he didn't nominate which one.

Late in the night of 1 October 1994, Warne went to Malik's room. The Pakistan captain was wearing a white salwar kameez, the long robe-like shirt and pyjama-type trousers commonly worn in Pakistan. He must have made an exotic, if not unnerving, sight to the leg-spinner. After some uneasy pleasantries, the Pakistan captain put his offer.

'You know,' he said, 'we cannot lose.'

Warne laughed, saying both teams had a good chance of winning.

Malik repeated, 'You don't understand. We cannot lose.'

Malik said he would give Warne and May $US200,000 – in a brown paper bag, delivered within half an hour – if they agreed to bowl wide outside the off stump the next day, stopping Australia from winning. Malik implied that the Pakistanis would leave the balls and the match would be drawn. Warne was too stunned to say anything, apart from reasserting his confidence that Australia would win. He went back to his room and told May, who replied, tongue in cheek, 'Hmm, $200,000, eh? Half an hour, eh?'

When Warne assured him he was serious, May said, 'I hope you told him where to go.' May then instructed Warne, who was badly shaken, to phone The Rat 'and tell him we're going to nail them'.

They told Taylor, who relayed the news to Simpson and the manager, Col Egar, who in turn told the ICC match referee, New Zealand's John Reid. The next morning, some, but not all, of the other Australian players were informed.

In a state of some confusion, Warne took the field but May, showing the effects of stress, had woken with a stiff neck and could not bowl. McGrath was out of the game with a strained quadriceps.

Warne, Angel and Steve Waugh took on the responsibility of taking the last seven wickets. Warne, fired up by the previous night's events, dismissed Akram Raza lbw with the fifth ball of the day. Saeed Anwar lifted a drive straight back to Angel, Wasim Akram skied Warne, and Basit Ali was trapped in front. Within the first hour, Pakistan were 7/184.

In a move that would have been odd in any team other than Pakistan, Inzamam had been pushed down the order to number eight. He put on fifty-two for the eighth wicket with Rashid Latif, the wicketkeeper, to keep Pakistan in the hunt. Steve Waugh trapped Rashid leg-before, then Waqar came in and put on twenty-two with Inzamam before Warne had him caught behind. With a lead of fifty-five and one wicket to take, Australia seemed to have the match in their keeping.

Mushtaq Ahmed joined Inzamam. The hulking Multani right-hander must have reminded those old enough to remember of Warwick Armstrong, the 'Big Ship' who had played either side of World War I. Edmund Blunden wrote of Armstrong that 'he made a bat look like a teaspoon and the bowling like weak tea.' Enormous men, Armstrong and Inzamam were both in the habit of poking around at bowling like a giant playing with his food. Armstrong, a notorious dabber and prodder, was also capable of enormous hitting on those occasions when he was in the mood. Likewise, Inzamam had come into international cricket with some mighty clouts in the 1991–92 World Cup, including a match-turning knock in the final, but most of the time he pushed and glanced and caused hands to wring and exasperated sighs to break out.

Sometimes, his mood changed. Until Waqar got out, Inzamam had fussed about for 25 runs in two hours. Alone with Mushtaq, he turned into the Inzy of the World Cup. He swatted Angel, who had set himself up for a caution after reacting volcanically to Khizer Hayat's rejection of an lbw shout, and floated down the wicket to Warne.

Inside forty minutes, a blink in cricketing time, Inzamam and Mushtaq had scored fifty-three runs and put Pakistan a shot away from victory. After such a tense wrestle of a match, the final act was rushing by.

Inzamam was on strike to Warne, who held a meeting with Taylor. They decided to remove the mid-wicket, tempting Inzamam to hit across the line. Warne would bowl around the wicket, hoping he might draw a leading edge if Inzamam played across the spin.

As Healy recalled, 'it worked even better.' Warne tossed it up, Inzamam stepped out of his crease to turn it through the mid-wicket gap, and the ball passed between his bat and legs. It kept a little low, but not too low for the ever-vigilant Healy. Healy had a flash of seeing the ball hit the stumps. Warne went up. Taylor went up. Healy didn't go up, but nor did he stay quite low enough. The ball spun between his legs and ran down to the boundary. Warne, halfway through an appeal, clutched his head. Taylor likewise. Healy, who had spun around on one knee to watch the ball roll away, bowed briefly in anguish. He roused himself to kick over the stumps. He would not talk for an hour, and when he would he could say nothing that didn't begin with F or C.

Happy with the win and still five months from being publicly exposed, Malik found himself standing beside Boon at the presentation ceremony. He asked the Australian what he was doing that night.

'What is there to do in Pakistan? Nothing,' Boon said.

'We've got a bit of a party going on,' Malik smiled. 'Do you smoke?'

Boon said he enjoyed a Benson & Hedges, but not the kind of thing he sensed Malik was offering. Malik still invited him, staying, 'We can talk about all sorts of things.'

ABOVE: Through the legs and to the fence, Pakistan win in Karachi.

Rebuffed again, Malik would also approach Mark Waugh during the tour, at a reception for the players in Rawalpindi. Malik and Waugh knew each other, having played together for the English county team Essex. According to Waugh, Malik said, 'I'll offer you $US200,000. I'll have it in your hotel tonight if you get four or five players and you throw the [one-day] game tomorrow.' He nominated Mark, his brother Steve, May and Warne as the players who might share the cash.

Malik then slithered away, leaving Waugh nonplussed. He told Warne, who said, 'Well, Junior, are you going to tell Stephen?'

Steve Waugh's recollection deserves full repetition.

'My first reaction was disgust that this low-life of a prick would even consider my name as a candidate for his vile plan. "Tell him to fuck off" was my only response.'

When he found the Pakistani captain an hour and a half later, Mark Waugh said, 'We don't play the game that way.' To underline his point, Waugh went out the next day, in the game under discussion, and scored 121 from 134 balls. When Anwar and Inzamam went on a spree and overtook the Australians' 250 runs, Malik found Waugh and said, 'See, you should have taken the money.'

Having dominated the Second and Third Tests with what would be arguably the best batting against Warne by anyone in fifteen years, Malik was feeling invincible. In the Second Test he scored a seven-hour 237 to save the match after Pakistan followed on with two days to go. In the Third, he hit 75 and 143. His stocks would never be higher.

It was established, over time, that the offers to Warne, May and Mark Waugh were not the first time Malik and some of his teammates had been involved in betting and bribery. With oceans of money swilling through illegal betting houses in the subcontinent and Middle East, it was inevitable that players from low-wage countries would be drawn in. One would hope that it was their integrity that kept Australian players from taking bribes, but credit can also be given to the high salaries they had earnt since the Ian Chappell-led revolution in the 1970s. The captains who were lured in by criminal money – Malik, Hansie Cronje, Mohammad Azharuddin – had one thing in common: they thought they were underpaid.

Australians had been approached with suspect offers before. During a tour of Sri Lanka in 1992, a member of a Mumbai-based illegal betting syndicate asked Dean Jones if he would provide 'preview' information for a substantial sum. After reporting it to Border and Boon, Jones declined. Then, on the last morning of the Fifth Test of the Australians' 1993 Ashes tour of England, the former Pakistani Test captain Mushtaq Mohammad phoned Border to offer a 'considerable amount of money' for arranging an Australian loss. At the time, Australia were 0/9, chasing 120.

Given their history when chasing small targets, perhaps it would have needed no organisational skills. Border told his teammates that he had treated the offer with the contempt it deserved. Later, Mushtaq would say it was a joke, but Border maintained that it was a genuine offer. Even allowing for Border's sense of humour deficit in the middle of Test matches, subsequent events in Pakistan would suggest that his interpretation of the offer was more credible than Mushtaq's.

The 1994 Australians, as was their wont, preferred to keep their heads in the sand. Warne and Mark Waugh would describe themselves as 'naive and stupid' for their part in the scandal. Seldom as competent with words as with bat and ball, this time they were spot on.

Throughout the Australian Ashes season that followed the Pakistan tour, when England were put away again, Waugh continued to fulfil his obligations to John the bookmaker. He claimed to make no connection between his and Warne's association with John and the approaches from Malik. From the outside, it seems clear that Waugh and Warne were being groomed, softened with easy money and set up for coercion. From the inside, perhaps because

WARNE AND MARK WAUGH WOULD DESCRIBE THEMSELVES AS 'NAIVE AND STUPID'

they saw their own sportsmanship and integrity as beyond question, neither Waugh nor Warne thought there was any connection.

In February 1995, Phil Wilkins broke the story of the Warne–May offer in the *Sydney Morning Herald*, and the *Age* named Malik as the Pakistan player who had offered the money. The Australian team manager, Ian McDonald, heard that one or two players had also received money from a bookmaker in Sri Lanka. Soon Waugh and Warne were making handwritten confessions. The chief executive of the ACB, Graham Halbish, and the chairman, Alan Crompton, interviewed Waugh and Warne at the Parkroyal

Hotel in Sydney the night before the players were to fly to the West Indies to contest the Frank Worrell Trophy. That timing cannot be brushed off. The Australians were about to embark on the most critical tour of the era, the tour that would determine whether they could call themselves world champions. They had their best chance in twenty years to beat the West Indies, to salve all those old wounds. Two of the most important Australian players had just been found to have acted in a corrupt manner – not so corrupt as to take Malik's money, or to be actually involved in match fixing, but putting themselves on a criminal payroll nonetheless.

Halbish and Crompton decided to fine Waugh $10,000 and Warne $8000. They also decided to keep it quiet. They informed the ACB directors and the top echelon of the ICC, but nobody else knew, aside from a coterie of senior players: Taylor, Healy, Steve Waugh and the two culprits. Four years later, when the *Australian* newspaper's Malcolm Conn exposed the secret deal, Waugh and Warne were forced to publicly apologise and acknowledge their wrongdoing, and went before an inquiry headed by Rob O'Regan QC, who wrote:

> They must have known that it is wrong to accept money from, and supply information to, a bookmaker whom they also knew as someone who betted on cricket. Otherwise they would have reported the incident to team management long before they were found out in February 1995. In behaving as they did they failed lamentably to set the sort of example one might expect from senior players and role models for many young cricketers.

But at the time, Waugh, Warne and the other players in the know thought that it was a minor matter that had been proper-ly – that is, covertly – dealt with. Their reticence betrayed guilty consciences, but the extent of their wrong-doing was not yet clear to them. What was most important to them was getting to the Caribbean and winning cricket games. Morally, they were chil-dren. They just wanted to play. Simpson, on the other hand, found out about the secret fines as the team was about to board the plane to the West Indies. The coach, who was taking the corruption issue much more seriously than the players, was furious. He said that if he had known a day earlier, he would not have flown to the West Indies at all. 'What am I doing here,' he asked himself, 'if these people don't trust me?'

Perhaps the best way to put into perspective the Australians' direct involvement in the world of match-fixing is to note the observations of Michael Slater, who was sharing a hotel room with Mark Waugh in the 1994–95 summer. Slater had a contract with the Sydney radio station 2DAY FM to provide match previews. One day, half an hour after Slater had made this call from his hotel room, Waugh picked up the phone and seemed to do much the same. He said the weather was fine, the pitch would take spin, so Warne and May would both play, and if Australia won the toss they were likely to bat first (it was a little more than just 'pitch and weather information', after all). When Waugh hung up, Slater asked him which radio station he was working for.

Waugh said it wasn't a radio station, it was an Indian man who paid him $US1000 each time he passed on this information.

Slater's recollection speaks volumes: 'I thought nothing of it, apart from – Wow, he's an experienced cricketer, he's been around – I hope someone will ask me to do that when I've been around for another couple of years.'

Stupid, naive, greedy? Most certainly. Corrupt? No – or not yet. Big-time corruption always starts with small-time gifts. As would emerge a few years later, there were others whose relationships with bookmakers started out, just like Waugh's and Warne's, with a few innocent-seeming phone calls, money changing hands, one little thing following another. Would Waugh, Warne or any other Australians have ended up in the same place? Perhaps not. Nobody would impugn their competitive integrity, but then, before 2000 nobody impugned Hansie Cronje's either.

The 1994 tour of Pakistan has become a cloak-and-dagger story of gangsters, corruption and huge bundles of US dollars in brown paper bags. Three inquiries later, two in Pakistan and one in Australia, Malik would receive a lifetime ban and his role in match-rigging would be well established. The ICC would set up an anti-corruption unit. Waugh and Warne would get over the embarrassment and retire with glittering records. In retrospect, there are many games involving Pakistan that now take on a suspect air; but match-rigging also appears to be a relic of the era.

On the field, Australia had played well but had noticeably missed their goals. In Karachi, they had again lost a Test match as close as Adelaide 1993 and Sydney 1994. They had lost a Test series overseas, again. They were no closer to the top. They might be able to go to the West Indies and win the Frank Worrell Trophy, but the benchmarks of success would shift just as they were being achieved. They may win in the West Indies, yes, but how long is it since they won in Pakistan or India?

'THE WEAKEST AUSTRALIAN TEAM I'VE PLAYED AGAINST'

Kingston, April 1995

IF REVENGE IS A DISH BEST EATEN COLD, AFTER SEVENTEEN YEARS IT MUST HAVE TASTED VERY, VERY WELL CHILLED.

It can be a bit sad when they end up as commentators. One moment they're on the field, in the changing room at the centre of the effort, and the next they're earning their bread by casting judgement on their mates. All public criticism hurts, but players can always brush off the opinions of some journalist. It's not so easy when it comes from a retired Australian captain.

But it wasn't sad that Allan Border was in the West Indies as a commentator, because there was a piece in the heart of every Australian player on Sabina Park that was playing for him. It was sad that he couldn't be in it as a player, yet at least he was there, on the island, in the ground.

This was redemption day. He would have preferred it to have come four years earlier, against Richards, Greenidge, Haynes and Marshall. It would have been better two years earlier, at Adelaide. But you can't pick and choose. If revenge is a dish best eaten cold, after seventeen years it must have tasted very, very well chilled.

By the beginning of 1995, the long-term plan was coming together. Australia had demolished the English. Taylor, who

THE SKILLS CAN BE BUILT UP, BUT THE DETERMINATION IS HARDWIRED

had recovered his form, and Slater were becoming as strong an opening pair as Simpson and Lawry. Boon was still at three, adamant. The Waughs, after much patience, had grown into their skins at last. Steve, in particular, had been unstoppable with the bat and sometimes the ball since the previous summer. In the middle-order, the new wave was coming through, in depth. Bevan had been dropped after an awful few Tests against the short ball, but his replacement Greg Blewett had stroked hundreds in his first two Tests. Healy was proving why it's always best to select a wicketkeeper on character; the skills can be built up, but the determination is hardwired.

So much for the batting and keeping, which appeared rock-solid. The bowling was another matter. For the summer, Taylor had enjoyed the dream trio of McDermott, McGrath and Warne. But then, during the one-day series in the West Indies, McDermott and Damien Fleming went amiss and the bowling was suddenly looking frayed going into a Frank Worrell Trophy series. With his boyish bowl haircut McGrath was a fine back-up for McDermott, but still green for an attack leader. His most likely support would be Paul Reiffel and Brendon Julian. Reiffel's Test figures were modest in the extreme, numbering

LEFT: After ten years in Test cricket, the Waugh machine was fully assembled.

twelve wickets in the nine Tests he had played outside England, while Julian was an erratic left-armer who wasn't even guaranteed a game for his State. The Waughs might jag an important dismissal here and there, but with fast wickets expected, Taylor would probably not be able to pair May with Warne. He was one paceman short.

In other words, everything rested with the leg-spinner.

If Australia had strength in their batting and question-marks over their bowling, the West Indian side presented a reverse image. Their bowling power remained with Ambrose and Walsh. It was true that they were getting on. The vertical lines on Curtly's brow were deeper and angrier, and the horizontal lines across Courtney's looked ever more harmless and simple-minded. Within the team environment, both appearances were deceptive: Ambrose was actually a class clown, while Walsh was emerging as a thoughtful tactician and leader. They were still two of the greatest fast bowlers on the planet. The prospect of duels between Ambrose and Walsh and the Australian top order was mouth-watering. Yet, in some ways, their outcome would be predictable. There would be wins and losses on both sides. All would rise to the occasion. Australia's batsmen against the West Indies' bowlers would be a titanic clash, but it wouldn't decide the series.

The series would be decided by the unknowns: Glenn McGrath and Paul Reiffel against Sherwin Campbell and Stuart Williams. Who? Precisely. Brendon Julian against Carl Hooper. Mark Waugh against Jimmy Adams. Keith Arthurton had looked very good coming in after Haynes, Greenidge, Richardson and Richards. But now?

The key was how the Australian bowlers would handle Richardson and Brian Lara. Richardson, who had a better record against Australia than any other West Indian batsman in the late 1980s and early 1990s, had been struggling with chronic fatigue syndrome. A likeable, sincere man, he was finding captaincy more burden than joy. He had taken some time out of the game. His authority in the team was lukewarm. Many felt that Walsh, who had led a victory in the subcontinent, should remain captain. In the middle, Richardson's face twisted up in a grimace, as if bothered by strong sunlight. He even took to wearing a helmet.

Lara was probably the key to it all. Since his 277 against Australia in Sydney in 1993, not a bad maiden Test century, he had achieved so much so quickly that the Australians' best hope was that he had done it all too soon. In 1994, he scored 375 in a Test innings in Antigua. It was only against English bowlers, and on a small ground, but nobody else had done it anywhere against anybody, not even Bradman or Sobers, and so Brian Lara was now the world record holder. To show how much he enjoyed big innings and English bowling, he followed it just over a month later with 501 not out for Warwickshire, the record for first-class cricket.

If he was a run-machine, however, he wasn't a machine. It was already suspected that Lara might turn out to be less a great batsman than a player of great innings. He flashed a florid backlift that gave bowlers hope that he might squirt loosely behind point. But more significantly, he was a passionate man, moody and willful. He was not a robotic Bradman or Tendulkar. He could be probed and shaken. He was restless with ambition. It was a double-edged challenge for the Australians.

THE PARTY ATMOSPHERE OF THE ISLANDS HAD ITS OWN MAGNETISM

They wanted to manipulate him into the wrong mood, but not into a bad mood. In the wrong mood, he might give up his wicket. In a bad mood, he might knuckle down and bat for two days.

So going into the First Test in Barbados, the series had more intrigue than an ICC board meeting. The West Indies won the five-match one-day series 4-1, with Australia out of sorts, all the more so when McDermott and Fleming went down. McDermott twisted his ankle while jogging and ended on crutches; Fleming, who had taken a hat-trick on the Pakistan tour, strained his shoulder. Some of the Australians were also succumbing to one of the subsidiary challenges of a Caribbean tour: not getting enough sleep. The party atmosphere of the islands had its own magnetism, and it could be difficult for cricketers to make what seemed a great sacrifice and go to bed. But in a meeting Simpson called after the one-dayers, the players agreed to spend more of their free time with teammates, rest more, and put cricket first. They would delay the gratification until after the Fourth Test.

The preparation intensified, particularly with the volume of chin music at net practices. It didn't take much of a cricket brain to predict the West Indian bowling tactics. The novelty in Taylor's approach, as captain, was to urge the Australian bowlers to strike back. In previous series, Australian fast bowlers had taken it relatively easy on their West Indian counterparts, hoping to establish some kind of détente. This time, someone convinced McGrath that he would be bounced anyway, so there was no point going softly on the West Indians in hope of a quid pro quo. The tactic, in Healy's words, would be 'Retaliate first!' Steve Waugh would write: 'For [McGrath] to face up to that must have been terrifying, because his skill level with the bat was akin to a featherweight taking on Muhammad Ali – and pain was a logical outcome.' McGrath's fearless – or hopeless – attitude was vital both psychologically and in its wicket-taking outcome. The West Indian tail would lie paralytic for the whole series.

To see the dividends of their aggressive preparation, Australia had to wait fifteen minutes into the Test series. Within that time, Reiffel and Julian had sent both openers and Richardson to the Kensington Oval pavilion. Hooper and Lara blasted back, but Lara was out after lunch, caught in the gully by a juggling Steve Waugh. The ball bobbled between his arms, chest and the turf, but he claimed the catch and Lara assented. Only later, with exhaustive replay and commentary, did the catch become a matter for disputation. Slow motion doesn't necessarily clarify. In any case, it started a run of very poor luck for Lara throughout the series.

McGrath took eight wickets in a low-scoring match, the Australian batsmen chipped away at Walsh and a lethargic Ambrose, and the tourists won with surprising ease, by ten wickets on the third day. It was Australia's first-ever Test win in Bridgetown. In both innings, the Australian pacemen rocked the West Indian lower order with the kind of short-pitched treatment that the West Indians had meted out for twenty years with impunity.

The Second Test in Antigua shaped up as a classic, with the West Indies chasing 257 on the last day. Richardson, who had

ABOVE: Down, boy: Richardson restrains Ambrose in Trinidad.

moved up to open, and Lara fell before storms swept in and turned it into a moot point.

In Trinidad, the West Indians welcomed a pitch that would have been perfect for the cultivation of mushrooms. Warne described it as the worst he ever saw for a Test match, biased no doubt because he had to bat and bowl on it. Boon, playing his 100th Test, thought the same. Ambrose and Walsh probably thought it was the best. Half the first day was lost to rain, and still the match didn't go past the third. The fans were getting their money's worth in quality of entertainment, if not quantity. On day one, the Caribbean pacemen were rampant, rumbling Australia for 128. It was here that Steve Waugh played possibly his greatest innings. Not only did he make 63 not out, but he dared to speak back to Ambrose, causing a brief but tempestuous on-pitch fracas. These things often pass in a matter of seconds, but time and telling elongates and amplifies them into epic battles. Ambrose, outraged by Waugh swearing at him, had to be pulled away by Richardson, a sight resembling a tug boat trying to move an aircraft carrier. The image of Richardson yanking on his fellow Antiguan's arm said so much, it was clear; yet exactly what it was saying, nobody quite knew.

Revved up rather than subdued by the fight, Australia's bowlers restricted the hosts to an eight-run lead, McGrath taking 6/47. At no point did he look as downright terrifying as Ambrose, but his figures were as good. The story of his cricketing life.

Australia went to stumps after day two with a sniff of Frank. They were 0/20 and felt they only had to bat all day to guarantee the knockout win. Next morning, they lost all of their wickets for 85. Despite, or because of, the rapidity of their capitulation, they still entertained hopes of rolling the West Indians for less than the target of ninety-eight. Instead, someone waved a wand over the pitch and batting became easy; the hosts only lost one wicket and squared the series.

And so to Jamaica. Interestingly, up to this point the anticipated big individual duel had fizzled. Warne, as would be the case throughout his career, was not hugely successful in the West Indies. In seven Tests on his two tours there, he would take 17 wickets at nearly 40. Partly this was due to the pitches: a leg-spinner needs pace off the wicket even more than fast bowlers. Partly, Warne was hampered by a right thumb bruised by an Ambrose steepler and a neck ricked by a fall off a 'Big Banana', an aquaplane towed by a speedboat. This *was* the West Indies. Partly also, Warne's relative weakness in the Caribbean was due to the batsmen being far better players of leg-spin than they looked. Warne's greatest bunnies, throughout his career, were the white teams: England, New Zealand, South Africa. Their approach was to study him hard and tighten their techniques, hold meetings and develop a plan for countering him. But they failed; with Warne, there was an invisible line, often crossed, between respect and fear. The non-white teams, by contrast – India, Sri Lanka and the West Indies – did not lie awake at night planning and worrying about him. They would take him on, without bothering too much about technique, and engage him head-on in the game of confidence. To contrast the white and non-white approaches in this way is gross racial and ethnic stereotyping, of course, but it's also true. Year after year, while Warne was playing Test cricket, the best antidote to bravado was more bravado. The player who handled him best of all the West Indians was Carl Hooper. QED.

Like any good argument based on racial stereotypes, the Warne theory does have a glaring exception: Pakistan, against whom he took 90 wickets at 20.17 in 15 Tests. But he only averaged 28 against them in Pakistan, where they were more confident, and as always, there were peculiar frailties in Pakistan's batting over the years that made them a singular case that had to be removed from any statistical sample.

Yet while Warne was relegated to support status, the West Indian wickets kept falling – to Reiffel, to Julian, to McGrath. Lara had not been able to capitalise on Warne's dry spell; the pacemen had picked him off and, on the verge of a century in Antigua, he had fallen to the catch of Boon's career. The pre-series prognosis, that the decisive contest would be between Australia's bowlers and the West Indies' batsmen, had been correct, yet it had been fought without match-winning contributions from either Warne or Lara.

For the fourth time of the series, Taylor called 'tails' and the coin landed heads. Sabina Park was a big, long slab of a ground with a unique microclimate: a cannabis cloud that hung over the field between wind gusts. The pitch was red clay rolled shiny and full of jigsaw cracks showing a tint of whiteness from the saline content in the soil. Richardson decided to bat first, or rather, to avoid batting last.

Reiffel took the new ball. Stuart Williams had strike. It is hard to imagine that the most important Test in world cricket for nearly twenty years could be started by two more unprepossessing names. But Reiffel was the perfect bowler for this opponent: he nagged like a mother of ten, he had great discipline, and he moved it off the seam just enough to cause problems. Certainly enough to trouble Williams, a fidgety, loose-looking right-hander. The second ball of the match popped off his bat and chest to Greg Blewett at short leg.

Now for the real match: Richardson batting with Lara. The left-armer Julian shared the new ball with Reiffel, but they couldn't break through. Lara and Richardson batted almost to the end of the first session, Lara in his most relaxed, sparkling form of the series. Some of his off-drives off Warne were good enough to preserve in amber. Richardson seemed scratchy and squinty, as he had all series, in the unfamiliar opening role wearing the even less familiar grilled helmet. Lara strolled to 65 just before lunch, cover-driving Warne to bring up the century stand.

Then, the pivotal moment – and it was Warne versus Lara after all. On the stroke of lunch, Lara pressed forward, the ball bobbed up ahead of the stumps, and Healy dived forward to take the catch. The umpire, Karl Liebenberg, thought about it. Not for the first or last time, Lara relieved the pressure from the umpire by walking. Personal criticisms of Lara would mount over the years, but he was a more honest walker than nearly every other batsman, and certainly all the great ones. Given the context – a pitch full of runs, a crucial match, an innings building nicely – Lara's honesty was all the more commendable.

For the first time in eight Tests, Warne had got Lara out.

In the middle session, the suspect West Indian middle-order was asked the question begged on Carl Hooper's T-shirt: 'Form is temporary, class is permanent.' So which of these definitions applied to Adams, Hooper and Arthurton? That day, as so often, after good starts they let their team down. Adams played some elegant straight drives on his way to 20 before trying an ungainly pull off Julian, scooping a catch to mid-on, his feet both mid-air as he played the shot. Hooper accumulated a patient 23 before wildly slicing Julian to slip. Arthurton made 16, including a towering six off Warne, then nicked McGrath.

Only Richardson stood firm, but Richardson wasn't enough on his own. He made his first century since the Sydney Test of the 1992–93 series, but was then becalmed for forty-five minutes while wickets fell at the other end. He was dismissed without adding a run and by stumps the home side was out for 265, two late wickets falling to a sharp Steve Waugh. As Border remarked, 'It looked ugly for a while, but it was a great day.'

Like the tennis player who can only claim a break of service by holding his own, Australia had to press home the advantage on day two. Again it looked ugly for a while: Taylor, Boon and Slater were out before lunch. The wicket had hardened and quickened. Taylor and Boon were unlucky perhaps: Taylor snapped up by an Adams blinder in close, and Boon caught off his helmet. Slater meanwhile had been slashing at everything, and used up enough luck for three men before Lara took a fine diving outfield catch off a top-edged pull.

Steve Waugh came in to join his twin, and as usual looked utterly incompetent against the short ball. A short leg was in place, of course, and Adams was moved right under Waugh's nose, almost on the pitch at an extremely silly point. Because he refused to hook, Waugh had no choice but to duck or twist or fend or take a thunderbolt in the ribs. For West Indian bowlers, this was a red rag to a bull. They could attack him without fear. Walsh came around the wicket and set a field of three slips, gully and two short legs. It was estimated that Waugh faced 150 short-pitched balls in his innings, an onslaught as close to Bodyline as the rules would permit.

But competence is not only a matter of aesthetics; effectiveness counts too. Counts, in fact, for more. As Waugh had resolved in the period from 1991 to 1992 when he was dropped from the Australian side, it would no longer be how, but how many. He had been an attractive, daring slasher early in his career. Now it was no more Mister Pretty Boy. He had been encouraging the West Indians to bowl at his ribs and head all series, and had so far emerged as the best batsman on either side. So he would again this day. His game had been transformed since 1992; after eight years in Test cricket, he was going to take all the cheap dismissals, all the disappoint- ments, all the grudges and lack of grace and surliness and sensitivity to criticism, and convert them into fuel. It was almost alchemy, the way he did it. As if maturity were a matter of will-power, Steve Waugh decided one day that he was going to make the most of his natural talent. And he stuck to it for ten years. What a contrast with the man standing at second slip, Hooper, a player of similar age and all-round ability who would manage to play 102 Tests with a batting average of 36, a bowling average of 49 and an incomparable record of under-achievement.

The easy comparative benchmark, for observers, was to take Mark Waugh. Because they were twins, the Waughs were an obvi- ous study – the first scientific twin-study in international cricket! But this would always be unfair to both. Because Mark was so pleasing to the eye, as a stylist, Steve was unjustly thought to be an ugly player. Many who saw Steve punch the ball off the back foot through mid-on, barely moving, pure timing emanating from the core of his body, would testify that there was no more beautiful sight in the game. And because Steve was so grimly determined, Mark was unjustly thought to be a carefree type. These contrasts appeal to poets, but they weren't accurate. Mark was just as steely as his brother. Some days he was even tougher, battling through periods that Steve couldn't handle. The truth was that, removing the stinky red herring of comparison – odorous as well as odious – both were gifted, crowd-pleasing, fast-scoring, ruthlessly deter- mined competitors.

Only rarely did their games synchronise, but this was it. In thirty-three previous Tests together, they had put on one century partnership. In four hours at Sabina Park, between just before lunch and just before stumps, they put on 231. Even though they would play together for Australia for another seven years, this would be the biggest Test partnership of their lives. They did it at a run a minute.

ABOVE: Sabina siblings: the Waughs in a rare moment touching each other.

They weren't just surviving the artillery, but were counter-attacking. Mark, who had been scratchy in the nets, lacking sureness and inconsistent through the series, batted with total control, barely mis-hitting a ball all day. Steve was ugly-beautiful and fully focused, later calling his state 'a certain type of loneliness that I found extremely peaceful'. Winston Benjamin, booed by the Jamaican crowd, sat down, apparently weeping beside the pitch. Courtney Browne, one of a rolodex of average wicketkeepers in the post–Jeffrey Dujon era, dropped a straightforward chance when Steve was 42. The noise from the West Indian fielders abated, over by over. The Waughs gave a run-out chance after lunch, but substitute Shivnarine Chanderpaul threw to the wrong end and missed too. As the pacemen tired, Hooper's off-spinners became more dangerous, showing how much potential lay in the wicket for Warne. In less than four hours of a backyard-cricket dream come true, from 3/73 the Waughs cruised past the West Indies' total and began building a lead. Both were driven on, and on, by a remembrance of beatings past. The only pity for Australia was that it didn't go on for longer. Mark was out prodding at Hooper, for 126, just before stumps. He complained that he had something in his eye, partially blinding him. But his job was thoroughly done.

Both twins scored their eighth Test centuries that day. Mark was playing his forty-eighth Test, Steve his seventy-sixth. The one thing Steve was definitely better at than his brother was not getting out. On the third day, batting with Blewett, he ground forwards. Blewett made 69, his first half-century of the series, rocking back and pulling the way he had in Australia, or going down on one knee to drive square through the off, before holing out to the seventh bowler a desperate Richardson used, Arthurton. Australia was more than 150 ahead.

Still Waugh kept going. Healy, Julian and Warne fell cheaply, but Reiffel helped him pile on another seventy-four runs of pain, and finally McGrath was there for an all-run four to bring up Waugh's first Test double-century. Both twins had played their best Test innings in the most important match of their life. Passing 200, Steve was mobbed by Australian spectators, among them the tired and emotional former player-turned-commentator-turned-tour-group-leader

Greg Ritchie. A girl kissed him. A little Australiana festival took place on the centre square: one fellow was holding a didgeridoo, another a Sherrin football. One wore an Essendon football jersey, another a lifesaver's cap. From the commentary box, Allan Border watched with pride. Being modest, he resisted the temptation to put on his cape and fly down to the wicket.

Then it was over. Kenny Benjamin produced a snorter that Waugh conceded would have got him out whether he was 200, 100 or 0. Waugh's double-century was only the fourth in the Caribbean by an Australian, after Neil Harvey, Bob Simpson and Bill Lawry, and the first in thirty years. His average for the series was 107. To place that into relief: of the other batsmen on both sides, Lara averaged 44, Mark Waugh 40 and nobody else bettered

WHAT WERE THE WEST INDIES MADE OF? NOT ENOUGH.

Richardson's 32. Waugh was a batsman in a bowlers' series, re-silient above all against the verbal buffeting he had taken since claiming Lara in Bridgetown.

Australia made 531, a lead of 266. A big first-innings deficit can have the effect of ultra-violet on dandruff: it shows up every weak-ness, technical and mental, in a Test team. This day, it was overlaid with the pressure of losing the Frank Worrell Trophy at home for the first time since 1973. What were the West Indies made of? Not enough. In the last session of the third day, Reiffel bowled three containing overs. In his fourth, he took a smart caught-and-bowled off Richardson. In his fifth, he found the jackpot spot on the wicket, the loose plate of turf (possibly a fraction outside the line of leg stump), and his shooter trapped Lara. In Reiffel's sixth over, Williams slashed one onto his stumps.

With the West Indies 3/63 and apparently doomed, the rain tumbled down. A pall of horror must have settled on Border – all that effort, and now rain? Just his luck. But as someone said, better to be a lucky captain than a good captain, and Taylor was one of the luckiest. The rain was falling on a rest day, when rest days were still taken. The tropical storm meant nothing. Simpson – ever vigilant, let's not say paranoid – made doubly sure of it by sending extra security to the ground to watch the covers stay put. By the scheduled day four, the weather was bright again and Sabina Park had drained dry.

Only a miracle would save the home side's seventeen-year hold on Frank. But if miracles didn't happen, nobody would watch sport. On the fourth morning, not miracles but Australian nerves kept the West Indians alive. The red clay was cracking white, but Adams was dropped by Healy in the first over, and then the night-watchman, Winston Benjamin, nicked one that Taylor and Mark Waugh waited for each other to go for.

Before and after lunch, though, the wrestle started breaking Australia's way. Steve Waugh caught Adams smartly at gully, then Reiffel ducked one in on Benjamin, who had made a gutsy 50. Less courageous was Hooper, run out going for a second when Julian's marvellous athleticism delivered a direct hit from deep backward square. These things always seemed to happen to Hooper, and over a twelve-year period they must have added up to something. Arthurton thought he was Garry Sobers after swatting a Warne full-toss for six; then he realised he was only Keith Arthurton, as he padded up to a massive turner.

Warne was spinning it so hard, forcing his way through his soreness, and the ball was spitting so unpredictably off the pitch, that on Taylor's suggestion Healy set a precedent: he would, as wicket-keeper, wear a helmet. The psychological value was as good as the protection. Who cared about Healy's nose? The West Indian tail-enders must have thought Warne was bowling bombs. He ran though the tail, finally dominant, administering the coup de grace when Kenny Benjamin took a swipe and Taylor held the thick edge.

For Australia, it was the day of days. The same eleven players had turned out in all four Tests. The West Indies squad was almost as stable, nine of them playing all four Tests and two playing three. None of the West Indians had lost a Test series in their lives. Some of them were in nappies when Clive Lloyd's 1975–76 team had lost in Australia. Ambrose wept openly. Richardson, in a rare lapse of sportsmanship, called the victors 'the weakest Australian

ABOVE: A kiss for Frank: the captain, Sabina Park, 1995.

team I've played against' – although to be fair, any team without Border and McDermott would have looked weak, on paper, to West Indian eyes.

What could have been weaker than a new-ball attack of Reiffel and Julian? But Reiffel was the bowler of the match, and took 15 wickets at less than 20 for the series; Julian and McGrath always popped up to take wickets when needed; Warne, despite falling short of expectations, played the containing role he would develop to great effect as he grew older and took vital wickets down the order. For all the dazzling days of Australian supremacy over the next decade, they would win more Test matches through the patient, slow-drip application of tight bowling and uncompromising fielding than by dynamiting their opposition. These wins, in the Caribbean, would set that pattern.

The Australian players chaired Taylor from the ground. His tactical acumen and man management had proven, in many ways, the difference between this series and those of the past. His pledge to bat aggressively, aiming at 300 runs a day, always gave his bowlers more time to close out a win.

Border, still behind his microphone before joining the players' party, said the win left a 'lump in the throat'.

'I am still very close to this side and it would have been wonderful to be out there sharing this moment with them,' he later wrote. 'But watching on this day was almost as satisfying.'

He went down to the changing rooms and joined in the party. Every player made an effort to include him, Taylor memorably handing the Worrell Trophy to his predecessor and saying, 'Here mate, this is for you too.'

The Australian Cricket Board must have been equally satisfied. It rewarded the players with a night out in Bermuda that was said to cost $13,000. Hush money? By keeping the Warne–Mark Waugh 'bookmaker' fines secret on the eve of the tour, the ACB had made its own special contribution to a harmonious, unified team effort.

SWALLOWING THEIR PRIDE

Lahore, April 1996

BACK IN 1975, SRI LANKANS WERE THE POOR LITTLE GUYS WHOM EVERY FAST BOWLER USED AS TARGET PRACTICE. NOW, AFTER A TWENTY-YEAR MARCH, RANATUNGA URGED THEM, JUST LIKE THE AUSTRALIANS IN THE WEST INDIES, TO RETALIATE FIRST.

As Border knew, it is the bowlers who turn history. If batsmen could win Test matches, he would have beaten the West Indies on his own. His history-changing bowlers, Warne and McGrath, had matured a year or two too late for him, and now Taylor was reaping the benefits. Without match-winning bowlers, a captain is armed with little more than empty threats.

Every country produces good and great batsmen. It is the absence of a great bowler that stops them from rising. But imagine this scenario. Imagine that the smallest, newest and poorest of the Test-playing nations, the easybeats, the tadpoles, produce the bowler who will become the greatest of all time. He is a fellow who can rip out entire batting line-ups within a session. Single-handedly, he can lift his nation to the top. Imagine that the fellow, likeable and free-spirited, comes from the ethnic minority in his war-divided country. Imagine the unifying symbol he can become. He is a good sport and a generous benefactor, a perfect role model. In him resides much of his nation's heart and hope. For the international game, too, he is a symbol of Third World power, the great leveller of economic inequality. Laden with all this responsibility, he keeps

THE WORLD GAME NEEDS HIM: IF HE IS BANNED, THE GAME ITSELF WILL SPLIT

smilingly winning matches. He is their Bradman, and more.

But there's a catch. Imagine that he is breaking the rules. Imagine that most of the balls he bowls, possibly all of them, definitely the most dangerous and unpredictable of them, are in violation of one of the laws of cricket. It is an ancient law, not necessarily designed to stop a bowler like him, yet a law all the same. Nobody really wants to call him on this breach. His own country has invested so much hope in him, to have him removed from the game would trigger a riot, bring the sky falling down. The world game needs him: if he is banned, the game itself will split. He is a symbol not only of excellence but of race. His continent needs him. So administrators look the other way, pretend it isn't happening. Umpires – solitary men, sometimes strange men, doing a lonely and often reviled job – can also be forgiven for looking the other way. Why should it be left to them? Opponents complain. Everyone who loses his wicket to him, perhaps their career and livelihood, mutter about this sanctioned cheating. Many are complaining, yet nobody does anything about it. Nobody asks him to correct his action. Nobody calls him. Nobody does anything. Until somebody does something, and then all hell breaks loose.

LEFT: Optical illusion or throw? Murali at Perth 1995.

Perhaps it was just a design flaw in international cricket that meant, when Australian umpires Darrell Hair and Ross Emerson no-balled Muttiah Muralidaran in 1995–96, the entire house of cards teetered. It should be simple: if an umpire sees a law broken, he takes action on the field. The umpire's decision may then be examined, and if his judgement is incorrect he will not be doing much international umpiring anymore. If he is right, the player is sent away to fix his fault, or else he won't play again. It's not a matter of opinion, as many said it was; it was a matter of fact. Did Murali's bowling arm straighten during his delivery or not?

Yet this fundamental question was left lying in the dust behind the stampede. When Hair no-balled Murali in the Boxing Day Test of 1995, the Sri Lankans cried injustice. They cried racism. They cried home-town, big-country bias. Their allies on the sub-continent and in Africa closed ranks, under the anti-racism banner. Nobody talked much about whether he was throwing or not; they were all talking politics and justice and morality and opinion. Questions were raised about process: how could the International Cricket Council, the ruling body, handle this better? How could it avoid the victimisation of either the umpires or the bowler? How could it avoid a split? Few questions were raised about the elephant in the room – was Murali throwing the ball or not? It didn't help that on the field, after Hair no-balled him seven times in three overs, Murali was switched to the other end, from which he bowled another thirty-two overs without New Zealand umpire Steve Dunne no-balling him at all. Unlike Hair, who stood back from the stumps to examine Murali's arm, Dunne perched on top of them and only checked Murali's front foot. Dunne, like Hair, had told the ICC previously about his concerns over Murali's ac-tion. The ICC did nothing. Dunne, in public, did nothing. Darrell Hair, who could never be accused of hiding from the limelight, did something. But being an attention seeker did not make him wrong. And being long picked-on, racially discriminated against, ignored, patronised and bullied thoughout their history did not, on this occasion, make the Sri Lankans right.

Being the meat in the sandwich of cricket's biggest controversy was a disappointing way for Taylor's Australians to celebrate their homecoming as world champions. After the Caribbean triumph they'd enjoyed tickertape parades in Sydney and Melbourne. They'd come out with all the expected bromides about this being not a summit but a foothill. They'd talked about the improvement still left in them, the beginning of a new era.

Simpson, sensitive to suggestions that Taylor had limited his powers, wrote an article claiming most of the credit for the Worrell win, titled 'They Did It My Way'. Like the man who only attracts attention when he is drowning, Simpson's desperate plea for relevance served to emphasise its opposite. Border, speaking of Taylor, captured the truth: 'He hasn't been inhibited by anything. He's said, "This is the way I want it," with no "umming and arrhing" about the old regime. He's come in straight away and stamped his own authority on the captaincy and now he's holding one of the greatest prizes of all.' For that, read Taylor had reclaimed the team from Simpson.

The Pakistanis came before Christmas 1995 and were thumped. Salim Malik looked like someone who had been dragged to Australia at gunpoint. Never again would he be the force he was in 1994. Wasim and Waqar were fiery and potent, but the Pakistan batting suffered its historic travel sickness and had no immunity against Warne, McDermott and McGrath.

The Sri Lankans followed, and gave Australia little opposition in the Test series. In the First Test in Perth, which Australia won by an innings, the Sri Lankans had to face accusations of ball tampering, which were quashed when the umpires continued to use the same ball rather than impound it. Strange days indeed. Ricky Ponting and Stuart Law made their debuts in Perth, but left through different doors. Ponting, given a terrible lbw decision by Khizer Hayat on 96, would become one of the Australian greats. Law, who stroked an unbeaten 54, would enjoy the unusual distinction of never registering a Test batting average.

But it was the fuse lit by Darrell Hair in the Boxing Day Test that ignited the summer. Sri Lanka claimed all sorts of dark conspiracies, compounded when Emerson no-balled Murali again in the one-day format. By no-balling Murali when the bowler switched to leg-breaks, Emerson confirmed Sri Lanka's suspicions that there was a preconceived vigilante attitude among the Australian umpires. It was claimed that no one could straighten their arm bowling leg-spinners. That is incorrect, though it is a lot harder than when bowling off-breaks. At the time, few were in the mood for rational analysis. Lines were drawn and trenches were dug. Sri Lanka had many advocates within Australia who pointed to Hair's baiting ways.

The outcome might have played out differently if the tourists had a different leader and a different mood, but Arjuna Ranatunga was a rebel looking for a cause and he found it in the no-balling.

Ranatunga was a small-town popinjay, a conceited man whose rage led him to mirror the prejudices of his nemeses. He was also a more than useful batsman and a leader his men would follow into hellfire. He was a product of Sri Lanka's small economic and political elite, with an upbringing that had no parallel in Australian cricket. Justifiably angry at years of condescension shown to Sri Lanka by Australia, England and others, he was condescending himself, referring to Australians as uncouth types and 'convicts'. Competitive to a fault, he had grown tired of being pushed around by the big strong countries with their big strong fast bowlers, and he urged his players to answer back in deed and word. Sri Lanka's bowlers went for more attacking lines and lengths, firing in short balls and following them with a verbal volley. Their spinners tried to take wickets, not just contain. Their fielders, packed around the bat, chattered noisily and never bridled their delight at success. It was in their batting, though, that they showed their spirit. This was the nation that had had its toes crushed, literally, by Jeff Thomson when they first arrived at a World Cup. Back in 1975, Sri Lankans were the poor little guys whom every fast bowler used as target practice. Some took pity on them. Australian cricketers tended to disregard them. Now, after a twenty-year march, Ranatunga urged them, just like the Australians in the West Indies, to retaliate first.

It didn't work in the Test matches, but as soon as the one-dayers started the Sri Lankan batsmen took the risks and got the rewards. Ranatunga played a guiding role in the middle order, but above him Aravinda de Silva, with his pot belly and his axe-like bat, had become one of the best two or three attacking players in the world. And above him, in turn, were Sanath Jayasuriya and Romesh Kaluwitharana.

Jayasuriya had been around for a while, a flashy but inconsistent middle-order player and handy left-arm spinner. Kaluwitharana was an unknown quantity, a jockey-sized wicketkeeper who had made a Test century on debut against Australia at Colombo four years earlier. During the one-day series in Australia, Jayasuriya and Kaluwitharana reinvented the wheel. With a new ball and only two fielders allowed deep, the pair went hard at McGrath. Jayasuriya perfected a technique of playing the ball purely on its length; that is, he had the same slash ready for the ball that pitched just short of a length, whether it was outside off, on middle or outside leg. The ball would fly off in any direction, but very often safely because he hit it so hard. He knew how to block the good balls, but he had worked out that one-day bowlers like McGrath picked out a predictable length. McGrath's greatest strength, his control, became his soft centre.

Before long the Sri Lankans had inverted the orthodoxy of conserving wickets and building steadily towards a slog in the last ten overs. Instead, Jayasuriya, Kaluwitharana and de Silva went for the slog in the first fifteen, frequently putting on eighty, ninety or 100 runs during that period. They might lose wickets, but then Ranatunga and the experienced Roshan Mahanama would work them through the end of the innings, nibbling away in ones and twos. The end result – scores of 250 became commonplace – forced every other nation to rethink their tactics. Eventually.

The Sri Lankans made the finals of the one-day series, but were not expected to shake a patient Australia. Early-innings slogs had been tried before, and had run out of puff. England had tried it with Ian Botham, New Zealand with Mark Greatbatch. It never lasted. It relied too much on luck, and the Sri Lankans' luck couldn't hold. Guided by Simpson, Australia stuck to their plan. Above all, it would be humiliating to be seen to be learning lessons from Sri Lanka. Even when Mark Waugh was promoted to open the innings with Taylor, it was put as an original idea, not one inspired by this opponent.

A win in the finals seemed to justify the Australians' stubbornness. After accounting for the Sri Lankans in Melbourne, Australia made 273 in the second final, on a humid afternoon in Sydney, before a storm reduced the target to a more gettable 168 off twenty-five overs. For a while, Ranatunga and Hashan Tillakaratne loomed ominously, and amid the tension and mugginess all the animosity of the summer was finally brought to the boil. Ranatunga, whose idea of a fitness session was to breaststroke to the end of the hotel pool and make his way to the buffet, asked for a runner early in his innings. Healy couldn't resist stepping up.

'Mate, you can't have a runner just because you're unfit.'

'It's nothing to do with you,' Ranatunga said, waving his finger. In Ranatunga's patrician mind the plebeian Australians barely merited his attention. 'I have cramp.'

'Have a look at yourself, Porky. That's why you've got cramp.'

Refused at first, Ranatunga began limping. Then he was allowed the much faster Jayasuriya as a runner. Soon afterwards Jayasuriya and McGrath collided and exchanged words, the umpires were drawn in, and at the end of the match Taylor had trouble finding an adversary to shake his hand.

No doubt Sri Lanka went into the subcontinent's World Cup, which followed hard on the Australian summer, with a sense of un-requited loathing. No doubt the Australians were happy to be rid of them. The Australians had, individually and collectively, received death threats – not an uncommon response from cheesed-off Sri Lankan cricket fans. This author once received a death threat in Colombo for writing about insects. It didn't take very much. But the Australians, seriously worried, were murmuring about not playing

'MATE, YOU CAN'T HAVE A RUNNER JUST BECAUSE YOU'RE UNFIT'

their scheduled World Cup fixture in Sri Lanka. Graham Halbish told them that if they boycotted the game after what had happened in Australia, 'it will take at least ten years to rectify the situation'.

In the end the argument was superseded by reality. A horrific bomb blast in central Colombo persuaded Australia and the West

Indies to stay out of Sri Lanka. A hundred innocents were killed and windows were blasted out of buildings a block away from the explosion. The Australian government and ACB counselled against the trip. Yet with their eye on money and politics, the body organising the World Cup, PILCOM, and the ICC ruled that the Colombo matches still had to go ahead. Australia's withdrawal heightened further Ranatunga's sense of grievance, if that were possible.

Australia duly lost their match in Colombo by walkover, as did the West Indies. Zimbabwe played there and lost. Kenya played there and lost too, but atoned by beating the West Indies in Pune, an upset so outrageous that Richie Richardson was forced to apologise to his country, his parents and friends, the whole world. But the West Indies then beat Australia in Jaipur to make the quarter-finals anyway.

Based in India, the Australians accumulated enough points to qualify for a quarter-final against New Zealand. In Madras, Taylor lost the toss and they fielded first in hellish heat and humidity. New Zealand's Chris Harris smashed a once-in-a-lifetime century, 130 off 124 balls, and the Kiwis amassed an imposing 286. Their captain-wicketkeeper, Lee Germon, made 89 off ninety-seven. The previous night at their team meeting, the Australians had spent no time discussing either Harris or Germon: 'Never made a run against us, won't do anything, forget him' was how the players recalled the discussion. Still, the target didn't daunt Mark Waugh, whose 110 was a brave one in the heat, and his twin's 59 not out helped secure a win with thirteen balls to spare. Mark Waugh had now notched three centuries in the Cup, an unprecedented feat.

The West Indies, belying their post-Pune obituaries, had not only beaten Australia but also South Africa, Lara's century inspiring a quarter-final upset in Karachi. Little went to plan in this World Cup, and sometimes it was not the fault of shoddy organisation. Not only were South Africa, the favourites, out, but Pakistan and India had found themselves opposed in the quarter-final stage. India won, and were drawn to meet Sri Lanka in their semi-final in Kolkata.

In the other semi-final at Mohali, Curtly Ambrose and a rejuvenated Ian Bishop had Australia 4/15 in the first nine overs. Law,

Bevan and Healy saved face, but only for a total of 207, lower than any other winning first-innings score through a batsmen's Cup.

Australia's second comeback of the day turned out to be even more dramatic than the first. Chanderpaul, Lara and Richardson steered the West Indies calmly to 2/165 before McGrath dismissed Chanderpaul for 80. Still, Richardson was there and the West Indians only needed another forty-three in nine overs. What followed must have sickened Richardson and driven him to retirement even more surely than what had taken place at home the previous year. McGrath and Warne accounted for Roger Harper, Ottis Gibson and Jimmy Adams. Harper and Gibson had been sent in as pinch hitters, showing a modicum of panic in the West Indian tactics. Then Fleming came on with his hooping swingers and had a slogging Arthurton caught behind. West Indies had lost 5/14 in five overs. But they were still favourites with Richardson there and McGrath having finished his ten-over quota. Bishop and Richardson brought down the required runs to 14 before Warne trapped Bishop.

Richardson and Ambrose took four runs off the penultimate over. Now Richardson was on strike to Fleming with ten runs needed. Fleming was the most underrated and unlucky of Australia's bowlers in this period. He was a swing bowler of rare ability, getting the ball to 'cross the eye-line', or loop above the horizontal, at decent pace. He could move it both ways in the air and off the pitch. On his day, in the right conditions, he was unplayable. If he had avoided injury to take a full Ashes tour in 1997 or 2001, he might have been the new Terry Alderman. But injury was his downfall, constantly interrupting his career when it was about to go into full flower. Nevertheless, in two of Australia's greatest World Cup semi-final wins, in 1996 and 1999, Fleming was the bowler in the clutch, the man who took the last over and came up with the result.

Richardson swiped the first ball to the mid-wicket boundary. Six to win, five balls. Should he keep strike, or take any run on offer? He elected the latter. From the second ball, he tried to steal a cheeky single from a bottom edge that ran through to the wicketkeeper. Healy ran Ambrose out, courtesy of a video umpire's verdict, exposing the bunny Walsh. Rather than lay bat on ball, run to the non-striker's end and stay there, Walsh tried to be the hero and took an almighty swing at Fleming's third ball. Where Walsh got the idea that he could bat, after so many years of proof to the contrary, is anyone's guess. The ball hit the top of the off stump.

Australia had taken 8/37 and scraped in with the luck and will of a team destined to win the World Cup. This kind of rite of passage had happened before, and would happen again, to winners – the five-set marathon a Sampras or Borg had to fight through in an early round, or Australia's miracle quarter-final win over Ireland in the 1991 Rugby World Cup. Final victory now seemed inevitable, and the Australian celebrations rocked the Punjab.

Richie Richardson had played his last match, a heroic failure to sign off with. Aptly, he was abandoned in the middle. Ambrose caused jaws to drop by actually speaking to the Australians. Seeing what a mood they were in, celebrating the greatest one-day win of their careers, he said, 'Don't waste it now.' From his great height, he must have seen something they didn't.

Sri Lanka had had to cap no such emotions. They only had to beat England in the quarter-final, achieved when Jayasuriya hit 82 off forty-four balls. Then, after an early scare when Jayasuriya and Kaluwitharana both holed out in the first over of the semi at Kolkata, they cruised home to beat a nonplussed India and their rioting supporters.

It's fair to say that Australia would have preferred playing anyone but Sri Lanka in the final. They said they were relishing it, but Australian instincts rebel against being favourite; like most sporting teams, they prefer to have a grudge, a reason to aim up and bring a more fancied opponent down. Life really is lonely at the top. There might also have been a lingering sense of irritation, a belief that the Sri Lankans didn't really deserve to be there. There was certainly a climbing blood pressure of ill will between the teams. With a kind of bravado, as if to talk himself into the right mood, Steve Waugh wrote in his tour diary: 'We are all very keen to have a crack at them. We haven't been impressed with the "cry baby" tactics that were employed during their summer tour of Australia …' Ranatunga played his part to the hilt, telling the press that Warne and the Waughs were 'overrated'.

As they recovered from a punishing celebration, things started to go wrong for Taylor's team. Sensitive tourists on the subcontinent at the best of times, they were unsettled by the move to Pakistan for the final. They had been comfortable with their routines in India but had now to adjust to a tortuous day-long trip, a new country and the usual shambolic PILCOM organisation. On the eve of the final, they were blocked from practising at the Gaddafi Stadium, there being only one netted area and another team, Sri Lanka, being in it first. Later, the Australians were invited to an interminable 'official' dinner, missing the opportunity the Sri Lankans had used to practise at the stadium at night – tellingly, because it was during that session that the Sri Lankans discovered how heavily the dew was settling on the ground after dark.

On the morning of the final, the teams were led to believe the match would be postponed due to overnight rain. The Australians, lolling about in their hotel, were roused by a hasty change of plans: the game would start on schedule. They arrived later than usual, harassed, out of kilter, tired, lacking their usual eagerness to play. The Simpson era was built on professional pre-match preparation; his last match as coach was one where preparation let his team down. At the last, they didn't do it his way.

When the game started, a subdued crowd of 30,000 was in the ground, kept well back from the boundaries. The atmosphere was less than a World Cup final deserved. After the national anthems, the Australians made to leave the field, only to be told to wait, because the anthem they'd assumed was Sri Lanka's was in fact a mistake. Another stuff-up turned into another perceived slight upon Sri Lanka.

Ranatunga won the toss and sent Australia in. This in itself defied orthodoxy. Batting first was mandatory in high-pressure matches. Every World Cup final had been won by the team batting first. It said a lot for Sri Lanka's pluck that they backed themselves to win batting second. But it was their way, and to his credit Ranatunga stuck with it.

On an overcast afternoon, the Australian batsmen couldn't find their rhythm against the Sri Lankan mix of medium pace and spin. As Warne said, 'there was a certain flatness about us from the start'. After losing Mark Waugh early, Taylor built a platform with Ponting, in the team to replace his Tasmanian mentor Boon, who had retired after being omitted from the World Cup squad. They cruised to 1/137, Taylor playing one of his best one-day knocks. But instead of exploding into the second half of the innings, Australia withered. The wicket began to take turn and the ball softened. Taylor and Ponting fell to de Silva's part-time offies, and then Warne, as designated slogger (a tactic loudly opposed by Simpson), charged, swished and missed. Steve Waugh scored 13, one more than his brother, before trying a chip over mid-off and instead spooning a leading edge to de Silva. Australia's launch pad was gone, and so too were the secondary boosters. They'd lost 4/33 in the gear-change part of the innings, and failed to score a single boundary between the nineteenth and forty-third overs. Law and Bevan steadied, but a total of 241 was only going to be enough if they could crack the Sri Lankan self-confidence.

The floodlights failed during the dinner break, then came on again. This was the 1996 World Cup. Again the Sri Lankan openers missed out, and again it didn't matter. Perhaps the slogging-openers theory wasn't all it was cracked up to be, and although Jayasuriya would win the award for man of the tournament, it was de Silva at number four who dictated the narratives of the semi-final and final. Asanka Gurusinha and de Silva put on 125 for the third wicket as the Australian fielders and bowlers sought but failed to find the required intensity. Sometimes it is reached for, but simply isn't there. Warne couldn't grip the dew-sodden ball, and Australia grassed four catches and a stumping chance. When Warne tried a flipper to Ranatunga which slipped and ballooned, the Sri Lankan captain hit it over the boundary and proceeded to poke out his tongue at the bowler.

He had every right to triumphalism. Ranatunga's decision to send Australia in had, because of the dew, been a masterstroke. He assisted the centurion de Silva home to a first World Cup, by seven wickets with four overs in hand. Not only had Australia lost the final, they had been absolutely hammered; from the moment they stuttered with the bat, they never looked remotely likely to win. That, as much as the fact of Sri Lanka being world champions, sat them squarely on their backsides as they endured the celebrations (which were themselves one final farce, ending with Taylor unwittingly committing an error of protocol by offering to shake the hand of Prime Minister Benazir Bhutto, the podium collapsing under the weight of humanity, and the oversized winners' cheque being stolen).

This Australian cricket team hated losing; loathed it. That was one of the traits that made them so good. But they were probably motivated, in this match, by a dread of losing that was so intense it shaded into fear. Swatting off the annoying Sri Lankans again was a deflating kind of incentive. The World Cup final might have seemed anticlimactic from the moment they achieved their miracle in Mohali. They would never have admitted this, but their greatest handicap was a shortage of genuine respect for Sri Lanka's cricketers, who, on slow wickets and small grounds, deserved favouritism. This was not the MCG, Toto, and Sri Lanka were playing better cricket than Australia throughout the World Cup. Australia could have been underdogs, and have motivated themselves accordingly, if they had taken a more unflinching look at the way the Sri Lankans had been playing. It took a very nasty shock in the final for the Australians to realise that they were not the best team in the world. They hadn't just lost a match; they had been overtaken at the top. From here on, they would have to swallow their pride and learn lessons in cricket from the world champs. Considering who the Australians were and what they had achieved, this psychological shift – to be the pupils – would pose an unprecedented challenge.

As for Muralidaran, he bowled ten overs in the final for thirty-one runs, dismissing Warne. His containment in the middle was an essential ingredient in Sri Lanka's win. His bowling action continued unchanged, and no umpire no-balled him. He said a birth defect left him with a right arm that couldn't straighten; biomechanical tests suggested that his bent arm twisted, rather than straightened, during his action to produce an optical illusion of straightening. Many Australian batsmen refused to believe in these results, saying that Murali bowled differently while being tested. Some deliveries were more suspect than others. Nobody knew what to do. There seemed no acceptable way to settle the argument. The last thing the ICC wanted was to encourage umpires to enforce the rules. Murali was tested, and tested again. Whatever was happening with his arm, his place in the game made him too hot to handle. The awkwardness was resolved, some years later, when the law was changed to allow up to fifteen degrees of straightening. Apparently, Murali's arm had been measured to straighten by between ten and fourteen degrees. He had an unusual action, there is no doubt – when Allan Border faced him before his retirement, he played and missed at five balls in an over, thinking he was facing a leg-spinner rather than an off-spinner. Steve Waugh called him 'the David Copperfield of cricket', which was far too great a compliment to the Las Vegas magician. Murali's magic was real, and bewitching. Perhaps his rubbery uniqueness was beyond the game's capabilities to cope. Within the rewritten rules, he continued to take cartloads of wickets. The adjustment to the laws didn't stop batsmen around the world muttering into their beer, but it did make him fully legal.

ABOVE: Dear oh dear: Warne laments another Ranatunga run in the World Cup final.

MARK WAUGH'S TEST

Port Elizabeth, March 1997

NOW HE WAS FOUR YEARS OLDER, AND SEASONED, AND WASN'T GOING TO LET HIS CHANCE SLIDE. STEVE HAD FAILED IN BOTH INNINGS – THIS WAS MARK'S TURN. AND HIS LUCKY DAY!

This would be known as Mark Waugh's Test, and, given how long he lived in one shadow or another, his moment of sunshine should be allowed its full colour. But the Second Test against South Africa at St George's Park in 1997 represented more than one in-dividual's triumph. It might as easily have been called Jason Gillespie's Test, or Ian Healy's, or even – considering it saved his career – Mark Taylor's. In short, it was Australia's Test, because they met three hitherto unachieved goals: they had beaten their number one challenger in a series away from home; they had won one of those low-scoring cliffhangers they had so often lost; and they had chased a target successfully in the fourth innings. But notwithstanding many telling contribu-tions, they couldn't have done it without Waugh's century.

After the glories of 1995, 1996 was a middling year for Australia. The World Cup final loss triggered a plummeting one-day performance. They were well beaten by Sri Lanka in a short tournament in Colombo, then failed to win a single one of their six matches against India and South Africa in the limited-overs Titan Cup, on a tour in which they were also monstered

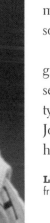

AFTER THE GLORIES OF 1995, 1996 WAS A MIDDLING YEAR FOR AUSTRALIA

by Anil Kumble in the one-off Test at Delhi.

Some notables were missing for the period. An injured Taylor and Warne missed the Sri Lankan tour, while the leg-spinner, recuperating from finger surgery, also sat out India. Bob Simpson was no longer part of the scene. He had asked the ACB for a contract extension, but eleven years was seen to be enough, and he was replaced by one of his most successful coaching projects, Geoff Marsh. The new arrangement was clearly driven by Taylor's needs. In Marsh, the captain had an offsider who would organise practice, throw endless balls at young batsmen and prove a friendly mentor. But Marsh was not the tactician or mastermind or, for that matter, the politician that Simpson had been. Simpson was not replaced so much as made redundant; the coach's role itself was being scaled back so that Taylor could run his team his way.

At home for the summer, Warne returned and the team re-grouped in defence of Frank. New adventures were tried at the selection table. Slater, after a run of patchy form, was not the type of player Marsh favoured, and after a wild swipe at David Johnson, a bouffant-haired Anglo-Indian fast bowler, at Delhi, he was dropped. His place was taken by Matthew Elliott, a country-reared Victorian left-hander with the finest-looking technique in the land. Elliott had made plenty of runs for his State and was a tall, textbook-perfect driver, cutter and puller. His mental fitness for Test cricket was unknown, but his obvious talent and domestic record compelled his selection.

Ponting moved up to number three to fill the Boon-sized hole, and Bevan had fought his way back through the one-day game to recapture the number six spot. With McGrath now the undisputed attack leader, Fleming injured and McDermott retired, Reiffel and Julian had not been able to sustain their Caribbean contributions. Instead, Australia tried two contrasting young right-armers. Jason Gillespie, at twenty, looked like a South Australian bikie with heavy-metal hair, earring and dry humour. With a lengthy run-up and a fluid side-on action, he was capable of generating McDermottesque pace. Michael Kasprowicz had played rugby and looked like it. His record for Queensland also demanded selection, though there were doubts about his penetrative ability at the top level. He had a lower arm action than Gillespie and a cocked wrist that suggested he bowled off-cutters, one of the less threatening variations against most international batsmen. Worst of all for him, though, he was a through-and-through gentleman, a sincere and friendly man without any nasty streak or chip on his shoulder. One journalist joked that his moniker was 'Nicekowicz' when a fast bowler ought to be known as 'Psychowicz'.

Against the West Indies, Australia won the first two Tests without much ado. Walsh and Ambrose were getting as long in the tooth as they were in the limb, and apart from Lara and Chanderpaul the batting lacked substance. Healy scored 161 not out in Brisbane, while McGrath took the bowling spoils. In Sydney, Elliott, after an encouraging start, collided mid-pitch with Mark Waugh and tore his knee ligaments. Warne's fourth-innings spell, including an astonishing leg-break to bowl Chanderpaul, settled the affair.

The selectors were still not entirely comfortable. For the Boxing Day Test in Melbourne, Matthew Hayden was rebirthed after three years for Elliott, and Justin Langer came in at number three to replace Ponting, who might have been the right choice to replace Boon but would take another five years to grow up and into the role. Greg Blewett was rotated back in for the unfortunate Bevan, found out again by short-pitched bowling. Kasprowicz was dropped for Reiffel. It seemed that raw talent had made way for endeavour.

Perhaps the selectors shouldn't have tried fixing what wasn't broke. On Boxing Day, Hayden and Langer were among the victims as the Walsh–Ambrose–Kenny Benjamin show gave a last encore on Australian soil. Having roared back to win in Melbourne, however, the West Indies lost their puff and surrendered meekly in Adelaide, Hayden coming good with his first Test century almost three years after his debut. He was dropped three times, however, and the selectors would be keeping a close and sceptical eye on him. What had been a sporadically competitive Test series then finished in the ugliest way in Perth, with Lara complaining about Australians sledging his junior partner, Robert Samuels, and Ambrose finishing his superb career in Australia with a mystifyingly churlish last spell, deliberately overrunning the crease from around the wicket and trying to maim Warne and newcomer Andy Bichel. With the Perth crowd gathering to give him a standing ovation, in gracious recognition of his three series spearing Australians on the WACA, Ambrose responded in character, arrogant and aggressive and fully focused on the contest, not the occasion.

After Perth, the Australians had five days with their families before flying to South Africa, via Hong Kong. Had the Perth Test gone the distance, they would only have had three. Following South Africa would be an Ashes tour. The scheduling was unrelenting, almost exploitative. It is a wonder that the Australians were then able to string together their best two Test matches since 1995. Their performances flattered the administrators, giving them the impression that players thrived on long flights and constant hard cricket. As far as professionalism was concerned, the administrators were still lagging somewhat behind the players, to put it kindly. To put it more directly, the ACB continued to reign like the Bourbons: they had forgotten nothing, and they had learnt nothing. If the players weren't happy, they could quit, couldn't they, and the Board could luxuriate in the idea of the teeming millions who would love to replace them. This attitude, uninterrupted since 1877 and not fundamentally shaken by the events of 1977, was soon to have a harsh light, that of modern industrial relations, shone upon it.

As the Australian team arrived in South Africa, the selectors were still fussing over those personnel issues, some old, others bubbling up after a long gestation. The top- and middle-orders were unsettled. Blewett had performed fairly at six, and Hayden's Adelaide century was enough to keep his tenure going for the time being, but both still played under question marks. Elliott, back from injury, would replace the unconvincing Langer at three. The simmering question was Taylor, who hadn't scored a fifty through-out the summer and appeared to be a whisker off the pace. His one-day form had dropped off alarmingly, to the point where he was a major factor in Australia failing to make the domestic finals for the first time in nearly two decades. As Edward de Bono would ask Steve Waugh some years later, why would you try to dismiss a one-day batsman who is aiding your cause by batting slowly? It seemed that Pakistan and the West Indies cottoned on during that summer, allowing Taylor to play and miss to his heart's con-tent. His Test output that summer amounted to 153 runs in nine innings at 17; his one-day tally was 143 from 325 balls in nine innings at 18.

His form was such an important issue because he was not just another player. As captain, he had to be cut more slack than an ordinary player, but not at any cost. So how much slack, and what cost?

This was the rising issue, and Taylor's form would set off a chain reaction through other selections. Bevan would be picked as a number seven batsman and support to Warne with his left-arm wristies, and Reiffel, whose naggers would have been at home in South Africa, was left out.

Warne was the other concern. McGrath had taken the man-tle as the team's premier wicket-taker, imperiously winning his duel with Lara through the summer. Gillespie was emerging as an excellent sidekick, raising hopes for a new Lillee–Thomson or Miller–Lindwall combination. But Warne's injured finger had not quite healed when he came back, and although he had hoped to bowl himself into form he had instead finished the summer sore and tired.

When the Australians arrived in Johannesburg, the South Africans were strutting even more than usual, having undergone generational renewal themselves. Wessels, de Villiers, Peter Kirsten and Craig Matthews had gone. Cronje was now the captain, a more dynamic and inspiring figure than Wessels. Their new breed, comprising Jacques Kallis, Herschelle Gibbs, Shaun Pollock, Lance Klusener and Paul Adams, were exciting talents. Kallis, a Western Cape 21-year-old, had a sturdy all-round game and would bat at number three. Pollock, the son of Peter and nephew of Graeme, was laying a claim to the title of best all-rounder in the world. He had a picture-perfect bowling action, with a smooth run and a high rocking delivery that produced movement in the air and off the seam. Klusener was a front-on skidder from wide on the crease, and a powerful left-handed slogger. Adams, the left-arm spinner with the action likened to a frog in a blender or a person trying to change the tyre on a moving car inside a phone box, could be anything. It wasn't often South Africa could promote such unpredictable talent, anchored by a hard nucleus of Gary Kirsten, Hudson, Cronje, Rhodes,

THE SPECTRE OF AN AUSTRALIAN CAPTAIN BEING DROPPED BEGAN TO LOOM

Richardson, McMillan and Donald. They had belted Australia in the one-dayers in India, and beaten India at home. Undefeated in South Africa since their return in 1991 – undefeated, there, since the 1960s – they had every entitlement to consider this series the world championship of Test cricket.

All the early eyes were on Taylor. He struggled in the warm-up matches, was unrelieved by a scratchy half-century against Western Province, and the spectre of an Australian captain being dropped began to loom out of the history books. Had it happened before? Not likely. To his great credit he maintained his composure, and showed his street smarts by always deflecting attention onto the team's results. A great deflector, Taylor always was. By the time the First Test at the Wanderers arrived, Taylor was downplaying the importance of his batting. He described himself as an 'all-rounder', a 'captain-batsman', and if the team won then it showed his value in one of his roles. It was observed that he was edging dangerously close to the English model, but he was unabashed.

He picked the right horse to back, because in Johannesburg his men played their best Test since Sabina Park. From the fourth ball of the match, when McGrath had Hudson caught behind, Australia had their old fire. South Africa recovered from 3/25 to score 302 on the first day, but the bowlers kept coming, refusing to let batsmen convert starts into scores. In the end it was the wicket-keeper Richardson, with 72 not out, who pulled South Africa back from 8/195.

Taylor nearly got going on the second day, lasting almost an hour before chopping Pollock onto his stumps. Elliott announced his arrival as a top-class batsman with 85 from 113 balls on a rain-interrupted second afternoon, playing one pull shot, a flat six off Donald, that will remain vividly in the memories of all who saw it. Elliott was that kind of batsman: memorable. But his moment would come to be preserved not in the amber of glory, but the aspic of regret.

By the end of that day, Steve Waugh and Blewett were in the middle. They were still there twenty-four hours later. On 2 March, Waugh and Blewett added 288 runs to the score and reduced Donald, Pollock and company to fodder. Blewett, enjoying what would be the highpoint of his career, made it to 214 on the fourth day, while Waugh scored 160. Australia declared 326 runs ahead, and Warne and Bevan, with four wickets each, spun South Africa out for 130. The world championship of Test cricket? Australia had not only won, but inflicted South Africa's worst loss in forty-seven years. A more thorough obliteration of a high-class side could not be imagined, until India did it twelve months later in Kolkata.

Yet the beauty of a cricket series is that games do not overlap. Once the mountain is climbed, both sides find themselves at the base again the next time they meet. Scores are even. As much as the Australians would have liked to meet a confused, disunited rabble when they next convened in Port Elizabeth, that is rarely the way it works among the elite. It only takes one good session for the momentum to pull a U-turn. This would change later, in the early 2000s, when Australia were so superior in every respect that they pitched their base camp, so to speak, higher up the mountain than their daunted opponents. But in 1997 Australia had no such aura. Cronje and the South African coach, Kentian Bob Woolmer, were able to con their team into forgetting Johannesburg and believing the Australians were beatable.

There was much head-scratching and dark muttering over the state of the St George's Park pitch. After the previous year's Test, involving England, Geoff Boycott said it should be dug up and replaced. The ground was small and right-angled, with quaint green-and-white painted stands that filled up for this Test with school children bussed in by the South African Cricket Board and a several-dozen-piece brass band complete with choir. St George's Park, in the heart of Xhosa country, could put on an atmosphere that felt more like the West Indies or India than South Africa, particularly compared with the rugby-and-sausage-loving high veldt. The pitch, however, was never going to break into song. It looked rough and patchy, certainly underprepared, and locals such as Wessels predicted tennis-ball bounce, poppy and dangerous on the first days, then low and spinning. After the trouncing on a good wicket at Johannesburg, the South Africans probably fancied their chances more in a low-scoring lottery, as the West Indians had in Trinidad in 1995.

ABOVE: St George's Park, Port Elizabeth: a ground with character.

Taylor won the toss and, no doubt with great relief, evaded having to bat first. He had been sending the manager, Col Egar, to the ground to keep an eye on what passed for pitch preparation, and Taylor's opinion of the strip was so low that he sent the opponent in for the first time in twenty-six Tests as captain.

The wicket played as it looked. Kirsten, Kallis, new opener Adam Bacher and Cronje were all out by the time the score reached 22, two each falling to McGrath and Gillespie, who were getting the ball to snort into the batsmen's armpits. Cullinan's technique was up to the task and he grafted a very good 34, alongside a youngster, Cape Towner Herschelle Gibbs, who had come in for Rhodes.

But Gillespie, having the best day of his fledgling career, struck with three wickets after lunch and when Pollock was lbw first ball South Africa were 7/95. Still, even if none of their batsmen averaged more than 40 in Tests, they had competent players down to number ten. The veterans McMillan and Richardson, 55 and 47 respectively – their scores, not their ages – put on eighty-five late in the afternoon in what would be the second-highest partnership of the match, getting South Africa to a competitive 209.

Just how competitive was becoming clear at the end of that day, when Hayden was caught off Pollock for a duck. Taylor survived without once laying a sure bat on ball, but edged Pollock early the next morning to deepen his mire. This was no wicket to be playing for your career on, and Taylor was probably glad for the excuse. Crucially, in light of what happened later, Pollock went down with a hamstring injury after taking two wickets in his six overs; but the slower medium-pacers, McMillan, Cronje and Kallis, were almost unplayable on that second day. As the band played and the choir sang ('Stand By Me' on perpetual rotation), wickets kept falling to McMillan and Cronje. Donald, with his high pace, was brutally difficult but took his wickets at the other end. Elliott top-scored with 23, run out in a mix-up with Steve Waugh, and Australia made 108. Their run rate was one and a half an over.

By stumps, the South African openers Kirsten and Bacher had cantered to 0/83, a lead of 184 with no wickets down. The jubilation of Johannesburg must have seemed a long time ago. There was no way Australia could fight their way out of this, and, going by his own formula of *L'équipe, c'est moi*, Taylor's career looked like it would be over the next day. Certainly, as players and press left St George's Park on the second night, it wasn't so much a case of the knives being sharpened as the dessert being planned. It was so inevitable that Australia would lose, and Taylor be dumped, that already discussions were taking place among the selectors and the Board on how to manage the transition of the captaincy for the third Test. Would it go to Healy, the vice-captain, or Waugh, the captain-designate? A curious situation had arisen whereby Waugh, who was widely expected to succeed his New South Wales colleague Taylor as captain, was not vice-captain because of interstate niceties. Healy, a Queenslander, was deputy to maintain cross-border balance, and had replaced Taylor as captain in Sri Lanka the previous year. His diplomacy had wobbled there, however, as doubts prevailed about a wicketkeeper's suitability to take on the job, and Healy himself had seemed to flick-pass the prospective captaincy to his good friend Waugh. The fact that the discussions had gone so far, midway through the Second Test, showed what a formality it seemed that South Africa would win.

Two events happened within the Australian team confines that night. Taylor held a rousing meeting, putting aside his personal problems and assuring his men that they could still win. It was a rev-up they all remembered later, and enhanced the myth of his magical touch. Meanwhile, Healy was changing his mind about the top job. While it had been off the agenda, he had happily shelved ambition. Now that it loomed as a real possibility, he 'couldn't help coming back to the fact that we'd gone into the Test with the wrong team because we were protecting the team from our captain's poor form …. Things needed to change. Tubby relinquishing the captaincy was one option we had to consider. And if there was going to be a new captain, then, yes, I wanted to be considered.'

Can there be a better game than Test cricket? Spry and plucky on the second evening, Kirsten and Bacher came out on the third morning with the wobbles. McGrath and Gillespie were bowling with great accuracy and extracting movement and variable bounce from the wicket, but there was a strange hesitancy in the South African attitude. Now that they had the match in their grasp, they seemed unable to close their hands around it.

Kirsten was bowled by Gillespie, then Blewett ran from square leg to mid-wicket, picking up and throwing the ball without looking, hitting the stumps at the non-striker's end, to remove Kallis. Freakish. Gillespie kept charging in finding incisive late outswing, and removed Bacher and Cullinan in the space of one run. South Africa had lost 4/17 in the first hour, and their lead was now 201. Still, it seemed ample. Australia turned to spin, and Warne and Bevan kept the path from the centre to South Africa's changing room well trampled. Only Cronje and Pollock made double figures as the South Africans fell for 168, losing 10/85 on the day.

But still, their lead seemed enough. Australia's first innings was their second lowest ever against South Africa. Now they were being asked to score nearly three times as many. There were few signs that the wicket was improving, and South Africa had oodles of time to defend their 269-run lead, complete their win and square the series. World championship back on.

The Australians had unexpected ways of showing the effects of the pressure they were under. On the third afternoon Warne had revealed his bullyish side again. Paul Adams had a cheeky disposition that had not so far been matched by his bowling figures. This irked the Australians – a young opponent 'chirping' at them when they didn't believe he had earnt the right. These Australians saw Test cricket like a club, in which the permission to enter was granted, in recognition of time served and achievements racked up, by the hardened veterans who had undergone the requisite initiations and humiliations. It was nothing new. As Gary Cosier told Christian Ryan in *Golden Boy*, Ryan's book about Kim Hughes, 'the Chappell era … had the same hangover from Benaud, Simpson, Lawry. Sit down, shut up and we'll tell you when to speak. And if you get a couple of hundreds and start to look all right then we'll let you talk sometimes. And if you're really good then you can open your mouth whenever you want to. There was still that really hardline ethic that you had to earn your stripes.'

And this was with teammates! The Waughs, Healy and Warne saw a clear hierarchy in the world and they were at the top of it, controlling admission to those below. They would grant entry to a Brian Lara, or a Courtney Walsh, or a Richie Richardson, or a Graham Gooch, and maybe, in good time, to a Ponting or a Hayden. But they would not grant it to a Paul Adams.

Adams had been playing some impudent shots to Warne, such as a reverse sweep which caused general merriment. Warne was one of those players who loved a joke except when he was on the wrong end of it, and when Adams played one silly shot too many, Warne reacted by putting on a showy belly laugh, to mock Adams and ask, 'How funny is it now, champ?'

It was schoolyard stuff. Warne had his reasons for humiliating Adams, and in the cosmos of the Test cricketer those reasons had validity; but whatever else the gesture betrayed, it advertised that the Australians were under the pump.

So, on the third afternoon of a match moving at timelapse pace, Australia embarked on its long haul. Again, Taylor failed: 13, trapped playing back to McMillan. Some in the crowd stood. Most thought they were waving him adieu, not au revoir. Hayden followed after a ludicrous mix-up with Elliott ended in the batsmen racing each other to the same crease. Hayden lost the footrace, and his career was suddenly in as much peril as Taylor's.

The next ball, Elliott top-edged a hook to fine leg, and Adams, who had been relishing some banter with the crowd, dropped it. 'The sky must have been too blue for him,' Woolmer quipped later. Mark Waugh steadied Elliott, and they avoided running into each other or for the same crease. The cloud broke up after three days, and with the sun beating down the pitch seemed to be settling. But then a ball would rear or shoot or pop or grip, and the batsmen were back in the minefield. But with their two best technicians at the crease, Australia began to look unexpectedly sound. The total grew imperceptibly, like mould.

WARNE LOVED A JOKE EXCEPT WHEN HE WAS ON THE WRONG END OF IT

Half an hour before stumps Adams had his revenge, snapping a low return catch from Elliott, whose 44 was then the highest Australian score in the match. The Waugh twins survived to stumps, weathering a last assault from Donald.

When they took stock, Australia's position was not all that bad. They were 3/145, only 125 from victory. A fourth-innings target of 270 on a poor pitch seems an Everest at first, but once it is broken into two chunks – 145 down, 125 to get, seven wickets in hand – it can appear almost gettable.

It was Steve, not Mark, who faltered the next morning, Cronje taking a brilliant diving catch at cover point off Kallis. These moments are quickly magnified in cricketers' superstitious minds. Everyone is looking for a sign of whose 'day' today will be. The sight of the South African captain pulling in a screamer to remove Australia's premier bat must have spread the belief that this would be South Africa's day.

Blewett could not find his Johannesburg fluency, and on a very different wicket his technical flaws were shown up. Having grown up in Adelaide, the slim, upright right-hander played brilliantly on true, bouncing wickets, but his early commitment to his shots and extravagant confidence, eschewing the safety net of keeping his bat and front pad close together, made him suspect on low, deviating ones. He hung around with Mark Waugh to put on twenty-five, but at 192 was bowled playing around a full ball from Adams.

Now, of all times, it seemed to be one of those arsey Taylor masterstrokes that Australia had played an extra batsman. Bevan had provided the shock factor with the ball in the second innings, taking 3/18, and must have felt, as he joined Waugh, that the day was his. They batted together for ninety-eight minutes. Bit by bit they chewed down the required runs. McMillan, who had lost his bite after bruising his heel, had to share the new ball with Donald. Mark Waugh was playing the innings he might have played in Adelaide back in 1993. He was the only man out there with the time, the eye and the straight-batted technique to handle a pitch as poor as this. Now he was four years older, and seasoned, and wasn't going to let his chance slide. Steve had failed in both innings – this was Mark's turn. And his lucky day! In his sixties, he fine-edged a ball from Adams. Richardson caught it from a metre away but didn't appeal. Cullinan stifled a shout. Nothing else was heard, and the umpire didn't have to answer the unasked question.

The medium-pacers kept putting the ball in the corridor, Donald roared in at high voltage, and Waugh was able to leave the nasty ones, deflect the in-duckers, and put away the rare loose ones. In the team meetings, he had said the pitch was not as bad as people were making out. He was the only one who genuinely believed that. He gave one other chance, a hard low one off the toe of the bat that Cullinan put down at first slip. It wasn't the most attractive batting, but context is everything and Waugh was making batsmanship look normal when few others had a clue. He was above doubt. Perhaps the difficulty of the situation was what was needed to rein in his moments of airiness. He did everything right, which is to say he did nothing wrong. He raised his century in five hours and kept going, his heart invested in being there at the end.

Bevan's 24 runs, in a partnership of sixty-six, were priceless. Cronje summoned Kallis for one last spell. Kallis, with his looping action and late swing, was emerging as the right pace for this surface. Cronje, encouraged by Kallis and snakebit by Donald's zero wickets, took the ball at the other end. But was it too late? Australia only needed twelve.

In the Australian changing room, Taylor bit his fingernails and looked like a defendant waiting for the jury to return to court. With precisely twelve to get, Steve Waugh turned to him and said, 'Wake up to yourself, Tubby, we're home here, we won't lose five for twelve.'

Then Kallis bowled Mark Waugh, a good ball that swung in late. Next over, Cronje had Bevan caught low by Cullinan at slip. The match had turned on its head, again. At 5/258, Australia couldn't lose. Now, at 7/258, it seemed highly unlikely that they would win. Healy and Warne were useful lower-order batsmen but this was one of those pitches where every new batsman (except Mark Waugh) was a duffer.

Warne and Healy conferred mid-pitch. The conversation was later recorded by Taylor.

Warne: What are we gunna do, Heals?

Healy: I don't know. I haven't worked it out for myself yet. How can I let *you* know what to do?

Warne: Well, I can't feel my legs.

Warne hit Cronje over his head for four in a precious seven-run partnership with Healy, but played back and was trapped. 8/265 – five to win, or two wickets.

Gillespie, since joining the team, had shown a sterling determination to never bat below McGrath. Few could entertain the notion of batting below McGrath, but at first Gillespie could. So set was he on learning to bat that he enlisted Geoff Marsh for arm-cramping throw-down sessions. He didn't learn how to bat, but he learnt how to block.

He blocked five balls from Kallis. McGrath waited with his pads on. The over seemed to take an hour.

Still five to win. Healy took strike to Cronje. Cronje moved a man from the off side to square-leg, and dropped his backward-square to the boundary. The intention seemed to be to give Healy a single on the on side and get Gillespie on strike. Healy sweated on an off-side ball which he aimed to late-cut to the now vacant third-man fence. He defended the first ball, and as Cronje was running in for the second, Healy backed away. He complained to the umpires that South African fieldsmen behind him, on the leg-side, were dropping back in the field while the bowler was running in. They were. South African teams had been doing it in domestic cricket for years. But the umpires told Cronje to stop them.

Healy defended the second ball, then Cronje came in for the third, angling towards leg. Off a good length, the ball rose into Healy's leading hip. Healy had a limited number of swing arcs, but those he did have he tended to play with a full 360 degrees. This ball was in one of his zones. He swung through the ball, helping it on its way, and it carried and carried and carried … over the boundary and into the choir.

A match like this, where every run was like gold, ended with a six. So stunning was it that most of the ground fell into silence. The band, the choir, the South African players. Cronje dropped his head. Healy ran around laughing, like the kid who has smashed the streetlight everyone has been aiming at. The Australians converged on him, Taylor foremost, and Mark Waugh got to see his great job finished in the style it deserved.

Taylor's captaincy was saved, Waugh had played the innings of his life, Bevan had played his best Test, and Healy had his delightful cream on the cake. Australia had won the unofficial world championship, won it away from home, and won the elusive nailbiter. The Port Elizabeth Test lodges so firmly in the memory not because Australia won but because it was such a great cricket match. Taylor called it 'the type of match that only comes along once every twenty or thirty years'. If there were statistics for how many times the advantage shifts between teams in one match, surely this would be among the all-time highs. Australia

ABOVE: I did that! Healy celebrates his six.

commanded the first two sessions of day one, then South Africa fought back with the McMillan–Richardson stand before taking over the running with two sessions of great bowling and the match-high partnership between Kirsten and Bacher. Then Australia won the next two sessions, but were still behind in the match. South Africa got further ahead by dismissing Taylor and Hayden on day three, but then Australia fought back – until Elliott was out. The pendulum hovered while the Waughs were in, but South Africa got a swing when Steve Waugh, then Blewett, perished. The Mark Waugh–Bevan stand was crucial, and even match-winning – until both were out, and then Warne too. It really was, in racing terms, a bob of the heads down the straight. Healy's six was the last stretch of the winner's neck across the line. Fabulous. Test cricket is the greatest game.

NORMAL BUSINESS WILL NOW RESUME

Manchester, July 1997

HE TOLD THE PLAYERS ONLY WHEN HE WALKED OFF THE FIELD, AND THEY REACTED WITH DISBELIEF. HE STRAPPED ON HIS PADS; IF HE WAS TAKING THEM OVER A CLIFF, AT LEAST HE WAS LEADING FROM THE FRONT.

The first unique aspect of Taylor's 1996–97 slump was that it went on for so long. Between 9 December 1995, when he made 96 against Sri Lanka in Perth, and 7 June 1997, a stretch of twenty-one Test innings, he did not score a half-century. As it extended, so it worsened: the first ten innings of the slump yielded 249 runs at 27.7, the next eleven 118 runs at 10.7. Greg Chappell wrote that he was in 'denial'. By early 1997, Dennis Lillee, Bob Simpson and Ian Chappell were among the Greek chorus of former greats singing him out of the team.

Meanwhile, behind a pleasant smile and impervious hide, Taylor was wriggling and scrapping and politicking with the skills of a backroom veteran. He was given grace to under-perform for so long because he was a very good captain of a very good team which kept winning series. How did we know this? Because he kept telling us. Nor did he spare any effort pointing out the contextual fact that his opening partners in that stretch – Slater, Elliott and Hayden – also struggled. He convinced the selectors and the ACB that the Australian team, as richly diverse in tone and tune as an orchestra, might lose their thread without him, their ever-calm conductor. He came

BY THE LATTER HALF OF THE SOUTH AFRICAN TOUR **HE STANK LIKE** A WEEK-OLD FISH

up with a long list of imaginative excuses: green wickets were being prepared to nullify Warne, openers were struggling everywhere, captains were struggling everywhere, and many more.

The other unique aspect of his slump is that it *enhanced* his reputation. Lying awake at night, he might have been boiling with frustration and resentment, but in company, Taylor was Taylor. He seldom let the pressure show, except in barely perceptible ways such as when he forgot to put Michael Bevan's name on the team list before the first one-day match of the South African tour in East London. Only once did he react to the press, confronting Malcolm Conn of the *Australian* in Port Elizabeth.

Taylor's enduring popularity, and authority, is all the more remarkable when we consider the number of teammates his slump managed to alienate. By the last half of the South African tour, when the team lost the Third Test and split into 'Test' and 'one-day' specialists – Taylor remaining with the latter – he stank like a week-old fish. Healy thought he had claims to be captain. When ACB chairman Denis Rogers went to South Africa to affirm his confidence in Taylor, it grated with Steve Waugh, who couldn't see why *he* shouldn't be captain. Reiffel thought he should have been playing in the Tests, but

LEFT: For months, Taylor had been forgetting to bat like Taylor.

couldn't because Bevan was being used as a stop-gap for Taylor. The trio of Elliott, Langer and Hayden, sent home after the Test series and clumsily informed during the calamitous Third Test, were justifiably resentful that Taylor was allowed to stay as a mostly non-playing one-day squad member. *Nobody* in the squad, except for Taylor, thought he should have remained for the one-dayers. His presence led Healy and Geoff Marsh to forcibly 'rest' him for the last five games while a newcomer, Adam Gilchrist, was tried.

Yet it was Taylor whose reputation grew. No matter what they thought of his stubbornness, his teammates would all marvel at his capacity to absorb pressure. To the press, who were doing everything but begging him to go, at the very least to give them something different to write about, he was unfailingly polite. Somewhere inside that square, heavy-rumped body and friendly face with its squinty right eye, he was able to seal away the pressure and criticism. Perhaps he chewed it all into his gum while he stood at first slip, directing traffic. Meanwhile, Healy cracked, throwing his bat in Pretoria and being banned for two matches. He was stripped of the vice-captaincy for the Ashes tour, and his short-lived dream of succeeding Taylor was over. Still embittered years later, Healy wrote that 'the way I felt about playing for Australia changed as soon as I heard that decision'. McGrath succumbed to a stress injury in his foot, Warne struggled with the wear and tear on his fingers and shoulder, and Mark Waugh split his webbing. Most of the other senior players showed the effects of severe strain. Not Taylor. He had a sore back, but didn't let it get him down. He embodied the qualities of a man in Kipling's 'If', treating the two impostors, victory and defeat, the same.

When the Ashes squad arrived in England in May the pressure ramped, if possible, up. As Taylor went through Heathrow, a customs officer asked him what his job was. 'Australian cricket captain,' Taylor replied. 'Ah yes,' said the officer, 'but for how long?' A tabloid newspaper presented him with a three-foot-wide bat. The whole of England was laughing at him. Back in Australia, the *Daily Telegraph* ran a front-page headline announcing that Taylor had dropped himself from the Test team.

As the one-day matches were scheduled before the Tests, Taylor was reinstated to the limited-overs team. He scored 7 and 11; the Australians lost. He then made a duck and 30 against Gloucestershire, and when he scored 5 in the first innings against Derbyshire it began to look unlikely that he would survive until the First Test. He wrestled with standing down, and openly canvassed the possibility with Waugh, now his vice-captain. What to do then? Go through the whole six-Test marathon with a non-playing captain? Retire and go home? These possibilities were real, and the back-up openers, Langer and the recalled Slater, were having their growth stunted by frustration. Which is not to mention the omitted Hayden, whose Test career had been cut down again, a victim of Taylor's form as much as his own.

Then, in the second innings of the Derbyshire match, photographers followed Taylor most of the way to the wicket. 'They all wanted the picture of me going out to bat for the last time,' he would say. 'Why I didn't belt someone, I don't know.'

The butter-fingers of fate touched him when, on 1, he edged a drive to the overseas professional, a fellow named Dean Jones, at slip. Jones grabbed at it too early, closed his knuckles, and put it down. The irony: Jones, unwanted in the Taylor era, was now giving the Australian captain a last lifeline. Taylor had just about had enough anyway. After Jones dropped him, he said to his batting partner, Langer, 'I just can't fucking play.' He needed the younger man, kept out of the Test team by Taylor's retention, to calm him down and

'IT WAS ALMOST AS IF HE WAS LEARNING TO BAT AGAIN'

reassure him. Afterwards, he asked Steve Waugh frankly if he should select himself in the First Test. Waugh – who was being asked, in effect, if he wanted to be captain of Australia – urged Taylor to back himself and play, but not to 'force it'.

Taylor made a three-hour unbeaten 59 that afternoon in Derby. His footwork at the crease led Steve Waugh to observe that 'it was almost as if he was learning to bat again'. He was out next day for 63, enough to make the beachhead of the First Test at Edgbaston.

Nevertheless, Christopher Martin-Jenkins described leaving out Slater as 'a decision of extraordinary folly which could only have been made by selectors so close to the wood that they cannot see the trees'.

In his tour diary, Taylor mulled over his feeling that something was not quite right with the team. He couldn't put his finger on it, but they didn't seem ready for a Test series. Talk about being unable to see the trees! Taylor must have been the only person on earth who didn't realise what was affecting his players. Paul Reiffel, who had not been picked in the original squad but was called in to replace the injured Bichel, observed:

> It was obvious to me that Tubby's string of failures and the huge publicity around them had created a negative atmosphere in the team. They were very low. These things can run through a team like a virus, and it seemed that everyone was looking at themselves and believing or at least imagining that they were also out of form.

On a spicy Edgbaston wicket Taylor won the toss, batted, and failed again, slicing Devon Malcolm into the cordon for 7. He wasn't alone: if Australia had made 1/300 Taylor might have given up hope, but his teammates gave him company by collapsing around him to 8/54, only Warne's 47 saving their blushes. By the end of the first day, the match was lost: Australia 118, England 3/200 and on their way to a 360-run lead.

With the luxury of a 288-run stand between Nasser Hussain and Graham Thorpe, Mike Atherton delayed his declaration until the third morning. He might have declared 300 runs ahead, late on the second day, to put Taylor in for a nasty pre-stumps session and perhaps the last rites. But the weather was uncertain and Atherton wanted more runs. Another stroke of luck for Taylor.

Elliott took the first over of Australia's second innings, from Darren Gough. Taylor faced up to Devon Malcolm: fast, inconsistent, and either juicy or unplayable with not much in between. As the bowler was about to come in for his first ball, off his long straight run, Taylor backed away – he had something in his eye. His last-chance saloon started with a leave, then a single. Soon he was into a slow-burning 133-run partnership with Elliott. Taylor top-edged a hook, but it flew to the rope. He didn't look safe, but he wasn't getting out either. He wasn't trying self-consciously to 'have fun'; he was simply batting like Mark Taylor. As he reflected later, he had been trying too hard to play the perfect innings, when all he had to do was play a Mark Taylor innings. For a year he had been trying to lift his batting by a cog, to be more aggressive and adventurous, when all of his success in the previous decade had come from playing within his well-grooved limitations. He had been trying to lift his game like a driver searching for a fifth gear, forgetting that his car only had four.

England's bowlers erred in giving him too much on his pads, while his vulnerability around off-stump went unexploited. They bowled as if they agreed with Martin-Jenkins and preferred to keep Taylor in the side rather than take another mauling from Slater. When the medium-pacer Mark Ealham came on, Taylor pulled him for a four and a six, possible signs of a return to fluency as opposed to survival. He only took sixty-six balls to reach his half-century, showing that at least he was turning over the strike.

Elliott fell for 66, then Taylor found an ally in Blewett, elevated to three in another reshuffle. Blewett relieved the pressure by unfurling some classical drives and pulls, and noticed a change in Taylor's behaviour. Having been unusually quiet early in the innings, as he progressed Taylor found his voice again, urging Blewett between overs, setting the next goal and making commentary on how well he was hitting the ball. Late in the day Taylor brought up his century with a push off Andrew Caddick into the covers. He raised his bat and his arms and looked much the same as he had celebrating any of his fourteen previous Test centuries. He went on to 129 the next day.

Australia lost the Test but had cleared the decks. The distraction was behind them. The captain would stay. They could play cricket now. As Healy said, 'our captain was back, our tour had begun'. Warne would call it 'the turning point of the series', an unusual comment to make about a match lost by nine wickets.

The catharsis was one of mood and atmosphere rather than hard facts. Taylor would only score 60 runs in the next three Tests, yet without raising a murmur about his form. It wasn't a question of how well or how badly he was batting, but of whether or not he would be replaced. After the First Test, his team knew that he would remain captain for the rest of the series. That, rather than any ongoing confidence in his form, was the thing that was settled at Edgbaston.

The Second Test, at Lord's, was virtually a washout, but not before McGrath roared back with 8/38 to rumble England for 77. Elliott made his long-promised maiden century, a classy 112, and Warne found better rhythm. Whether they admitted it or not, the entire team had been in disarray, but now the pieces could fall into place. Individuals would stop imagining that they were as out of form as Taylor. Nevertheless, they went to Old Trafford one-down to a newly confident foe. As miserable as the English could seem when they were down, once they were up they were unbearable. Their players had carried on with unbridled, incautious hubris after winning at Edgbaston, and their crowds, adapting a song from the Euro 96 football championships, were singing 'The Ashes Are Coming Home'. As Old Trafford revealed, the only things that were coming home were their chickens.

When he went out to toss, the wicket Taylor faced was more like a creekbed: damp and grassy in the middle, bare and dry at each end. He must not have relished batting, but if he won the toss he had to consider the devastation Warne might wreak bowling last. He also remembered 1993, when Australia had won easily after batting first on a similar-looking track. But when he told Steve Waugh he was thinking about batting first, Waugh thought he was joking.

Taylor won the toss and decided to bat. Pointedly, he didn't signal his decision to the changing room. He told the players only when he walked off the field, and they reacted with disbelief. He strapped on his pads; if he was taking them over a cliff, at least he was leading from the front.

Dean Headley, playing his first Test, took the new ball and promptly hit a ducking Taylor in the head. Headley was long and whippy and while not as fast as the man he replaced, Malcolm,

ABOVE: Supreme: Waugh at Manchester.

he had better control and movement for what were turning out to be seam-friendly conditions. He was also the first third-generation Test cricketer. His grandfather was the West Indian great, George, and his father, Ron, had also represented the Windies. Taylor became his first Test wicket in his third over and Blewett followed, chopping on to Darren Gough. The England attack was probably the best they fielded during the 1990s. Gough was fast and willing and could extract surprising bounce from his low action and hyperextending right arm. The Australians tended to think his bubbliness disguised a brittle self-esteem, but when he was up he was hard to bring down. Andrew Caddick looked like a parking inspector with a pebble in his boot, but the Waughs respected him and that said enough. Headley could, on his day, run through any batting order, and Robert Croft was a more useful off-spinner than he looked. Backed by a sound batting order, it was no wonder they thought the Ashes were homesick.

Mark Waugh had lost his South African touch, and only Elliott of the top order could hold out, with a stabilising 40. At the other end, Steve Waugh looked reasonably comfortable, or as comfortable as possible after the third wicket had fallen at forty-two, while he was on the toilet. Moreover, he had been awake most of the previous night looking after his infant daughter, Rosalie. To old hands, this was why families didn't come on tour. To Waugh, the challenges of cricket and of life were indivisible. The dicey wicket and bracing temperature were just the tonic to sharpen his concentration. He could sniff out a fight better than Don King, and was straight into the ring, sensing that this was a Test that could be won by an individual performance. He was irked anyway, having made a golden duck at Lord's.

He survived an early lbw appeal when he lost sight of a Caddick full toss. But at the other end the wickets kept falling, as Elliott edged one, Bevan again failed to keep down a riser, and the technical shortcomings of both Healy and Warne were exposed. Yet there are few things that build a batsman's confidence more than the fall of wickets at the other end, and Waugh was looking stronger with every dismissal. He was the only batsman in the Australian innings to strike at better than 50 runs per 100 balls. In Reiffel, flown in for Kasprowicz, he eventually found a long-term relationship. As they had in Kingston two years earlier, Waugh and Reiffel paired to blunt the bowling with a mix of evasion and counterthrust. The English bowlers, impatient, fell into the West Indian trap of bouncing Waugh. Reiffel's batting had gone off during his stop-start 1996–97, showing the effects of the selectors' lack of confidence, but he was reborn in England. When he had made 13, Stewart dropped him off Headley. Atherton grew confused over whether to continue his attacking but run-leaking fields to Reiffel, in whom Waugh was happy to vest confidence. That first afternoon, Reiffel's two-hour 31 helped Waugh add seventy runs and take the score past 200 and Australia to stumps. Waugh cut against what there was of Croft's spin to reach his thirteenth century in Tests, in semi-darkness, having refused the umpires' offer of bad light.

The last three wickets fell quickly on the second morning. A first-innings 235 was not as bad as it could have been, and looked all the better as the second day went on. McGrath performed what was becoming his 'Atherton routine'. Like Merv Hughes, McGrath exerted a mysterious force over the university graduate. This was the fifth time McGrath had dismissed Atherton in seven innings, in a run of nineteen dismissals in twenty Tests. Who knows why? McGrath was very good. He would develop a similar hold over Lara, who was a much better player than Atherton. But it is tempting to think there was something of a clash of civilisations personified in the contest, a triumph of pig-shooting over pen-pushing.

Alec Stewart and Mark Butcher, very much players rather than gentlemen, dug in and took the score to 1/74 before Warne got in on the act, ripping a mighty leg-break past Stewart to Taylor at slip, kissing the outside edge on its way. This was Warne's ground from 1993, and Jim Laker's, and Derek Underwood's – spin heaven. The previous day's damp surface, chopped up by spikes and seam, had hardened into a crusty moonscape. In thirty unchanged overs Warne took 6/48, tearing out English hearts and winning them at the same time. Amazingly, it was his first five-wicket Test haul since 1995. In the two years prior to 1995, he had taken ten.

Between 1995 and 1997 he had been contributing with containing spells and crucial wickets, maintaining a good strike rate and an average in line with his career rate, but his dry spell between five-wicket hauls was a long one. If not in the Taylor category, as slumps go, it had been worrying the spinner, with his post-surgery right finger playing on his mind. He'd only taken three wickets in the first two Tests. His first innings at Old Trafford restored his strut and, correspondingly, England's flutters.

From such a poor start, Australia emerged with a seventy-three-run lead. In their second innings, Taylor failed again (his post-century Test scores had been 1, 2 and 1, but now, exhausted by the subject of his form, nobody cared). Blewett was caught controversially by slipper Hussain, who no doubt thought he had taken the ball on the full but was shown up by the video replay. From 3/39, Mark Waugh's 55 in a ninety-two-run stand with Steve, the younger twin's first substantial contribution, put the Australians over the horizon. The wicket was still uneven in bounce and pace, and Bevan's agony continued, but Steve Waugh dug in for more than six hours. Hampered by a bruised right hand, he pulled it off the bat on impact with a tight grimace. All his down-the-order partners outscored him. Healy made 47 in a partnership of seventy-eight; Warne 53 in a partnership of eighty-eight; and Reiffel 18 out of 35 before Waugh was finally out, nicking Headley, for 116. Steve Waugh's reputation was built on matches like this, where batting was so hard that his scores stood out like oases in the desert. His twin centuries were the first by anyone in an Ashes Test since Denis Compton and Arthur Morris both achieved it at Adelaide in 1946–47. It didn't happen every day.

England, chasing 469, soon found themselves reverting to old fears and habits. Victory having slipped away, their batting wobbled then stopped like a set of blown tyres. Gillespie made early inroads before Warne was back again, taking the prizes of Stewart and Thorpe. Healy went for the helmet again, and Warne passed Richie Benaud's 248 Test wickets. McGrath helped the clean-up operation but Australia would win by a definitive 268 runs. In the performances of Steve Waugh and Warne, something more than a single Test victory was asserted: it was the return of the past, a restoration of normal operations. Waugh would rate his first innings alongside Sabina Park, and Australia would go on to win by an innings at Headingley and 264 runs at Trent Bridge, wrapping up the Ashes with a match to spare. In the tradition of throwing the English some crumbs from the table, they lost the Sixth Test at The Oval, bowled out for 104 chasing 123, a nasty little reminder of the past. As they had in 1993 and 1995, and would again in 1998–99, 2001 and 2002–03, England celebrated winning a dead rubber as if they'd regained the Ashes. It tended to keep them keen for next time.

OPPOSITE: First in 51 years: Waugh celebrates his second Manchester ton.

THE PRETENDERS

Adelaide, January/February 1998

MACGILL WAS THE OSCAR TO WARNE'S FELIX. WHEREAS WARNE WAS USUALLY BROWNED WITH DIRT FROM THE FIRST OVER, MACGILL LOOKED LIKE A MAN WHO WOULD COLOUR-CODE HIS LEGO.

There were three matches in the late 1990s that broke the heart of South Africa. The first and third are glittering ornaments on the Australian mantelpiece: the Port Elizabeth Test in 1997 and the Edgbaston World Cup semi-final in 1999. Between them, though, was a less celebrated game, a draw no less, but one which did as much as the others to sap South Africa's self-belief and ensure another decade would lapse before they won a series against Australia.

If they were ever primed to nail the Australians, it was in the summer of 1997–98. After returning from the punishment of nine overseas Tests in 1997, the Australian players were distracted by an acrimonious but overdue clash with their board over payments and conditions. The newly formed Australian Cricketers' Association, headed by Tim May, allied itself with a management operation called Sports and Entertainment Limited. The men behind SEL were James Erskine, an oleaginous Englishman who had previously headed the International Management Group's Australian arm, and Graham Halbish, the former chief executive of the ACB who had departed after a never publicly explained tiff with chairman Denis Rogers. Both Erskine and Halbish, in their different ways, had an axe

'HE MIGHT BE A BASTARD, **BUT HE'S** *OUR* **BASTARD'**

to grind. The overbearing, moustachioed Halbish knew the ACB's books inside-out and if he didn't know the players were underpaid, nobody knew it. Erskine, starting his own business, saw a nice stream of commissions pouring out of cricket. While not a cricket man himself, he earnt the players' confidence; as one of them said, 'He might be a bastard, but he's *our* bastard.'

But the agents needed a power base, and that came from the discontented senior players. There is no doubt that when they looked at the salaries being thrown at Australian rules, rugby union and rugby league players, the international cricketers suffered from relative deprivation syndrome. It hadn't gone unnoticed that some two hundred Super League–pumped rugby league players were earning six-figure sums, an amount matched by only a handful of Test cricketers. The second tier of Test players earnt much less, and – the real scandal – the average State player was on an annual income of around $30,000 to $50,000. Seeing that cricket demanded full-time participation, it was only right that State players be paid a full-time salary.

The complexities of the dispute were tortuous, but at bottom it was a dispute like all employer–employee fights. The ACB didn't want to pay the players any more than they were,

LEFT: Patriots: Cullinan, Donald and Cronje were amped-up for Australia.

and marshalled all sorts of arguments to maintain the status quo. Emotions were muddled by the presence of Halbish and Erskine, and in the end the players only had one bargaining chip, which was the threat to withdraw their labour. Thanks to a last-minute intervention from Kerry Packer's Channel Nine, a strike was averted. Thanks to a last-minute attack of commonsense, the ACB offered a more reasonable pay deal. Halbish disbanded with Erskine and disappeared from the scene; Erskine went off to manage other kinds of show business, but bobbed up again a decade later to finally give Warne the quality of personal management the leg-spinner could have done with earlier in his career.

On the cricket front, the Australians did well to keep their minds on the New Zealand Test series, which they won. The ACB and ACA agreed to take their negotiations behind closed doors just in time for the arrival of the South Africans. Later in 1998, a deal was struck whereby State players would collectively receive an extra $300,000 from the board's revenues, and international players' pay would be calibrated by whether they were required for Test or one-day duties, or both. The ACB also agreed to increase the portion of overall revenue it paid players, from eighteen per cent to more than twenty per cent, and to institute other reforms such as appointing a full-time professional team manager. Up to then, going on overseas tours as 'manager' had been a nice little perk shared among ACB directors. At best they were harmless, at worst useless. Most of them, said Greg Chappell, 'didn't have a clue. We spent more time managing them than they spent managing us'. Steve Bernard, the former New South Wales bowler and national selector, would hold the role as a full-time professional from 1998 for more than a decade.

The major onfield change that summer was the formalisation of the 'two teams' strategy. Taylor didn't even belong in Australia's top thirty in coloured clothes; unluckily, Healy was dumped too. Steve Waugh became captain, and Adam Gilchrist wicketkeeper, alongside a host of other fresh faces. The Australian selectors, under new chairman Trevor Hohns, were unafraid to take the long view, and the 1999 World Cup was their target. Of course, sections of the public and media were unafraid to take the view of the day, and Hohns was their target. Taylor, so long excoriated, became a martyr; even more so, Healy. A magazine polled the country's first-class cricketers, and seventy-eight per cent said Healy should be one-day keeper ahead of Gilchrist. In a terrible misjudgement of the public mood, the ACB arranged a one-day game at the SCG between the new-look Australian team and an 'Australia A' outfit spearheaded by none other than Healy. Gilchrist had already played the role of villain when he moved to Western Australia and replaced the local favourite Tim Zoehrer; now he had to represent his own country in Sydney, with crowds booing him and chanting Healy's name. Waugh proceeded to make no runs in his first four innings as international captain, South Africa took the whip hand in the series, and the experiment went very close to combusting in the laboratory phase. Fortunately the Melbourne and Sydney Tests intervened.

South Africa had come with a familiar team, led by Cronje. This time Kallis, Klusener, Gibbs and Pollock were a year older; but then, so were Richardson, McMillan, Symcox and Donald. Nevertheless, they were formidable on paper and, having just beaten Pakistan in Pakistan, again had a legitimate claim to be contesting the Test world championship. They had now won twice in the subcontinent, where Australia hadn't won at all since 1969.

The intensity of the South Africans' mood glowed like radiation. Upon their arrival in Perth, the brooding Cronje and Bob Woolmer sat in the stands watching Australia. Woolmer, an early adopter of the laptop

HE WANTED TO WIN AS ACHINGLY AS CRONJE

computer and imaginative software as a coaching aid, as well as delving into the science of biomechanics, was bringing an unprecedented level of analysis to the job. He was a highly intelligent man with a bright red face and a nice line in dry quips. But – and this is a big but – he wanted to win as achingly as Cronje. These relationships, as Australia had learnt, are all about the individual dynamics. As John Buchanan later showed, a scientific approach can yield pure gold. But the twin intensities of Cronje and Woolmer often seemed to cancel each other out. Pressure often seemed to build up for no good reason. Approaching the series, Cullinan was reprimanded for dissent in a lead-up game, Symcox was pelted with a whole roast chicken from the crowd in a one-dayer, and Cronje was caught apparently tampering with the ball in Devonport. The South Africans, who could have walked around like favourites, the conquerors of India and Pakistan, were soon skulking from venue to venue like a hunter's quarry.

The First Test, at the MCG, ended in a draw after Kallis put himself between the Australians and what they wanted. In an era of attack, Kallis was a throwback to a dour defensive time, even as a young man. He was rarely exciting, the type of batsman who could go on for days without an increase in his pulse rate. He batted six hours in the second innings on a dying MCG deck, and kept Warne out. Australia ended up three wickets and South Africa 108 runs short of victory.

Sydney's New Year Test belonged to Warne. He captured five wickets in South Africa's first innings 287, aided by Bevan. This time the South Africans' defensive batting had become a disease. Facing an Australian attack worn out from its efforts in Melbourne, on a placid wicket, South Africa only scored 197 runs on the first day. Given their big chance, they seized up. Taylor was able to use his part-timers for twenty-four overs, and still the Proteas treated them with respect bordering on fear.

The Waughs led Australia's grinding reply of 421, memorable for the pummelling Donald gave them late on the second day. For Donald, it was the old story. He bowled fast, he bowled brilliantly, he bowled the highest quality express pace – Mark Waugh said it was up with the best bowling he'd ever faced, on a par with the West Indians at their peak – yet he failed to break through until it was too late. The Australians reckoned they could see it in his eyes, that unrequited effort, that presentiment of failure. There was no justice. His parallels with McDermott were eerie at times. At the end of a riveting contest of bat and ball, Mark Waugh upstaged Steve's hundredth Test by scoring a century to Steve's 85.

Leading by 134, Australia closed the noose. McGrath and Reiffel removed the openers, and then on the fourth day Warne took the levers. By the end of his career he would look at these years, 1996 to 1999, as his fallow ones. But there were still some grand days. Rain and darkness loomed, but Warne kept charging in – can a leg-spinner charge in? Yes, but only Warne. Maybe Abdul Qadir, and Tiger O'Reilly. But Warne really was a thundering paceman trapped in a spinner's body. First he dislodged Cronje, snapped up by Ponting in close, then Gibbs, McMillan, Pollock and Richardson. Kallis remained, the roadblock as always, and he received overdue support from the grey-haired Symcox. For a while it looked like a fathers-and-sons match. The players were on and off, wild approaching storms threatened to steal Australia's thunder, but finally Warne got the breakthrough, bowling a full, dipping ball from around the wicket and somehow sneaking through Kallis. It was game, set, Test match and 300 wickets for Warne. He was now behind only Lillee in Australia, and the far-off Himalayas of Botham, Walsh, Hadlee and Kapil Dev were in sight. His mentor Terry Jenner said he might take 500, and everyone laughed.

Between the Second and Third Tests, South Africa had the chance to regroup in the one-dayers. The format suited their all-round athleticism and the even spread of their skills. They could all bat, they could all bowl and they could all field. It wasn't a bad formula, and until the finals series Australia went nowhere near beating them.

When it counted, however, the mood took a shift. In the first final in Melbourne, Steve Waugh had a brainwave over his ice-cream and strawberry sauce during the meal break and asked Gilchrist if he would like to open the batting with Mark. Gilchrist started by running Mark out, but the pairing showed some promise and then, in the second final in Sydney, Gilchrist hit a century so exhilarating that the series was won, the South Africans wept, the career of an all-time great was launched, and coach Marsh, a guiding hand in Gilchrist's development, leapt up so excitedly that he forgot there was a 200-kilogram table in the way and put himself on crutches.

Beating South Africa in the one-day finals was an unexpected interim vindication of the new approach. The calls to reinstate Healy and, to a lesser extent, Taylor, were quelled. But the exasperation it wrought on the Proteas brought a wave of heat to the final match of the summer, the Australia Day Test in Adelaide. South Africa were a fine and proud team who had, on a tour that promised so much, won nothing. Not a sausage. They were on a face-saving mission going to the Adelaide Oval, bitter with need.

An attritional summer had taken out the top pacemen, McGrath, Gillespie and Donald, and Warne's shoulder was hanging by a tendon. Bevan had been dropped, for the last time as it turned out, after eighteen Tests in four separate tries. He would continue as the world's premier middle-order batsman in the compressed game for another five years, winning two World Cups, which emphasised both how gifted he was and what a mystery his failures in Test cricket had been. He had no problems with short-pitched bowling at first-class level, scoring prolifically in Australia and overseas. Perhaps it was just luck; perhaps one more Test innings could have been the breakthrough. There were some who were shown more patience. Others less. He was without doubt the best batsman of the era to average less than 30 in Test cricket.

The outcome was a deep-green Australian attack: Bichel and Kasprowicz taking the new ball, with Stuart MacGill partnering Warne. MacGill, from Western Australia via New South Wales, was a late bloomer who flung the ball with a front-on action, imparting greater sidespin than Warne. MacGill was the Oscar to Warne's Felix. He had neat short brown hair, long sleeves and a little towel, like an apron, on his front. Whereas Warne was usually browned with dirt from the first over, MacGill looked like a man who would colour-code his Lego. Their spinning styles were different enough to encourage Grimmett–O'Reilly dreams. MacGill had a better wrong'un than Warne, who had largely given his up. Warne's variations were more subtle and his control tighter, but MacGill had a happy knack of taking the wickets of overconfident batsmen. The only weakness in the partnership was that, deep down, and sometimes not so deep down, Warne didn't really have his heart in it. That the greatest spinner of all time could also be insecure and jealous of the limelight is a lesson in human nature. Warne was a good teammate to MacGill's face and a sniper behind his back. Had MacGill arrived a couple of years before, when Warne was at his height, the partnership might have gelled better.

ABOVE: Taylor, redeemed, shows Symcox his good side in Adelaide.

Warne might have allowed it to. But by the beginning of 1998, notwithstanding his match-winning performance in Sydney, Warne grizzled about the second leg-spinner and – quite objectively, of course! – wondered aloud if it would dilute the novelty effect of the ball spinning away from the bat.

The first innings in Adelaide appeared to bear out his worries. South Africa won the toss. Bacher, Kirsten and Cronje made half-centuries, but Australia had high hopes at 7/305. With Donald missing and Richardson having gone in at nightwatchman, South Africa's bottom four were McMillan, Pollock, Klusener and Symcox. They all made runs, McMillan topscoring with 87 not out and Symcox slogging 54 off forty-two balls in a tenth-wicket stand of seventy-four. The tired and inexperienced bowlers took a flogging in the heat. South Africa had batted for 166 overs, scoring 517.

Donald had strained a muscle in the one-day finals, and for the first time against Australia Pollock stood up as the attack leader. Like Cronje, the redheaded Pollock was a head-prefect type, clean-cut and God-fearing and talented at everything he tried. Unlike Cronje, Pollock was the real thing right through to the core. His bowling on the second and third days, on a road of a wicket, was among the best seen at Adelaide. With his rocking action and balanced delivery, he controlled his length like McGrath but often extracted more movement. In forty-one overs, he took 7/87.

Only one Australian stood in his way. While his 334 not out later that year at Peshawar would stand as the conclusive redemption day for Taylor, his unconquered 169 in Adelaide was his real comeback innings. For the first time since his slump, his batting stood above his teammates' failures and had a decisive impact on a Test match. Alongside him, Mark Waugh scored 63 but Elliott, Blewett, Steve Waugh, Ponting and Healy, playing his hundredth Test, all went cheaply. As the temperature kept rising, Taylor watched ten wickets fall at the other end. After a scratchy first hour, he struck the ball as close to the middle of the bat as he ever did and in nine hours gave the bowlers little hope, carrying Australia past the follow-on and winding his own form clock back to 1989. He was the first Australian to carry his bat throughout a Test innings since Boon in Auckland in 1986.

With Australia having batted until the fourth morning, South Africa had to set a target quickly. The kiln-like heat was cracking the wicket, and they hoped to get Australia back in long enough before stumps to grab an early wicket or two. It went more or less to plan, if only because Gary Kirsten's 108 not out staved off a MacGill-induced collapse. For the game, MacGill took five wickets and Warne three. Clearly bothered by his shoulder, Warne privately pronounced the leg-spin partnership a failure.

This was a match of towering individual efforts: Pollock, Taylor, Kirsten. Would an Australian stand up in the last innings, or would it be Pollock, or another South African bowler? In an hour before stumps on day four, having declared 360 ahead with 109 overs to bowl, the Proteas grabbed the vital break. Pollock winkled an edge out of Elliott, and Klusener bowled Taylor, who, having been immoveable for two days, could only last half an hour. Taylor must have been beyond exhaustion. In forty-degree heat, he had been on the field for every minute of the match from the opening ball to the last minutes of the fourth day.

Australia should have lost a third wicket by stumps. Mark Waugh, notorious as a rubbisher of off-spin, was goaded by the garrulous Symcox to come down the wicket. Symcox's first ball popped straight off the bat to Bacher at short leg, then straight out onto the turf. The miss didn't shut Symcox up, but it would give the fieldsman and his captain nightmares.

There were always doubts about this Australian team's ability to bat out a draw. They were entertainers, attackers. Taylor instilled the belief that games should never be allowed to drift. Australia must always press for victory, and a draw was as bad as a loss. But this time, with no hope of winning the match and a series win to be gained by a draw, they had to knuckle down and block out a day. Accordingly, on day five they batted for time, not runs. Blewett was the only man out in the first session, his 16 having taken 104 minutes. Steve Waugh joined Mark and batted for 110 minutes before falling to Klusener. Ponting supported Mark for another two hours either side of tea, and it seemed Australia was going to last the day. Importantly, what they had done was stop the fall of one wicket from turning into a cascade. Mark Waugh was, as in Port Elizabeth, unruffled by the up-and-down bounce. Pollock, Klusener, McMillan, Kallis and Symcox kept at him, but he had the measure of this opponent. His innings went into its seventh hour, his longest in Test cricket. Continually, he was assisted by the fielders, who dropped him three times in the last two sessions.

Then, half an hour after tea, Ponting was caught by Symcox off Klusener. No heroic sixes today for Healy, who was caught behind after twenty-four minutes. The last fifteen overs were called with South Africa needing four wickets and Bichel supporting Waugh, who passed his century. South Africa heaped on the pressure, but Bichel soaked it up, as nerveless as his senior partner.

Amid excruciating tension, the moment arrived about forty minutes from the end, with seven overs to be bowled. Pollock flung down a bouncer at Mark Waugh, which hit him above his left elbow. The ball fell harmlessly. Stunned for a moment, Waugh turned away from the crease. The nerves in his struck arm, holding onto the bat, had gone dead. He took three steps towards backward square leg, and as he did so his bat swung out and knocked off the bails. The South Africans, most of whom hadn't seen Waugh hit the wicket, noticed the bails on the ground and appealed. Cronje rushed up to Waugh from mid-wicket and said, 'You've trodden on your stumps.' Waugh said he hadn't. The onfield umpires, Steve Randell and Doug Cowie, referred the decision to Steve Davis in the video booth. Waugh tried again to explain to the South Africans what had happened, and Davis turned the appeal down, ruling correctly under Law 35 that Waugh was neither playing his shot nor setting off for a run when he broke the wicket. Cronje remonstrat-

THE NERVES IN HIS STRUCK ARM HAD GONE DEAD

ed for another five minutes, arguing that Waugh's hitting the wicket was a direct consequence of the ball he faced, and therefore part of the continuous action. 'If somebody gets hit on the head, and he's a bit wobbly and he walks onto his stumps, he's out,' Cronje said later.

Enraged, the South Africans resumed. Three balls later, Waugh popped another catch into Bacher's midriff. Bacher dropped it again. None of his teammates offered him any consolation. Klusener surged in and trapped Bichel. The Zulu-speaker's zippy skidders, angled in from wide on the crease, had now taken four wickets. Warne joined Mark Waugh with half an hour to go. Cronje gave the last responsibilities to Pollock, and Waugh was dropped again – the tenth missed chance in the innings. When the game ended in a draw, Cronje didn't miss the door of the umpires' room, spearing a stump through it. As he said, his team had worked desperately hard for two and a half months, and had nothing to show for it. His own captaincy, as much as the lack of variety in the bowling attack and the absence of a damaging attacking batsman in the top order, had more to do with the barrenness of the quest than he could acknowledge. Cronje relied on plans and patterns; he didn't trust his gut, and consequently he often failed to see opportunities when they cropped up unexpectedly. As Steven Lynch wrote, watching Taylor and Cronje as captains was comparable to watching Doctor Who battle with a Dalek. For the last time, as it would turn out, Cronje left Australia a loser. A draw, even more than a win, can be the most decisive result in Test cricket, and after this one Cronje's South Africa would never be the same threat.

OPPOSITE: Cronje shakes Waugh's hand. Minutes later he'd destroy a door.

ROUTED

Chennai, March 1998

JOURNALIST ROBERT CRADDOCK FIXED TENDULKAR WITH A LONG LOOK AND SAID, 'THIS TOUR IS YOU AGAINST WARNE. SHANE WARNE WILL BE AT YOU, AND AT YOU; HE WILL NEVER LET UP, MENTALLY OR PHYSICALLY; HIS ACCURACY AND FLIGHT WILL GRIND YOU DOWN.'

By now Australia had been playing for sixteen months. Warne's shoulder, as shown by his weary bowling in Adelaide, was zinging with pain. McGrath, Gillespie and Reiffel were all injured for that Test. The batting of the rising youngsters Elliott, Ponting and Blewett had gone off the boil. And now they were being sent to India – but not before a quick tour to New Zealand, shoe-horned into a free fortnight.

Only Reiffel and Warne of the main bowlers would go to India. The pace backup was Kasprowicz, Queensland swinger Adam Dale, and a Novocastrian playing for South Australia, Paul 'Blocker' Wilson. Wilson was nicknamed without irony: he could stop anything smaller than a freight train. His determination was such that he had gone to the Cricket Academy uninvited, camping on the doorstep until they had to either call the police or let him in. Chosen for Australia in one-day cricket during the summer, he had performed creditably. Warne's spin support was MacGill and, showing Warne's nostalgia for the Tim May days, New South Wales journeyman off-spinner Gavin Robertson.

While the Australians were queuing up for the ministrations

HE COULD STOP ANYTHING SMALLER THAN A FREIGHT TRAIN

of their evergreen physio, Errol Alcott, the Indian players were quietly preparing to destroy them. Over in Mumbai, there was a touch of Doctor Evil in Sachin Tendulkar's planning. Tendulkar might not have known much else, but he knew how to bat. He had been scoring centuries since he was a child. In Australia as an eighteen-year-old in 1991–92, he had hit two of the best hundreds ever seen here, in Sydney and Perth, in a decimated team. And that was before he really got going.

There was not much to Tendulkar, except for a calmly ruthless application to the task of scoring runs. In his small stature, wristwork and tendency to keep the ball down, Tendulkar reminded Bradman of himself. In other eyes, what was also Bradman-like about Tendulkar was that he had seemingly excised, or been born without, those dimensions of the human personality that might have caused him problems as a batsman. He was not afflicted by the passions of a Lara, a Waugh or a Richards, nor the technical limits of a Border, nor the glumness of a Gooch. In short, there was nobody like him. Except Bradman.

Warne and the other Australian bowlers, prone under the

physio's touch, were dreaming of a holiday at the far end of the Indian tour. Meanwhile Tendulkar was at home relaxing, which for him meant going to the nets of the Madras Rubber Factory cricket academy with the former Test leg-spinner Laxman Sivaramakrishnan and some young leggies. With his spikes, Tendulkar roughed up the area outside the leg stump to simulate a wearing Test wicket. He asked Sivaramakrishnan, a bigger turner than most Indian spinners, to bowl from around the wicket. Tendulkar focused on the bowler, and saw Warne. In the nets, Tendulkar pulverised him. Sivaramakrishnan was attempting a comeback at the time, but did not progress far.

The weary Australians flew into Mumbai, saying all the right platitudes about embracing India and taking on the challenge. Yet the light had dimmed in their eyes. One exception was Michael Slater, restored in place of Elliott. Full of beans, Slater was again batting well. For nearly all of the sixteen-month cricketing marathon, Slater had been exiled from the Australian team, which was arguably the best preparation for this tour of India.

On the second night of the tour, some Australians attended a testimonial function for the retiring Indian and Mumbai batsman Sanjay Manjrekar. Tendulkar was there. During a short speech on the Australians' behalf, the journalist Robert Craddock fixed Tendulkar with a long look and said, 'This tour is you against Warne. Shane Warne will be at you, and at you; he will never let up, mentally or physically; his accuracy and flight will grind you down.'

Tendulkar, in all crowds, had the ability to stare into some middle distance — a distance of about twenty-two yards. As Craddock spoke, Tendulkar's eyes formed a glaze.

On the first morning of Australia's match against Mumbai at the picturesque art deco Brabourne Stadium, Slater, with 98, was the only batsman to show much pep in a total of 305. The next day started in routine fashion, Dale and Wilson taking early wickets. The surprise, in a warm-up match, was that Tendulkar was playing for his home town. Key players usually wanted to avoid a confrontation with a visiting side before the Test series, reasoning that there was too little to gain and too much, psychologically, to lose. Tendulkar saw it differently. Perhaps, after his net sessions with Sivaramakrishnan, he wanted to try a few things out. Such as the slog-sweep over mid-wicket. It certainly seemed premeditated.

The crowd chanted: 'Ganpati moraya!' meaning that the Hindu god Ganesh, or Ganpati, the elephant-headed remover of obstacles, was returning. Tendulkar was seen as Ganpati's reincarnation – not a warrior god, but a considerate, intelligent one. He was the son of a Brahmin school teacher, an intellectual, not a brute. The remover of obstacles between India and victory, the god who takes sadness away.

Warne was an obstacle. When he bowled to Tendulkar, his second delivery was a regulation leg-spinner pitching outside leg stump. For any mortal batsman, it posed enough questions that the only sane response was to cover it up, smother it down into the pitch. But this was Tendulkar, and the next time the ball connected with the earth was several rows back in the stand beyond the mid-wicket boundary.

A contest can never be decided in the first couple of balls. Or can it? Didn't the Gatting ball set the tone for the 1993 Ashes series? Didn't Slater's cover-driven boundary off Phil DeFreitas in Brisbane in 1994–95 dictate the course of that Ashes series? What about Steve Harmison's first-ball blooper in 2006–07? Who is to say? What is certain is that that game at the Brabourne was the most influential provincial tour match Australia played in twenty years. Tendulkar proceeded to score 204 not out from 192 balls. Warne's figures were 0/111 from sixteen overs. Mumbai declared at 6/410 in the seventy-ninth over, putting Australia back into bat that same afternoon, and snatched three quick wickets on their way to a ten-wicket win achieved in eight sessions.

Somewhat dizzily, Australia retreated from Tendulkar to Vishakapatnam, where they found a Board President's XI prepared to grind them down with a boring draw. In the Australian rooms, the whinge was on and the fatigue was bubbling to the surface. India was spurning their embrace. Slater was almost booked for dissent over a bad lbw decision – after he had scored 207!

An ill Steve Waugh hadn't had a bat on tour yet, and Warne had only taken two wickets. But perhaps tins of Australian baked beans and spaghetti would be his version of Popeye's spinach – famously, comfort food was flown over for Warne on Test eve. Taylor's teams habitually lifted for Test matches, and their mood on the first day in Chennai was bright. New series, new start. The real thing. The Chidambaram Stadium, on the aromatic banks of the Buckingham Canal (an open sewer), was packed and noisy and hot, generating more atmosphere than India's larger grounds. Mohammad Azharuddin won the toss and batted, and the first two days portended a classic Test match with savage swings of momentum.

India opened with Nayan Mongia and Navjot Singh Sidhu. Mongia was a typically talkative wicketkeeper who had batted down the order until, in Delhi eighteen months earlier, he had blitzed Australia with a 150 so convincing that it sentenced him to a stint against the new ball. Sidhu was a very interesting character. Physically, with his sparkling dark eyes, beard and pronounced overbite, he resembled a character from *The Simpsons*. He had been playing Test cricket, on and off, since 1983. Now thirty-three, he had plenty of history behind him, including a double century against the West Indies and charges of murdering an elderly man in a road rage incident in 1988. Sidhu was later convicted of homicide, then had his conviction stayed by the Supreme Court, worked as a commentator and entered politics. In 1997 he had walked out of India's tour of England when Azharuddin told him he was dropped as he was padding up for a Test match. He batted with a dirty plank of wood taped against disintegration, looking like something he'd kept since his school days. But beyond the local colour, as it were, he was a superb

ABOVE: Sikh and ye shall find: Sidhu the destroyer.

orthodox right-handed opening batsman with a lovely straight technique and a commitment to shotmaking. Steve Waugh called him 'the cleanest and most consistent hitter of sixes against spinners I ever saw. Sidhu used to literally throw himself into the shot with such force that he finished in a front-on position rather than the conventional side-on.' Warne would say that Sidhu's impact on this series was even greater than Tendulkar's or Azharuddin's.

Though he didn't score a century, Sidhu's top-of-the-order consistency and belligerence would soften Australia up for the big names in the middle-order.

Sidhu and Mongia put on 122 for the first wicket. Ominously, Kasprowicz and Reiffel couldn't break through and Warne was bowling against the openers well before lunch. Mongia finally nicked Kasprowicz, and Tendulkar came in to face Warne. It is said that a billion people stop to watch Tendulkar, and the strangest thing about this assertion is that it is true. They flock into grounds when they know he is going to bat. They go home and turn on the television. And they leave the ground, or go back to work, when he gets out.

That day Warne won. Tendulkar drove the first ball for four, then sliced an edge to Taylor at slip. With the run-out of Sidhu for 62, Australia had India 3/130.

The spinners, Warne and Robertson, maintained the advantage for the first day, taking four wickets each. This, his first, was the most fruitful of Robertson's four Tests. Unlike his teammates, he had a real job at the time, working as a junior executive for the groceries firm Davids. He needed it. In three years prior to this date, he had only been selected for one first-class match. A few months later he would be closer to selection for Australia than he was for his State. But in Chennai he loomed as a potential man of the match, especially when Australia faltered in reply to India's 257 and he came in at 8/201 to join Healy, who was playing the long top-class innings he seemed to muster once or twice a series.

HIS FIRST BALL WENT OFF LIKE AN EXPLODING CIGAR

India's attack was three-parts spin. The medium-pacers, Javagal Srinath and Harvinder Singh, were only there to take the shine off the ball and prepare it for the wrist-spinner Anil Kumble, the left-arm orthodox Venkatapathy Raju, and the most blatant thrower in a decade of throwers, Raj Chauhan. It was Kumble, predictably, causing the most problems. His first ball went off like an exploding cigar and hit Slater on the arm. He bowled Steve Waugh with an inswinger, the batsman not offering a shot. More of a top-spinner than a leg-spinner, he bounded in like a kangaroo and broke through the surface of the dusty wicket, causing bounce so unpredictable that the Australians were in a funk of indecision. He bowled too fast for them to come down the wicket. The temptation was to play back, but his top-spin was so vicious that the risk of lbw was too high. Yet when the batsman pushed forward, the variable bounce was just as likely to kick up at the gloves or shoulder of the bat and pop to the squad of close-in fielders.

Only Mark Waugh's technique had coped at the top, and now Healy's clean counter-hitting was effective while it lasted. Robertson, a bowling all-rounder batting at ten, scored 57 to go with Healy's 90 and lift Australia to 328, a potentially winning lead of seventy-one. Healy only got out, he said, because his brain was starting to melt in the heat.

Enter Sidhu, again. This time Blewett was able to pick off Mongia early, but Sidhu went after Warne with bloodthirsty intent. The sight of him charging down the wicket, his helmet bouncing around over his patka, must have been genuinely frightening for the Australian spinners. Sidhu was such a straight hitter and so fast on his feet that it didn't matter what the bowlers did, he was there first. 'He had a fantastic eye for the ball,' Warne said. 'Three or four times I thought I had beaten him through the air, only to see him swing the bat and hit the ball ten rows back into the stand.' He smacked 64, eradicating the Australians' lead, and set them on their heels for the arrival of the master. (Sidhu's scores in the series were, for the record, 62, 64, 97, 74 and 44.)

The constant roar in the Chennai ground is hard to describe. There was no power-on, power-off to the crowd's enthusiasm when Tendulkar batted. It was a wall of sound, voices, the percussion of empty plastic bottles banged together and the wind section of horns, the very air vibrating, and in the middle of it a tiny man carving the ball to all points. Steve Waugh said the Indian euphoria was so infectious that it made home batsmen feel 'bulletproof, as if they've signed an indemnity form against getting out'. It didn't matter where the Australians bowled,

Tendulkar had ample time to devise the shot and place it between the fielders with such force and timing that if he beat the inner ring by a yard it was a certain four. Rahul Dravid (56), Azharuddin (64) and Sourav Ganguly (30 not out) were able to say that the privilege of being an Indian batsman that day was to have the best seat in the house. Between balls Tendulkar nodded sharply, once, to himself, as if conducting a vigorous interior conversation. He squatted to spread his thighs and loosen his knees, then settled into his stance. He choked down on the handle of his three-pound bat, fifty per cent heavier than Azharuddin's, and waited for every ball with his firm, straight, orthodox stance. In a reprise of his Mumbai innings, when he scored at a gallop yet never seemed to be taking a risk, Tendulkar hummed along to 155 off 191 balls. In three swift sessions Australia were swept away. Azharuddin declared at 4/418, an hour before stumps on day four, and the bowlers closed in on the shell-shocked visitors. Slater and Blewett fell early, and Taylor was three balls from surviving the day with nightwatchman Reiffel when he pushed Kumble into Srinath's waiting hands.

At the start of that fourth day, Australia had been on parity in a seesawing Test match. By day's end, they were gone. You could see it in their rounded shoulders, in their slightly dazed expressions. They were tasting what the English tasted: disappointment, yes, but despite themselves a creeping admiration and feeling of being blessed to have witnessed cricketing history. It is no disgrace to be blown away by greatness, as Mark Waugh reflected: 'When you play against Tendulkar, you almost want to see him get a few runs just to see him bat.'

The fifth day, like the fourth, was simply overwhelming. India's seamers didn't bowl after the first four overs. Kumble was unplayable on the crumbling wicket, taking four wickets, while the underrated Raju chimed in with three and Chauhan pinged the ball in for a highly suspect brace, including Robertson first ball. Some poor umpiring from the tie-wearing, illness-affected Englishman George Sharp helped, but bad decisions, like dry leaves, always seem to go the way the wind is blowing. There was no doubt Australia were outplayed. Only Healy, not out on 32, remained unbowed. Hurt by losing both his vice-captaincy and one-day position, gutted by his father's death, he had gone into a period of soul-searching at the end of the summer, but now he was falling back on his core personality trait. Sheer bloody-mindedness and defiance would ensure that Healy went on for another year, breaking the world record for dismissals and playing some of his best cricket for Australia.

Australia had lost by 179 runs, and if they felt that things could get no worse they were sadly mistaken. The Second Test, at Eden Gardens, flowed like a second act of the first. Srinath became the second bowler in history, after South African paceman Tip Snooke in 1909–10, to take two wickets in the opening over of a Test (Slater and Blewett) and Australia lost 4/29 in the first ten overs. That was as good as their position got. Azharuddin made 163 not out for India and the lowest score of their dismissed batsmen was Ganguly's 65. Sidhu and his new opening partner, Vangipurappu Venkata Sai Laxman, both made nineties and Tendulkar was barely noticed with his 79. Warne, now bowling through increasing pain in his shoulder and extracting little turn, had to resort to a line wide outside the off stump, hoping for a batsman to feel enough pity or overconfidence to hand him a wicket. He took 0/147 and Australia lost by an innings and 219, their heaviest defeat since Len Hutton's Test in 1938.

Not only had Australia come to India and lost, but they had been routed. There were times in Calcutta, with Reiffel injured, Wilson broken down mid-match, and everyone else powerless to affect events, that it seemed Steve Bernard was going to have to bowl. Pressmen stretched with the expectation of being called upon to field. The Australian second innings again needed Healy's lower-order starch to prevent outright embarrassment.

Having lost the series, Australia managed to pick themselves up and win the Third Test, in Bangalore, when an ill but just ambulant Mark Waugh made his career-best 153 not out, Kasprowicz took 5/28 in the second innings, and Taylor hit 102 not out in the chase for 195. But that Test was as dead as an England victory at The Oval. The Australians' consolation was scant. In little more than two weeks, they had been reduced from world champions to a listless rabble. Their powers of recuperation could give them some heart, but they now had another three years to wait before another crack at the final frontier. As Mike Coward summarised in the *Australian*: 'Australia are world champions in Test cricket except in one regard – they cannot win on the subcontinent – and if they cannot win here, what sort of world champions are they really?'

A LUCKY LOOK
Peshawar, October 1998

AS WAS SO OFTEN THE CASE WITH TAYLOR, HIS FEAT WOULD BE REMEMBERED AS MUCH FOR ITS HUMAN AS ITS CRICKETING QUALITIES.

O nly once would Mark Taylor's batting be mentioned in the same breath as Sir Donald Bradman's, and this was it: the third week of October 1998 in the north-west frontier's Dodge City. In the lead-up to the Peshawar Test match, the Australian cricketers staged a public-relations blunder by posing for photographs with AK-47s, unbecoming for ambassadors of a nation still mourning the Port Arthur massacre. Their response was that in Peshawar playing with guns was an almost unavoidable temptation. If there was not much else to do in the city, Taylor would present an alternative spectacle over the next few days.

Still in search of the win in the subcontinent that would legitimate Australia's status, Taylor brought a very different squad from that beaten in India. Back from injury was McGrath, whose absence had been telling, if not decisive, against the Indians. Back also was Fleming, who had taken his Test hat-trick in Pakistan in 1994. Warne had finally put his shoulder under the surgeon's blade, so MacGill had his chance to play as the alpha leggie. The fourth bowler would be Colin 'Funky' Miller from Tasmania.

Miller was thirty-four when the selectors chose him; yet he

LIKE HIS BOWLING, HIS HAIR COLOUR WAS VERSATILE

was seen as a daring experiment, a work in progress. He wore an earring and his hair was blond at the time, or perhaps dark brown, on the road to green and blue. Like his bowling, his hair colour was versatile. The bare facts of his journey tell an epic story. A native Victorian, he had been playing first-class cricket since 1985–86, the year Steve Waugh first played for Australia. Miller was even older than Waugh, and had covered more of Australia than a Telstra lineman in the intervening thirteen years, playing wherever he was wanted. His employment record included first-class stints in Victoria, South Australia, Tasmania and most recently Holland, where he plied his trade as a professional right-arm medium-pacer, not fast-medium, not slow-medium, but just right, medium-medium, when it came to extracting movement in the air and off the seam, both ways, in all conditions. He was well known in the English minor leagues, amateur baseball competitions, late-opening bars and in the Netherlands, where he was in love with a girl. He was obsessed with the Tone Loc song 'Funky Cold Medina', of which he carried something like a dozen different recorded versions. His was a nickname hard-earnt.

The turning point in Miller's tale came in a club game in

Hobart when, nursing an ankle injury, he tried some off-spin. It wasn't a lot slower than his medium-pace, but it created more problems for batsmen. In 1997–98, he broke Chuck Fleetwood-Smith's 63-year-old record for the most wickets in a Sheffield Shield season, snaring sixty-seven scalps by being two bowlers for the price of one. He took the new ball, had a rest, and returned later with spin, using an unorthodox grip he had adapted from his baseball days. On the Pakistan tour, if Taylor bracketed himself in history with Sir Donald Bradman, Miller could put himself in the same group as Sir Garfield Sobers.

The Australian batting order in India had been Taylor, Slater, Blewett, Mark Waugh, Steve Waugh and Ponting, who was replaced in the Third Test at Bangalore by Darren Lehmann. In Pakistan it would be Taylor, Slater, Langer, Waugh, Waugh and Lehmann. Langer slipped back smoothly into the line-up after several years going on every tour but playing not much more than the team porters. After such a courageous debut in Adelaide in 1993, he had still not sealed a regular place, and looked destined to be one of those batsmen who fell into that crack between Shield and Test class. Lehmann's story was quite different. Chosen as a teenage twelfth man for Australia against Pakistan in 1989–90, he had still not played a Test match until Bangalore. True, the Waughs had stood firmly in his way, but in the mix of number sixes over the previous two seasons – Ponting, Law, Blewett, Bevan – Lehmann had been overlooked, perhaps a victim of his age, perhaps of the flux of form, perhaps of a selection-table opinion that he wasn't quite as good as the others. Now, after more waiting than a public hospital patient and a decade of so many runs for South Australia and Yorkshire that he might well have been getting bored with it – 10,187 at 51.7 – he was given his chance.

Pakistan awaited. After the shenanigans and revolving doors of the mid-1990s, they had settled down with much the same team, only now the captain was the squeaky-clean Aamer Sohail, while Salim Malik occupied a place in the middle-order between trips to a judicial commission investigating allegations of match-fixing. He was not the only member of the team whose bank accounts were under the microscope of Judge Malik Mohammad Qayyum.

Fast bowler Ata-ur-Rahman had accused Wasim Akram of offering him money to bowl badly in a one-day international and was now retracting his statement. Rahman, Malik and Wasim were on the commission's long, long list of witnesses. Talent was never an issue, however, and they had just whipped the West Indies.

Before the First Test in Rawalpindi, the Qayyum inquiry summonsed Taylor and Mark Waugh, the only one of the trio on this tour who had been offered bribes in 1994. May had retired, and Warne had chosen an opportune moment to have surgery. Taylor and Waugh flew to an awkward forty-minute hearing in Lahore, which included a cross-examination guided by none other than Salim Malik! They repeated what they had said in earlier written statements, and raced back to Rawalpindi and the relative comfort of trying to achieve something that had never been done in any of the players' lifetimes.

With a fresh team, Australia brought a fresh attitude. Having learnt from their flat-footed start in India, they pulverised a Karachi selection team as if playing a Test match. On their previous tour to Pakistan, Steve Waugh wrote: 'we used to count down the days left on tour, starting from our second day'. On the 1982 tour, Rod Marsh had watched one movie thirty-three times in his hotel rooms. This time they were determined to be cheerful and aggressive. Warne's absence, rather than bringing them down, inspired them to prove they could win without him. Accordingly, on the first day at Rawalpindi, MacGill took five wickets as Pakistan fell for 269, the majestic Saeed Anwar scoring 145 but the rest melting around him. Miller had a lucky look about him, and with his fifth ball in Test cricket Taylor took a fine first-slip catch to remove the nemesis, Malik.

In Australia's reply, Wasim Akram and Mushtaq Ahmed had Taylor, Langer and Mark Waugh out for a combined three runs, but then Slater and Steve Waugh first arrested and then reversed the tide, both making centuries before Lehmann showed how overdue his elevation was with a sparkling 98 and Healy chimed in with 82. Australia's 513, finishing at the end of day three, was a superb assertion of good intentions and a fine demonstration of the lessons learnt six months earlier in India.

Pakistan were no competition in the fourth innings as McGrath, Fleming and Miller each took two wickets and MacGill four. Healy caught Wasim Akram off Miller, his 356th dismissal in Tests, passing his idol Marsh. Healy, like Marsh, was a once-in-a-generation wicketkeeper. His record looked like it would stand for decades.

Only Salim Malik, with an unbeaten 52 in nearly four hours, survived the Australians' pace-and-spin assault. Australia's win, by an innings and 99 runs, was their third Test match victory on Pakistan soil and their first since 1959–60.

Now the lead was Australia's to defend, the series theirs to lose. For the Second Test, in Peshawar, Pakistan adjusted the balance of their attack. With Waqar Younis ruled out of the series with a neck injury, they had gone into the First Test with three spinners assisting Wasim. It backfired, as MacGill and Miller proved more adept; so for the Second Test a hard, true, bouncy track was prepared. It might have been Perth, not Peshawar.

HIS RECORD LOOKED LIKE IT WOULD STAND FOR DECADES

Just before the Test, Wasim pulled out with a throat infection and off-spinner Saqlain Mushtaq flew to London to be with his sick father. Such was the murk of conspiracy in Pakistan cricket politics at the time, a throat infection and a sick father could have meant anything. The outcome was that, having gone into Rawalpindi with too much spin, Pakistan came out at Peshawar with two lightning-fast but inexperienced fast bowlers, Shoaib Akhtar and Mohammad Zahid, the leg-spinner Mushtaq Ahmed, and the all-rounder Azhar Mahmood. Yousuf Youhana and Salim Malik's brother-in-law Ijaz Ahmed came in to bolster the batting, but the bowling line-up was a pale and somewhat hopeful imitation of what was usually Pakistan's strong suit.

The hazy first morning started without a hint of what was to follow. Taylor had fallen into another lean patch. His scores on tour had been 1, 19, 3, 13 and an unbeaten 63 down the order in a last-day batting practice against the Rawalpindi Cricket Division XI. As Geoff Marsh and Steve Waugh inspected the concrete-like surface of the Arbab Niaz Stadium strip in Peshawar, Marsh made one of those comments that deserves its place in an alternative history: 'I can't see Tubs getting too many. What are we going to do if he fails here?'

It would quickly be forgotten how sternly the young Pakistani pacemen tested Australia's batting in the opening session. Akhtar and Zahid bowled at express pace, faster than 150 km/h, and the Australian openers could barely get it off the square. Akhtar, with his movie-star leaping black locks (the Australians' nickname for him was 'B-grade actor') and a round-arm throw-like action, bowled faster than anyone since Michael Holding. Zahid had been clocked even faster in a one-dayer in Australia, and for a short time was possibly the fastest bowler in world cricket since Jeff Thomson at his peak. Taylor's first runs came off an inside edge slipping past his stumps. The ball flew off the hard deck. Slater, after making 2 in nearly an hour, was out slicing Akhtar to gully.

Langer, to this point, had played nine Tests spread over five and a half years. His half-century in his first Test, back in Adelaide in 1993, remained his career highlight. At Rawalpindi he had been out first ball.

To his first ball at Peshawar, he shuffled across to Akhtar, missed it and looked plumb to everyone in the world except Steve Bucknor. Langer thought, Two golden ducks, Test career over. But Bucknor shook his head and Langer was on his way. He and Taylor would bat out a first day truncated by bad light. After their opening hour, Akhtar and Zahid tired quickly and could muster neither the same pace nor accuracy in their later spells. Taylor lofted a drive to the covers off Mushtaq on 19, before popping a sharp chance to silly point on 27. Saeed Anwar was the snatcher both times; his spills would cost Pakistan 315 runs.

When he hit his sixties Taylor found his flow, and soon, he would say, he was batting with a kind of prescience, as if he knew where the bowlers would bowl it and which gap he would thread it through. He was also benefiting from an off-season fitness campaign, and stayed ahead of fatigue. By day's end he was 112, Langer 97.

In truth, the batting on the second day was not the most exciting. The Pakistanis, acknowledging the state of play, bowled a defensive line as Australia ground to 4/599. Langer was out for 116, his maiden Test century, Mark Waugh 42 and Steve Waugh, his fighting qualities surplus to requirements, a third-ball 1. Lehmann, after his First Test 98, had made twin tons against Rawalpindi but injured his groin and Ponting, his replacement, now cashed in with an unbeaten 76. Taylor was immovable, not giving another chance until he was 325. As an innings it was a wonder of endurance more than shotmaking, but was monumental nonetheless. He defended the good balls, left most of what was pitched outside off stump, worked the straight ones off his pads, and relied on his matter-of-fact pull shot to dispatch the short ball like a silly question at a press conference. The bad memories of 1997 must have steeled him, given him an extra spur of determination when he grew tired. He hit a boundary for each of those Test innings he had gone without a fifty; one for each Test win of his captaincy. In all he hit 32 fours and one six off 564 balls in six hours. He only grew nervous in the 290s. When Mushtaq looped up a tired long hop, Taylor punched it away for his triple-century, the first by an Australian since Bob Cowper's 307 in 1965–66.

Finally, there was the Bradman matter. When Taylor reached 334, there were still three balls left in the day's play. It became a myth associated with the innings that Taylor did not want to, or try to, pass Bradman's 1930 Australian record. As Steve Waugh wrote, Taylor 'did try with all his might to sneak past the great one'. On the second-last ball of the day, Taylor drove Sohail confidently wide of mid-on and would have passed Bradman's score if Ijaz Ahmed hadn't flung out a hand. As a fielder, Ijaz normally made a fine batsman. His stop was a fluke. Then, on the last ball, Taylor tried a similar shot. Ijaz stopped it again. It was pure coincidence that when the players went off at stumps, Taylor was 334.

Bradman, by the way, wrote Taylor a letter thanking him for not passing his record. As *Wisden* remarked: 'The thanks might have been better directed at Ijaz.'

As was so often the case with Taylor, his feat would be remembered as much for its human as its cricketing qualities. After stumps on day two, he consulted his teammates, who dead-batted

ABOVE: Taylor drives towards a 425-run Test at Peshawar.

the decision straight back to him. He phoned his wife and his father, telling them his only consolation was that the batsman on 334 was himself: he would have hated to cut short Steve or Mark Waugh on the same score. At 2 am, lying awake in his hotel, too exhausted and over-stimulated to sleep, he was resolved on declaring. Some time later, he changed his mind. When he woke up the next morning, he breakfasted with Waugh and gave his vice-captain the impression that he was going to bat for another forty minutes. Then he gathered the players at 8.45 am and told them he was going to declare. They rewarded him with a round of heartfelt applause. Thus, a decision to try to get Pakistan in to bat and press for a victory would be seen as a great act of personal sacrifice. Cricket followers around the world were perplexed that he would not try to exceed Brian Lara's world record 375, or give Ponting a chance to make a Test century. But those opinions were ignorant of Taylor's instincts, which were to seek team victory first, individual glory second. And after 1997, he owed it to his players. His declaration can be seen as a thankyou note.

The pitch and some good Pakistan batting rendered the declaration a moot point anyway. Anwar's grace and Ijaz's bottom hand inked the scoresheet on the third day and the Australian bowlers could not find the assistance they had received in Rawalpindi. The extraordinary also eluded them. Pakistan's reply, 9/580, ensured they would not lose the match and go 0-2 in the series. In Australia's second innings, Taylor was seeing

HIS DECLARATION CAN BE SEEN AS A THANKYOU NOTE

the ball as big as a pumpkin and lashed a breezy 92, chopping on to Aamir Sohail when thirty short of Graham Gooch's world record for the most runs in a Test.

A tighter, tenser match followed in Karachi. Slater's 96 underpinned Australia's first innings 280, then McGrath took 5/66 and Sohail made a hundred as Pakistan almost reached parity. Needing to bat for a long time to put the match and series beyond Pakistan's reach, Australia lasted for 142 overs in its second innings, being all out for 390 on the fourth afternoon and setting Pakistan an impossible 419 on the last day. Mark Waugh buttressed Australia's crucial second dig with 117, completing a quartet of truly masterful innings in a two-year period. He was very much at the height of his powers, and could boast that his Third-Test centuries in Adelaide and Karachi, while lost in the fog of draws, had ensured Australia won both series.

Salim Malik made a pair in Karachi. In the second innings he was out lbw to Colin Miller, a man as honest as Malik was mendacious. Taylor wrote that he 'had never seen our guys so jubilant'.

As selflessly as he had declared in Peshawar, the series win over Pakistan was a personal crowning moment for Taylor. While the Pakistanis batted out the last day in Karachi without much urgency or hope as the knowledge sunk in, Taylor could pause to reflect on the completion of his cycle as captain. He had come into the job to lead a team on the brink of great things. His first Test and series were lost here in Pakistan. Now he would retire from cricket, two months after the Karachi Test, after beating England again at home, and ascend to the heavens of the Channel Nine commentary box knowing he had harnessed the energies and personalities of his great players, and melded them with the comings and goings of the less-established. The centre of Warne, McGrath, Healy and the Waugh twins had held during Taylor's time.

Despite his own troubles and in the face of some immense challenges, things did not fall apart. He had encouraged, demanded even, a bright and entertaining style. His ACB-friendly diplomatic stance had threatened to alienate him from his players during the dispute of 1997, but as always he managed to slip through like teflon. Indeed, apart from his 7000-plus runs, his 43-per-innings average and his winning record as a captain, Taylor will be remembered as a kind of non-stick man, emerging squeaky clean from all the turbulence beneath and behind him. His last summer as captain was marred by the discovery of the Warne–Mark Waugh imbroglio with John the bookmaker and the secret deal to fine them in 1995 – but none of it reflected poorly on Taylor himself. He was a treasured Australian captain, albeit, unlike some of his champion players, the type who would be more admired by the nation's parents than capture the imagination of its children.

His captaincy would be compared with that of his predecessor and his successor. Between 1994 and 1999, Taylor was perceived to have taken the team's cricket to heights beyond Border's reach. They had won in the West Indies and now the subcontinent. Those two feats could not be gainsaid. Taylor curbed some of the excesses of onfield behaviour, improving on Border's record but not asserting himself strongly enough to iron it out, or not wishing to dull the edge completely. Further improvement would be left to his successor. If the image of the team had plenty of room for amelioration, its playing record was seen to be unimprovable. The burr in Taylor's saddle during those five years was his own fluctuating form with the bat. But he had survived 1997, held his place for two more years, and in Peshawar he had built his memorial for the ages. As Peter Roebuck wrote, it was a feat not of sport so much as of survival: 'The greatness of the innings lay in the fact that it was played at all.'

LARA

Port-of-Spain/Kingston/Bridgetown,
March 1999

SOMETIMES, VERY RARELY, CRICKET CAN BE AN INDIVIDUAL RATHER THAN A TEAM SPORT. THIS WAS ONE OF THOSE TIMES. LARA WAS A MARVEL TO WATCH.

I is a mark of the Australians' greatness that their losses were often more remarkable than their wins. They lost very few 'live' matches in the era, and when it happened, their opponent had to pull out a history-making exploit.

What live Tests had Australia lost? Sydney 1994, when Fanie de Villiers had his career day; Karachi later that year, when Pakistan's last-wicket pair had staged a miracle partnership; Trinidad 1995, a rogue match on an unfit wicket. Twice they were rumbled in India. It invariably took something extraordinary to beat them, a demand that would continue over the years: witness India's incredible comeback in 2001, Mark Butcher's day out at Headingley later that year, and the West Indies' world record chase in Antigua in 2003. But none of these reversals was quite as brilliant, or as unexpected, as Brian Lara's two match-winning innings in the 1999 series in the Caribbean.

The first was in Jamaica, the second Barbados. But before we get there, it is crucial to understand the prior transformation of both teams.

Taylor's retirement after the home Ashes series set off a brief flurry of competition for the captaincy. Warne had some

WHETHER REALISTIC OR NOT, WARNE'S ASPIRATIONS WERE GENUINE

influential fans, not least the former captains Border and Ian Chappell. Chappell believed Waugh to be a 'selfish' player, less likely to get the best out of his team than Warne. There was never really any chance that Warne would be captain, but it seems he never divested himself of the belief that he would have been better than Steve Waugh. That Warne could even imagine himself becoming captain two months after he admitted he was 'naive and stupid' for accepting the Indian bookmaker's money was proof positive of how naive and stupid he really was. Or perhaps they are just synonyms for the peculiar and necessary brand of self-confidence he needed to succeed at this level. In fairness, he did lead the Australian one-day team with conspicuous flair while Waugh was injured during the 1998–99 home series. Whether realistic or not, Warne's aspirations were genuine. As were Mark Waugh's. The younger twin had few supporters for the captaincy, and it rankled with him. Just as Warne would have to swallow his disappointment at missing out on the job for what he perceived as irrelevant reasons, Mark Waugh would have to get used to taking orders from his brother.

Elliott was recalled for Taylor, the selectors holding faith that technique would triumph over temperament, and Warne

LEFT: Gladiators: the one-man teams enjoy a friendly moment.

returned from his shoulder surgery in the tail-end of the home summer. He ran into a juggernaut in the shape of MacGill. Throughout the Ashes series against one of the more woeful England squads of recent history, MacGill had done everything possible to prove he was not just a seat-warmer. As in Pakistan, the team thrived in Warne's absence, and MacGill now had claims to have surpassed the great one. Warne returned for the fifth encounter, in Sydney, for what would become known as MacGill's Test.

Slater hit a stirring century on a grippy, hard-turning wicket, but MacGill was unmanageable, taking twelve wickets. Warne took two, and looked about one-sixth as dangerous as his partner. Taylor made his perfectly timed exit, and the Steve Waugh era was underway.

Meanwhile, the West Indies had stuttered along since their loss to Australia in 1995. Walsh, succeeding Richardson as captain, led the team well but the undercurrents of Lara's ambition were so pervasive that it was hard to imagine any key issues being settled until he became captain. He might not have white-anted Walsh, but sometimes the presence of so strong a personality, and so fierce a self-belief, amounts to the same thing. Lara created instability merely by being there, waiting for the captaincy to fall to him. After a disastrous tour of Pakistan under Walsh in late 1997, Lara got what he wanted. A series win at home over England followed, but the wheels wobbled again during a tour of South Africa, which ended in a straight-sets wipeout: 5-0 in the Tests, 6-1 in the one-dayers. Lara was the lightning rod for home criticism, blamed for everything from not scoring enough runs to playing too much golf to not talking enough to his junior players.

As bad as the overseas results were, West Indian crowds' firm expectations of victory at home were not without foundation. Up to this point, the loss to Australia in 1995 remained their only home series defeat since the early 1970s. There was a divergence between most teams' performances at home and away, but in the West Indies' case it was extreme. Since 1995 they were a rabble on the road, but on home soil their body language and cricketing output was imperious, even arrogant, as if their golden age had never ended. It is difficult to explain why playing away was such an obstacle. The best guess is that the variance between a team playing at its peak and being thrashed was a lot less than it seemed. A five per cent shift in confidence could be transformative. Playing at home, in familiar conditions and in front of supportive crowds, could give any group that crucial bit extra, and conversely, sap their visitors' confidence by the same pivotal quantum.

Not that it could be assumed that the 1999 West Indian crowds would be fully supportive. The reason was Lara himself. Throughout his career he would give the impression of being thwarted. Perhaps he never got over the bad luck of coming into a once-great team during its decline. But his moments of joy seemed to flicker against a backdrop of niggling frustration. The West Indies is not one country but a group of separate nations and when things went wrong Lara was identified as a Trinidadian.

LARA CREATED INSTABILITY MERELY BY BEING THERE

For Bajans, Jamaicans, Antiguans and the rest, he was a ready-made scapegoat. The expectations he set in 1994 were impossibly high; unless he could score centuries, or double- or triple- or quadruple- or quintuple-centuries, at will, he would be perceived as not having tried hard enough. Like Tendulkar in India, Lara was asked to work miracles. Unlike Tendulkar, the public's love for him seemed to have conditions attached.

His reappointment as captain for the Australian series, ahead of Walsh, brought a chorus of dismay. Michael Holding called it 'a shocking decision ... Being captain of the West Indies is a huge honour and a huge job. It needs a big man to do it, someone well-rounded as an individual. Brian Lara is not. He is a spoilt child.'

He was given the captaincy against Australia on a two-match probation. He could get it right in Trinidad and Jamaica or face the axe. His series could not have started worse than it did on his home ground at Port-of-Spain (where he had never scored a Test century). On a dreadful Queen's Park Oval pitch and over-lush outfield, both teams struggled to amass runs over the first three sweltering Trinidadian days. Elliott batted beyond tea on day one in scoring

44, and Blewett just as long for his 58. When Healy fell lbw, Walsh became the third man in history after Richard Hadlee and Kapil Dev to take 400 wickets. But McGrath and Gillespie put on an improbable 66, pushing the Australian score towards solidity.

The West Indies fell 102 runs behind Australia's 269, Lara's slashing 62 cut short when Healy fumbled the ball in a close-in melee but was adjudged to have completed a run out. In Australia's return dig, for the second time in successive Tests Slater stood head and shoulders above all others. His second-innings 106 is a neglected masterpiece of the era. Walsh and Ambrose were bowling just short of a length on a devilish up-and-down wicket, meaning that to play forward meant risking a ball in the fingers, body or face. But to play back risked the ball darting in or running along the ground for a leg-before-wicket or a bowled. Walsh in particular kept finding the unplayable length. Batsmen were damned if they did and damned if they didn't, and wickets kept falling. Slater alone had the courage to play forward and the technique to cover the ball movement. He was fifth man out at 193, when Australia's lead was unassailable. His century would be overshadowed by subsequent events, but it was one of the mightiest single innings by an Australian batsman in the Taylor–Waugh period. Alongside his 123 at Sydney a month earlier – out of a team score of 184 – this innings' doughtiness and watertight defence showed Slater's full maturity as a Test opener.

Slater's ton was more or less forgotten when the West Indies collapsed for 51 on the last day. McGrath and the finally fit Gillespie ran amok, and did to the Windies what Walsh, Ambrose and their predecessors had done to so many visitors. The procession of West Indian batsmen was so rapid as to border on the farcical. They looked like they had given up. The total was their lowest in seventy-one years of Test cricket.

Lara was outgunned by Gillespie, edging his second ball to slip. He wasn't alone, but more was expected – demanded – of him. West Indian cricket writer B.C. Pires wrote: 'All we have left is faith healing. And if anyone can work the miracle that so many West Indians still seem to expect surely it must be Lara, our lad of Fatima College.'

There was one fly in the Australian ointment from Port-of-Spain. They went into the Test with an attack of McGrath, Gillespie, Warne and MacGill. Warne bowled tidily but without bite, taking 0/35 in his fourteen overs in the first innings. MacGill took 3/41. Following his twelve wickets against England in Sydney, he had taken 13/74 in a warm-up match under the oil refineries at Pointe-a-Pierre in Trinidad, while Warne struggled to take four wickets. In his first innings at Port-of-Spain, Lara went after both MacGill and Warne. The second innings was such a capitulation that neither spinner was needed, but Lara's intentions had been ominous. All he needed was some support. Still, this was ignored in the light of the capitulation. All out 51. Australia had McGrath and Gillespie. Against this opponent, who needed support bowlers?

From Trinidad the teams went to Jamaica. For Lara even more than the Australians, this was hostile territory. Jamaica was Walsh's nation, and Jamaicans believed Walsh had been stabbed in the back. When Michael Holding spoke of a 'big man', his fellow Jamaicans heard 'Walsh'. At practice the day before the Test, locals ringed the training ground and jeered Lara. He embodied the damaged pride and fallen glory of West Indian cricket. Meanwhile, the mayor of Kingston presented Walsh with the keys to the city.

Lara had missed the team bus to training that Friday. Malcolm Marshall, a coach in despair, cited medical reasons, but the truth was that on the Thursday night Lara had been partying until about 4 am at a Kingston nightclub called the Asylum. It's true. If you were a fiction writer, you wouldn't be allowed to invent a metaphor so clunking.

As Waugh and Lara walked to the centre of Sabina Park on the Saturday, even the people in the good seats booed and heckled Lara. 'Play well,' Waugh said after winning the toss. Lara replied, 'This is the last time I'm gonna have to put up with this shit.'

Lara would prove himself wrong.

In the changing room, Waugh told his teammates that Lara was ready to quit and his fragility should be exploited. Langer said, 'Just be careful, we've heard that from him before.'

Lara would prove him right.

Walsh was in bristling form, meanwhile, and the West Indian bowlers restricted Australia to a modest 256 on the first day. Only Steve Waugh, returning to the scene of his 1995 heroics, showed the requisite fibre, making an even hundred. Aside from Mark Waugh's 67, the next best was Slater's 22. But it didn't seem to matter: by stumps, the West Indies were a weak-kneed 4/37. Perhaps they would not even make it to 51. The not-out batsmen that evening were Lara and nightwatchman Pedro Collins, who had gone in ahead of him.

Fourteen wickets had fallen on that Saturday. Fourteen fell on the Monday. But on the Sunday, not a one. And the West Indies scored 340 runs, of which Lara made 205.

What happened? Sometimes, very rarely, cricket can be an individual rather than a team sport. This was one of those times. Lara, battered by his countrymen, turned all the powers of his resentful genius against the Australian bowling. He was a marvel to watch. What made him such an exciting proposition, for both sides, was how early and whole-heartedly he committed himself to his forcing strokes. When he wound up with his circular backlift, he was going to hurl his bat through the line of the ball. Most of his life he never seemed able to make up his mind; yet with a bat in his hands, in this kind of form, he was as free of doubt as any player who ever lived. His off-side play was particularly devastating as he thrashed the leg-spinners time and again through cover. When he was not going for the boundary, his defence was a decisive wall. The result was either one thing or the other, the ball dropped at his feet or denting the fences, and in both facets he was peerless. As Mark Waugh said, 'He hits the ball so hard that it's almost impossible to stop the run flow. You try to limit the boundaries and work on the other guy but you've sometimes got to accept he's too good for you on the day.' This was an uncustomary concession from the confident Australians, but a realistic acknowledgement of Lara's genius.

Twenty-two runs into the morning, Collins retired hurt after being hit and 'the other guy', Jimmy Adams, came to the crease. On his home pitch, the Jamaican finally played an innings of substance against Australia. He had been disappointing so often,

ABOVE: Staying ahead of the crowd: Lara after his 200th run in Kingston.

but this time his brief was comprehensible: stay with Lara. Adams again merited the nickname 'Padams' for his play against the spinners, but he did not get out and never looked like it.

It was perplexing to watch the Australian bowlers. They did not seem to be bowling all that badly. McGrath was accuracy personified, Gillespie likewise. Warne bowled tightly enough, and Lara treated him with high regard. MacGill received more punishment, but with his greater flight and hopes of buying a wicket, that was to be expected. But he couldn't buy a thing and nor could anyone else. Waugh set aggressive fields and Australia continued to attack, feeling that one breakthrough would bring down the house of cards. But it never came on that Sunday. Lara gave one chance, an edge off McGrath on 44, but it was a sharp low one and if Mark Waugh couldn't catch it, no one could. When Lara reached his hundred he was swamped by Jamaican fans – they loved him now, adored him – a chaotic scene given that Lara had only passed the mark by scampering for a tight single and Blewett's direct hit was still being examined by the third umpire. When Lara passed his double-century he had learnt his lesson and was ahead of the mob, running to the changing room before the sprinting well-wishers, among them a man who, with a baby in his arms, might have been asking for a baptism, and another who seemed, from a distance, to be naked but for a bandana. When the field was cleared Lara re-emerged from the changing room, arms aloft, to take the frenzied apologies of those who had, twenty-four hours earlier, wanted him impeached.

Sunday 14 March was a dream, or a nightmare. Tony Cozier, one of Lara's sternest critics, wrote: '… with apologies to George Headley, Sir Garry Sobers and a host of other greats, I cannot identify a single innings by any West Indian batsman in our 71 years of Test cricket of such significance.' Michael Holding said, soberly, 'Brian is a changed man and a better captain.' Mike Coward recorded in *Wisden*: 'On one fantastic, sunny, windy Sunday, Lara seduced the people of a bankrupt nation, resurrected his career as a batsman of rare gifts and reignited cricket throughout the Caribbean.'

Neither Lara nor Adams lasted long into the third morning, Lara edging McGrath to be out for 213. The damage was well and truly done. Australia, 175 behind, batted as if they were 175 ahead. Perhaps it was the nimbus of ganja over Sabina Park. Wickets fell like inhibitions to Walsh and off-spinner Nehemiah Perry, over-attacking shots accounting for most, and by the Monday night the match was as good as over. Only by two runs did Australia avoid an innings defeat.

The tourists regrouped in Antigua, their base throughout the tour, but the strains papered over by the First Test were stripped bare by the Second. Steve Waugh's newborn captaincy had gone from the penthouse to the outhouse in the space of a day. Did he look in-

PERHAPS IT WAS THE NIMBUS OF GANJA OVER SABINA PARK

decisive in Kingston? Would Taylor have let that happen? How sure was Waugh's authority over his senior men? On that Sunday at Sabina Park observers remarked, and no doubt his teammates recalled, how Taylor always had the happy knack of making just the right bowling change, or altering the atmosphere with a shift in the field, to conjure up the vital wicket. Taylor had this mystique about him, the trick of luck. Waugh was starting all over again, just a man with two arms and two legs and no magic wand. These things are so mercurial that they belong to the realm of myth and superstition more than to reality, but cricketers rely heavily on imagined 'X' factors. Taylor had it, and Waugh, so far, had yet to show it.

There were form worries, too. Elliott was struggling to stop his head from being turned by the Caribbean's nocturnal excitements, and it was beginning to show in his batting. Heraclitus, the ancient Greek philosopher, was right: character is destiny, and the brittleness of Elliott's character, not the beauty and fluency of his strokemaking, would play the decisive role in his cricket career. There were no doubts about Healy's character, but in his mid-thirties his wicketkeeping was a fraction slower than its usual perfection. His batting, often a barometer of a wicketkeeper's state of mind, had been poor, with scores of 12, 0, 6 and 10, the last two being run-outs in both innings in Kingston. Also, Warne was not threatening any batsman. He was bowling conservatively and containingly, but he was not threatening. He and MacGill, turning the ball into the pads of the left-handers Lara and Adams, were easy pickings. Perhaps Miller, turning the ball away from them, would provide the necessary variety. Yet before the Third Test, in Bridgetown, it was unthinkable that Warne's or Healy's positions could be more than mere talking points. Champions always fight back, don't they?

Again, the first stanza of the Barbados Test was Australia's. After stumbling to 3/36 on the first morning when Ambrose came to life, Steve Waugh's 199 and a fine 104 from Ponting, in for the injured Blewett, dominated the first afternoon and the second morning. They put on 281 runs in presto time. Uncharacteristically, Waugh confessed that he was lucky, playing and missing countless times. Ambrose was bowling fractionally short for the amount of movement he was extracting, and his leg-cutters continually shaded past Waugh's searching outside edge.

Showing how much life remained in the wicket, the last six Australia wickets fell for 65 (Healy making a duck), and then the hosts collapsed to 6/98. Normal business seemed to have been resumed. Gillespie bowled a snorter which Lara fended to gully, and Australia entered the third day with few fears.

But Sherwin Campbell played his best Test innings against Australia, a six-hour 105, beginning a run of good form for the Bajan opener. With the tough left-handed keeper Ridley Jacobs (68), Campbell put on 153 for the seventh wicket, then the tail gave an unwonted wag, with Perry, Ambrose and even Walsh helping to eke 78 runs out of the last three wickets. Still, the West Indies' 329 was well in arrears of Australia's 490.

Walsh was simply magnificent on the fourth day, running through the Australians for 146. With everything at stake, he and Ambrose found their rhythm and, more importantly, a fuller length. As in Kingston, the Australians went down breezily. And yet they still set the West Indies 308 to win in little more than a day on a pitch offering plenty of perk. The visitors' advantage was confirmed late on day four when McGrath trapped Campbell for 33 and Lara sent out the nightwatchman Collins ahead of him for the third time in three innings. Collins was out for 1, MacGill rediscovered his luck to add Dave Joseph, and Lara, booed onto the ground for having hidden behind Collins, was 2 not out.

Opener Adrian Griffith batted for just on four hours but fell on the fifth morning, as did the hapless Hooper, and the West Indies were soon five down with more than 200 to get. Lara, as ever, stood alone.

If there had been something operatic about his 213 in Kingston, his innings in Bridgetown had more of a jazzy pace, an improvisational tactical component. In Kingston, he had been rising from rock bottom, both personal and team. Throughout that innings he had seemed to be batting for dignity. Only as it progressed into its sixth and seventh hours did the possibility arise that he might also be winning the Test. That win had been a bonus. The restoration of pride in Caribbean cricket was the main thing.

In Bridgetown, he had a specific cricketing task: to chase down a target, to win the match. The common denominator in both innings was how much depended on this one small man. Both performances were triumphs of the art of batting, true, but more than that they were unparalleled triumphs of the will to win.

He had started late on day four, scoring two runs in half an hour while wickets fell at the other end. On day five, after losing Griffith and Hooper, he found Adams again a willing sticker. They tracked steadily until lunch. Lara made one error, chipping a drive down the wicket to Warne, but the chance went down. Lara's strategy was much the same as in Jamaica. He watched and waited while seeing off McGrath and Gillespie, then went on the attack to the spinners, jumping down the wicket more to MacGill than Warne. All parts of Warne's game were deserting him. As soon as spin arrived, the pressure eased noticeably. What an unusual situation for Australia. Adams was as patient as in Kingston, and Lara began to unfurl some drives on both sides of the wicket, as well as his reliable cutting and pulling. The target began to shrink fast. Gillespie, the best of the bowlers, had to leave the field with back spasms. McGrath hit Lara on the helmet and snarled and griped, but no words could put Lara off. It was dawning on the crowd that he was doing it again, playing a second impossible innings. This time he was more daring than in Kingston, taking more risks and getting further down the track. Missing the ball never crossed his mind. You have never seen such absolute control.

After tea, however, there was another whiplash: Adams was bowled by McGrath for 38 after a stand of 133 with Lara. McGrath steamed in, trapping Jacobs for 5 and Perry next ball. The advantage was back with Australia. Three wickets had fallen for ten runs and sixty were still required. Only Ambrose and Walsh remained. Oh, and Lara.

As the Australian bowlers tired, Lara kept the score moving. Improbably, Ambrose rediscovered some of his better defensive style and stayed with Lara for a fifty-four-run partnership, almost, but not quite, to the end. Waugh entrusted the final task to Warne and McGrath. MacGill stalked around the field and wiped his clammy right hand on his little towel, but only needed it for collecting Lara's drives.

After the partnership with Ambrose had been going for nearly an hour and a half, at 302, with six runs needed, Gillespie, back on the field, drew the edge, at long last, from Lara. After what seemed like days of resistance, they had him.

They didn't. Healy was a mite slow on the hard, high chance to his left and it went to ground. It took one bounce before Warne collected it at slip.

That was it. That was the chance. But then Gillespie had Ambrose caught by Elliott at fourth slip. Incredible game! Walsh, indubitably the worst Test batsman since India's polio-afflicted B.S. Chandrasekhar, was all that stood between Australia and re-taining the Worrell Trophy. The former captain strode out, his bat looking like a toy, to join his controversial successor. Walsh's 12 in the first innings had been his first venture into double figures in two years, a period in which he had scored 46 runs at an average of 3.5. With that 12, he must have thought he was in sparkling touch. When he let go a ball from Gillespie and twirled his bat like a bandleader's baton, the crowd went into hysterics. Walsh survived five balls, and a wide and a no-ball from McGrath brought the target within one shot.

Lara got on strike to Gillespie and flashed a drive through covers; it was over. Kensington Oval erupted, Lara and Walsh embraced and ran joyfully from the ground. The Australians looked and felt extinguished. They were behind in the series; after nearly two decades trying to win Frank, they were about to lose him on their first Caribbean defence.

The Barbados *Daily Nation* called the Third Test the Match of the Century, and certainly it holds its place with Port Elizabeth 1997 and Sydney 1994 as the greatest Test matches played anywhere on the globe that decade. All three involved Australia, and two were losses.

Australia was taking no consolation from having contributed to such an epic encounter. Steve Waugh's tenure was now under serious fire, and in the few days before the final Test he had to ask himself the hardest question of all: with two wickets for 268 runs in the series, and such demoralising losses in the last two Tests, was Shane Warne worth keeping – or worth risking – for the match that would decide the series?

The answer, of course, was that Waugh and the third tour selector Geoff Marsh, in consultation with Allan Border on the tour and Trevor Hohns at home, would drop Warne from the Fourth Test in St Johns, Antigua. The attack had clearly been out of balance in Kingston and Bridgetown, and arguably the selectors should have bitten the bullet at the beginning of the series.

Unlike most players, Warne had the chance to argue his case. As vice-captain he was a selector in the touring party. He didn't disagree that three pacemen should play, but he believed he should stay and MacGill go. His strongest argument was that with Gillespie's back too sore for the Fourth Test, the attack would lack critical experience without him. In so arguing, he put Waugh and Marsh in an even more invidious position. Could this really be happening? Could the greatest spin bowler in the history of the game, with 317 wickets to his name, be dropped? Bradman had been dropped, yes, but that was after one Test. Warne himself had been dropped after his second and third Tests. But had any cricketer as successful as he now was been left out of a Test team?

Waugh, Warne, Marsh and Border sat in the team room at the Rex Halcyon Cove resort on the north coast of Antigua. Marsh and Waugh said that Warne was not fully fit and Miller's variety was

ABOVE: After dismissing last man McDermott, Courtney Walsh breaks Australian hearts and takes flight. Phil Simmons leads the chase, Adelaide, 1993.

RIGHT: Darrell Hair's liking for the limelight didn't necessarily make him wrong. No-balling Muralidaran in the 1995 Melbourne Test lit a fuse that would take a decade to put out.

LEFT: Monument, or monumental obstacle? Allan Border leads his team onto the field in what would be his last Test, Durban, 1994.

BELOW: Where Courtney Walsh got the idea that he could bat, after so many years of proof to the contrary, is anyone's guess. Damien Fleming bowls him and the Miracle of Mohali was complete, World Cup semi-final, 1996.

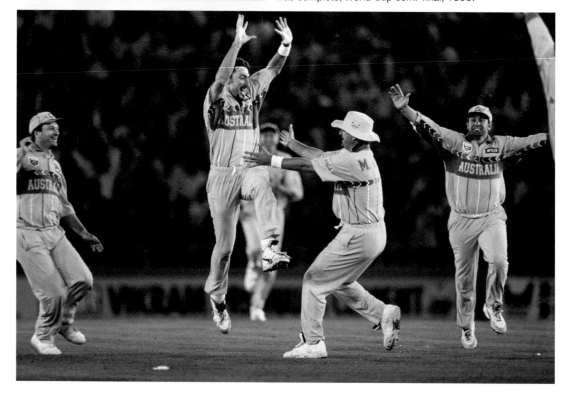

Given how long he lived in one shadow or another, Mark Waugh's moment of sunshine should be allowed its full colour. Port Elizabeth, second innings, 1997.

LEFT: Looking like a defendant waiting for the jury to return with their verdict, Taylor chews the last of his fingernails as Australia falter at Port Elizabeth, 1997.

BELOW: Warne's spinning finger back to its best as Australia returned the Ashes to normal service, Old Trafford, 1997.

The rich man's Angus Fraser. Nothing much to him except an unerring ability to hit the off bail, take hundreds of wickets and win Test matches. McGrath, full tilt, 1997 Ashes.

Darryl, be my bunny? South Africa's Cullinan had a fine Test record against everyone except Australia – and Warne, seen here bowling him for a duck, Melbourne, 1997.

A rare breakthrough for Warne in India, 1998. The taped-up hunk of old wood at right of picture belongs to Navjot Singh Sidhu. This dismissal, in Bangalore, was too late. The bat had been whacking Warne over the fence for three Tests.

ABOVE: Saeed Anwar was the best performed batsman against Australia in the golden age. Another silky stroke on the way to a century at Rawalpindi, 1998.

RIGHT: Too long in the tooth? Not yet. Ambrose, written off after Trinidad, roars back in Jamaica, 1999.

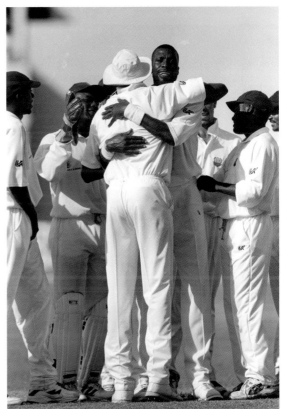

If Jamaica was opera, Barbados was jazz. Lara, 153 not out, in pure ecstasy after leading the West Indies to a second miracle in two Tests.

needed to force the West Indians to rethink their tactics. Warne put up what Waugh described as an 'emotional argument that included some very valid points', but the three others, including Border, agreed on omitting him from the Test XI.

Warne asked for another hearing. He knew he wasn't bowling well, but wrote later that he felt his 'record in tough situations and big matches should have counted in my favour ... All the way through my career I had pro- **THEY HAD NO FAITH** duced when it mattered and **IN HIS ABILITY TO** I thought the selectors should have backed me.' This time **CREATE MAGIC** Border, stirred by Warne's impassioned plea, changed his mind. By not choosing him, they would be doing more than making a judgement on his form: they were stating that they had no faith in his ability to create magic, to pull success out of thin air. Warne had always relied on this perception, this mystique, and by dropping him he felt they were sending a message to opponents that might cripple him forever: the message would not just be that he wasn't bowling well, but that he was mortal.

Waugh and Marsh stuck to their decision, however, and had the final say (Border, while on the national selection panel, was not a tour selector.) Warne left the meeting. Border, never much good with the complications of team politics, now told Marsh and Waugh that he thought they had made the right decision.

But the omission of Warne would send repercussions through the team that would not be resolved until the semi-final of the 1999 World Cup, and perhaps not even then. It could be argued that Warne's resentment would not fully be assuaged while both he and Waugh were playing for Australia.

So without Warne, Waugh led his team onto the St John's Recreation Ground. To win the match and retain Frank, he had the unlikeliest bowling attack: Glenn McGrath, Adam Dale, Colin Miller and Stuart MacGill. Everything was on the line now.

Having settled on their selection, the Australians went about dismantling the West Indies. Waugh won the toss, and a grinding first innings was underpinned by his 72 not out and an enterprising

43, including a one-handed leg-side six off a nonplussed Ambrose, from Miller. Ambrose actually seemed to smile. Miller could not confirm this, saying he had been too scared to look.

The West Indians' reply, and their chances in the match, would pivot on Lara. He came in at 2/20 after Miller, bowling medium-pace, had removed both openers and provided a strong case that he should not have had to wait until now for a game.

Lara wasn't the only individual to dominate this series. Indeed, the 1999 Frank Worrell Trophy series was in large part Steve Waugh and Glenn McGrath versus Brian Lara, Curtly Ambrose and Courtney Walsh. Among the Australian batsmen who played all four Tests, Waugh made 409 runs at an average of 58.4, when the next best was Langer's 291 at 36.4. McGrath took 30 wickets. The next best was MacGill with 12. On the West Indian side, Lara overshadowed everybody with 546 runs at 91. The next best was Campbell with 197 at 28.1. Walsh (26 at 20.9) and Ambrose (19 at 22.3) didn't leave many wickets for the rest. Only Perry, with 10 at 32.6, made any other impression.

With such gladiators so far out in front, it was natural that the final battle would come down to one man against another: Lara against McGrath. Wicket by wicket, McGrath had assumed the leadership of Australia's attack. By 1999, Warne was a sideshow attraction, while McGrath had become the star of the Big Top. Throughout their careers, McGrath would mostly have Lara's measure, but not in this series. In Antigua, Lara came out blazing, almost carefree. He had been cautious in Kingston and perfect in Bridgetown, but now he was stepping up to take the match by the scruff of its neck. He didn't score off his first thirteen balls. Miller dropped him early, and he almost ran himself out. But when he decided to accelerate, he was murderous. After those first thirteen dots, he went from nought to fifty in forty-eight balls. That was pacing himself. He went from fifty to one hundred in twenty-one balls. He hit fifteen fours and three sixes, most of them in that second fifty. Coming five days after his Bridgetown epic, the innings was, as Mike Coward wrote in *Wisden*: 'as though Lara had neither the time nor the energy to play conventionally'.

McGrath laughed last, though, and longest. Lara could spank

as many boundaries as he liked, but McGrath could undo it all with just one ball. After reaching his century, Lara tickled a lifter down the leg side. Of the 116 runs and extras scored while he was in the middle, Lara had contributed 100. Again there was little support, with Hooper running himself out, and the West Indies' 222 was eighty-one runs short. Langer then hit his third and so far best Test century, a second-innings 127, to engineer a lead of 387, while Lara showed such despair over the quality of his back-up pacemen, Collins and Corey Collymore, that he gave forty overs to the phlegmatic spin of Hooper and Adams. Once McGrath fooled Lara with a slower ball to have him lbw for 7, Australia's win was a formality. Dale, MacGill, Miller and even Blewett, a true ensemble cast, popped up with important wickets.

For Waugh, the Antigua victory brought immense bullet-dodging relief rather than jubilation. The Australians were convinced that they were the better team, but twice Lara had seized Test matches away from them and for a time on that second day in Antigua he looked as if he might steal the series. Without Lara, the West Indies would almost certainly have lost all four Tests. Waugh's anxieties – losing Frank would be some start to his captaincy and possibly its end too – were put to one side, thanks in large part to his own efforts with the bat.

The end of the Test series would also signal the beginning of the 1999 World Cup campaign. Seven one-dayers in the West Indies would be the warm-up and final experimentation phase before the squad, staying together rather than coming home, continued on to England. But this campaign would start with a serious overhang from the Test matches: the problem of Warne.

'ARE WE IN? ARE WE IN?'

Edgbaston, June 1999

WAUGH GATHERED THE
TEAM FOR A FINAL PEP TALK,
UNTIL AT THE LAST MOMENT
WARNE WANTED TO MAKE AN
ADDRESS. RATHER THAN LET
THE CAPTAIN'S WORDS BE THE
LAST, WARNE HAD HIS OWN
PIECE TO SPEAK.

When he started as captain, Steve Waugh had struggled with his changed status. He said he felt 'out of the loop' when it came to the team's ambient conversation. 'I found that they tended to give me a little extra space,' he said, and the stories of nights out or other off-field events in the West Indies tended to weave their way around him. Rooms fell silent when he walked in. His teammates were treating him differently and, he found out later, some were making secret pacts to stay out beyond curfews. Gilchrist said the team had a 'weird vibe' during the Antigua Test, and one night, when he was out with some colleagues, it was 1.30 am before one of them laughed: 'Too bad about the curfew!' Gilchrist hadn't known about any curfew.

Waugh found little reassurance from Healy, engaged in a final battle with fitness and motivation, or from his twin brother, who stepped away from any leadership initiative off the field. 'What I needed,' Waugh would write later, 'was a strong lieutenant. In Warney, as vice-captain, I had a good mate with a sharp cricket mind and a desire to form a strong partnership, but what he sometimes couldn't do was tune into the mood of the side.

ROOMS FELL SILENT WHEN HE WALKED IN

Often he stayed indoors, avoiding the public due to his enormous popularity, and he didn't eat anything you'd find served at a restaurant, so he didn't spend a lot of time with the guys socially. All this meant that I was left a little unaware of how the team was functioning off the field.'

After retiring, Healy was mildly critical of the new captain's efforts in this period: 'On tour, the atmosphere at early team meetings was a little stiff, as Tugga attempted to stamp his mark on the team by imposing his team plans and goals. By doing this he unwittingly denied the ranks any ownership of those plans and goals, which reduced their value.'

Put it another way: the senior clique of Healy, Warne and Mark Waugh had their noses out of joint. By the Fourth Test, Warne was more hindrance than help. Dropped, he gave a press conference canvassing retirement. In the changing rooms, he passed unsubtle critiques on the bowlers, particularly the honest Queensland swinger Adam Dale, whom Warne seemed to particularly resent being in the XI ahead of him. The squad's unity fragmented to the point where Elliott, who had also been dropped, commented that being able to relax and not play was preferential to the pressure of competing.

LEFT: Where's the loop? The new captain seeks his own counsel.

As a benchman for the Fourth Test, Warne was a non-contributor. Rather than support the playing XI by throwing balls or running drinks, he lingered in the back of the changing rooms before mooching off to the toilet cubicles to smoke cigarettes. At the time he was receiving a $200,000 sponsorship from a quit-smoking company, but, in the recollection of Gilchrist, who had been called in as cover for Healy: 'He thought nobody knew ... but there was a great grey cloud of smoke coming out [of his cubicle] and ash mounting up like the pile of birdseed in Road Runner cartoons.'

The playing XI were able to ignore Warne and even, as in Pakistan the previous spring, use his absence to their advantage. As Steve Waugh recalled, 'The pressure valve of our team had been released with Shane not being there. This isn't meant to be unkind, but when a great player is for some reason unable to achieve what he's used to achieving, players begin to tread on eggshells around him in an attempt to not make his life harder than it already is. A new freedom showed in our play ...'

Moving into limited-overs mode after the Test series, Warne could not be ignored. Indeed, as the only front-line spinner he had to be nursed back into the fold, his confidence rebuilt game by game. The seven-match one-day series in the West Indies provided that foundation, Warne reconstructing his self-belief ten overs at a time. The series was squared 3-3, with riots intervening in Guyana and Barbados, but Australia could go on to England feeling more secure about Warne, who had been their best and most economical bowler throughout the seven matches.

Once they hit English soil, however, the campaign tripped again. A win over Scotland was achieved despite three dropped catches and the kind of sloppy outcricket which is the surest indicator of an unhappy team. New Zealand beat them easily in Cardiff, and at Headingley the unbeaten Pakistanis romped away to 275, which they defended thanks in large part to Shoaib Akhtar's thunderbolt into Steve Waugh's stumps. Australia then beat Bangladesh at Chester-le-Street. Three teams from the group would go through to the next phase, the Super Sixes. Pakistan were top of Australia's group, and the other two places would be a game of musical chairs between New Zealand, Australia and the West Indies, with the crucial match being Australia's against the West Indies at Old Trafford.

Internally, the Australians were in disarray after the Pakistan loss. Warne had not maintained his form and spirits from the West Indies one-dayers, and was again spreading his self-doubt through the team. He was in trouble with the ICC for writing a newspaper column criticising Arjuna Ranatunga. Steve Waugh criticised the team in public, maybe for the only time in his career, after the Scotland match. Internal discipline was inconsistent, with Waugh and Marsh trying to instil stricter rules on socialising but being voted down by the players.

The circuit-breaker, before the Bangladesh game, was to bring Tom Moody into the starting XI. Tall as a basketball centre, Moody had been given his chance in Test cricket between 1989 and 1992 but seemed, somehow, too far from the earth to negotiate the ground-level trickery of subcontinental spinners. He was another of those enormous batsmen who spent a lot of time pecking at the turf like a hen between occasional bouts of monster hitting. His bowling, while accurate, also tended not to put his natural height to its best use. But Moody's inclusion had less to do with his crick-eting skills than his maturity. At thirty-three, he was younger than only the Waugh twins, and was universally looked up to as a voice of reason and calm. While Warne was falling short as an off-field vice-captain, Moody stepped in and played de facto deputy, me-diating between Waugh and the players and enjoying unalloyed respect from all factions. It helped that he was man-of-the-match against Bangladesh, taking 3/25 and scoring an unbeaten 56 that shored up his position as a player.

Waugh decided to institute some respect for tradition by having each player's one-day number – where in the order of Australia's 139 limited-overs international players each man stood – embroi-dered on his cap. It was a move that would be copied by other teams. A psychologist, Sandy Gordon, was brought into the squad. Waugh raised the question of player support, particularly Warne's, at team meetings and one-on-one, and received assurances that everything was hunky-dory. Later, though, he learned that Warne was causing friction over the captaincy, still stewing over his omission in Antigua and griping over the inclusion of other players, notably Dale, in the World Cup team. Waugh asked Moody to take Warne under his albatross-sized wing. Other senior players were asked to go out of their way to reassure Warne, telling him he was and always would be The Man. As Waugh remarked, 'He loves to be loved.'

The inevitable soul-searching sessions started to produce results when Australia crushed the West Indies. McGrath had been used as a change bowler, letting Dale and Fleming exploit the big-swinging Duke balls. The South Africans had been using Allan Donald that way, with some success. But it hadn't worked in Australia's first three games. Now, with the new ball, McGrath routed the West Indians, bowling Lara for 9 on the way to dismissing them for 110. Bevan and Steve Waugh blocked their way to victory, in the ultimately misplaced belief that they could help their cause by assisting the West Indies' relative run rate. It didn't matter, as New Zealand won its match over Scotland, and the tactic attracted criticism for its cynicism. Waugh responded that he was only adapting to the tournament rules.

Australia finished second in the group, between Pakistan and New Zealand, a creditable result given their losses to both teams. But in this tournament, teams would carry into the Super Sixes the points they had won against other Super Six teams. (This was why Australia had wanted the West Indies to go through.) Having lost to Pakistan and New Zealand, Australia carried no points into the Super Six round – putting them in last place for the next phase. The permutations were, as often in the World Cup, the bewildering outcome of a new formula, but the bottom line for Australia was refreshingly simple to understand. They couldn't afford to lose another match.

Their first authoritative performance against good opposition was a seventy-seven-run victory over India at The Oval. McGrath was at his best, getting Tendulkar for a duck with a short ball and also snaring Dravid and Azharuddin. Against Zimbabwe, a Mark Waugh century set up the win, though Warne again struggled as Neil Johnson scored a century in Zimbabwe's 259. Australia's form was far from convincing, and it was little surprise when at Headingley Herschelle Gibbs reeled off a hundred for South Africa in a total of 271. At 3/48 in reply, with Mark Waugh, Gilchrist and Damien Martyn out, Australia's undistinguished World Cup campaign looked to be dying its natural death.

Steve Waugh joined Ponting, a transformed cricketer since his Test hundred in the famous Barbados match. Ponting, a State player at seventeen and a Test cricketer at twenty, had taken another four rocky years to civilise himself. His fondness for a drink had led him into embarrassment in nightclubs as far apart as Kolkata and Kings Cross. After admitting to an alcohol problem in the summer of 1998–99, he had applied himself more conscientiously during his time outside the Test team, and was using one-day cricket as his springboard back to the big time, perhaps to a fulfilment of his vast talent. Back in 1999, Ponting was a walking question-mark: his future as an Australian cricketer was in his hands, but doubts persisted over the safety of those hands. A greyhound-loving, cricket-breathing boy from the tough Launceston suburb of Mowbray, Ponting had none of the worldliness of a Taylor or time-tested hard-bittenness of a Waugh. He had risen as fast and young as Warne, but hadn't ridden a similar wave of success. His highlights had been sporadic, interspersed with barren runs of failure and lapses into indiscipline.

At Headingley he scored 69 as Australia chased a mountainous target, but his main role was to support his captain. Early in his one-day international career, Waugh had been used more as a bowling all-rounder and down-the-order slogger; consequently he had few one-day centuries to his name. This time, with everything to play for and time on his side, he constructed a mighty run chase. And he did, literally, have everything to play for. After fourteen years as a one-day international player, he had been told by Hohns that if Australia underperformed in this World Cup, another spring clean would follow. Waugh's would be the first name swept out.

That day at Headingley, Waugh was Lara-like in his tactics, sitting watchfully on the pace bowling of Pollock, Donald and Steve Elworthy, then unleashing upon the spin of Nicky Boje and Hansie Cronje's wobblers.

For nearly two decades, he was perceived to have a weakness to the straightening ball on his pads, which he could clip uppishly to mid-wicket. On 56 he did just that, and gifted a catch to Herschelle Gibbs. Gibbs was one of the best fielders in the world, as catlike as Rhodes and even quicker on his feet. So skilled was he that he had a habit of flicking the ball in the air in celebration a split-second after taking a catch. It has been reported that he was doing so when he dropped Waugh. Watching the footage carefully, Gibbs is not quite in the action of flicking the ball in the air when he drops it; but it seems that he is thinking about it. Whatever went through his head, he had just dropped the World Cup. Mythology had it that Steve Waugh told him as much, but Waugh confessed later that all he said was, 'Hey Herschelle, do you realise you've just cost your team the match?'

Cronje would maintain, on the field and off, that Gibbs had in fact controlled the ball. This was Adelaide all over again, when Cronje said Mark Waugh had stepped on his wicket. Cronje can't have watched the Gibbs incident, or the replays, very closely. His habitual refusal to face the facts probably protected him from asking himself why he hadn't previously told Gibbs to cut it out. But that was Hansie Cronje: able to ask Herschelle Gibbs to throw away his wicket for cash in a brown paper bag, but unable to ask him to desist from silly stunts in World Cup matches.

A footnote to Herschelle's howler: in the Australian team meeting the previous night, Warne had raised this very issue. He said that Gibbs's habit of throwing the ball up before controlling it meant that no batsman should walk, if Gibbs caught them, until he had caught it coming down. Mark Waugh recalled, 'Warney does speak some good stuff but most of the time you don't really listen to it. He raves on and you think, "Oh yeah, good one Warney," but this time look what happened.' It is interesting to read other players' memories of how that meeting ended. Warne recalled that everyone laughed and said, 'Shut up, Warney.' Steve Waugh said: 'With a hint of scepticism, someone said, "Good point, Warney," and the meeting was over.' However Warne's suggestion was treated at the time, the events of the next day reminded them all of his gift for the uncanny.

Waugh went on to play his finest one-day innings, an unbeaten 120. It included, on 91, what he called the greatest single shot of his career, a slog-sweep for six off Elworthy when he swung himself off his feet and lay on the ground watching the ball sail over Headingley's longest boundary. After adding 126 with Ponting he still needed the aid of Bevan, in a partnership of seventy-three, and the steely Moody, who helped him add

HE RAVES ON AND YOU THINK, 'OH YEAH, GOOD ONE WARNEY'

the last twenty-five runs, victory coming off the third-last ball which Waugh stubbed off the bottom of his bat past the wicketkeeper.

It was Steve Waugh's match, but against one of his favourite opponents Warne had also come good. He had conceded just thirty-three runs in the South African innings, dismissing Cullinan for 50 and Cronje for a duck. In the highly flammable laboratory of his mind, he had turned some kind of corner that day. With Waugh making his century, the two players were sending each other a message: If we can't come to terms as captain and vice-captain off the field, we will do so with our performances on it.

The South Africans only had to wait four days for the rematch, the semi-final at Edgbaston. Pakistan had finished top of the Super Sixes and thumped New Zealand by nine wickets in their semi-final. Australia's relative run rate was marginally higher than South Africa's, due mainly to the Proteas' shock loss to Zimbabwe three weeks earlier, a quirk of mathematics that would ultimately decide the World Cup.

Cronje, visibly taut, won the toss at Edgbaston and put Australia in. Back in 1996, South Africa had entered the World Cup as favourites but were shock losers in the quarter-final stage. Cronje was under pressure. In a group match, he was found to be wearing a radio earphone to receive instructions from Woolmer. He defended the apparatus's legality but stopped using it. Then, in the Super Six match at Headingley, after Steve Waugh had sledged him while batting – a highly unusual, even courageous, ploy – Cronje had lost control and begun ranting and swearing at his counterpart. Waugh had never heard Cronje erupt like this.

Nevertheless, South Africa's bowling and fielding were at their best at Edgbaston and they restricted Australia to 213. Cronje was playing his aces: Pollock took five wickets and Donald, twice taking two wickets in an over, took four. Only Steve Waugh and last-man-out Bevan, with painstaking half-centuries, and a useful late 18 from Warne saved Australia from an indefensible total.

Before taking the field, Australia's preparations proceeded normally. Waugh gathered the team for a final pep talk, until at the last moment Warne wanted to make an address. Rather than let the captain's words be the last, Warne had his own piece to speak. He told his teammates that 'a few of the boys' might be retiring after this match, so everyone should try to make it memorable. He could have been referring to Tom Moody, but nobody believed he was referring to anyone other than Shane Warne. Some of them found it strange, even slightly offensive, that he should step in like this, drawing attention to himself and inferring that the team should be lifting its efforts for his sake. But none was surprised, for Warne's attitude throughout the campaign had bordered on pure solipsism, as if the entire team's fortunes were external manifestations of his personal ups and downs.

Australia's progress in the 1999 World Cup had stuttered from the start, and although they had survived the Headingley match, it had seemed like a stay of execution. Their form was too unreliable. Needing to win their last seven matches was deemed too tall an order; eventually they would stumble, and this seemed to be the day – 213 was not enough, surely.

Kirsten and Gibbs blunted McGrath and knocked up a quick forty-three runs. McGrath, Fleming and Reiffel had shared the first ten overs but Gibbs in particular was in fine form. Making amends after his famous fluff at Headingley, he punched his way to 30 off thirty-four balls.

Waugh called Warne into the attack. This, really, was it. Both must have had those conversations at the Rex Halcyon Cove in Antigua in the back of their minds: when Warne had said he still possessed his magic, and Waugh had rejected him. Did Waugh believe the leg-spinner could save this match? With his head, no. With his heart, all he could do was hope. Did Warne believe it? He had a point to prove. Waugh said later that he was in a state of desperation when he gave Warne the ball. Warne said, 'It was strange to think that my argument about being the man to perform when it mattered had cut no ice in the West Indies two months earlier, but I had an opportunity now.' He might have been forgetting that it had mattered in Kingston and in Bridgetown, yet he had failed lavishly. And his shoulder operation was now two months further behind him.

Warne's first over was a quiet one, Gibbs and Kirsten taking three singles. The action started in his second over, the thirteenth of the innings, with South Africa 0/48.

Warne's first ball was a dot; his second was a diamond. Gibbs received his Gatting ball, the one that pitched in the rough outside his leg stump, spun across him and clipped the off stump. At first Gibbs refused to believe he had been bowled. His reaction was as incredulous as Gatting's. The Australians, like believers given proof of a second coming, converged on Warne, who was so pumped up he had to take deep breaths to slow himself down and concentrate. His excitement, his emotions flying off him like sparks, bordered on frightening. What meant most to him was that the ball had been the first big leg-spinner since his operation that he had dared to bowl under pressure which had drifted and landed and done what he wanted. Confidence is God, and now he had found it again.

Cullinan defended Warne's next four balls, before five runs came off Reiffel from the other end. With his seventh delivery, Warne spun the ball from hand to hand, steadied at his mark, feet together, and walked in. The slight Kirsten crouched. This one was similar to the Gibbs ball, only Kirsten, being a left-hander, attempted to follow the spin and drag it over mid-wicket. The ball gripped and turned, Kirsten missed and was bowled. Warne, looking like the winner of a game show, went into some private pandemonium. Yet again he was the star, the centre of not only his team's but the cricket world's attention: right where he loved to be.

Cronje, the best South African player of spin, was next. He blocked his first ball. The second was a fuller one which he shaped to drive. It curved and dropped and hit him on the toe. It might have taken some bat as well, or the bat might have struck his toe or the turf as it came down. The ball squirted to slip like an orange pip, Mark Waugh pocketing the catch. Cronje looked disgusted – with himself, with the umpire – and left the scene. In eight balls, Warne had taken three wickets for no run. South Africa had gone from 0/48 to 3/53.

Gilchrist remembered it thus: 'It sums up what Warney can do to you emotionally. One minute you'd be asking yourself why he was carrying on a certain way. And the next, he was engineering one of the greatest experiences of your cricketing life … I was frustrated with Warney for some of that tour, but I also owed him some amazing moments I will never forget.'

The afternoon wasn't to go all Warne's way. He was bowling in the belief that he could dismiss a batsman with every ball, but two hours would pass between his third and fourth wickets. Kallis and Cullinan sat on him for his fourth, fifth and sixth overs, deciding that as long as they stopped him taking wickets they had ample time to gather runs off the other bowlers. Kirsten and Gibbs had given them the priceless asset of a fast start, and even with three wickets down the task required them to be sensible, not heroic. After six overs, Warne had only conceded two more runs but took no further wickets.

Then, with Fleming bowling, Kallis drove wide of mid-off. Cullinan either heard a call or decided on his own brain-snap to run. He turned to see Bevan pick up the ball and throw down the non-striker's stumps. Cullinan had failed against Australia again, all his good work shutting down Warne gone to waste.

The key to the result would lie in the next partnership, between two of South Africa's level heads in Kallis and Rhodes. Inch by inch, over eighteen overs they wore Australia down. Reiffel could not penetrate, and Mark Waugh's off-spinners began to leak boundaries, with Rhodes edging a four then slog-sweeping a six. With ten overs to go, two of them to be bowled by Warne, South Africa required seventy runs. They had slowed down considerably but had six wickets in hand, the present pair plus Boucher, Pollock and the man of the tournament designate, Klusener, whose late order axework had so far brought 250 runs in the Cup at a strike rate of more than 120.

After a quicksilver 43, Rhodes panicked, mis-hitting a pull shot off Reiffel and spooning the catch to Bevan running in from the mid-wicket rope. For some reason best known to Cronje and Woolmer, Pollock came in before Klusener. He and Kallis took eight off the next nine balls. There were eight overs remaining, with sixty-one runs required, when Waugh gave the ball back to Warne for his last two overs.

INCH BY INCH, OVER EIGHTEEN OVERS THEY WORE AUSTRALIA DOWN

Again the South African tactic was to keep him out. Two runs came off his ninth over. No wickets. Eleven runs had come from the last three overs; fifty-nine were needed off the next seven.

Six runs came off McGrath's next over, his eighth, and the ball went back to Warne. Last roll. South Africa were 5/161, needing fifty-three runs from thirty-six balls with Klusener still in the rooms.

With the first ball of his final over, Warne induced the error. Kallis came down the wicket and chipped the ball to long-off. Reiffel ran around, and in, and dropped the catch. The South Africans scampered for three. Fifty to win.

Pollock, as if remembering who was in next, went on the charge. He ran down the wicket to Warne's second ball and deposited it over the long-on rope, then stroked the third lusciously to the cover boundary. From the fourth ball he collected a single. The game had just turned on its head. During that crucial last over from Warne, South Africa had gone from potentially losing a wicket to harvesting fourteen runs off four balls. The game was theirs.

No it wasn't. Warne pitched up and Kallis drove airily, willing the ball over Steve Waugh's head at short cover, but the Australian captain stuck up his hands and said thank you. Warne, and Australia, had clambered up off the mat for one last flurry. South Africa were 6/175: thirty-nine needed off thirty-one balls.

Klusener, at last, emerged with his arm guards and chest guard and power tool, looking like a forester or a meatworker. He took a single, and Warne had given up fifteen runs in his last over. But fifteen runs to buy Kallis's wicket was, for the Australians, a fair price.

In the forty-fifth over, bowled by Fleming, Klusener smacked a four and two singles, but Pollock dragged a slog back onto his stumps and was out for 20. Thirty more were needed, four overs to go, Klusener and Boucher more than capable enough.

McGrath sent down a Scroogely forty-sixth over, giving up five unthreatening singles and squeezing South Africa into a three-over corner, with twenty-six needed. Fleming bowled three dot balls to Boucher then gave up a single. Twenty-five needed off fourteen balls, the pendulum swinging back towards Australia, until Fleming went around the wicket to cramp Klusener and the batsman went slap-whack, a four edged over gully and a two to mid-wicket.

Nineteen were needed off the last two overs. McGrath, of course, took over number forty-nine, and McGrath, of course, took a wicket. Boucher backed away from a yorker, trying to cleave it through the off, and lost middle peg. Facing his first ball, Elworthy popped an edge to gully but Ponting couldn't get in fast enough from backward point. The batsmen ran one.

Klusener drove the next ball down the ground and took what could have been an easy single. But so desperate was he to get back on strike, he called Elworthy for another. Reiffel fired it in from long-on, the ball struck McGrath's hands and ricocheted onto the stumps. Elworthy was out of his ground, but several replays were needed to confirm that the ball, not McGrath's hands, had upset the bails.

So, with eight balls to go and sixteen runs needed, Allan Donald came in. Poor Donald, so magnificent for six years against Australia, yet never enjoying any meaningful win. And now, like McDermott back in 1993 against the West Indies, he was being asked to annul all that disappointment with his bat.

At least he was at the non-striker's end. The field, batsman and crowd settled, and McGrath pitched up to Klusener. The man used his bat like Tony Soprano in a back alley. It wasn't a bad delivery, but Klusener clubbed it high down the ground, far enough to clear the rope.

Far enough to clear Reiffel? The unfortunate Victorian, a ball magnet that afternoon, got under it, but the ball arrived with such force that it parted his hands and pitched in the cheap seats. A dropped catch, a six. Ten to win. Klusener kept the strike with a single to mid-wicket off McGrath's last ball.

Warne was racing around, hectoring the batsmen, geeing up the fieldsmen. Then he said something many of the Australians hadn't taken into account: 'A draw will get us through!' The cricketing parts of his cerebral cortex were ever active, and he was right. Due to their higher position after the Super Sixes, a draw or tie was a win for Australia.

So, Fleming. The man who had bowled the last over in the miracle of Mohali was being asked to do it again. Injuries over the past four years had punished his body but not his happy nature. Fleming took the ball with his usual simple optimism. He was a fine bowler. He believed in himself. He came around the wicket and aimed at the popping crease about thirty centimetres to the off-side of middle stump, as Klusener's most obvious strength was hitting through the leg side. The inner fielders dropped back to the perimeter of the marked ring. The idea was to give him a single, get him off strike. But Klusener wasn't bad through the off either. Reading Fleming's intentions, he backed away and bludgeoned the first ball for four through covers. Waugh could have packed nine fielders into the off-side, and they still wouldn't have stopped it. The deep fieldsman had only a few steps to take, but that was too many.

Five to win off five balls. Klusener had just gone six-one-four. Fleming had a plan. It was the same plan as the first ball. Around the wicket, pitch it up, off-side. But Klusener knew the plan too. He waited for the off-side yorker, backed away and smashed another four, this one a little straighter than the last, whizzing bullet-like past Mark Waugh at long-off. Waugh said he had never seen balls hit harder than those two.

And so, with four balls to go, the game was South Africa's. At the wicket they had Klusener. It didn't really matter who was at the other end, did it? Waugh brought the entire field up to save a single, but grimly. It was all over.

South Africa could relax. But nobody told Klusener and Donald. On Mark Waugh's suggestion Fleming switched to over the wicket. To the next ball, Klusener mistimed a slog and bumbled it to Lehmann at mid-on. For reasons known only to himself, Donald went for the run. He was a third of the way down the wicket before Klusener sent him back. With Donald stranded, Lehmann picked up the ball and dive-passed it to the stumps, only three or four metres away. A training drill, completed a thousand times – and he missed. Everyone chokes under pressure, and the winner is not the one who doesn't choke but the one who chokes least. This time, Australia choked, Lehmann missing the easy run-out. Steve and Mark Waugh, and probably their team, thought that was it, the last of their nine lives.

Donald made it back, so the winning run had not been taken. Surprisingly, Klusener and Donald didn't talk to each other between the third and fourth balls. Perhaps they thought they could communicate telepathically. Perhaps Klusener should just smash another four and be done with it. After his let-off, Donald evidently decided that he couldn't risk a quick single. Nor should he! There were plenty of balls left.

But he hadn't told Klusener. The Australians were amazed that the South African batsmen didn't confer. Instead, Klusener asked the umpires what the score was and how many balls remained. Gilchrist recalled: 'There were three balls, we all knew that. It was clear to me that his mind was all over the place. But I still didn't think we'd get them.'

The fourth ball, Fleming again pitched full. Klusener jammed it towards mid-off and believed that if Lehmann was going to botch a run-out, so would Mark Waugh. Klusener ran, screaming at Donald. Donald didn't hear him, and stayed in his ground. Klusener kept coming. Mark Waugh flicked it, backhanded, a moment of rare elegance amid the mayhem, to Fleming. Klusener was halfway to the bowler's end before Donald realised he had to run. Donald froze. Donald dropped his bat. Donald ran.

The Australians had recently visited a ten-pin bowling alley. Had it been a practice session? Fleming bowled it to Gilchrist at the other end, straight as a die, staying clear of the gutters. Strike!

ABOVE: Are we in? Donald in agony, Waugh in ecstasy.

Fleming's action, as compared with Klusener's and Donald's, in those wild five or six seconds showed the difference between clear and clouded minds. The ball beat the batless Donald, Gilchrist broke the wicket, and the Australians ran and danced like performers in the finale of a rock opera. Their veterans, not to mention the tyros, would describe it as their most exciting moment in a lifetime of cricket. Running off the field, Steve Waugh was still unsure about the result, shouting at Warne, 'Are we in? Are we in?'

Warne replied, 'We're in, mate, you beauty!' And so: reconciliation at full sprint across Edgbaston.

A decade later, the spine still tingles and the palms go moist. The South African players and supporters must be spending the rest of their lives either wondering how they failed or trying not to think about it. The Australian players, for all their self-assurance, must also wonder how they got through, but not as deeply, because winning was their birthright and that was why they kept on doing it. *Wisden* said: 'This was not merely the match of the tournament: it must have been the best one-day international of the 1,483 so far played.'

Edgbaston is often, and naturally, thought of as a great Australian win. It wasn't; it was a tie. But the tie put Australia through to the final, which they won in a canter over a Pakistan team that played poorly enough to raise questions about their seriousness, on top of the questions already lingering over their loss to Bangladesh in the group phase. That was the problem with being Pakistan in the post-Malik era: every loss, and even some of the wins, had a bad smell.

But the final at Lord's was an afterthought. The real final was Edgbaston. There is much to savour, going over and over it. There was Warne's behaviour, veering from the self-indulgent to the Herculean. There was the bowling of McGrath and finally Fleming. There was the bowling of Pollock and Donald, easily forgotten; but there was also their batting, at the end. There was Klusener's schizophrenic half-hour of genius and madness. And there was the incoherent sadness of Cronje, who could barely speak a word at the presentation. He tried to talk, but his mouth opened and closed and the words stayed inside.

The legend of Australia's invincibility – and South Africa's fatal flaw – was forged out of games like this. In truth, standing back from the events of those years, Australia lost more of the very close matches than they won. But that World Cup semi-final was not just another match. It delivered the greatest finish in limited-overs cricket between the two best sides in the world, with such a history between them, and it decided a World Cup. It came at the end of an Australian campaign that had been teetering on the brink of chaos and recrimination for days, weeks and even months; a campaign that never, until that afternoon, looked like succeeding. There has been nothing like it. And for the first time since the West Indies secured their second World Cup in 1979, the world titles in the Test and one-day games were unified: cricket had an undisputed champion in both forms. 'Hindsight,' wrote Matthew Engel in *Wisden*, 'made it look like manifest destiny. It was obvious all along, wasn't it? But it was nothing of the kind.'

OPPOSITE: We're in! Australians converge; Donald reunites with his bat.

A NEW MOOD

Hobart, December 1999

GILCHRIST'S CHEERFUL MANNER AND ETHICAL APPROACH TO THE GAME WOULD ATTRACT SOME MUTTERING AMONG TEAMMATES WHO SUSPECTED HIM OF THE GREAT AUSTRALIAN CRIME OF ARSE-LICKING, **BUT THAT WAS SIMPLY HIS UPBRINGING AND CHARACTER.**

In the narrative of Steve Waugh's captaincy, the West Indies tour and the World Cup of 1999 were the baptism of fire, the harsh introduction to leadership that ended, by dint of will and skill, in victory. Yet he was only gradually becoming comfortable in his skin, always a slow process when a captain is inheriting a ready-made team. Bit by bit, however, the transformation was taking place, and this was turning from Taylor's team into Waugh's. The World Cup win gave him legitimacy: at that moment, he said, he was able to step out of Taylor's shadow.

Selections were in flux, and would remain so over the next two years. The Waugh twins were the fulcrum of the batting line-up, though it would turn out that for Mark, the years 1995–99 were his high tide, and the next three years its ebb. The other four positions would turn into a competition between Slater, Blewett, Elliott, Langer, Hayden, Ponting, Lehmann and finally Damien Martyn, who had been rehabilitated in Shield cricket and eased back into the one-day international line-up since 1998. The selectors recognised his potential and did not want to see it wasted; it had been a long time since the New Year's Test of 1994. This squeeze of eight batsmen into

MCGRATH NEVER MANAGED **HIS CRANKY ACT** VERY WELL, OFTEN OVERDOING IT

four places would take another two years to shake itself out.

In the bowling, McGrath was the leader, notwithstanding Warne's Edgbaston heroics. McGrath was the man who took the new ball on day one, who performed the containing role in the middle days on flat wickets, and who rolled opponents on the last-day crumblers. McGrath did it all, reliably, without any more fuss than what was required from the fast bowler's stage persona. McGrath never managed his cranky act very well, often overdoing it, a sign of someone to whom theatre did not come naturally. Merv Hughes was always a better villain, if half the bowler.

When fit, the first-choice back-ups to McGrath and Warne would be Gillespie and Fleming. But both suffered from periodic injuries, Fleming the more frequently, and the filling agent was Miller, who would turn into an essential Test bowler over the next two seasons. He had a Hughes-like knack for taking the vital wicket when it mattered most. His hair went to blue, blond and black, jewels filled his piercings, and he added the pleasing sight of a wrinkled face and crooked teeth to an otherwise collectors-card line-up.

In the wings would be a bowlers' collective of MacGill,

LEFT: The professor: Buchanan would bring scientific method to coaching.

Kasprowicz, Dale, Reiffel, Angel, Bichel, and two emerging pace bowlers, Brett Lee and Scott Muller. Lee, from New South Wales, was an out-and-out speedster with a fast athletic approach and, early in his career, a susceptibility to back injuries and a worrying kink in his arm. Muller was in the McDermott mould, smooth and easy in his action, slower than Lee but able to bend the ball around.

Over the next years, Waugh would earn the freedom to sculpt a team in his image. Of course, this would rely on subtle judgements of character and ability when it came to the emerging players. Less certain, in 1999, were where Healy and Warne would stand in the new era.

Healy, as he would admit later if not at the time, had had a difficult series in the West Indies. His batting was poor and his keeping, while never dropping to mortal levels, fell short of the standards he had set. His enthusiasm, since losing the vice-captaincy and his one-day place, came and went. Every time Gilchrist arrived on a tour as 'cover' for one of Healy's injuries, Healy furred up like an old dog and dug in his heels to preserve his spot. In eleven years he only missed one Test, ceding to Phil Emery in Pakistan in 1994; if any testament is called for to demonstrate Healy's stubborn genius, it is that resilience in the face of the weathering and erosion his body endured.

As for Warne, he appeared rejuvenated in the World Cup but was still talking about retirement. MacGill was the incumbent Australian Test leg-spinner, a fact Warne would not accept. His continuing to play for Australia was, at that point, conditional: upon him being the first pick, and upon him taking wickets. If things didn't go his way, he was prepared to walk out and enjoy a long twilight of county cricket for Hampshire, where he felt valued, loved, idolised, unquestioned, all of which was, in his mind, his due.

Australia's spring 1999 tours of Sri Lanka and Zimbabwe (against whom they played their long-overdue first Test match) sealed the Healy and Warne issues, albeit in different directions. Warne regained his place for the next Test Australia played, in Kandy, and nearly spun a victory, taking 5/52 in a match Sri Lanka snatched under Jayasuriya's captaincy. The memorable moment was when Gillespie, chasing a high ball, broke his leg against his captain's nose. Australia lost the series, rain stopping any kind of charge in Galle and Colombo, but won by ten wickets their only Test in Zimbabwe. Warne would never again relinquish his place for reasons of form. Only reasons of stupidity would push him out again.

For a wicketkeeper at number seven, meanwhile, it is unfortunately the case that he must hold his position through his batting. In the twelve months after his 134 against England in Brisbane in the 1998–99 series, Healy scored 170 runs at just under nine an innings. Through his last two tours, his Test scores were 12, 0, 6, 10, 0, 3, 6, 16, 11, 3, 4, 7 and 5. For such an underrated batsman, who had averaged more than Rod Marsh for much of his career, Healy's decline was a sad sight. He had made four Test centuries and deserved to be remembered as a doughty contributor, an added bonus, and superior to the more naturally gifted Marsh. But even though his wicketkeeping was good on difficult wickets, in Sri Lanka, Healy's batting was in terminal decline. He would not be a part of the new Waugh era.

The other significant change was the appointment of John Buchanan as coach. After the Sri Lanka tour, Geoff Marsh had had enough of being away from home for nine or ten months of the year. Too much wandering; he wanted to go back to Wandering, Western Australia.

Buchanan's elevation was the first deep impression Steve Waugh could stamp as captain, because this was a position of some permanence, relying not on the vagaries of form but on the captain's determination of how he wanted to run his team. As a message, it was the equal of Taylor's backing for Marsh to replace Simpson in 1996. A new coach is always a reaction to the old coach. Taylor wanted a subordinate, a practice coach, a helper, rather than the Svengali that Simpson had been for Border. But Marsh had his limits. His response to problems was simple and lacking in variety, which was fine under such an authoritative captain as Taylor. Yet Waugh wanted more, something indefinable and new. Taylor had inherited a team rising towards its peak. Waugh inherited a team that had been peaking for a few years and would curdle if it wasn't kept stimulated.

As Queensland coach, Buchanan had certainly offered stimulation. Never a player of great note, he came to the game with a reputation as a boffin, an enthusiast for laptop computers and mathematical analysis. He liked to challenge the players with unconventional thinking, and was an articulate communicator not only to thoughtful opening batsmen but equally to burly fast bowlers and instinctive middle-order hitters. Under his tutelage, Queensland had won their first Sheffield Shields after a long and at times tragicomic history of failure.

Some, such as Ian Chappell, were sceptical about a cricket coach's relevance per se. Being a non-Test player was a double strike against Buchanan. Many in the tightly hierarchical world of Australian cricket dismissed him because he was not one of the Test club. How, they asked, could he understand the minds of Test cricketers if he had never done it himself? An earlier version of Buchanan had been Western Australia's multiple Shield-winning Daryl Foster, who might have become Australian coach but for the question, posed by querulous senior players at moments of their choosing: 'And how many Tests have you played, Fos?'

But Waugh was adamant, about the way he saw the role as much as about Buchanan the individual. 'I saw him as a "performance manager" more than a coach, in that he would address a variety of issues, many not necessarily cricket related, and would endeavour to have each player prepared for his cricket with a clear mind so that the actual playing side would be easier.'

So after Border acted as caretaker coach on the spring tours, Buchanan came into the set-up for the Australian summer of 1999–2000, when Pakistan and India would tour for three Tests each. Initially Buchanan stood back. He wanted to allow Waugh the space to lead in his first home summer, and he wanted to watch the players, understand how their minds operated, look and learn before taking any action. In the early Tests, Buchanan came along as a fly on the wall.

Knowing he was about to be shuffled out, Healy had a dear wish to play one last Test, at his beloved Gabba against Pakistan.

But the selection panel had never been interested in awarding laps of honour, no matter how distinguished the player's service. Told he would not be chosen for Brisbane, Healy retired, giving Gilchrist a gracious endorsement as they passed in the doorway.

Nonetheless, Gilchrist feared that for the third time in his young career he would be cast as villain. When he had left his insecure position as a middle-order New South Wales batsman to go to Western Australia in 1994, he had endured a whole summer of 'home' crowds taunting his mistakes and calling for the return of Tim Zoehrer. When he had replaced Healy in the Australian one-day side, in one match in Sydney the South African bear-baiter Pat Symcox asked him how many people were in the ground. 'Thirty-five thousand,' Gilchrist replied innocently. 'Well,' said Symcox, 'that's thirty-five thousand who hate you.'

Gilchrist had subdued those protests with success, and now, mellowed by Healy's backing him in a newspaper column, the Gabba crowd applauded his sharp first-day keeping. Raised mainly in Lismore, in sub-tropical far-northern New South Wales, he had spent most of his youth facing his schools' inspector father Stan and a bowling machine in the full-length synthetic net Stan had built in their backyard. Stan Gilchrist had been

HE WASN'T TRYING TO BE A GOOD BLOKE; HE COULDN'T HELP IT

a first-grade leg-spinner in Sydney and brought both his cricket acumen and uncompromising commitment to sportsmanship to the education of his third son. (The first and second, Dean and Glenn, were also more than useful cricketers.) Adam Gilchrist's cheerful manner and ethical approach to the game would attract some muttering among teammates who suspected him of the great Australian crime of arse-licking, but that was simply his upbringing and character. He wasn't trying to be a good bloke; he couldn't help it. He had been picked for New South Wales without scoring a century in first-grade cricket, had been picked for Western Australia without having kept wicket in Sheffield Shield, and had been picked for Australia's one-day team without a compelling record in the domestic game. So some thought he had been favoured. Yet by 1999 he had done his time in the waiting room. He had played seventy-six one-day internationals, a world record for patience, before his first Test. His first eight one-dayers, and fifteen of his first twenty-one, had been in the cauldron against South Africa. He had blitzed centuries as an opening batsman and hit a half-century in the World Cup final. By November 1999, there were few who still thought he had enjoyed an armchair ride.

At Waugh's initiative, the 1948 Invincible Bill Brown came to the Brisbane Test match and presented each of the debutants with their baggy green caps. The two lucky young recipients were Adam Gilchrist and Scott Muller.

Test cricket started brightly enough for the pair. Pakistan made 367, with Gilchrist taking three catches and Muller dismissing Abdul Razzaq and Wasim Akram. Australia replied with a flood, Slater cracking 169, Blewett 89 and Mark Waugh 100. Gilchrist did come in under some pressure, Australia having lost Slater, Steve Waugh and Ponting in half an hour and still trailing Pakistan. But he was quickly into his rhythm, and cracked 81 off eighty-eight balls, including one over from Mushtaq from which he harvested a David Hookes–like five boundaries. Along with Warne's 86, Gilchrist turned the course of the innings; from 5/342, Australia got to 575. A close contest had been turned into a wipeout for Pakistan, thanks to the batting of Australia's bottom half. If Gilchrist could make a habit of this, he could transform the game itself.

Saeed Anwar made another of his fluent centuries for Pakistan, but Fleming, with nine wickets in the match, was close to unplayable as the ball began to wear. Just when Pakistan looked like building a challenging lead, Muller removed the elegant Yousuf Youhana, and Australia won by ten wickets. Against a very strong Pakistan team, Steve Waugh had given a hint that he was starting something that might even eclipse the glories of the Taylor era.

The Second Test was the first great Test match hosted by Bellerive Oval, a Test venue used only four times since 1989. The Bellerive wicket had a tendency to play slow, low and overly friendly to batsmen. In first-class matches, mammoth totals were piled up by moderate teams.

ABOVE: Scott Muller wouldn't, unfortunately, be remembered for his seven Test wickets.

For the Second Test, though, the Bellerive wicket was damp and both captains would have liked to bowl. Waugh won the toss and immediately McGrath tore into the Pakistani top order. The upright Mohammad Wasim and Inzamam-ul-Haq put on a stabilising partnership, counter-attacking against Warne, who found the pitch too slow and was carted for twenty-six off his first four overs. After Inzamam dragged one on from Muller, Wasim put on another forty-nine with Youhana and appeared to be strolling towards a well-crafted century until Muller induced the edge and got him for 91. Pakistan fell for 222, a disappointing total even accounting for the conditions, with Muller and Warne, coming back to snip the tail, taking three wickets each.

Slater, Blewett and Langer again built a firm platform for Australia's reply, with Pakistan dropping Slater four times in his 97. Australia was one wicket down and almost up to parity before a nervous collapse, the last nine wickets falling for 55. Pakistan had an all-star pace attack of Wasim Akram, Waqar Younis and Shoaib Akhtar, but after a breakthrough spell by Waqar, a throwback to his glory days, it was the both-ways off-spin of Saqlain Mushtaq that did the damage. Normally a conventional off-spinner with more drift and dip than spin, Saqlain fooled Steve Waugh and Gilchrist with a ball that squirted through his fingers and, rather than turning back like an off-spinner or running straight on like a top-spinner, hit the seam and turned marginally away from the right-hander, or into the left-hander.

It was called 'the other one', or the 'second one'. In Hindi and Urdu it was called the 'doosra'. Moin Khan, Pakistan's wicketkeeper, is credited with giving it its name. But doosra bowlers tend to be nonconformists, and Saqlain himself termed his the 'teesra', or 'the third one'.

Immediately, the bowler's arm was examined, but Saqlain's was less suspect than some other finger-spinners' (among the notable doosra bowlers, such as Muralidaran, Shoaib Malik, Johan Botha and Harbhajan Singh, Saqlain was the only one whose arm didn't need to be straightened out). Through a pure application of the finger-spinner's art, he cut Australia down to 246, a lead of twenty-four.

Pakistan went to stumps at 1/61, and considering their recent performances in Australia a capitulation on day three was widely expected. The contrary happened. Amid increasing local anxiety and frustration, Anwar (78), Ijaz (82) and Inzamam (116 not out) reefed the match away from the home team. Anwar was only stopped by a giant turner out of the footmarks from Warne. Inzamam and Ijaz, both of whom had been mentioned adversely in match-fixing inquiries, applied their tremendous skill to dismembering Australia's attack. No bowler could tie them down. Ijaz had an unorthodox style with an almost non-existent top hand, but would amass a fine record against Australia. In sixty Tests in a stop-start fourteen-year career, he would average 38 against all-comers but 47 against Australia, including six of his twelve Test centuries. Sometimes diffident and even surly, he might have suffered a form of guilt by association by being related through marriage to Salim Malik, but on this day he switched on against Warne and McGrath and plundered Muller, who was beginning to wilt. Inzamam was imperious, showing the broad bat and easy timing that had characterised his work on the subcontinent. His recent weight-loss program, which was meant to aid his mobility between wickets, was not entirely manifest but seemed to have done him no harm. One looking like a matinee idol, the other like a nightclub bouncer, Ijaz and Inzamam formed a delightful contrast of styles in their partnership of 136.

Ijaz's departure saw a late flurry of wickets, four falling in the last session, but at stumps Pakistan's 7/351 gave them a lead of 327 and a sleeper-hold on the match.

Warne, after taking early punishment, was Australia's most dependable bowler. The pitch had dried out in the sunshine and he was at least containing the Pakistani rush. Early on the fourth morning he contrived the match-turning wicket. He bowled a backspinner to Inzamam, who had added two runs to his overnight score. The big fellow leaned back, cut, and got a hard edge. The ball flew to Mark Waugh's right at first slip. He stepped backwards, anticipating where the ball might go if Inzamam edged it, and somehow his hand was in the same place as the ball as it flew past. Of all Test cricketers, was there ever one with superior hand-eye coordination? The catch, one of the greatest in Waugh's world-record-setting career, did not stop Pakistan from building a 368-run lead, but it stopped that lead from becoming a lot greater.

So, Australia had 369 to win. In their favour, they had five full sessions: time would not be an issue. But the size of the chase was daunting and unequalled on Australian soil. To put it into context, it was eighty-seven runs more than the epic chase in Port Elizabeth. It was only thirty-five fewer than the unthinkable Bradman–Morris pursuit at Leeds in 1948. And it would have to be scored against the most varied and dangerous bowling attack in world cricket.

Blewett and Slater, establishing what was widely predicted to be a ten-year opening partnership, again blunted the new ball, but both fell soon after, for 27 and 29 respectively. When Mark Waugh was trapped first ball by Azhar Mahmood, Australia were 3/81 and in a deep pit. They sank even deeper late on the fourth day when Steve Waugh gave Saqlain a return catch and Ponting commemorated his first Test in front of his home crowd by completing a pair, lbw to Wasim Akram.

Pakistan had neither won a 'live' Test match in Australia nor threatened to win a series since 1979. Now, with Australia 5/126, their moment had surely come. When Gilchrist marched assertively to the wicket there was an hour remaining on the fourth day, and many on the field, in the stands and in the Australian changing room believed the game might be finished by stumps. Langer, who had just seen four wickets fall at the other end, smiled at Gilchrist when he arrived and made some brave remarks: 'You never, never know,' he said. 'We could just make Test history here.'

Gilchrist didn't take him too seriously, admiring his bravado but feeling that what Langer really meant was 'Let's have an honourable last crack on our way down'.

In that hour, the pair managed to set the Pakistanis on their heels a little by adding sixty-two, of which Gilchrist made forty-five at nearly a run a ball. It was probably only a rearguard slog, but when the batsmen returned to the changing room the mood surprised them with its buoyancy and hope. If this had been an England changing room, Gilchrist and Langer would have returned to find most of their colleagues lining up for the bus, making dinner plans and looking at them reproachfully for dragging out the agony for another night. But the Australians were cheering and back-slapping, optimistic about a win and revved up by Gilchrist's late hitting. The only problem was, there were still 181 runs to get. They were barely halfway there.

As part of his program to take his players on an adventure into the past as well as the future, Waugh had arranged for four of the 1948 Invincibles to dine with the team and spend time in the Hobart changing rooms. Bill Brown, Doug Ring, Ian Johnson and Arthur Morris were part of the team group for five days. On the fifth morning, Brown saw Gilchrist at breakfast. 'We'll need a century from you today,' he said. Gilchrist thought: No pressure or anything! An Invincible's just told me I need to score a century!

The forecast rain held off: the Test match would be decided one way or the other. Langer and Gilchrist strategised to set themselves small, achievable targets rather than think of the whole 369. The plan was that Langer would focus on ten runs at a time. They would tick off each chunk and start afresh. Gilchrist, meanwhile, would set targets of ten minutes. At the end of each chunk, each batsman would notify and encourage the other. This worked tremendously well in the first session. Akram, with perhaps too many options at his disposal, kept changing his bowlers. Every wicketless over increased the bickering in the field and improved the Australian pair's mood. Every bowling change, Langer and Gilchrist felt that they had won another of their small, interim victories.

On the hill, a group in the crowd sang the *Brady Bunch* theme. In the changing room, Steve Waugh put a ban on anyone switching position. The captain even followed Border's tradition of playing with the worry ball, perhaps forgetting that its luck-making properties hadn't been exactly bounteous for Australian teams.

The game could have ended early and differently but for an umpiring error. On 76, with the score at 5/237, Langer pulled at Akram and appeared to inside-edge to Moin Khan. Umpire Peter Parker gave him not out, and Langer did not walk. Parker, coincidentally, had given Langer out to a bat-pad catch in the first innings which appeared to be incorrect the other way; he had even apologised to Langer afterwards.

The Pakistanis, outraged, fell to pieces in the way Australian teams used to in Pakistan. The captain set the tone, muttering and raging and eventually taking it out on his fieldsmen and bowlers. Soon they were all at each other. Langer, accepting his luck – he would later say, tongue-in-cheek, that his bat might have 'clicked' in the handle as the ball went past him – went on to make a fine and much needed Test century. Shoaib bombed him with 150 km/h bouncers, hitting him on the chin; Langer responded with a gappy grin.

Langer's hundred had taken a day; Gilchrist's took barely a session. Before lunch, he had clattered his way to 100 off 110 balls, not as fast as some later in his career, but he was only just beginning to set the new benchmarks and this was the fastest Australian century since Ray Lindwall's eighty-eight-baller in 1946–47. His free-wheeling ways, as much as his results, inspired teammates and spectators; Steve Waugh would say that even in these circumstances Gilchrist batted as if in his backyard. Perhaps, given Stan Gilchrist's skills as a spin bowler, taking on Pakistan in a Test match felt easy.

The record-making day passed remarkably quickly. An hour after lunch Australia was on the brink. The Pakistanis' morale and discipline were in high-speed reverse. When Langer was finally out for 127, top-edging Saqlain to Inzamam, Australia only needed another five to win. Langer's father, Colin, embraced him at the gate. The partnership, amounting to 238 runs, was the third-highest by an Australian sixth-wicket pair since the beginning of Test cricket. Gilchrist lifted Saqlain over the infield later that over, and the win, coming at three o'clock in the afternoon, seemed almost comfortable, with four wickets in hand. The excitement was almost too much for Warne, the non-striking batsman, who had to be reminded by Gilchrist to finish the run before celebrating.

ABOVE: Gilchrist, a centurion in Hobart, starts to make the extraordinary routine.

Gilchrist's contribution was 149 not out off 163 balls. A tiny elite of Test wicketkeepers had scored any centuries at all; some, such as Marsh and Healy, played for more than a decade and rustled one up every three or four years. Gilchrist had done it in his second Test, having nearly done it in his first, too. He had now scored 230 runs in two innings, at virtually a run a ball, and had played match-winning roles in both Tests. The Australians celebrated as if they had achieved a once-in-a-lifetime feat. For most wicketkeeper-batsmen, it would have been. For Gilchrist, it was just the first.

With the Australian cricket team, however, there was often a cloud wrapped around the silver lining. The nation was still marvelling at the Gilchrist–Langer partnership, its panache and its aggression, the size of the chase and the manner of its achievement, when the teams got together for the dead Test match in Perth. Australia won that Test easily, but it was achieved beneath the shadow of a most unusual incident.

After the Second Test, a television talk show called The Panel played some footage from the third day in Hobart, when Inzamam and Ijaz appeared to be taking the match away from Australia. In the footage, Warne bowled to Inzamam, who swung the ball towards the mid-wicket fence. Scott Muller ran around, picked up the ball and threw it to Warne's end. As the ball flew wide, a nasal voice was picked up by a microphone saying: 'He can't bowl, and he can't field.'

Fingers were immediately pointed at Warne. The voice certainly sounded like his. Only Gilchrist and Mark Waugh were near the stump microphone at the other end, and it didn't sound anything like them.

Warne went on television to issue a strong denial. The incident, while trivial-seeming, caused an uproar. Why? With everything else Warne would be caught doing in his career – philandering, taking money from an illegal bookmaker, smoking in violation of a sponsorship deal, gorging on junk food, taking banned diuretics – this one touched the rawest nerve. To let himself down was, it emerged over the years, just typical Warne. He was naive and stupid. But lovable, in his way. This time, the alleged crime was a crime against the team, and that, in the self-made moral universe he inhabited, was beyond the pale. To sledge one of his own, with such cruel and dismissive words, was a violation of all that Warne claimed to hold dear. If he said it, he could not admit to it under any circumstances, especially having denied it so firmly when first questioned. If he was lying, he had breached the sanctity of the team, a mortal sin compared with which all the other indiscretions were peccadillos.

It is possible that Warne did not admit to it because he didn't do it. The head of Channel Nine sports, Gary Burns, came up with a number of explanations before settling on the one that stuck. A cameraman had said it, and the comment had been picked up by an effects microphone on the fence near where the cameraman was working. This cameraman, Joe Previtera, went on television admitting he had said the words. Warne continued to deny it was himself.

There was said to be footage showing that Warne's mouth had not moved when the words were spoken, but nothing was proven and nothing could be. A voice analyst contacted by the *Australian* opined that it was not Warne, but this failed to sway Muller, who said in a phone conversation to Warne, 'You can give me all the proof you want, but it was you.' Warne denied, vehemently, that it was him, and said that if it had been, he would have had no problem owning up to it. Previtera, an employee of Warne's good friend James Packer, made a smiling confession in which he apologised to Scott Muller. No explanation was ever given for how, for the first and only time in the history of live sports coverage, the words spoken by someone on a boundary fence could have achieved the miracle of hopping through the circuitry of an outside broadcast to emerge through viewers' television speakers.

Warne might well have been innocent as claimed. But not all of his teammates believed him. For a short time during the Perth Test, Warne pointed the finger at Mark Waugh and Gilchrist, saying it could have been them. Only two people knew for certain if Warne didn't say it: Warne himself, and the bowler's end umpire, Peter Parker, who did not issue any conclusive public statement on the matter.

Muller, however, left cricket believing the culprit was Warne. On the fifth night of the Hobart Test – before the revelation on The Panel – Muller was already feeling shut out of the inner circle. He refused to come out of his hotel room to celebrate with the team. There was already something wrong. Muller was dropped after the Test, and thought, with some justification, that he had been harshly expelled from the 'club'. He had taken useful wickets in both of his Test matches – the accusation that he couldn't bowl was extremely harsh, given his seven wickets at 37 in four Test innings, all seven being good batsmen, and he was unlucky to be dropped. He lost confidence and played little first-class cricket thereafter. He believed Warne was the type who would criticise a teammate, as it was known through the Australian and Queensland teams that Warne had ridiculed Adam Dale earlier in 1999. Warne had, however, tried to make Muller welcome in the team. Muller's riposte was that Warne had only been pretending.

Correctly or not, Muller would not be shaken from the belief that Warne had humiliated him publicly and been somehow complicit in the end of his Test career. 'The sad thing,' wrote Gilchrist, who had known Muller for twelve years, debuted on the same day and 'shared the same dream', 'is that it left him with a sour taste of what should have been the greatest experience of his life: playing for Australia.'

Warne continued to deny he had anything to do with it. Joe Previtera acquired the nickname, among some players, as 'the man who never had to pay for another dinner'.

THE RUN

Harare, October 1999–Chennai, March 2001

BUCHANAN WROTE ON A SHEET OF BUTCHER'S PAPER WHICH HE STUCK ON THE CHANGING-ROOM WALL: 'TODAY IS THE FIRST TEST OF OUR JOURNEY TO THE INVINCIBLES.'

The win over Pakistan in Hobart instilled in the Australians the belief that no situation was insurmountable. They could win from anywhere. They duly did.

Here is a summary of the world record run of 16 successive wins they achieved between October 1999 and March 2001.

Zimbabwe, Harare, 14–17 October 1999
  Australia won by ten wickets.

Pakistan, Brisbane, 5–9 November 1999
  Australia won by ten wickets.

Pakistan, Hobart, 18–22 November 1999
  Australia won by four wickets.

Pakistan, Perth, 26–28 November 1999
  Australia won by an innings and 20 runs.

India, Adelaide, 10–14 December 1999.
  Australia won by 285 runs.

India, Melbourne, 26–30 December 1999.
  Australia won by 180 runs.

THEY COULD WIN FROM ANYWHERE. THEY DULY DID.

India, Sydney, 2–4 January 2000
  Australia won by an innings and 141 runs.

New Zealand, Auckland, 11–15 March 2000
  Australia won by 62 runs.

New Zealand, Wellington, 24–27 March 2000
  Australia won by six wickets.

New Zealand, Hamilton, 31 March–3 April 2000
  Australia won by six wickets.

West Indies, Brisbane, 23–25 November 2000
  Australia won by an innings and 126 runs.

West Indies, Perth, 1–3 December 2000
  Australia won by an innings and 27 runs.

West Indies, Adelaide, 15–19 December 2000
  Australia won by five wickets.

West Indies, Melbourne, 26–29 December 2000
  Australia won by 352 runs.

West Indies, Sydney, 2–6 January 2001
  Australia won by six wickets.

LEFT: Mr Fix-It: Miller going the spin
option in New Zealand.

India, Mumbai, 27 February–1 March 2001
Australia won by ten wickets.

As with most stupendous sporting achievements, little comment is necessary. All we can do is stand back from a distance and admire it. (And it's well to remember that during the same span they also had a run of thirteen straight one-day wins, also a world record.) With the twelfth win of the sixteen, over the West Indies in Perth, Australia passed the previous world record set by Clive Lloyd's team of 1984. Comparisons between Australia of the present era and the West Indians of the 1980s were attracting more than passing consideration; until Waugh's captaincy they had still been inconceivable.

The likelihood of a Test draw intervening in the period is so great as to make the run of wins all the more laudable: this team played to win, not to avoid losing. Under Waugh, there was a resolution against boring draws. Taylor had hoped for the same, but Waugh was taking on a fanatical zeal for innovative thinking and 'bursting through' preconceived ideas of team and individual limitations. A washout, of course, could have nipped the run in the bud, but so many of Australia's wins were achieved within three or four days that they even made allowances for acts of God.

Ten of the wins were by an innings, ten wickets, or a welter of runs. The Hobart win over Pakistan was the only one achieved from a position where Australia were outsiders going into the last day. The first two Tests against New Zealand were tight affairs, and the Adelaide Test against the West Indies – when Gilchrist led the team in the absence of a buttock-sore Waugh – was recorded after a fine Lara century and late Australian nerves. But for the most part the victories were by such large margins that none of them, aside from Hobart, would be remembered as a great contest in its own right.

The quality of the opposition varied. Zimbabwe was well beaten, but this was a side that still included the best of a generation: the Flower brothers, Neil Johnson, Heath Streak and Alistair Campbell. This was not a bunch of ring-ins selected on the basis of race but the last of the strong Zimbabwe teams before the late-Mugabe madness dragged cricket down with it.

Pakistan had a strong team on paper, but, as we have seen, surrendered dominant positions under pressure. India disappointed during its 1999–2000 tour, with too much weighing on Tendulkar after the retirements of Azharuddin and Sidhu. New Zealand posed the toughest challenge to Australia during this period. Their team included Chris Cairns, Nathan Astle, Stephen Fleming, Craig McMillan and Daniel Vettori, all close to their peak. After Hobart, Auckland and Wellington were the two closest Test matches during the run. Yet the Australians were still able to accomplish the first-ever 3-0 'blackout' of New Zealand, away from home no less. By contrast the West Indies, touring Australia for a five-match series, offered little resistance apart from Lara and occasional contributions from Walsh. McGrath's hat-trick in the Perth Test, collecting Campbell, Lara and Adams in his fourth over of the game, provided great excitement for the fast bowler and his teammates but a general sense of mourning through the cricket world. Australia was overwhelming the sense of the unexpected that was vital to the game as a competitive spectacle.

PERSONNEL

Openers
Slater (16 Tests)
Blewett (9 Tests), Hayden (7 Tests)

Batsmen
Langer (16 Tests)
M. Waugh (16 Tests)
S. Waugh (15 Tests)
Martyn (4 Tests)
Ponting (13 Tests)

Wicketkeepers
Healy (1 Test)
Gilchrist (15 Tests)

Bowlers
Warne (11 Tests)
MacGill (4 Tests)
Bichel (2 Tests)
Fleming (8 Tests)

Lee (7 Tests)
Miller (7 Tests)
Gillespie (5 Tests)
Muller (2 Tests)
Kasprowicz (2 Tests)
McGrath (16 Tests)

There were many individual highlights. Langer, who had been lined up for the selectors' axe before his 127 in Hobart, peeled off a succession of centuries and one double-century, seeming to establish himself finally as the successor to Boon at number three. Ponting cemented his place at number six. When he was injured for the New Zealand tour, his replacement, Martyn, back after six years, showed that he was ready to step into the next vacancy when it arose. And it would.

Langer, Slater and Mark Waugh were the only batsmen to play all sixteen Tests during the run, yet it would be those three who would be dropped from the Test team in the following eighteen months. Such are the swings of fortune. Mark Waugh played his hundredth Test during the run, against India in Sydney, a testament to his durability and consistency. Those who expected him to build his batting average to the fifties, as his talent might have merited, were only looking at one statistic; Mark Waugh won or saved as many games with his bat as did his brother. In the run, Steve Waugh played all but the Adelaide Test against the West Indies. Gilchrist played in every match after succeeding Healy, whose last appearance, in Harare, was the first of the sixteen.

Australia's personnel during the run was remarkably stable. The only batsman dropped for form was Blewett, who made way for Matthew Hayden in the New Zealand series. In four different bursts over a period of six years, Blewett had played forty-six Tests for Australia. But there were always doubts about his technique against spin and against the fast ball moving into him – he left a wide 'gate' when driving – and he had not scored a Test century since his 125 in the Edgbaston match of 1997, Mark Taylor's comeback Test. Three years were too long for the selectors to wait, and they recycled another in-and-outer. Hayden was having

ABOVE: Slater, who played all 16 Tests, showing his approach to the nervous nineties.

his third crack at Test cricket, after one Test in South Africa in 1994 and six against the West Indies and South Africa in 1996–97. Extreme doubts hovered over his technique, too, but there was no other response to the thousands of runs he piled up year after year in domestic cricket. And this time, at last, the selection would hold. The Third Test against New Zealand in Hamilton, the tenth of the run, would be the first of ninety-six more Test matches for Hayden, a future that nobody on earth would have guessed when he returned with scores of 2 and 37.

Among the bowlers, there was similar stability. McGrath played all of the sixteen Tests and was at the very top of his game, moving up into the highest shelf of Australian bowlers. Again, few would have suspected five years earlier that McGrath could be as damaging and effective a strike leader as any of Lillee, Lindwall, McKenzie, Miller, Thomson and Gregory. But without a se-

AND THIS TIME, AT LAST, THE SELECTION WOULD HOLD

quin's worth of the retired greats' glamour or pizzazz or obvious threat, he was all that and soon he would surpass every one of them.

Warne played each Test in the run aside from the home series against the West Indies, when he was forced out with a finger injury. He was very much back in his pomp after his years of uncertainty from 1996 to 1999. When he dropped out of the 2000–01 home series, MacGill was an able substitute and Miller, the Spakfilla of Australian cricket, turned out to be more than useful. He was Australia's Test player of the year in 2000, and played with the enjoyment befitting a man who had seen enough of life to keep all of this ballyhoo in perspective. Fleming played eight of the Tests – the first seven before being injured again, then returning when he was fit. Gillespie, likewise, came back into the team after recovering from his broken leg. When they were injured the depth of Australian cricket was shown in the replacements: Bichel, Kasprowicz and Brett Lee all helped win matches. Lee, blasting onto the scene with 5/47 in his debut innings, against India in Melbourne, seemed to be the answer for the long-term future.

Beneath the statistics of constant triumph – partly explaining them, but partly coinciding with them – a cultural change was reshaping the Australian team. Buchanan, a bower bird gathering ideas from wherever he pleased, was introducing new methods of stimulating and preparing the team. Whereas Bob Simpson had innovated constantly in the types of drills and games the Australians played in practice, Buchanan was often looking away from cricket.

Sometimes the change came from the advance of sports science: specialised gym sessions, ice baths, power naps, recovery sessions and chats with sports psychologists. At other times, Buchanan's methods came from the 'science' of management. He gave out 'Player Feedback Cards' categorising and analysing performances to the most minute detail. He encouraged 'dressing room contracts', where players would pledge anything from supporting their teammates to banning mobile phones. He introduced a new language of 'values', seeing the worth of encouraging players to articulate their feelings about tradition, honesty, integrity, ambition and so on. Under Buchanan, Australian players were urged to write poems for each other and lead show-and-tell sessions, broadening their experience of the world when on tour. It is impossible, from the outside, to know how much of the team's success owed to this influx of ideas. For some players, it kept them fresh. For others, it was all a bit silly and over-complicated. Out of context, recorded on paper, many of Buchanan's 'innovations' come across as an empty and almost risible borrowing of self-help and management-speak. In themselves, it is hard to see his buzzwords helping a player hit or bowl the ball better, but with raw talent more or less equalised at the highest level, preparation and the mental game become vital.

Context is everything. When Buchanan started as coach, for the First Test against Pakistan in 1999, he wrote on a sheet of butcher's paper which he stuck on the changing-room wall:

'Today is the first Test of our journey to the Invincibles. Let's make the ride enjoyable and attainable.'

Having been on top for so long, some of the older players didn't take to being told to aim higher. But that was what Buchanan did, and his urging was infectious. Damien Fleming, when asked in a team meeting what he wanted from that summer, said, 'Sing the team song after all six Tests.' Nobody was used to that kind of ambition. It was crazy. But by shaking up the players' thinking, Buchanan helped to make the realisation of such ambition believable.

Speaking of 'older players', the selectors did have a concern during this period that the team's average age was over thirty. The senior men were thirty-five. Even Gilchrist, a newcomer, was twenty-eight. If they were to avoid a clean-out at the selection table in the near future, this team was going to have to recalibrate perceptions of time itself.

Buchanan came into the team at the right time for his methods, and went into harness with a captain looking for something extra. With a coach and captain following the old-school methods, Australia would still have won Test matches; but it is hard to imagine them winning so many in succession without growing jaded. Ultimately, to use a Buchananism, the only reliable feedback is that which is posted on the scoresheets. Going by the wins they had recorded, it was arguable that Australia not only had its greatest team but its greatest coach.

The sixteen matches of the run were bracketed around two controversies. One spelt the end of Warne's ambitions to be Australian Test captain. He was finally caught satisfying what his wife Simone would describe as his 'sex addiction'. In this case, an English newspaper exposed Warne's attempts to seduce a nurse. The episode was squalid and had nothing to do with cricket, but the public protests lit up the ACB switchboard and email inboxes to the point where the board stripped Warne of the vice-captaincy in mid-2000. Warne argued, not without validity, that it was none of their business. The Board often had a keener eye for the winds of public opinion than for principle. But Warne had such a long run of form behind him that this was the final straw for those Board members who had never wanted him anywhere near a position of responsibility in the first place. He was replaced as vice-captain by Gilchrist, who at that point had only played nine Tests and would, three Tests later, become Australian Test captain himself when Steve Waugh got injured.

The other controversy had nothing to do with Australia, except insofar as it affected everyone in the cricket world. In April 2000, the world woke to headlines stating that Hansie Cronje had been caught up in the match-fixing business. Initially the South African captain denied any involvement, but over the following weeks phone-tap evidence from Indian police forced him to admit that he had received money and gifts to influence performances from his players in one-day matches. Among his teammates, Herschelle Gibbs was also implicated. Cronje was sacked as captain, and some years later would die in a light plane crash.

When the news broke, Australia and the Proteas were about to start a one-day series in South Africa. Among the Australians there was disbelief and uncertainty over what exactly had been alleged, admitted or proven. Among the South Africans, there was a period of rallying around Cronje. Among all cricket followers, there was complete puzzlement that he, of all people, could let greed get the better of him. Cronje's devout Christianity, family-man image and ferocious will to win seemed to place him on a higher plane than the other cricketers drawn into the ongoing scandal. Also, there might have been a hint of Western racism: it was easier to imagine such sly fellows as Azharuddin and Malik being caught up, but not a clean-cut white man such as Cronje.

The ICC would take on the issue in greater earnest, setting up an Anti-Corruption Unit that would again examine Mark Waugh's dealings with John the bookmaker but ultimately unearth no new evidence of ongoing match-fixing. Yet the temptation would remain as long as oceans of illegal betting money were swilling around the game. Sanath Jayasuriya, who came from a very poor family in Matara, Sri Lanka, once revealed that he had been offered up to $US500,000 to enter into a relationship with a bookmaker. For Cronje, an ambitious man who fought for better payments for South African players at a time when the rand was in free-fall, the lure of financial 'freedom' must have been overwhelming. A commission of inquiry in South Africa later in 2000 led to more confessions and greater details: Cronje had been taking money to twist cricketing performances for years. The shock, as Warne said, was 'mind-boggling'. No one could believe it of Cronje.

Gilchrist would write: 'It was amazing not because he was an international captain, but because he was Hansie Cronje. Next to Stephen Waugh, I couldn't think of a captain I would less suspect of being capable of this ... He was quite an inspirational character. He commanded absolute loyalty from that team, but he seemed fun as well, genuinely popular.'

Steve Waugh was more poetic: 'Mentally he pushed himself so hard that, like a piece of pottery in a kiln when the heat became too much, he cracked.'

In early 2001, Waugh and his own men were about to crack under a different kind of heat.

GREATNESS IN DEFEAT

Kolkata, March 2001

IN THE AUSTRALIAN CHANGING ROOM, SLATER PRODUCED A CIGAR, SNIFFED IT, AND MURMURED, 'OOH YEAH, BABY, TONIGHT, HERE WE GO, TONIGHT!' NOBODY WARNED HIM ABOUT TEMPTING FATE.

If they weren't so knowledgeable about cricket, Indian fans might have been wondering what all the fuss was about. This so-called world champion team had visited India in 1996 and left without winning a game, crushed in a Test and impotent in six one-dayers. It had come again in 1998 and was knocked over by a wave of runs from Tendulkar, Azharuddin and Sidhu. Nor did the Australian batsmen look remotely capable of countering Kumble on dry wickets. On Indian soil, Australia looked anything but world champions.

India could remember the great West Indian teams, who had gone to the subcontinent and, even without effective spinners, won series. The Australians were good, yes, but the West Indies had won everywhere on the globe, not losing a single series between 1980 and 1995. Beat that, world champions.

Yet the Indian cricket community was well enough informed to know that Australia was a prize catch. The glories of satellite television brought year-round cricket into Indian living rooms, so when an Australian team arrived it was confronted with more knowledge than it knew how to deal with. Michael Bevan was once shown a baby boy named after him: 'Bevan'. Shane Warne, toothless in India in 1998, remained

THE AUSTRALIANS WERE GOOD, YES, BUT THE WEST INDIES HAD WON EVERYWHERE

a hero because of his achievements elsewhere. Technology had fed not only the Indian fervour for cricket but the national appetite for facts as well. No country could have been less insular or parochial. Indian cricketers, and their supporters, were always looking outwards. As a result, they would take all the more pleasure in cutting the Australians down. Their exuberance would be a measure of their respect.

Unlike in 1998, the Australian team of 2001 would be arriving at full strength. McGrath and Warne were both there, and in form. Gillespie, Miller, Kasprowicz and Fleming would back them up. The batting line-up was stable after a year of uninterrupted Test victories. And just fourteen months earlier, Australia had whitewashed India 3-0 at home.

The auguries were promising, with reasonable performances in the warm-up phase, at least compared with the previous tour. This Australian squad was relatively seasoned in India, bringing memory and experience as well as boots, bats and pads. As well as the usual exhortations to 'embrace India', Buchanan allowed those with negative feelings to express them rather than bottle them up. It seemed a more mature, thought-out approach.

LEFT: It all looked so good: a McGrath wicket before the drought hit.

Two nights before the First Test in Mumbai, the Australians received news that Sir Donald Bradman had died at ninety-two. Senior team members such as Steve Waugh, Warne and Gilchrist paid public tributes to the Don. What took them aback was the genuine mourning among Indians. Bradman had never played there – in fact, he had rather undiplomatically declined to get off the boat at Bombay on the Invincibles' journey to England – and yet Indians were clasping the Australian players' hands to pass on their condolences. Cricket's beating heart was meant to be Lord's; by these gestures, the Australians were made to feel that the centre was here, in India.

Playing with black armbands, the Australians finally lived up to their billing and in Mumbai continued their run. Waugh won the toss and put India in on a grassy wicket, hoping to confront their batsmen with the 'recent trauma syndrome' of their last tour of Australia. Only Tendulkar resisted, with 76 of India's 176. Warne, in his best performance in India to that point, took 4/47. This time he had McGrath to apply the top-order choke, and by the time Warne was given the ball India were three down.

After a bright start Australia's reply stumbled on the second morning, and they were 5/99 when Gilchrist joined Hayden. Mark Waugh and Ponting had fallen without scoring, and the finger spin of Rahul Sanghvi and Harbhajan Singh was threatening to cast a 1998-like spell even in the absence of Kumble, who was out of the series with a bung shoulder. But Gilchrist, who had talked himself into a spell of his own, kidding himself into the belief that he was starting his innings already well-set after half an hour's batting, got to work sweeping, cutting and driving the spinners as if he was in Perth. His method was simple in conception: he would hoick everything pitching on his stumps into the mid-wicket gap that Ganguly had left open to tempt just such a shot in the expectation that any batsman silly enough to try it against the biting spin would miss or miscue. After taking a hammering in this fashion, Harbhajan aimed more defensively, wide of the off stump. Gilchrist leaned back and cut through the point area. It was a perfect plan, but without the greatest skill Gilchrist would have looked foolish and let the team down. He took sixteen balls to score his second run, another thirty-nine to get to his fifty, and a mere twenty-nine to go from fifty to 100. His century, off eighty-four balls, was the fastest in history against India and the second-fastest by an Australian, after Jack Gregory's sixty-seven-ball hundred eight decades earlier. In thirty-two overs Gilchrist and Hayden blitzed the bowling for 197. Hayden, whose heavy footwork and muscular build had seemed the wrong design for Indian conditions, was a delight to watch, tripping down the wicket so lightly as to make the bowlers feel he would get to the ball on the full no matter where they pitched it. The batting, from two men more accustomed to bounce and pace and with techniques developed accordingly, was a lesson in intimidation. On their own pitch, with their own raucous crowds and close-in fields, the Indian bowlers looked as timid as if they were playing away.

Despite a handy 39 from Warne, the last wickets fell quickly after the loss of Hayden, for a five-hour 119, and Gilchrist, for 122 off 112 balls. He had made a habit of scoring centuries from number seven, but this was the best since Hobart in 1999 and arguably the best of all.

Trailing by 173, India's batting was more patient in the second innings, but the Australians were comfortable with this kind of game. The main bowlers settled in for long spells and arrested the growth of large partnerships. Mark Waugh, given fifteen overs on the drying wicket, dismissed Tendulkar for 65 among three important scalps. The Tendulkar dismissal typified the way things were running for Australia. Waugh bowled a long-hop which Tendulkar smashed to leg. It hit the back of short-leg Langer, then ballooned into the air into what appeared to be clear space until Ponting materialised and swooped like a seagull to take the catch. That it happened at all was freakish. That it happened to Tendulkar closed the deal for India's spirits. From a competitive 2/154, they lost Tendulkar, Ganguly, Dravid and Laxman in the space of twenty runs and only made it to 219, leaving a target of forty-seven runs which Hayden and Slater gobbled up in seven overs.

The final frontier? Who was overrated now? Australia had won the match inside three action-packed days, their only flaw the customary excess of fire. It was Slater, this time, who claimed to have caught Dravid at square leg off Fleming's bowling but was overruled when umpire Venkataraghavan referred the question to the video official. Slater, offended by not being trusted, had words with both Venkat and Dravid. When Dravid swore at him Slater flew off the handle, taking voluble exception to being called, he felt, a cheat. His outburst was out of all proportion to the dispute, betraying a state of mind that was as stable as a two-legged stool. Slater had been going through the break-up of his marriage as well as being accused, by ACB officials, of using hard drugs and fathering a child in Tasmania, victim of a cornucopia of rumours gone feral. Perhaps recognising the combined effects of heat of the moment and an unsteady temperament, the match referee Cammie Smith let Slater off with a warning. (This was later increased to a fine and suspended ban, not for the original incident but for the subsequent sin of discussing the incident in a radio interview.) But no matter what the mitigating circumstances, the images of Slater raging against Dravid, one of the game's universally admired gentlemen, raised hackles in Australia and India alike, confirming the view, held widely if in this case a trifle unfairly, that Steve Waugh's team were unable to leaven their ruthlessness with grace. They didn't seem able to win well. One of their finest moments, winning in Mumbai, bore their mark of Cain.

The Australian team in the Taylor–Waugh–Ponting era deserved the epithet of great not only for their achievements but for the qualities of some of the Test matches they played. Some of these they won; others they lost.

When they travelled to Kolkata for the Second Test, losing was the last thing on their mind. In fact it is fair to say that they had less reason to think about losing than any team in the history of the game. Their confidence was supreme; even if they lost early wickets, Gilchrist would dig them out of any hole, however deep. And finally the partnership of McGrath and Warne was fit, flourishing and giving India an overdue demonstration of why they had nearly 700 Test wickets between them.

Waugh won the toss at Eden Gardens; everything was going his way. Hayden and Slater rolled through the first session, encountering few challenges from the left-armer Zaheer Khan and the recalled veteran B.K. Venkatesh Prasad until Slater edged one from Zaheer on 42. Hayden went on to make a forceful 97 and Langer 58 as the Australian top order set about batting India out of the match; in just two innings Hayden had dispelled all doubts about his ability, at a mature age, to perform in Test cricket under all conditions.

In the final session of the first day, Australia's juggernaut hit a bump. In his sixteenth over, Harbhajan Singh, who had the great capacity to maintain his abrasiveness whether he had taken 5/20 or 0/200, dismissed Ponting lbw with a slider for another failure in India, to make the score 5/252. Never mind: Gilchrist strode out. But this time, unaccountably, his state of mind was a reverse image of Mumbai. He had been practising with Buchanan, so confident as to play reverse-sweeps and a clown's bag of trick shots not normally in his repertoire. After his Mumbai century, hubris might have been creeping in. Batting in India was a piece of cake. Now, with the din of 80,000 Eden Gardens fans in his ears, he walked out and glanced Harbhajan's first ball onto his pads. The crowd noise was too loud for the Indian umpire S.K. Bansal to hear the nick, and Gilchrist was given out.

Harbhajan skipped in again, his elbows characteristically flapping like the wings of a waterbird in take-off. The ball was full, Warne turned it to leg, Ramesh held onto the catch tight against the turf, and the young Punjabi had a hat-trick. It wouldn't bring India back into the match immediately, but, like an early tremor before the big one, it signalled that they had a bowler who could change a match in a trice. That Harbhajan had come back from several months of exclusion to rectify a suspect action, overlapping with the death of his father, Sardev Singh, wove layers of significance into his achievement. He was the first Indian bowler, including all the great spinners and the peerless swing bowler Kapil Dev, to take a hat-trick.

Test cricketers who have played in India say the same thing: matches can doze along for hours, or sessions, with nothing much happening, and then five wickets can fall in an hour. It is so hard to get started, with fielders crowded around the bat, the noise dizzying and the atmosphere closing in claustrophobically, that the fall of one wicket can feel like a loud crack on a slope prone to avalanches.

ABOVE: A matter of trust: Slater loses it with umpire Venkat.

Steve Waugh, who had watched the hat-trick from the other end, would have none of it. This was his team, in the land he had embraced. For decades Australians had been talking the talk about opening their arms to the foreignness of India, but Waugh put the fine statements into action. He was sponsoring an orphanage, Udayan, near Kolkata and walking the streets with his camera, happy to open his senses to the teeming impressions of Indian cities. As Australian captain, not only was he a great ambassador but he wanted desperately to achieve something that had eluded Taylor.

IF THE OTHER BATSMEN COULDN'T DO IT, HE WOULD CARRY THEM

He'd done it with a World Cup, but a Test victory in India was his personal holy grail. If the other batsmen couldn't do it, he would carry them. With Gillespie, he dug in and batted until just before tea on the second day. Gillespie made a three-hour 46 and then McGrath, in one of those occasional innings that convinced him not to give up completely on his dream of a Test half-century, stuck around, hit some shots and helped Waugh to his twenty-fifth hundred, his first in India and one that set off an unwontedly emotional celebration. The shudders caused by Harbhajan's hat-trick were a distant memory as Australia's last wicket, Waugh, fell at 445.

India's top order coped even worse with McGrath than they had in Mumbai. As *Wisden* recorded, they 'batted as though they were collectively beyond therapy'. Wickets kept clattering, seven between tea and stumps, and Australia was eyeing another three-day win. Only V.V.S. Laxman, batting at number six, prevented a complete debacle. Laxman was a bit of a mystery. In a team of millionaire superstars, he had the demeanour of a librarian. He had come into the side in 1997–98 as an opener, showed some promise with a fluent 96 against Australia at Eden Gardens that year, and done frustratingly little else until an incredible 167 in the lost Test at Sydney in the New Year of 2000. When Laxman got into full flow, it was impossible to imagine anyone getting him out or stopping the runs. He stood in a crouch, with his bat jiggling at shin height, as he waited for the bowler, then moved into position for his bread-and-butter shot, the whip of the wrists firing any ball, regardless of line and length, like a bullet through mid-wicket. A batsman who could take straight, good-length balls and dispatch them regularly for four was a bowler's nightmare. Yet there was also a looseness to his technique, an uncertainty in shot selection, that got him out when he was set. Indian fans were perpetually waiting for more from him; until now he had never converted his talent into a Test century at home. He had twice scored triple-centuries in domestic cricket, so there was a suspicion that he could do much better. But the selectors were still unsure whether he was worth their patience. Had India lost in Kolkata in 2001, he would certainly have been dropped. In the first innings, batting with the tail, he showed a glimmer of form by scoring 59 off eighty-three balls and, with Prasad, saving some face with a last-wicket stand that took the score from 129 to 171. Laxman was unlucky to be given out, caught sweeping when the ball hit his forearm; nevertheless he was described in the Indian press as merely having shown his 'penchant for strokemaking in lost causes'.

Laxman kept his pads on when Waugh asked India to bat again. It was unlike the Australian captain not to grind the opponent down by batting again and setting them about 600 to win in five sessions. That was the Australian playbook, but Waugh departed from it this time. The bowlers had gone through India in fifty-eight overs. They weren't tired. The Indian batsmen were demoralised. Kick them when they're down, and you can plant your flag on the final frontier.

So an hour before lunch on the third day, India went in again. Nobody had lost a Test after enforcing the follow-on since Kim Hughes at Headingley in 1981. India's openers, Sadagoppan Ramesh and Shiv Sunder Das, survived until the break, but soon afterwards Warne broke through to have Ramesh caught, then Das hit his wicket trying to counter Gillespie. On 10, Tendulkar perished, flashing at a Gillespie riser outside off stump and giving Gilchrist the catch. Australia rioted; India slumped. It was all over. India was 3/115, still 159 from making Australia bat again.

The wicket was playing well, however. There had been nothing in it to explain or excuse India's dismissals. Between tea and stumps, Laxman, in at number three, and his captain staged a little counter-attack. Ganguly's batting in the series had been much like his captaincy: on the late side. With the captaincy, his lateness to tosses and press conferences seemed intended to rile others, particularly his opposite number. With the batting, he just didn't seem quite sharp enough. Almost in mockery of him, Waugh set a field with all his men on the off side. But Ganguly, notwithstanding the 'Prince of Bengal' moniker and regal mannerisms, possessed fighting qualities which the Australians had seen in Brisbane and would forget at their peril. In thirty-one overs of lengthening shadows he and Laxman scored freely, adding 117 as Australia's pacemen began to tire. Laxman reached his second Test century just before stumps, but McGrath, gnawing away from around the wicket, finally drew a nick from Ganguly. Although India were 4/254 at the close of play, they still trailed and were, at best, fighting a rearguard action to avoid a second thrashing. Still, Laxman had achieved the rare feat of playing two wonderful Test innings in the one day.

The fourth day dawned brightly, a typical humid, warm Kolkata spring morning. In the Australian changing room, Slater produced a cigar, sniffed it, and murmured, 'Ooh yeah, baby, tonight, here we go, tonight!' Nobody warned him about tempting fate.

The day came and went without a wicket falling. Nothing really happened except Laxman and Dravid scored 335 runs. They didn't give a catchable chance, and only once did the ball strike the pads with a reasonable possibility of going on to hit the stumps. Australia could do nothing. Everyone had a bowl except Steve Waugh and Gilchrist. Slater, Hayden and Langer got to bowl. Warne and Gilchrist, standing behind the wicket, went through their desert island music, movies and supermodels. Laxman and Dravid went on and on.

What was it about that date, 14 March? It was two years to the day since the Lara–Adams bat-a-thon in Kingston. Unlike that stand, though, this was a partnership of equals. Dravid, more correct and upright than Laxman, distributed his shots evenly around the wicket. Out of form at number three, Dravid had temporarily swapped positions with his present partner. It seemed to work! Laxman preferred easing the ball through the on side, but forced Australia to bowl so wide of the off stump that he was able to feast on cuts and back-foot cover-drives. There was nothing hurried or frenzied about the batting. Dravid showed why he was nicknamed 'The Wall'. As in Jamaica, the all-day pair went about their work dismantling Australia with patience and without risk. Their biggest threat was cramp.

As in Jamaica, Australia appeared to lack a Plan B. Waugh's credo had only one plan of attack, which was just that: attack. When attack failed, he would keep attacking. Everybody praises this aggression when it comes off. When it doesn't, everybody asks what he was thinking.

The simple fact of 14 March 2001 was that two batsmen with peerless technique, ability and concentration were too good for everything Australia could fling at them. By stumps, India was 5/589, leading by 315. The earth was turning in reverse; the sun was rising in the west and setting in the east; the water was going down the plughole anticlockwise; the wind was being carried by the dust. Magic was afoot.

All this on a day when there was not a player, official or press-man who did not think he would be boarding a flight to Chennai by nightfall.

And on the fifth day, Ganguly pulled a Clive Lloyd. The great West Indian captain was famous for batting too long before declaring. For years Lloyd was criticised for leaving his bowlers only two and a half sessions on the last day to take ten wickets. After he'd been doing it for a while, and winning every time, his over-caution was perceived to be a masterstroke of aggression. The extra time in the field addled the minds of the batsmen, the shorter time in the middle shook their determination, and somehow less became more, five hours being ample when six or seven might have been too little.

So Ganguly let Dravid and Laxman bat on. Showing his full talent for perversity, the Indian captain did a Lloyd and a half: even when Laxman fell for 281 and Dravid for 180 – the stand being worth 376 in 104 overs – he allowed the tail-enders to have a merry old time at the Australians' expense, with seventy-eight runs being reaped from thirteen overs in the morning. The secret to getting Dravid and Laxman was: there was no secret. Laxman slashed

ABOVE: Very Very Special: Laxman, with Dravid, enjoying another milestone.

a loose, wide ball to gully and was caught. Dravid was run out. They dismissed themselves. There was nothing Australia could do about them.

By this stage the Australians didn't know what Ganguly was up to. He let the score rumble on to 657, a lead of 384. When he declared Australia only had to face twelve overs before lunch, then two sessions, on a perfect wicket.

Or perfect-looking. To Australian eyes in India, truth always lay somewhere beneath the surface and nothing was as it seemed. On the last day of a cricket Test, truth lies inside the mind. Waugh told his men not to think about the end of the run but to fight this match out to a draw, placing as high a value on it as on any other Test match. 'But deep down,' Gilchrist said, 'there was disappointment already, a feeling that a draw was as bad as a loss.'

Hayden, Slater and Langer batted much as they had in the first innings, enjoying the hard new ball coming onto the bat and putting away the Indian seamers. As in the first innings, they failed to convert their starts into innings that would have a bearing on the match. They were more culpable than the middle-order, in that they had a chance to get set while the batting was at its easiest. Once set, by getting out they exposed their teammates.

Slater went first, for 43 to follow his 42, giving Harbhajan the wicket that put his tail in the air. Then Langer spanked 28 runs in sixteen minutes, Hayden contributing four to the partnership, before the West Australian gave a close-in catch off Harbhajan. Three hours still remained. Mark Waugh came and went, trapped by Raju's arm ball, but Steve Waugh and Hayden settled things until tea. Australia went in at 3/161 and relatively safe.

Or relatively safe-looking. Three overs after tea, Hayden watched aghast from the non-striker's end as it all fell apart. Harbhajan had Waugh and Ponting caught in the same over. The next over would be bowled by Tendulkar. Reassuringly for Australia, Gilchrist was coming in. Yet all he could think of was the golden duck he had made in the first innings. 'Don't sweep, don't sweep, don't sweep,' he urged himself. Tendulkar rifled in a faster leg-break … and Gilchrist swept. He missed it, and this time he was plumb. Two balls in the match, two lbws. He had never known anything but victory in the fifteen Test matches he had played; this was not only defeat but debacle. A king pair.

Disorder turned to mayhem in Tendulkar's next over, when he trapped Hayden for 67 – a good innings, but not good enough. When Tendulkar got Warne in his next, five wickets had fallen in thirty-one balls in less than half an hour after tea. Who said cricket was a slow game? The Australians were being chased out of town. The noise in the batsmen's ears was so loud that Langer compared it to having headphones on, turned up to maximum. Knowing they were not going to win, they did not know how to change direction and play for a draw. Sometimes a boring draw is the best result; yet it was anathema to the way Waugh and Buchanan had been leading them, and again, this time with the bat, they had no Plan B. Kasprowicz and Gillespie attempted a miracle of Kline–Meckiff proportions, hanging around for nine overs, and then when Gillespie was out McGrath held out for another nine, but when the last wicket fell India had ten overs and 171 runs to spare. Ganguly's declaration, which had set off a pounding of keyboards condemning his conservatism and lack of adventure, four hours and a lifetime ago, had not even cut things fine.

This was the greatest win in India's sixty-year Test cricket history, no doubt about it. Laxman, in passing Sunil Gavaskar's 236, had made the highest score by an Indian. Harbhajan had taken his country's first hat-trick, and his thirteen wickets were the best by an Indian against Australia. But those achievements would have faded if they had come in the cause of defeat. India was only the third team in history to win a Test after following-on, Waugh joining an ignominious club of Kim Hughes and bearded Jack Blackham, whose Australians had been caught on a sticky Sydney wicket in 1894–95. To stop the Australian juggernaut after eighteen months was one thing; to do it in such circumstances, coming from the impossibility of day three, was the type of reversal that happens once in a blue moon.

For all the records that had toppled in Kolkata, there was no time to fully digest what had happened. The deciding Test match, in Chennai, started seventy-two hours later. The Australians would say it felt like a continuation of the one match, the one nightmare, their dreams turning to dust.

Morale fractured. They were already peeved after being told to rush from Eden Gardens to Kolkata airport to pick up a flight to Chennai, only to find that the Indians, who were meant to be sharing the flight with them, were still partying at the ground. The Australians sat in the cabin and stewed. Then, in Chennai, Buchanan gave a misjudged press conference in which he said Warne was 'overwrought' after his ineffective toil in Kolkata. Warne lost his temper with the coach, and told the media that the team had been winning in spite, not because, of Buchanan's 'robotic' methods and 'school teacher' manner. Steve Waugh told the press that Buchanan should have kept his implied criticism in-house, about as close as Waugh ever got to publicly flogging his own coach.

Once the Chennai match started, both teams were still regaining their breath from Kolkata. Hayden was again a tower, making 203 with support from the Waughs. Australia looked like making 500 until Steve Waugh swept at Harbhajan. As the fielders and bowler appealed, the ball popped in the air and Hayden called out to Waugh: 'Look out!' Reflexively, Waugh punched the ball away from his stumps. He was out handled ball, the sixth in history, but more importantly his dismissal exposed fresh out-of-form batsmen and the tail. Sure enough, Ponting and Gilchrist failed again and the last seven wickets tumbled out like the contents of a giardia sufferer's bowels for fifty-one. Australia's overnight 3/326 had fizzled to 391.

This time India's batsmen massed together in their first innings, Tendulkar's 126 leading a reply of 501. Australia's top order all made starts in the second innings but Mark Waugh's 57 was the highest score. Ponting's 11 left him with 17 runs in five miserable digs for the series, to go with the 105 at 21 he had scored in 1998. Gilchrist, promoted to number three to shake him out of his Kolkata funk, now had a most unusual run of scores: 122, 0, 0, 1 and 1. Harbhajan added 8/84 to his first innings 7/133, taking his series tally to thirty-two of the fifty Australian wickets to fall. The next best Indian bowler took three.

But there was a last twist or two; this was a classic series, with another classic finish. While the name Kolkata will contain the deepest memories of 2001, Chennai was just as dramatic. Defending a lead of 154, Australia showed their amazing resilience. McGrath, Gillespie and a recalled Miller worked their way through the Indian batting; only Laxman, with 66, prospered. Just before tea, Dravid scooped a drive to mid-off and India went to the break at 5/132, with 23 to win and five wickets in hand. When Mark Waugh caught Laxman acrobatically off Miller, India had collapsed from 2/101 to 7/135 and suddenly looked like the team that would crumble in the end-game. Self-belief was pinging backwards and forwards like a tennis ball; neither team seemed to possess it at the same time. Now Australia were the ones with the buzz. But Waugh's options were limited. Warne was surprisingly ineffective, bowling six overs for 0/41, and Zaheer Khan hung around while the replacement wicketkeeper Samir Dighe hit a few fours and took the score to within a shot of victory. Then McGrath winkled Zaheer out. The stage was left, in the end, for the man of the series: Harbhajan's last shot, angling McGrath through point, concluded the matter, and India had a two-wicket win.

For such ruthless sportsmen, the Australians' reflections on the series showed how the greatness of the game can transcend the competitive drive. Each of the senior men would comment on a certain pride in having been a witness to history. Defeat can be glorious. Steve Waugh would say he felt much prouder, and more fulfilled as a cricketer, for having played in the lost series in India compared with the empty feelings that followed the barely competitive 5-0 win over the West Indies a few weeks earlier. We will always think of this Australian team as one that would win at all costs; but in this case that wasn't true. They loved the game itself enough to know greatness when they saw it.

'Every match in the series was a great Test match to watch regardless of the result,' said Mark Waugh, 'so we went away with that thought. Although we'd lost, we contributed to a very special series, and that's what Test cricket needed at that time after all the match-fixing dramas.' He, of all people, would know.

A MAN OF INFLUENCE

The Oval, London, August 2001

TEAMS OF THE PAST, AT 2-0 UP, MIGHT HAVE BEEN PLAYING GOLF AND CHASING BARMAIDS. BUT WAUGH'S TEAM HAD TURNED INTO SOME KIND OF TRAVELLING SELF-IMPROVEMENT SESSION. WINNING WAS NO LONGER ENOUGH.

The losses at Kolkata and Chennai, coming in a manner that was both unforeseeable and unrepeatable, could have crushed Steve Waugh's team. They had been one session, then one wicket, away from their grail, only to see it whisked away. The period of Australian ascendancy had lasted for a solid six years; Kolkata and Chennai 2001 might have been their Operation Barbarossa, their failed final conquest.

Instead, defeat had a remarkably galvanic effect. After that 2001 contest, Australia didn't lose a series for four years. They would enter a period of dominance so total it sometimes became boring. They would achieve generational renewal. And they would win in India.

The rally started in the week after the Chennai Test. Another nondescript five-match one-day series loomed. Australia's 3-2 victory was, Steve Waugh said, up with the best limited-overs achievements in his entire career. It 'rates just about top of the pile for me', said a man who had won two World Cups. The logical result of the Test losses would have been a dispirited, exhausted team who just wanted to get home. Instead, they played sparky and pugnacious one-day cricket to beat

ENGLAND HAD **A** BETTER TEAM NOW; SURELY AUSTRALIA WAS THERE FOR THE TAKING

India, with Ponting and Gilchrist rediscovering their form and Hayden maintaining his; far from being spent before their arrival in England for a full Ashes tour, they were finding new reserves of enthusiasm.

Until then, the English might have been licking their chops. What better preparation for them than to see Australia have their heart ripped out in the Kolkata sun? Such a run-in to the Ashes had nearly worked for England in 1997, when Australia brought the wounds from an emotional and sometimes nasty ten weeks in South Africa and lost nearly every game they played until the middle of their tour. England had a better team now; surely Australia was there for the taking.

But Australia parcelled up the Ashes in eleven days of cricket. The Indian tour had hardened them up, putting them in the mood, excising the last vestiges of weakness from their collective and individual make-up.

On their way to England, the Australians stopped at Gallipoli. They toured the sites, laid wreaths, listened to a lecture, re-enacted the 1915 diggers' cricket game at Shell Green, and took a bollocking in the press for wearing army slouch hats. No desecration was intended. Buchanan wore his father's war medals and players asked each other if they had a forebear who had fought there. Few knew one way or the other. From the outside, there was a lot that seemed a bit Open University about Buchanan's and Waugh's scholastics, but it had to be taken in context, and while their intellectual exertions – getting the team to read books such as *Tuesdays with Morrie* and *Who Moved My Cheese?* – might not have stood up to full peer review, it was genuinely meant and a big improvement on what had taken place in the past. Australian cricket teams' sacred sites had always been the changing room after a win, their holy relic the empty beer can, their hymn the drunken rendition of 'Underneath the Southern Cross I Stand'. Rod Marsh, he of the forty-five-can London flights, said he didn't need to eat if he'd had his 'ten malt sandwiches'. Steve Waugh wouldn't hold with it, asserting: 'To me, "bonding" is an overrated term normally linked to reminiscing about past escapades with a truckload of grog on board. I've had my fair share of these nights, and while they can create a few laughs and a better understanding of each other, the experience is shallow and soon forgotten. True bonding experiences stand the test of time and become part of you and, most certainly, visiting Gallipoli together … had a profound effect on most of the squad.'

With an adult sensibility in charge after 124 years, Australia began the tour by thrashing England and Pakistan in a triangular one-day series. From the start, England's only lead was in the sick bay: while Brett Lee was back and bowling fast, Nasser Hussain and Graham Thorpe were being treated by the doctors. Old Trafford staged a day/night match, a first in England, and the night owl Gillespie felt right at home, blitzing the hosts on a rain-freshened wicket. Waugh set Test-like fielding positions and England rolled over for 86. When Australia had qualified for the final against Pakistan, the English paid them the courtesy of a centre-wicket practice session at The Oval. Australia bowled them out for 176 and only needed thirty overs to pass them. England were relegated to the status of whipping boys in semi-opposed practice sessions, and were not very good at that either. In the whole series the only blow Australia suffered, as the ABC's Jim Maxwell reported, was a beer can hitting Michael Bevan at the presentation after the final.

For the Tests, Australia spiced up the batting order. Langer seemed to have cemented the number three position before India. But now he was pincered between his failure to capitalise on good starts against a hard ball in India and the growing recognition that Ponting was the champion Australian batsman of the future. Ponting's poor figures in the Indian Tests, a result of his losing his faith in his technique, had been buried under an avalanche of one-day runs. It was tough on Langer, but sometimes, as News Limited's Robert Craddock would say, 'The selectors just have to forget the numbers and look at the two guys and ask, which one's a better player?' When this fundamental question happened to be the one the selectors were asking, Ponting had a history of receiving the nod.

Down the order, Damien Martyn's one-day batting paved his road back from purgatory. Again, the selectors recognised that he was too good not to be playing Test cricket. He had done well when called in as a replacement since 1999, and he oozed class in the one-dayers. It was impossible to conceive of Martyn not succeeding in Tests. Compact, steady, blessed with that extra moment of time, he had added the supposedly missing determination to his character during his wilderness years.

So the order was: Hayden, Slater, Ponting, Mark Waugh, Steve Waugh, Martyn. An Australian captain never wrote a more talented top six on his team sheet. Add Gilchrist at seven, and then Warne, a fully fit Lee and Gillespie, and McGrath, throw in the relief and joy of English turf, English hospitality and English opposition, and no more explanations for an eleven-day Ashes contest are entirely necessary.

At Edgbaston, Martyn recorded his maiden Test century in his twelfth appearance, eight years after his debut. He would average 76 in the series. Gilchrist and Steve Waugh also made hundreds in the First Test, Gilchrist contributing 59 out of a 63-run last-wicket shindig with McGrath, and Gillespie broke one of England captain Hussain's infamous poppadum fingers. Australia won by an innings and 118, then followed up with a brisk, routine-seeming victory by eight wickets at Lord's, where the egg-and-bacon mob, not to mention Australian cricket traditionalists of an altogether different stripe, were scandalised by Waugh's request to invite wives and children into the winners' changing room. 'A happy family man,' Waugh said, 'was a more contented player who could focus better on his game.' Not to mention a better husband and father, perhaps. And brother? Mark Waugh, who was to enjoy a vintage Ashes series, passed Taylor's world record of 157 catches at Lord's too.

In the build-up to the Third Test at Trent Bridge, Buchanan slipped his pre-match motivational notes under the wrong door, and the world learned that his chief advisor on field placings was Sun Tzu, who emphasised, among other lessons, that a leader must be able to understand 'unfathomable plans'. As the word spread of Buchanan's interpretations of 'Ground of Intersecting Highways' and so on, the grounds for cringing on his behalf were too diverse to detail, but perhaps the captain put it best when he said that the sole weakness in Buchanan's approach was that it required listeners who were able to make head or tail of what he was on about.

But it showed that the Australians were still thinking, still making an effort to extend themselves. Teams of the past, at 2-0 up, might have been playing golf and chasing barmaids. But Waugh's team had turned into some kind of travelling self-improvement session. Winning was no longer enough.

Waugh tore his left calf in the Ashes-deciding win at Nottingham, Australia squeaking home in a low-scoring affair. England had tried the Trinidad '95–Old Trafford '97 trick, of underpreparing a wicket and making the game a lottery, but Australia made it through and Waugh heard the news that he was an Ashes-winning captain from his wheelchair in hospital.

England enjoyed their customary dead-cat bounce earlier than usual, at Headingley, where Gilchrist received some criticism after setting them 315 to win in a day and a bit. Nothing in England's recent history suggested they could do it, but Mark Butcher had the day of his life and no Australian begrudged him. The Australians' anxiety about losing dead rubbers had clearly become a kind of phobia, so Waugh rose from his sick bed to take the field for the last Test at The Kennington Oval.

Form-wise, the only Australian who had not made hay in the shining English sun was Slater. Like Langer, he had been able to enjoy the best of the batting conditions in India yet was unable to convert his starts into the kind of contributions Hayden had made. If Slater and Langer had turned their thirties and forties into hundreds, Australia might have won 3-0. Instead they got out just when the conditions were turning nasty on the middle-order. Langer had been punished with omission at the start of the Ashes tour and advised by Waugh to think about opening. Slater had kept his place, due to large deposits made in the previous two years, but through England he was steadily running down his balance. In the first four Tests he made 170 runs at 24. His personal life, moreover, was, in his words, 'in free fall', with the trouble in his marriage, which was public knowledge, and the encroachment of his bipolar disorder, which was not. As a Test-only player, he felt alienated from the one-day squad who had been to Gallipoli. Like Langer, he had offered to buy his own ticket, but the ACB refused. Then, Slater had embarrassed himself by joining Ponting and Mark Waugh on a trip to a London tattooist to have their Test numbers permanently marked. Slater compounded the dumbness by getting the wrong number. He and Brendon Julian had made their debuts in the same Test at Old Trafford in 1993, but Slater thought mistakenly that batting, not alphabetical, order determined the number. Oops. Or rather, ouch.

On the afternoon of the first day of the series, Slater had played the last of his great Test knocks. England had collapsed to 9/191, but Alec Stewart and Andrew Caddick contrived a 103-run stand for the last wicket. With little more than an hour to play, Slater went out and crashed the first ball, from Darren Gough, for four, took seventeen off the opening over, and cracked 76 not out off seventy-eight balls. He was out early the next day, but by the end of the tour Steve Waugh would acknowledge that innings as being comparable to the famous 66 Allan Border scored in the First Test of the 1989 series: a tone-setter, an opening statement. 'But by the time he said that,' Slater would recall, 'I was already out of the team.'

The subtext to all this was Waugh's intensifying concern about Slater's state of mind. During the Headingley Test, Slater went off the deep end at his stand-in captain Gilchrist, who had mildly berated him for being late to practice. 'Don't ever forget where you came from,' Slater snarled. To turn on Gilchrist, with whom he had played since junior days, was an inflammation caused by the more worrying tension in his relationship with Waugh. Never natural friends, the pair had grown increasingly uneasy with each other since India. Waugh was not one to look kindly on such temptations of fate as Slater's cigar-sniffing display in Kolkata. Waugh was not one to look kindly on any over-enthusiasm, a quality which

THE PAIR HAD GROWN INCREASINGLY UNEASY WITH EACH OTHER

he had utterly stamped out of himself. When Slater had been questioned by officials about his supposed drug habit and Tasmanian child, he suspected that information about his mental health had come from 'in-house', and the number one suspect was his own captain. The more uncomfortable Slater felt in Waugh's company, the more he idealised past leaders such as Taylor and Healy. This in itself only stoked the new captain's fires.

The last straw was Headingley, where on the first morning Slater batted like a tourist attempting a Fijian fire walk. The minutes before his innings were just as chaotic. In the changing room, he had been unable to find his helmet. Borrowing another, he had cut his finger on the grille, and Ponting had had to pad up in case Slater achieved the singular distinction of being retired hurt before stepping onto the field. Or timed out. He put himself together but then put himself in all sorts of contortions across the crease; his batting had throughout his career been a 3-D depiction of his mental state, and judging by the way he hopped about at Headingley he was not travelling well.

Before The Oval Test, Waugh and Gilchrist, intimate with Slater's late nights and foul moods on tour, talked over the phone to Hohns in Australia, eventually overruling the chairman's reservations and electing to drop Slater. Waugh invited Slater to his hotel room and composed himself to inform his seventy-four-Test teammate that, as in 1996, he was being left out for his own good. Trying to soften the blow, Waugh explained that there were disciplinary and health issues involved, and that Slater should get some professional help for his personal problems. It was a new-age, holistic, become-a-better-person approach to dropping a player. Slater's response rocketed straight out of the old days: 'You can all go and get fucked!'

(Slater's recollection was somewhat different. He wrote that he left the room with the words: 'Well, stay on your high horse and continue to play God.' What actually came out of his mouth, and what Waugh heard, might have met in the middle.)

During training at The Oval, Waugh was trying to explain the situation to the team when Slater again cut him off, shouting expletives before storming out of an Australian playing squad for the last time.

(Slater, in fairness, remembered this differently too. He said that when he asked Waugh to explain to the team why he had dropped him, Gilchrist interjected and told him it was inappropriate to discuss the issue while the team was trying to focus on its Test preparation. Slater, in tears, tried to join the practice session but was unable, and 'stormed away from training' despite Hayden's pleas to stay. Shane Warne consoled him with a cigarette before Slater returned, alone, to the team hotel.)

The episode left lasting regrets. Slater never played for Australia again and took years to come to terms with his bitterness. Waugh, for his part, had more confirmation that dropping his mates was the ugliest part of his job. A year later, with some relief, he would give up his role as a tour selector. Not much was too hard for Steve Waugh, but this got the better of him.

The match at The Oval, then, meant significantly more than a dead rubber at the end of a 3-1 series. It brought together Hayden and Langer as openers. They added 158 in forty-two overs, and from then on only retirement would part them. Thus was born a love that perhaps too often spoke its name. Indeed, the Langer–Hayden bond could have been Australian cricket's first open bromance. Their partnership, which embodied the sensibilities of the Waugh era, brought together two battlers who had been dropped from Australian teams a cumulative seven times, yet yielded more runs than any that came before them. They can stake a claim to being known as Australia's greatest opening partnership. Waugh was in the business of match-making, and by jettisoning Slater to pair Langer with Hayden, he had contrived a union that ended happily ever after.

Australia's win at The Oval would also seal an Ashes series in a way that had eluded previous tourists: with a victory. Australia won the dead rubber and were able to accept their crystal 'Ashes replica' trophy while in a winning mood. They only needed six batsmen, amassing 4/641 before bowling England out for 432 and 184, Warne – I'm still here, everyone! – capturing eleven wickets. As in 1997 and 1999, he made noises about this being his last tour to England with an Australian team. He had taken thirty-one in the series, just behind McGrath's thirty-two. Gillespie took nineteen and Lee nine. Astonishingly, Australia had completed a full Ashes series with only the four bowlers. England, contrastingly, had tried almost a full XI of bowlers. Caddick and Gough played all five Tests, but were supported by a moveable feast of one-Test ideas: Robert Croft, Dominic Cork, James Osmond, Alan Mullally, Ashley Giles and Phil Tufnell. Alex Tudor played two Tests, and Craig White was a veritable stalwart with three. Batsmen Ian Ward and Usman Afzaal were other names whose careers began and ended, more or less instantly, against Australia.

England was denied the customary south London consolation in large part due to Waugh's unbeaten twenty-seventh Test century. This was a titanic, if ultimately self-harming, effort. He batted in constant fear of re-tearing his calf. On 30, he tweaked a different leg muscle and also strained his buttock. On 99, he bolted through the pain and dived into the crease for his hundredth run, raising his bat while lying in the dust. And then, because Waugh was Waugh, he decided against slogging and kept batting properly, limping to another fifty-seven runs. And they still couldn't get him out.

Mark Waugh also made a century at The Oval in 2001, a fine 120 played in his twin's shadow. What's new? It would be his last Test innings in England, too.

Steve's innings was awe-inspiring and probably rather injudicious at the same time. The injury would complicate itself with the effects of deep vein thrombosis during the flight home, and immobility would metastasise into self-doubt. His Oval century was an apotheosis: a highest peak and the beginning of the end. His runs in that innings came perhaps too easily, against an opponent too easily beaten. Since 1993, he had been determined, almost perversely, to stop anything from coming to him easily. Crisis had been his mantra. As the Australian team flourished over the next two seasons, it would do so almost in spite of his individual qualities as a batsman. By creating a team that scaled heights unthinkable even in Taylor's time, Waugh would effectively make his job, as middle-order salvage artist, redundant. Although he would score another five Test centuries after The Oval, he would never be quite the same player again.

ABOVE: This time it's permanent: Langer, a hundred at The Oval.

WARNE'S WORLD
Cape Town, March 2002

WHEN GILCHRIST WENT OUT TO BAT, LATE ON THE FIRST DAY, HE WAS BLINDED BY TEARS. HIS PARTNER, MARTYN, ASKED HIM IF HE WAS ALL RIGHT, BUT GILCHRIST WAS BATTING IN A STATE OF 'PURE ANGER'.

In Eddie Perfect's 2009 rendition of Shane Warne's life as a stage musical, there is a touching early number where the young football-playing slob discovers, and is transformed by, the hypnotic qualities of the leg break. Of all Warne's foibles and addictions, the leg-break was his constant friend, the loyal companion that would not let him down or be condemned as a bad habit. Warne's many personal indulgences led him into mendacity and compromise, but not the leg-break. The only people he deceived with his leg-break were the world's batsmen.

His consistency and endurance, year after year, would eventually shed the off-field soap opera from his reputation like a dead skin. When all was said and done, none of that mattered as much as his 708 Test wickets. No scandal affected his leg-break. As Louis Nowra wrote in his book *Warne's World*, 'when Warne is playing cricket, incidents off the field vanish into a cosily hazy distance. He has the optimistic disposition of an entrepreneur like Alan Bond, whose wife was amazed that even in times of great financial crisis he would sleep like a baby and wake up, as Warne says he does, "with a smile on his dial".'

The scandals were today's news, tomorrow's fish and chips

NO WARNE, NO GOLDEN AGE FOR AUSTRALIAN CRICKET. IT IS THAT SIMPLE.

wrapper. The prattishness, the petulance, the stupidity and the naivety made wonderful fodder for journalists and singer-songwriters, but the bowling was for the ages. The growth of his popularity and mellowing of the public's view of him once he had retired can only owe to this fact. His legacy was not that he rejuvenated leg-spin bowling – there is scant evidence of the predicted generations of young Aussie kids rolling the ball out of the backs of their hands. Leg-spin is too hard to bowl, and requires too much faith from captains and selectors, too much bluff and nous and subtlety and perseverance, to be picked up and copied at will. Warne could not be imitated. But his legacy was even greater than that: he rejuvenated the game of cricket itself. His gifts with the ball and his contribution to the game's entertainment value are what will be remembered. Nobody could take his record of achievement away from him; the puzzle, with Warne, was why he so often acted as if frightened that somebody could.

No Warne, no golden age for Australian cricket. It is that simple. His career span correlates with Australia's era of greatness. No Warne, no defeating the West Indies at Melbourne in 1992, no thumping Ashes campaigns, no demoralisation

LEFT: Grip and rip: A hundred Tests in, Warne still had the technique.

of South Africa and Pakistan, no Edgbaston 1999. In a different and more Shakespearean way, if there was no Warne, there would be none of the dramatic rivalry that gave Murali's rise such texture. No Warne, no operatic duels with Malik, Cronje, Cullinan, Stewart, Lara, Tendulkar, Laxman and Pietersen. No Warne, less colour. As feted as were the efforts of the Waughs, Taylor, Healy, Gilchrist, Ponting, Hayden, Martyn, Langer and others, each was, to a greater or lesser degree, dispensable. Not Warne. Only McGrath was as essential as Warne.

He turned his hundredth Test, against South Africa at Cape Town in 2002, into an all-round showcase: his bowling, his batting and his first-slipping. Every now and then a universal public fondness would well up for Warne, where all was forgiven and glossed over under the radiant light of his talent. This was one of those times.

The Test came at the tail of a five-match winning streak against South Africa. None was a close result. In Australia, the Proteas were beaten by 264 runs in Adelaide, nine wickets in Melbourne and ten wickets in Sydney. This was no soft transitional South African team: it boasted Kallis, Kirsten, Donald and Boucher under Pollock's captaincy. But Australia had its A team of the decade, with multiple centuries raining down from Hayden, Langer and Martyn and swags of wickets from McGrath, Warne, Lee and Gillespie. The Hayden–Langer partnerships at home were 80, 8, 202, 7 and 219 before an unbeaten 54 to cap off the series. Collectively they had turned the confrontation with their toughest rivals into a bit of a yawn.

The one-day series went in the opposite direction, with Australia's failure to make the finals resulting in the omission of Steve and, a few weeks later, Mark Waugh. In an echo of the Taylor–Healy one-day sackings of 1997, Steve had lost form and was no longer one of the best eleven one-day players and deserved to lose his place. Mark, meanwhile, was a victim of forward planning. Looking to the 2003 World Cup, to be played in South Africa, the selectors were obviously wanting to groom a younger team under new captain Ponting. Still, there was no missing the historical significance: a Waugh-less Australian one-day team would take the field for the first time since 1986.

The Australian Test team marched into Johannesburg in belligerent form. Always seeking the vital chip on the shoulder, they found it in a quirk of the ICC world 'rankings' system promising that if South Africa managed to draw the series, they would take the world championship away from Australia. At the Australian team's pre-Test meeting, the theme was 'let's embarrass them on their home turf'. Waugh told them, 'We know we are the best, the South Africans know it, and that's all that counts.'

Two days later, South Africa's new captain Boucher, standing in for the injured Pollock, inserted Australia on a damp Wanderers track. Hayden reduced a strong bowling line-up – Donald, Ntini, Andre Nel, Kallis, Boje – to rubble, becoming the fourth Australian to score centuries in four straight Tests. His driving on the up, walking into the ball and dispatching good-length deliveries to the off-side fence, prompted his captain to rank him alongside Tendulkar. Then, coming in at 5/293, Gilchrist produced the latest out of his cabinet of astonishments.

The background to Gilchrist's innings has to be considered, as it contributed both to his attitude in the middle and his emotional collapse at the end. In Potchefstroom, where Australia was playing its warm-up game a week before the First Test, Gilchrist received a message from his manager, Stephen Atkinson, alerting him to an email that was circulating around the cricket world. The email alleged that Michael Slater was the father of Gilchrist's two-month-old son Harry. Gilchrist laughed it off at first, then stewed on it. 'As I re-read it,' he recalled, 'my eyes dimming over, I got a sick feeling in my stomach.' The email, which had originated from a cricket website in the United Kingdom, defamed Slater and Melinda Gilchrist as well as humiliating Adam Gilchrist. It was also patently false, inventing speculative links between Slater's falling-out with Gilchrist in England to other events in Slater's private life before and after his sacking from the Australian team. Gilchrist had also left the Australian camp during the summer one-day series to attend to a serious health problem the newborn Harry was suffering. That too was somehow cast in a sinister light.

The rumour was untrue, and Slater and the Gilchrists all later sued the site and received damages. But the falsity of the rumour did not quell Gilchrist's immediate pain. He entered the First Test 'dizzy with fatigue and the whole cocktail of emotions'. Nor did the falsity of the allegation stop some South African fans from pouncing on it. During the match, there were offensive signs on display taunting Gilchrist. He tried to ignore them, but couldn't ignore the awkwardness among his teammates. Finally, the bench man Andrew Bichel stormed out of the changing room and ordered security guards to take the signs down.

When Gilchrist went out to bat, late on the first day, he was blinded by tears. As he walked down the race onto the ground, some of the crowd 'were giving me a spray about it, and I walked onto the field thinking, It's not just two guys with a banner: everyone in South Africa knows about it'. His first shot, off Kallis, was an ungainly attempted pull-turned-into-cut-shot that ended up popping back down the wicket. His partner, Martyn, asked him if he was all right, but Gilchrist was batting in a state of 'pure anger'. Sections of the crowd were chanting, 'Slater, Slater'. Gilchrist was lucky to survive to stumps on 25. When Martyn stopped on the way up the race to confront some spectators, they showered him with beer. Gilchrist fled to a cubicle inside the changing room and 'totally broke down, bursting into tears'.

That evening, a still-distraught Gilchrist dined with two of his more emotionally attuned colleagues, Langer and MacGill. They gave him reassurance, and Langer left a fortifying note under his door later in the night. 'You know the truth, my friend. Be strong, have courage and enjoy today. If nothing else, today is just one day closer to seeing and cuddling and kissing and loving YOUR champion little son … PS It's not every day you have a chance to score a Test hundred.'

On the second morning, Waugh hoped to add another hundred runs. Gilchrist and Martyn had other ideas. It helped that Donald had buckled with a career-ending injury the previous afternoon. Gilchrist started circumspectly, but then a pulled four off Nel set pulses beating. When Kallis dropped him low at second slip off Nel in the ninth over, Gilchrist was 35 not out off sixty-four balls. He reached his fifty on his eighty-ninth ball, then went on a kind of controlled rampage, taking another thirty-two balls to reach his hundred just before lunch. He stumbled to the side of the pitch, his knees turning to water. 'This was the first time,' he wrote, 'I cried on a cricket field.'

After the break, riding a downhill wave after the struggle of the previous twenty-four hours, he collected himself while Martyn took over the running, notching his fourth Test century of the summer. Then Gilchrist erupted, taking twenty off Neil McKenzie's seventh over of spin and moving from 150 to 200 in thirty balls. With his unorthodox high grip, he was able to release the bat in an arc through the ball that drew comparisons with big-hitting golfers like John Daly and Tiger Woods; there is a photo of him driving Nel during that innings where his bat is moving so fast that his hands are virtually losing contact with the grip. In passing the double-century mark, the first Australian wicketkeeper to do so, he eclipsed Ian Botham's world record for the fastest 200 in Tests, a 212-ball onslaught. (New Zealand's Nathan Astle broke it two weeks later in a blur of 153 balls. Botham said to Gilchrist, 'After 20 years you broke my record, and you've held it for 20 days.')

'AUSTRALIA,' CONCLUDED BOUCHER, 'ARE A BETTER SIDE THAN US'

Martyn was out for 133. The partnership between the long-standing friends, which had started with one asking the other if he was capable of batting, had realised 317 runs, 190 of them coming in a memorable session between lunch and tea. Waugh, who likened the spectacle to 'four hours of non-stop highlights', declared at 7/652, and South Africa batted as if on death row. Kirsten nicked McGrath's second ball and the Proteas lasted a combined eighty-six overs in two miserable innings, losing the match by their worst-ever margin, an innings and 360 runs. 'Australia,' concluded Boucher, 'are a better side than us.'

Warne took six wickets at Johannesburg, his ninety-ninth Test, moving past Kapil Dev's 434 wickets to stand behind only Walsh's 519. He had made one of his periodical efforts to lose weight, dropping eight kilograms, he said, by giving up 'pizzas, beers, vanilla slices, chips and potato chips' in favour of 'cereal, baked beans and water'. The only thing that was not exaggerated about him was his talent, which mesmerised the South African batsmen. In the second innings he took the second, third, fifth and sixth wickets, the heart of the home batting, and was controlling the ball as well as he had on the same ground five years earlier. The Australians injected some symbolic defiance into their celebrations: they sang their team song at the point in the race where Martyn and also Steve Waugh had been abused by the crowd, and set on fire their complimentary tickets for the redundant days four and five. Waugh called it 'the perfect Test; no team could have touched us … The intent and purpose that we displayed in the field had been predatory and remorseless, so intense and concentrated, that it was reminiscent of the great Windies team of the early 1980s.'

Five years earlier, after a similar defeat at the Wanderers, South Africa had bounced back to all but beat Australia in the Second Test. This time they tried to recall Cullinan to replace the diffi-dent Boeta Dippenaar, but Darryl didn't want to play because he wasn't being offered enough money. Instead, then, they brought in an opinionated left-handed debutant called Graeme Smith, as well as the combative Andrew Hall and Paul Adams, signal-ling that South Africa would at the very least make some noise if they were to go down again. Off the field they showed an unusual pugnacity, having the Australians ejected from the coincidentally named Cullinan Hotel in Cape Town, saying they did not want to be in the same hotel as their guests.

On the first day at Newlands, at the foot of Table Mountain, the Australian speedsters maintained their dominance. South Africa were 6/92 before the street-fighter Hall, with a defiant 70, lifted them to 239.

Australia was in no mood to take the foot off the opponent's throat. The top three took the score to 2/162 and it was looking like a Johannesburg encore before a collapse in which Ponting, the Waughs and Martyn fell in the space of twenty-three runs. For the first time in five Tests, a real contest was on. Gilchrist and Warne came together in the forty-eighth over, with four wickets in hand and fifty-four runs in deficit.

ABOVE: Gilchrist, that series in South Africa, was rated the world's best batsman.

Warne was a prouder traditionalist than his fashion sense might have indicated. He was deeply honoured by passing one hundred Tests. He had brought his family to Cape Town to watch him, and in the first innings he had toiled away on a green wicket for 2/70. He always fancied himself as a batsman, harking back to his junior days as a batting-footballing all-rounder. He was having one of his better summers, having so far scored 298 runs at 33.1 Now he had a chance to contribute more than some late-innings hit-and-hope.

He found Gilchrist in full flow. Something had been unlatched by that dank late first afternoon in Johannesburg. Like Warne, if for different reasons, Gilchrist had flown his family to Cape Town. So often, when the stronger emotions rule, batsmen fail. Not with Gilchrist, who had the luck and gift of being able to harness intense feelings and pour them into the swing of his bat and the steadiness of his eye.

Warne joined him just before drinks in the middle session on day two. By tea, the pair had hit sixteen fours and one six, plundered eighty runs, and manoeuvred Australia into the lead by twenty-six.

It got better after the break. In six overs they put on another fifty-two runs before Warne was out for 63 off sixty-five balls, in a match-turning partnership of 132 in 138 balls. This was one of Warne's best innings, though for pure comedy none could match the 99 he had scored against New Zealand two months earlier, caught on the boundary trying to bring up his ton in the grand style. 'I'm sure Shane would have swapped 100 wickets for that one extra run,' Steve Waugh reflected after Warne walked off with that How-did-that-happen-well-I'm-in-for-it-now face he often wore, that of the school child who has kicked the football unexpectedly cleanly and sent it crashing through the principal's window.

One of the myths about Warne and Gilchrist was that they disliked each other. They spent too many hours over a nine-year stretch standing side by side in the field and batting together in the tail, enjoying each other's company, for men who didn't get on. There was laughter and playfulness rather than mere toleration. But it is probably fair to say they weren't too keen on the idea of each other, much as the lair at the back of the class and the head prefect can't quite reach mutual approval. Warne was often too self-indulgent and undisciplined for Gilchrist's taste; Gilchrist too clean-cut and conformist for the man he replaced as vice-captain. But this found expression in articles, press conferences and other fora when one was half a world away from the other. The ultimate truth about Gilchrist and Warne was that they each hated confrontation and liked to be liked, so when they were with each other, that day in Cape Town as on any number of days playing in the same team, they got on very well. It was when they were apart that their differences, such as they were, would blow up, as if absence were a distorting amplifier.

Once Warne was out, Gilchrist continued his lark, lofting and lashing another 63 runs off twenty-nine balls to end up unbeaten on 138 off 108 balls. He rated the innings even better than his tear-streaked 204 not out in Johannesburg. Certainly for the team it came at a more useful moment. Australia, from 6/185, had got to 382, a threatened deficit turning into a surplus of 143.

The wicket had flattened out, however, and South Africa finally mustered up some rebellion in the second innings. It took Australia twenty-nine overs to get a wicket, that of Gibbs for 39, but they could turn neither that nor any other into a cascade. Kirsten ground out 87, new boy Smith 68, Kallis 73 and McKenzie 99. South Africa passed Australia with one wicket down and proceeded to make a real Test of it. They got to the end of day three at 4/307, leading by 164. Steve Waugh described the day, under baking heat, as one of the toughest in his career. Salt was rubbed in when the Australian team bus was delayed by half an hour from leaving the ground, while security staff dealt with a death threat.

When Boucher dug in with McKenzie on the fourth morning, South Africa inched to 5/431, the lead nearly 300 and the match edging out of Australia's reach. Shades of Port Elizabeth 1997? Gillespie, heroic there as a fledgling Test cricketer, was now a seasoned hand, the leaping ponytail a distant memory. With Australia growing desperate in the middle session, he fired in an accurate skidder at Boucher and beat the bat, a triumph of persistence. Two overs later, the first cheap wicket in 147 overs fell, McKenzie and Hall getting greedy for an extra run on Brett Lee's throw. Again the bowler was Gillespie.

Drinks were taken with South Africa 7/436 and suddenly shaky. McKenzie was 97, looking for his first Test century against Australia. An introverted cricketer, McKenzie had a two-eyed stance, economical backlift and sweet timing. He had made massive scores in domestic cricket but was hampered by nerves at the top level, at one point so riven with superstitions and tics that he was diagnosed with obsessive-compulsive disorder. He avoided lines on the pitch as if they were electrified, insisted on walking precisely

MARTYN'S THROW, OF COURSE, HIT ALL THREE PEGS

halfway down the wicket to meet his batting partner, and before each ball looked around the field in a set number of directions. The Australians didn't need a psychiatrist to know that they had a customer who might get nervous in the nineties. It didn't help that McKenzie had the perpetual jackrabbit Adams as his batting partner.

In Warne's first over after drinks, McKenzie pushed a single to deep mid-wicket. Lee bowled the next over, McKenzie taking another run off the first ball to move to 99. Adams opened the face and stole a run, getting McKenzie on strike. Although the match was so delicately poised, all attention was on McKenzie and his milestone. Not least McKenzie's own attention. He left Lee's next ball outside off stump. The next was almost a half-volley, which he leaned into and drove through extra cover.

Or not quite through. Martyn, with four centuries in eleven Tests, could walk on water. He flung himself across the turf, cut off McKenzie's drive with his left hand, switched the ball to his right, pivoted on his knees and hurled the ball at the bowler's-end stumps, where McKenzie was closing in on his hundredth run. Martyn's throw, of course, hit all three pegs.

It had to go to the video umpire to confirm what the players knew: McKenzie, run out by 30 centimetres. Ninety-nine. Run out. Poor McKenzie.

South Africa made 473, a lead of 330, right back in the game. They would, in fact, have been deeper in charge if not for Warne, who had bowled seventy overs and taken 6/161. Seventy overs of the eighty-one possible for him to bowl. He came on at the Kelvin Grove end with a shiny new ball in the sixth over of the innings, replacing McGrath, who went wicketless throughout. Warne's first spell went unchanged for sixteen overs, taking Gibbs's wicket and conceding 39 runs. Mark Waugh gave him two overs' relief, and then he came on from the Wynberg end, for a second spell of seven overs with the wind behind him, taking 0/25.

He had a forty-five minute break before resuming into the breeze from the Kelvin Grove end. He bowled ten more overs unchanged, conceding twenty runs and taking the breakthrough wicket of Smith. Gillespie had two overs with the second new ball, and then Warne bowled unchanged again for another eight overs, removing Kallis and conceding fifteen runs. In the day, he had bowled forty-two of a possible forty-five overs, taking 3/100.

Day four, more of the same. He took the first over of the morning and would not relinquish the ball until lunch, adding another wicket, that of Ashwell Prince, in his fourteen overs. He had his baked beans and water and came back after for yet another fourteen-over spell, and another two wickets. He was given a standing ovation. This was something from the early years, when Border flogged him day after day and Warne loved every minute of it.

Now it was up to the batsmen not to let his labours go to waste. In the session before stumps Hayden and Langer put on a rapid 102 before Langer played on for 58. At 1/131 at stumps, Australia needed an even 200 to win. The chase would be only thirty-odd runs fewer than the fourth innings against Pakistan in Hobart two seasons earlier, yet this was a mature team with more belief than hope. Hayden and Ponting hit a four each in Adams's first over of the fifth day, and piled on sixty-six in the first hour. Hayden's aggression should have been rewarded with another century, five in five Tests, but, looking for the boundary to take him to three figures he threw his bat at a wide from Kallis and feathered it to Boucher.

The Waughs fell cheaply either side of lunch, but Ponting wanted fervidly to assert himself as the new keystone of Australia's batting. Through the summer he had been consistent, but consistently overshadowed by Hayden, Langer, Martyn and Gilchrist.

This was his day. Martyn made a duck and Gilchrist 24, his first time out in the series, leaving Australia with twenty-six to win when Warne joined Ponting.

Ponting's day, but Warne's Test: in the seventy-ninth over, delivered by Kallis, South Africa still thought they had a chance. Ponting was 94. Warne went four-four, the latter a spanking cover drive in all likelihood ruining Ponting's chances of making a century. Next ball, Adams generously dragged down a long hop and Ponting hoicked it out of the ground to raise an even hundred, and Australia had won by four wickets. The six-hitting conclusion did have an echo of Port Elizabeth 1997, but this was a thumping Australian victory. Steve Waugh rated it as one of the best Test matches he had played in, and he might have thanked the gods that it was Warne's hundredth. There was no way the leg-spinner, with his instinct for theatre, would have let it pass without making it his own.

When *Wisden*'s poll of one hundred experts had voted Warne the fourth-greatest player of the twentieth century, Greg Baum described the theme of Warne's career, set by the Gatting ball, as 'extraordinary performances, extraordinary production values'. Not even a musical could seem as theatrical as Warne's real life. 'Always,' Baum wrote, 'it was the stage that invigorated him as much as the challenge', contrasting his bowling average of 40 for Victoria in front of empty stands with his exploits in Test cricket. The Gatting ball 'was not just early in his spell, but his very first delivery – in the match, in the series, in Ashes cricket'. There followed a series of orchestral climaxes: his hat-trick on the MCG, his 300th wicket 'accompanied by lightning and apocalyptic thunderclaps'. When *Wisden* took its poll, Warne still had another eight years to play. Now he had done it again, pulling out one of his greatest all-round games, winning the match in his hundredth appearance. As Baum concluded, 'The only caveat on making him one of the cricketers of the 20th century is that he may yet figure in deliberations for the 21st.'

ONE PERFECT DAY

Sydney, January 2003

HIS VISION BLURRY,
NAUSEATED TO THE POINT
WHERE HE THOUGHT
'CARROTS [WOULD] HAVE
A DATE WITH THE DECK',
WAUGH HOPPED AROUND
THE CREASE WITH DELIRIOUS
INSTABILITY, HIS FOOTWORK
REMINISCENT OF SLATER'S
LAST TEST

The big themes never play out in sequence, one after the other. Instead, they overlap. Australia's ascendancy over South Africa in 2001–02 was achieved in the conspicuous absence of large contributions by the Waugh brothers, which might have been very healthy for the team and the selectors' future planning, but not so good for the twins themselves.

Their centuries at The Oval in 2001, as pointed out earlier, signalled the beginning of a long final act. The following summer, against New Zealand in Australia, Mark averaged 35 and Steve 19.5. Against South Africa at home, Mark averaged 32.2 and Steve 35.2. In South Africa, Mark averaged 33.8 and Steve 19. The brothers were notoriously, and sometimes amusingly, prickly when interrogated about their averages, and in their defence batting averages can deceive if taken over a short period of time. But now the period was mounting: nine Tests, and neither brother had made a century. Steve's Test scores since England were 3, 0, 8, 67, 8, 13, 90, 30, 32, 0, 14, 7 and 42. Mark's were a less wrist-slitting 0, 12, 42, 86, 2, 74, 34, 19, 53, 25, 16, 45 and 30. During this period, both were dropped from the one-day team. It might have irked them that they were

HE PLAYED, AS HE HAD PROMISED, UNTIL THEY DROPPED HIM

being asked, in early 2002, if they were going to retire together, but if the numbers tell fibs over a short time, they become more and more truthful over a whole summer.

The sands in Mark's hourglass would run out in the spring of 2002, during a Pakistan series moved for security reasons to Sri Lanka and Sharjah. He scored 80 runs in four innings. A first-baller to Shoaib Akhtar in Colombo was followed by 2 and 23 in the two Tests reconvened to the Middle East, and that, after 128 Test matches and twelve years at the top, 8029 runs, 59 wickets and 181 catches, was that. Mark Waugh played his last Test in an empty inferno in Sharjah in October 2002. He played, as he had promised, until they dropped him. No laps of honour, no emotional farewells. And no greater contrast with his brother. Like the sibling who chooses brown bread even when he doesn't like it, but because his brother has chosen white, Mark Waugh did things differently.

His absence saddened his teammates, none more so than his erstwhile one-day opening partner Gilchrist. 'Being a sentimental bloke,' Gilchrist said, 'I felt the acute pain of the end of that era.' He called Waugh to express his sadness, until Waugh interrupted, 'It's okay, I'm not dying.'

LEFT: Local lap of honour: the retired Mark Waugh received by a bigger crowd than in Sharjah.

Mark Waugh's omission from the 2002–03 Ashes series both relieved and increased the pressure on Steve. Relieved because, with one of the old guard gone, the selectors would not have wanted Steve to go too soon afterwards. Since 1984, Australian selectors had worked with a dread bordering on phobia of several big-name players retiring at once. The exits of Taylor, Healy and the Waughs would be managed so as not to replicate those of Rod Marsh, Greg Chappell and Dennis Lillee. But Mark's demise also increased the pressure on Steve, because his form was even patchier than Mark's, and if Mark didn't deserve a place in the XI, why did Steve?

After two ducks against Pakistan, an unbeaten century in hellish heat in Sharjah bought the captain an extension. Australia won that series 3-0 against a Pakistan side too inexperienced to deal with Warne in any conditions, let alone under a fifty-degree sun. Steve Waugh's century had started with a taunt from Waqar Younis. 'Let's make his last Test finish with a duck,' he called to his men as Waugh was scratching centre. Waugh shot back, 'Not today, buddy.' He completed his hundred with back-to-back sixes, a first in Test cricket. But that was Sharjah. A Test was a Test, but in the eyes of the Australian public and to a lesser degree the selectors, that series had been a virtual non-event.

England arrived in Australia refreshed by some new faces – Michael Vaughan, Matthew Hoggard, Simon Jones, Marcus Trescothick and Ashley Giles – but lumbered with the old leadership. In most of their Ashes losses in Australia they had buggered things up from the first day, almost the first moment. There had been Slater's cracking boundary off DeFreitas's first-ball long-hop in 1994–95, the timid preference for going to the hotel rather than onto the Gabba under floodlights in 1998–99, and there would be Steve Harmison's wild first ball in 2006–07. In 2002–03, Nasser Hussain saw demons in the Gabba wicket and after winning the precious opportunity to bat Australia into a corner on the first day, he instead sent the home team in. What on earth was he thinking? He couldn't be blamed for Jones's shocking knee injury, his foot snagging in the Gabba turf while fetching a ball, but Hussain did have to take responsibility for his bowlers being out there at all when they should have been drinking tea and watching their batsmen pile on runs. Australia, who didn't need to be asked twice, were 2/364 by stumps on the first day and amassed 492. Waugh described the bowling as 'tame, lame stuff'. Hayden made 192 and 103 for the match, McGrath took eight wickets, and England's second innings 79 was a depressing reflection on their captain and team spirit.

Wins by an innings followed in Adelaide and Perth, and once again Australia had only needed eleven days of cricket to retain the Ashes. Was England getting worse? Hard to say. Hussain was only intermittently up to the job as a batsman and captain, and injuries afflicted a number of bowlers and the all-rounder Andrew Flintoff, who barely played a minute on tour. There were signs of promise in Vaughan's three-century series and Harmison's bounce and pace, but it looked like England would need to go through another full generational renewal, their fourth or fifth since they had last held the Ashes, before they could challenge again.

Australia was getting better, which obviously didn't help. Hayden, Langer, Ponting and Martyn had built a top-order battle-ment that was now the equal of Greenidge, Haynes, Richards and Lloyd. Darren Lehmann, who had replaced Mark Waugh, was finding his way, and at number seven of course there was Gilchrist.

The only query over Australia's batting was the most improb-able: the captain. Every time Steve Waugh batted, Caddick and Harmison were brought on to attack his ribs and chin. His sup-posed weakness to risers had been a sucker punch to bowling attacks for years, but now he was struggling to cope. To add insult to potential injury, Hussain dropped the fieldsmen back for the last balls of each over when Waugh was on strike, to give him a single, as if he were a tail-ender. After failing in Brisbane and Adelaide, Waugh made a half-century in Perth before being bowled by Alex Tudor. With little else to write about, the Australian press found fertile territory in the captain's form, or lack of it. Waugh hated every minute, but the team he had built looked like it was moving on without him. In the Ashes celebrations he was a slightly bashful senior figure, less at the centre of things than supervising Hayden, Ponting and company's enjoyment of their moment. Waugh told Gilchrist 'he'd have liked more of a dogfight so we could feel we'd earned our win'; the occasion of retaining the Ashes had 'a hollow feeling'. Waugh might also have been shading over the sharp edges of his own anxiety.

Hohns had asked him for a meeting before the Perth Test. With his dark colouring and tendency to grimace painfully as an expression of good humour, Hohns had an air of the grim reaper about him at the best of times. An invitation for a chat couldn't have been good news. But from Waugh's recollection, their conversation was 'amicable and mature'; he said he would like to play through the 2003 West Indies tour and possibly the 2004 tour of India. 'I let him know that a big score wasn't far away,' he said. They never are, Hohns must have been thinking. 'I left the meeting accepting that two more Tests without runs,' Waugh said, 'would make the decision easy for all concerned.'

THE OCCASION OF RETAINING THE ASHES HAD 'A HOLLOW FEELING'

Hohns must have remembered the conversation differently, perhaps unsurprising when players talked with selectors. Hohns put out a statement saying, 'Stephen has our support until the Sydney Test. The decision is then up to him whether he wants to continue or not. If he does, he will be judged on form like any other player.' Waugh was deeply offended by what looked like an expression of indulgence. Since when had he not been judged on form? Was he now to go through the agonies of Taylor's 1997?

Beyond the confines of Waugh's personal slide, the Boxing Day Test followed the usual template, at first anyway, with Langer (250) and Hayden (102) putting on 192 before the halfway mark of day one. Waugh, coming in at 3/265, decided to flush out his bad form with some shot-making, and hit the fence fifteen times in his 77. It should have brought his confidence back, but in the second innings he came in at an unexpectedly challenging moment.

Replying to Australia's 6/551, England had made 270. Australia's attack was missing Warne, who had hurt his shoulder diving for a ball in a one-day match, but MacGill deputised with the usual impact. Waugh sent England back in. Capitalising on the tiring attack, Vaughan made 145 of the tourists' 387. Thanks to MacGill's five wickets, Australia retained the advantage, and needed only 107 in the fourth innings. But Hayden, Ponting and Martyn fell by 58, and the atmosphere was different this day. There were only 18,000 in the MCG but they were all English, making a noise that was as inspiring as it was three Tests too late. Caddick and Harmison, picking up on the mood, were tearing in. The pitch was up and down in the usual Melbourne way. Australia was almost in crisis.

Waugh was debilitated by a migraine. He tried to find Martin Love, the listed number six, to go ahead of him in the batting order, but as he was doing so, Martyn was dismissed and it was too late. His vision blurry, nauseated to the point where he thought 'carrots [would] have a date with the deck', Waugh hopped around the crease with delirious instability, his footwork reminiscent of Slater's last Test in 2001. Harmison aimed everything at his throat. While this tactic had usually been fool's gold for bowlers over the years, on this day it was working: Waugh was fending and popping and turning his face away and inciting the Barmy Army to a frenzy. In an eventful half hour, he was out for 4 to Harmison, caught behind off an outside edge – but nobody appealed until they saw it replayed on the big screen, by which time the umpire was no longer listening. Next ball, he lofted a drive to cover and Hussain caught him. It was a no-ball. Waugh survived to make 14 before backing away from a Caddick lifter, the ball following his gloves and Mark Butcher taking the leaping catch at slip.

Australia won the match by five wickets; crisis averted, but Waugh's decline now seemed terminal. He could point to two half-centuries in the series and the hundred in Sharjah, but the statistics didn't tell the story as much as the evidence before our eyes. Migraine or no migraine, he was all at sea in that second innings in Melbourne, and the English knew it.

So the teams arrived in Sydney to unusual excitement and tension, unusual given that Australia was carrying a 4-0 lead. The focus was less on the possibility of a whitewash than on whether this would be Waugh's farewell. A spectator told him he had driven twelve hours from Broken Hill to watch him bat in this match. He was equalling Allan Border's world record of 156 appearances. As much as Warne, he had embodied the golden age. It was the narrative of his reconstruction from the ruins of the loose, extravagantly talented and ultimately dropped basher of 1985–91 into the run machine of the next decade that said most about the Australian ascent. He had transformed himself by placing winning on a higher plane than entertainment, yet he remained entertaining in spite of himself. He could have ended up with a career like Kim Hughes; he ended up with one like Border.

As a captain, he had been a revelation. Some, such as Warne and his supporters, would struggle to give Steve Waugh due credit. They didn't go much on the self-improvement side of his and Buchanan's work. They just thought Warne should have been captain. But from the outside, it was clear that Steve Waugh had achieved what had eluded the West Indian leaders Richards and Richardson. He had taken a great team and made it greater. Whereas the West Indian teams after 1985 steadily ran down Clive Lloyd's legacy, Steve Waugh was never content to sustain the level of achievement of the Taylor years. When his men were winning everything, he demanded that they win more. He demanded a consistency of intensity that had only come in fits and starts under Taylor. He instilled an outward-looking mindset and an unashamed avowal of the tender side of mateship. Under his guidance, his players did genuinely like each other and got on as friends rather than just drinking buddies. Notwithstanding his image as grizzled warrior, his pair of stink eyes challenging all comers from under the age-ruined peak of his baggy green cap, Waugh was the nearest we have had to a new-age cricket captain.

So, at Sydney, all the eulogies had been written and the tributes were lining up to be spoken. Waugh deserved recognition. Waugh deserved every accolade. His seventeen years of Test cricket had made him the most popular and respected sportsman in the country. He deserved a national salute.

But Waugh did not want it. Waugh was not ready.

Australia went into the match without an injured McGrath and Warne, neither of them playing for the first time in a 118-Test stretch since 1992. England built a total of 362 around Butcher's first-day century. Waugh gave his injured body a bowl, as he had in Melbourne, where he had taken his first Test wicket in four years. Now he had four overs and trapped Robert Key lbw. As a blast from the past, there seemed something valedictory about it. He was giving us a last thrill for old times' sake.

In the middle of day two, the Australian top-order slumped in quick time: Hayden, Ponting and Langer had a slash but were all out to Caddick, the score 3/56 in a sprightly eleven overs. Three overs before tea, Waugh entered to a standing ovation: a retirement ovation from his home city. He rushed out before Langer was halfway off the ground. He didn't want the grand finale, or the emotions associated with it. Being shy, he was embarrassed. Being bloody-minded, he was infuriated by others, as he saw it, writing him off. But he was humble enough to recognise the significance of the game, his game, in the faces of the crowd.

Langer had been out hooking Caddick to fine leg, and the batsmen had crossed. Martyn saw off Caddick's over, and then Hussain brought on the 'white West Indian', Harmison, as a welcome gift for Waugh. Harmison bowled six short balls. Six! The day a bowler decided to pitch it up was usually the day Waugh failed. He evaded all of Harmison's risers, engulfed, he said, 'by an amazing cloak of tranquillity', like a near-death experience.

Martyn blocked out another Caddick maiden, then Waugh faced the outswing bowler Hoggard, who was replacing the one-dimensional Harmison. Waugh hit Hoggard's first two balls to the fence: one through square leg, the next through point. He took a single off the sixth ball and went to tea 9 not out. The crowd rose again.

After tea, while Martyn became mired on 4 for nearly an hour, Waugh tried to force the pace, but on 14 gave the chance, turning Harmison off his hip into the hands of Richard Dawson at short leg. Dawson dropped it. Next over, Waugh had had enough poking around, and carved three fours off three short Caddick balls. Here he was, up on his toes, head rock-steady, the late commitment to the shot, that signature firm-wristed flick. He cracked another two fours off Hoggard, and within a few overs he was 40. Martyn was 5. For all of Martyn's struggles, his inability to score pushed a wave of confidence towards the other end. Waugh was the scoring batsman; he was the aggressor; he was helping a weaker partner through a rough patch.

At drinks, Waugh was 47 and Martyn 16. Waugh raised his fifty with a slash through extra-cover off Caddick. He was pulling out all the Steve Waugh shots, this one the flat-footed cover drive, his weight transfer and steel wrists making up for the lack of foot movement. Having seen the shot thousands of times over the years only deepened the pleasure for the crowd, which applauded him with a throaty roar and rose again to their feet. The SCG members might have been aching from so much up-and-down, but it had only just started.

Seven overs after drinks, Martyn surprised no one by finally spooning a pull to mid-wicket. Australia were 4/146. In the partnership of 90, achieved in even time, Waugh had made 59.

Ah, a crisis. He must have felt right at home. Love arrived but left quickly, edging Harmison. Waugh, in his element, in a dog-fight, welcomed Gilchrist. Australia was more than 200 runs in arrears with a nasty little half hour remaining till stumps.

Waugh attacked. He hammered Dawson through point to raise his 10,000th run in Tests. Backs were aching as the crowd rose again. Border, Gavaskar, Waugh: a club of three. What a fine time to retire! But Waugh kept attacking. He dusted the cover boundary with driven fours off Harmison until the bowler decided to drop short again. Gilchrist, enjoying all of this immensely, got in on the action, spanking three straight fours off Harmison, who was now missing home again. The sightscreen broke, and two streakers invaded. It was, as Bill Lawry would and probably did say, all happening.

With three overs and one ball remaining until stumps, Waugh, on 83, had slowed down. Gilchrist, taking the wind, had raced to 40 off forty-two balls. Then Waugh whacked Hoggard through cover and started thinking three figures. But he only got a single off the next over, and with Hoggard to bowl the last, on 88 Waugh needed things to go his way.

Hoggard bowled a full outswinger with his first ball; Waugh waited, and squirted it behind point for another four. He took a two and a one later that over: 95. Gilchrist left the last ball and started to walk off. Only then did the batsmen realise that there

ABOVE: The late show: classic Steve Waugh cover-punch in Sydney.

was time for another, and Waugh was on strike. The knowledgeable in the crowd applauded Gilchrist for having left Hoggard's
last-ball bouncer. Stewart, walking past Waugh, asked: 'Do you
write your own scripts these days?'

Waugh didn't start the last over as if he was thinking about the
century. He played it like the mature batsman he was: surviving
until stumps, not his own milestone, was his priority. He defended the first three balls. Sure, a twenty-ninth Test century would
put him on the same figure as
Bradman, but it didn't really matter if he got it tomorrow, did it?

But they had been sacking
him two hours ago. His friends,
two hours ago, were standing for
him and shedding tears of farewell. Dawson dropped short and

A WICKET HERE, AND THE TEST MATCH COULD BE ENGLAND'S

Waugh clouted him through cover point. It wasn't going for four,
but he and Gilchrist could run them – perhaps. But no. They had
to settle for three.

So Waugh was on 98 when Gilchrist faced the second-last ball.
Gilchrist had so much experience spoiling things for senior men:
Zoehrer, Healy. Gilchrist dreaded going through it again. He just
wanted to be off strike. The crowd chanted the name of someone who wasn't playing: 'Single! Single!' Dawson aired the ball,
Gilchrist came down and turned it through mid-wicket. He got his
own ovation for that.

The cheers were followed by boos as Hussain took an eternity
to set his field and instruct Dawson. A slip, a silly point, a short leg.
A short mid-wicket. Hussain could be excused for his somewhat
unoriginal theatrics. The tension in the ground, the numbers who
had waited, the last-session blitz: that was all about Steve Waugh's
century, which didn't interest Hussain at all. For Hussain, the tension of the century presented an opportunity. A wicket here, and
the Test match could be England's.

Waugh took a splay-footed stroll down the wicket and said to
Gilchrist: 'Make sure you're backing up.' So much for the maturity
of the elder statesman.

Now: what should the off-spinner Dawson bowl? Hussain, like many close watchers, suspected Waugh would premeditate his bread-and-butter shot, down on one knee and slog-sweeping over mid-wicket. He told Dawson to rifle one in full and straight. If Waugh went for the slog-sweep, the fast full one was the wicket ball, the lbw a big chance.

But it was as if Waugh read their minds. He thought, If they think I'll go for the slog-sweep Dawson will bowl a full ball. So he stood and waited and, instead of going down, took half a step forward and laced a beautiful, orthodox drive through cover. Pandemonium, joy, chills down the spine. Gilchrist ran up to fling a high five, but Waugh never saw him. He had not saved the Test, to which he would contribute a grand total of six more runs: none on the third morning, and 6 on the fifth day. England would win, but few can remember that. As with Taylor at Edgbaston in 1997, Waugh had not really batted himself back into form, but he had settled the question of his retention in the team. Like Taylor, he had won the right to go out at a time of his own choosing. The Prime Minister, John Howard, was one of the first into the Australian changing rooms. Always one to identify with his cricketing heroes, he no doubt took inspiration from Waugh's comeback. Perhaps, as it turned out for him in 2007, too much so.

But this was a time for the holder of Australia's second-most important office. To have regained control over his future, passed 10,000 runs, equalled Bradman's twenty-nine centuries and re-alised a childhood dream ignited by seeing Doug Walters raise his 1974–75 century at the WACA by hitting Bob Willis for six off the last ball, made it, he said, 'the perfect day in cricketing terms'. The hour that followed stumps, surrounded by family, teammates and well-wishers, 'was a period I wish everyone could experience just once in their life'.

OPPOSITE: Not Finished Yet: A moment of tranquillity amid the bedlam.

WALKING TALL
Port Elizabeth, March 2003

DARRYL CULLINAN EARNT SOME APPLAUSE AND ACKNOWLEDGEMENT WHEN HE REPLIED TO WARNE'S 'I'VE BEEN WAITING MONTHS FOR YOU, DARRYL' WITH A QUICK, 'AND YOU LOOK LIKE YOU'VE BEEN SPENDING IT ALL EATING PIES.'

The Australian cricket team could bat, bowl and field, but when it came to the ethics of the game they showed the skills of supreme circus contortionists. In the moral realm, as in the cricketing, they believed they could bend reality to their will.

Reviewing the logic and rationalisations of the senior players is instructive. Mark Waugh, one of the side's more prominent sledgers over the years, said: 'Since I've been playing, the Australian team has been accused a lot of sledging. But it depends what you mean. If you mean you are attempting to unsettle the opposition players' mental skills, then sure we sledge, but if you mean being immoral, unethical or personal, then we're against it … I wouldn't say we overstep the mark at all. I'd say it's been overdone by the media. We play hard but fair.'

Shane Warne was unapologetic about using sledging as a tactic: 'If I can get a batsman out by saying something that affects his game so much, why not? That is a chink in his mental armoury.' Nevertheless, 'it should not become too nasty or personal.' Steve Waugh, who did care about the image his team projected, gathered them to draft a code of conduct in 2003. In many areas, such as dissent, the Australians had improved. But

AUSTRALIAN PLAYERS **HAD LONG ADMITTED THAT** THEY USED SLEDGING AS A PLOY

when the code came to sledging, all it would do was condemn 'personal abuse'. Otherwise, 'body language' and 'banter' were legitimate tactics and integral parts of the competitive nature of cricket'.

Here is an ethical starting point: verbal abuse is fair when it is a supplementary tactic to gain advantage in the match, but unfair when it is 'immoral, unethical or personal'. In the words of the ICC code of conduct, this was translated as: 'language that is obscene, offensive or of a seriously insulting nature'.

But what is 'immoral, unethical or personal'? What is 'seriously insulting'? And should the fairness of verbal tactics be judged by their intent or the way they are perceived by the recipient? And why should the freedom to judge what is 'personal', 'nasty' or 'immoral' be something that the perpetrators grant to themselves?

To go back to the matter of intent, Australian players had long admitted that they used sledging as a ploy. When it was an outpouring of passion, and indiscipline, such as Warne's sending off Andrew Hudson at Johannesburg in 1994, they weren't so proud of it. But when it was carefully targeted, it elicited the opposite response. Merv Hughes, who called such abuse

LEFT: Nothing personal, Hicky: Hughes claimed a quarter of his wickets came through sledging.

'verbal pressure', boasted that a quarter of his 200 Test wickets were indirectly a result of sledging. Boasted!

There was even peer pressure to join in the sledging. Steve Waugh, a prolific sledger (albeit out of the side of his mouth) for most of his career, said disapprovingly of non-sledgers: 'There were occasions when I thought other guys in our team could have taken more initiative to lift the team during periods of staleness, but they weren't inclined to get involved. Each to their own ...' Note the euphemistic 'lift the team during periods in staleness', when what that actually meant was a group of bullies getting together to verbally abuse a batsman. Note also the cowardice in the inference that sledging is something that fielding teams do as a group.

Mark Waugh concurred: 'If three or four other players are saying something, you generally join in.'

This probably captures what so many watchers found repugnant in the Australian approach. Someone like Mark Waugh was so courageous with a bat in his hand, alone in front of a baying crowd and a charging West Indian paceman, yet so weak and cowardly when standing in a group around a timid batsman. Only a timid batsman, mind: the Australians weren't silly enough to taunt a Lara or a Tendulkar. Picking on the weak seemed to be another rationale for sledging, because picking on the strong didn't work so well.

Often, sledging was excused on the basis of humour. Merv Hughes was famous for shop-worn lines like 'Maybe I should bowl you a piano, see if you can play that.' Darryl Cullinan earnt some applause and acknowledgement when in 1997–98 he replied to Warne's 'I've been waiting months for you, Darryl' with a quick, 'And you look like you've been spending it all eating pies.' As the height of good-humoured, and therefore acceptable, sledging, Steve Waugh cited a line from the former New South Wales paceman Richard Stobo, who was so unimpressed with the batting of Dean Waugh in a Sydney club match that he said, 'For Christ's sake, you must have been adopted.'

The problem with all of these 'guidelines' and 'standards' is their pure subjectivity. What is humour anyway, and why should it be a mitigation for abuse? 'Deep down,' Steve Waugh wrote, 'all players know what is acceptable behaviour and what isn't.' But do they? It's a very comfortable cop-out to assume that everyone, including the target, knows what you mean and how you mean it.

Under Waugh's captaincy, the truth of the matter was that Australian sledging was very often not humorous by anyone's definition, nor acceptable, nor inoffensive, nor impersonal. It wasn't just 'gamesmanship'. Nor was it very clever. (Not that cleverness should be any excuse. In a Shield match for Victoria against New South Wales, Warne and his wicketkeeper Darren Berry unnerved Michael Slater by doing a call-and-response routine with one saying 'Tick' and the other 'Tock', to imply that Slater was a ticking time bomb about to get himself out. Slater and his batting partner Mark Waugh objected. It might have been clever, but it was unacceptably personal – among Australian teammates, that is …)

The lid was blown on all this in 2002 when the South African newcomer Graeme Smith revealed in an interview the true content of Australia's on-field verballing.

'All Warne does is call you a c— all day,' Smith said. 'When he walked past me he said, "You f—ing c—, what are you doing here?" And I remember looking at [umpire] Rudi Koertzen and he just shrugged his shoulders as if to say, "I know it's rough, kid, but that's the way it is".'

That fine Christian gentleman Hayden, meanwhile, 'stood on the crease for about two minutes telling me that I wasn't f—ing good enough … "You know, you're not f—ing good enough," he told me. "How the f— are you going to handle Shane Warne when he's bowling in the rough? What the f— are you going to do?"'

Smith and Brett Lee had a slight collision in the match, after which Smith 'apologised, but [Lee] said nothing. Then I hooked him for four and then a one and then it was drinks. As he walked past me he told me that he would f—ing kill me right there if I ever touched him again,' Smith said.

Of McGrath, Smith said: 'He's like a grumpy old man. He doesn't stop cursing you. He called me a f—ing c— and told me go away, that I didn't belong there. He starts off quietly, but the minute you hit him for a boundary he loses the plot and it never stops.'

Smith named Langer, Ponting, Gilchrist, Warne and Mark Waugh as having attacked him personally.

This, then, was what they were really like: offensive, insulting, personal, lacking any redeeming style or humour. If 'deep down' they knew what was right and wrong, how did they justify this kind of thing? It seems to any objective eye the worst of schoolyard bullying, kept under the lid of another part of the 'code', which Smith had violated, as Lara was accused of violating on other occasions, which is that 'what is said on the field stays on the field'.

Only late in his career, when he started thinking about the way posterity would view his captaincy, did Steve Waugh seem to worry about verbal abuse. On his retirement, he said, 'Occasionally abuse did arise, and it was an area we needed to clean up as we were aware kids were copying our every move and such an example was not the one we wanted to set.' He didn't want it 'as part of our legacy'.

Accordingly he 'guaranteed' that Australia would 'play in the right spirit'. This was in 2001, a year before the sledging Smith revealed.

To some sections of the Australian cricket public, the team's on-field behaviour was embarrassing and unforgivable. Not much seemed to have changed since English journalist John Thicknesse damned Border on his retirement in 1994, saying he would be 'respected but never loved' because of his team's sledging. Other sections of the Australian cricket public accepted sledging and even agreed that it was in some way necessary to the team's manner of play, and justifiable because other teams sledged as well. The tradition of verbal abuse runs deep in Australian cricket, right down to the lowest grades in the smallest town on a Saturday afternoon. At the grassroots of the game, it's fair to surmise that giving someone a spray is seen as the essence of what it is to be Australian. But that's a narrow and, to be frank, self-indulgent idea of 'Australianness'. No Australian captain could be more patriotic than Brian Booth, who wrote in 2003: 'Sledging is unsportsmanlike. It is bad manners and

THE TRADITION OF VERBAL ABUSE RUNS DEEP IN AUSTRALIAN CRICKET

an example of discourtesy in sport. It is an admission by those who use it that they do not believe they can win fairly.' He was right on the mark there. For all their aggression and ability to 'back themselves', the Australians still revealed, through their sledging, an ingrained insecurity.

If nobody in the Test team could quite get their head around the ethics of sledging, the issue of walking was even more vexed. Steve Waugh praised the non-walking of Dean Jones, who 'quite obviously nicked one' before he had scored in a Test against England in 1986–87; Jones went on to make 184 not out. 'He was one tough cookie mentally,' Waugh said. 'Most guys find it hard to settle down after not walking because of the nagging guilt.'

The rationalisation most often given for not walking is that umpiring decisions 'even out' over time. There is no evidence that they do, but this is what players tell themselves when they cheat, that is, when they stay at the crease when they know they are out. They allay the 'nagging guilt' by telling themselves that they are balancing some kind of karmic balance sheet against the times umpires have dismissed them, or will dismiss them in some notional future, incorrectly. And because everyone treats walking this way, a form of cheating becomes normal and the person who stands up and declines to cheat becomes something of an oddity and a threat.

An oddity and a threat was what Gilchrist became in the 2003 World Cup semi-final, when his response to being given not out against Sri Lanka was to walk. On 22, batting first, Gilchrist swept Aravinda de Silva onto his pad, The ball popped to Kumar Sangakkara. Rudi Koertzen said, 'Not out', but Gilchrist heard a different voice, which said, 'Go. Walk.'

Where did that voice come from? Whose was it? Why was it so compelling, in the face of disadvantage for the team and ostracism for the individual?

There are two strains of background to follow up to this moment: one was Australia's 2003 World Cup campaign, and the other was a narrative of events in Gilchrist's own consciousness, that found their denouement in his walking. In the end it was not so much a decision as a moral reflex.

In contrast to the 1999 World Cup, Australia had powered through the 2003 event, undefeated if not incident-free. They had beaten Pakistan by eighty-two runs, India by nine wickets, Holland by seventy-five runs, Zimbabwe by seven wickets, Namibia by 256 runs, England by two wickets, Sri Lanka by ninety-six runs, New Zealand by ninety-six runs, and Kenya by five wickets. What appears to have been a triumphal march was not quite that. The team had been unsettled in the lead-up by a continuing public campaign in sections of the press to recall Steve and Mark Waugh, by doubts over some of the bowlers' fitness, and by the political agitation, in which the players found themselves out of their depth, over whether or not they should play their scheduled match in Zimbabwe. Certainly for the new captain Ponting this would be a strenuous initiation.

But none of it compared with what happened on the eve of the first match on 11 February. On 10 February, Ponting sat beside his vice-captain Gilchrist on the team bus and said, 'I've got the biggest cricket story in the world.' That evening, Warne, who had made a very fast recovery from his shoulder injury to declare himself fit for the Cup, sat in a chair in a hotel room surrounded by his teammates and broke the news that he had tested positive to a diuretic, not a performance-enhancing drug but one on the banned list because of its common use as a masking agent. Fighting back his shame, he told them that he had taken the diuretic before a match in Sydney. Then he choked up. Ponting recalled: 'I think there was plenty of shock in the room already, but to then see the greatest bowler in Australian cricket so distressed in front of us all was as sobering a sight as you could ever wish to see.'

Warne was too overcome to finish his planned address. Ponting, who had known the news for about ten hours, asked the players to go out and have dinner, separately or together, think about what had happened, and then reconvene in the hotel. Three hours later they met again and Warne, re-composed, bade the team farewell and good luck.

Warne did have the option to wait several weeks until receiving the 'B' sample of his test, thereby playing in the Cup. But he showed that he had learnt one lesson from the bookmaker affair,

ABOVE: No piss-take: Warne wondering if that diuretic was worth it.

which is that a cover-up can have a multiplier effect on the initial transgression.

Warne would tell the world, later, that he had been given the diuretic by his mother Brigitte. His reason for taking it, he said, was that concern about his appearance prompted him to use it to reduce the fluids he was retaining in his body. This may have been true, although the use of his mother as an alibi was greeted with scepticism by many in the public and even in his team. Conspiracy theories abounded: was he taking the diuretics to mask banned medications that might have hastened his recovery from injury, or recreational drug use? Unfortunately for Warne, this was the price he paid for his lack of public candour on many previous occasions. Joe the Cameraman might have been the guilty party. Brigitte Warne may have supplied him the diuretic to look good. But for all his emotional transparency, and his deep-down likeability, Warne had a history of spinning more than just the cricket ball. Now he suffered a frontal attack from rumour and its bowling partner, innuendo. But to give him due credit, he was not compelled by any rules to reveal his positive Test before the World Cup; that he did so showed that in this respect at least he was growing up.

As it had previously, Warne's absence galvanised the players to prove they could win without him. The possibility of a one- or two-year suspension for the leg-spinner lurked at the back of Ponting's mind, but the World Cup was the challenge before his eyes. Australia's subsequent wins were by heavy margins, with one exception, after Andrew Symonds's breakthrough 143 not out against Pakistan in the opening fixture at the Wanderers. They did go to Zimbabwe, where, on Robert Mugabe Way, Jimmy Maher memorably remarked that it 'would have to be a one-way street, wouldn't it?'

The exceptional match was against England in the group stage on 2 March at St George's Park. Australia was safely through to the Super Sixes, but England needed to win to progress. So it was a match where Australia's motivation was to eliminate an opponent rather than save their own skin – this was how far the earth had tilted since the 1999 World Cup. Australia's progress through the 2003 event was irresistible and, one imagines, in the minds of their opponents, intimidating. Survival in the Cup began more and more to look like a matter of getting out of Australia's way.

Hussain won the toss and batted on a typically mysterious St George's Park wicket, which Ponting called 'totally unfit for a one-day international'. But Marcus Trescothick and Nick Knight repelled the new ball and added sixty-six in nine overs before Knight fell to Bichel, setting off a collapse of 5/11 in half an hour: the notches on Bichel's bedhead were Vaughan (2), Hussain (1), both with textbook leg-cutters, and Paul Collingwood (10), while McGrath chipped in with Trescothick (37). Andrew Flintoff, herniated for most of the tour of Australia, staged a comeback with the soon-to-retire Stewart before Ponting brought Bichel back with eight overs left in the innings. England was looking at a prospective 230. But Bichel dismissed Flintoff, Stewart and Giles to cut off any kind of late flurry, limiting the pay-off from the last ten overs to thirty-three runs.

England's 8/204 didn't look enough until Australia suffered a collapse of its own. This time it was Caddick taking the top four wickets to reduce Australia to 4/48. Lehmann and Bevan consolidated, adding a patient sixty-three, before Lehmann's brother-in-law Craig White did a not very familial thing and had him caught behind for 37. Symonds, Brad Hogg and Lee fell in quick order, leaving Australia 8/135 and seventy short at a run a ball.

Bichel had just taken 7/20, so if he was ever going to feel that he could bat, this was the day. Over the previous few years, according to Steve Waugh, Bichel had been the world's best twelfth man. He was getting enough practice at it. But the comment was not meant flippantly. Bichel was one of those happy, committed, genuine, honest cricketers who was a pleasure to have around any team camp. A lot of nonsense is spoken about players talking themselves into 'enjoying' their cricket; often it is anything but enjoyable, particularly when the individual is failing or, for that matter, asked to carry the drinks time and again. Bichel must have minded, but he never seemed to. He roared into the crease at nets practice, giving the batsmen the best work-out they could hope for. He even loved weights and fitness training. Ponting termed him 'the heartbeat of the team', and the remark was more than just a consolation for being twelfth man. Nobody was more popular than Bichel. He was unfailing in all he did; and when given his chance, he unfailingly took it. This day, he was only in the team as a replacement for the injured Gillespie.

At the other end he had the world's best middle-order one-day batsman. There was a significant difference between the way Bevan played one-day and Test cricket, and perhaps it explained the divergence between his results in the two formats. In one-day cricket, whenever he came in to bat Bevan was presented with a mathematical problem to which he needed to provide a solution. So many runs off so many balls. Such and such a bowler having so many overs left. The fieldsmen placed here, here, here and here. The gaps here, here and here. A single needed off the last ball – put it here. A boundary needed this over – put it there. The problem, and its solution, was always external to Bevan himself. He didn't have to think about what he was doing; he only had to think about what to do with the ball, where to place it, and how to transform the accumulation of runs into a spreadsheet. He was almost too gifted for his own good. When he played Test cricket, however, the focus was reversed: here was Bevan, surrounded by a claustrophobic and talkative ring of catchers. Here comes the bowler, who might swing or cut the ball or drop it short or bowl it full. Rather than thinking about placing the ball around the field, Bevan had to concentrate on what he was doing with his feet, with his hands, with his head. His focus was not on scoring, but on sur-viving; not on the external task, but on himself. Between Test and one-day cricket, he might as well have been playing two totally different sports.

This World Cup problem against England produced a typical Bevan solution. Although he had only been required to play one innings in the Cup so far, he stepped right into his professorial rhythm. He took Bichel aside and gave him a thorough briefing on what was required and how they would go about it. They paced the pursuit until the last possible minute, when Bevan allowed the walking-on-air Bichel to unload. As they inched closer, the Australians could sense the quickened movements of anxiety in the English fieldsmen. Bevan and Bichel needed fourteen off the

ABOVE: The world's greatest twelfth man: Andy Bichel firing in the 2003 World Cup.

last twelve balls and were waiting for Caddick's reappearance. Hussain, somehow, made the decision to leave a man with 4/35 off his nine overs chasing balls on the rope. Jimmy Anderson and Flintoff were given the last two overs. Bichel slogged a square six and showed a pristine high elbow with a straight-driven four to get Australia home with two balls to spare, square-swatting the last boundary off Flintoff. Caddick scratched his head and looked glum. Bichel celebrated his coup de grace with a man of the match award.

Gilchrist, meanwhile, had for several months been nagged by interior questions about his responsibilities as an international cricketer. He had been disillusioned by the ACB's prosecution of him for comments about Muralidaran's bowling action in 2002. Asked at a private Carlton Football Club function if Murali chucked, Gilchrist had confessed, 'I think he does. I say that because, if you read the laws of the game, there's no doubt in my mind that he and many others throughout cricket history have.' The private became public, and although initially the chief executive of the ACB, James Sutherland, gave Gilchrist a friendly warning about the perils of speaking his opinion in front of crowds, soon afterwards Sutherland called Gilchrist again with an entirely different tone and charged him with 'conduct detrimental to the interests of the game'. Gilchrist was sat down in a kangaroo court in Sydney and reprimanded for having said what he thought. So much for cricket 'having a distinct place in Australian society and history', as it was put in the ACB's Code of Conduct. So much for freedom of speech. 'The game is healthier if opinions are freely expressed,' Gilchrist wrote later. 'And it was a mild comment. I certainly didn't personally abuse Murali.' (There is that word 'personal' again. Sure, Gilchrist mightn't have meant it that way, but how was Murali to take it if not 'personally'?) But Gilchrist had a more justifiable defence on a higher plane. He said that for all the

GILCHRIST WAS REPRIMANDED FOR HAVING SAID WHAT HE THOUGHT

lip-service the ACB paid to 'Australian values', it was 'crushingly disappointing' to see the Board bowing to the pressures brought to bear upon it by international politics.

Gilchrist didn't know it at the time, but the affair would set off a slow chain reaction within himself. The next summer, in the Second Ashes Test in Adelaide, Michael Vaughan sliced a drive to backward point, where Langer claimed the catch. Vaughan stood his ground and the video official had enough doubt to decline the appeal. The Australians were furious that Langer's word, and the team's, was not taken. Of course, the Australians might have been victims of their own 'play hard' reputation. Why would an Englishman trust them? But from Gilchrist's point of view, the loss of trust between players was a shame: 'I really do think there are disputes that can and should be resolved on the field between the players, and if the players are given this responsibility they will live up to it'.

The next steps in Gilchrist's internal journey involved irritations in one form or another. There was the vexation about whether or not to play in Zimbabwe, what effect this would have on the country, what signal it would be sending, how it would be manipulated by the Mugabe gang. The players felt unqualified to answer the political questions and distracted from their cricketing mission. There was also, for Gilchrist, the distraction of comments he had made about Warne's positive drug test, which had upset Warne back in Australia. And in the first match of the Cup, against Pakistan, Gilchrist was at the centre of a racial abuse charge involving the Pakistani wicketkeeper Rashid Latif.

All of this led, in ways that were not yet clear, to the World Cup semi-final in Port Elizabeth. Ponting won the toss, and Gilchrist and Hayden opened the batting with the aim of approaching the game like a Test match: watchful start, keep out the new ball, sit on Murali, keep wickets in hand for a late flurry. Instead, Gilchrist saw the ball large and followed his instincts, hitting the paceman Pulasthi Gunaratne for a four and a six in the second over. 'Did you premeditate that?' asked Hayden. He might as well have been the frog asking the scorpion why it had stung him. It was simply Gilchrist following his nature.

Soon Australia and Gilchrist were rattling along. To disrupt their rhythm, in the sixth over Sanath Jayasuriya brought on de Silva with his off-breaks: 'An early victory for us,' Gilchrist said, 'as my hitting had brought forward their plan to use their spinners.' Gilchrist blocked the first ball, then went down to sweep the second. 'I got a thick, loud bottom edge. It went into my front pad, just above the ankle. I heard cries of "Catch it! Catch it!" and turned around to see Kumar Sangakkara with the ball in his gloves. Well, that's that, I thought.'

But umpire Koertzen was shaking his head.

'I felt strange,' Gilchrist said. 'So much discontent about umpiring, video decisions, and trust between players had been bubbling away in the back of my mind that when I saw Rudi shaking his head I heard an emphatic voice in mine. "Go. Walk." So I walked.'

This action, just like the six-hitting, was unpremeditated and instinctive. Unlike the hitting, it was not necessarily part of Gilchrist's history. Throughout his career, he had walked sometimes but not always. He hadn't held a philosophical position on the issue. It was just that at that moment, out of the flux inside his head, he heard a voice telling him that the only thing to do was to do the right thing.

As the minutes, hours and days passed, the consequences began to emerge. Gilchrist's teammates were puzzled by why he had walked when the umpire had given him not out. At first they thought he hadn't seen Koertzen. Then Ponting was out for 2 and Australia was 2/37. Soon after, Hayden was out and the position had plunged from 0/34 to 3/51. The changing room became very quiet around the wicketkeeper. 'I suddenly felt very lonely, knowing how my walking was going to look to the others. Why now? Why in a World Cup semi-final? Why do something to appease my conscience when the whole team's fate hung in the balance?'

As it turned out, Australia won the match easily and followed it up with another 'perfect' World Cup final. Just as they had demolished Pakistan in 1999 by bowling first, they did it this time to India by batting first, Ponting blitzing 140 not out and Martyn 88 not out, then McGrath excising Tendulkar early. Australia cruised home by 125 runs.

But the enduring memory from that World Cup is Gilchrist's walking in the semi-final. *Wisden* spoke for much of the world when it said Gilchrist's act 'astonished everyone unused to such Australian magnanimity'. From within the Australian cricket community, Gilchrist received as much condemnation as praise. Ex-players lined up to say they would never have walked. Steve Waugh said walking was on a moral par with owning up to speeding. Present players gave Gilchrist the impression that he was acting selfishly, trying to be a 'moral policeman', trying to make himself seem purer than everyone else. This was never Gilchrist's aim, but he was probably asking too much when he said, 'I never thought my act reflected badly on other players ... I do not think there is anything dishonest or dishonourable in a policy of not walking.'

No doubt this is what Gilchrist believed, and wanted to believe, but the consequence of his action was to throw a somewhat murky tint over the majority, from every nation and every local club for that matter, who do not walk. Gilchrist was a reluctant, unwilling and even regretful standard-bearer for doing the right thing, but when he walked in Port Elizabeth he threw a burst of sunlight upon all the moral dilemmas about sledging, dissent, Zimbabwe, free speech, video umpiring and trusting a player's word. Sometimes all the ethical spaghetti junctions around these matters can be brushed away when someone listens to a voice in his head that says, even to the detriment of himself and his team, Do the right thing. Abusing opponents on the field, even when it is not 'personally' meant, is just wrong. It doesn't matter how many times a player says how 'tough' a game cricket is, how it's a 'man's game' and verbal attacks are a legitimate part of 'mental disintegration'; it's not the right thing to stand at silly point and tell a batsman he is a f—ing c—. It doesn't matter how often Merv Hughes or Shane Warne say they took wickets with their tongue; it's not something anyone with a conscience can be proud of. It doesn't matter how many times umpires give bad decisions; those are just human mistakes, whereas standing one's ground when one is clearly out, and knows it, is a form of cheating. They belong in different categories and never 'even out'. Bad behaviour can be rationalised and mitigated and explained away, but it can't be made good.

Gilchrist was made to feel uncomfortable by what he had done, because it did reflect badly on the others. His action was all the more heroic for his knowing that he would be ostracised and criticised for breaking a kind of accepted cheats' code. He didn't want to be a hero, because he loved belonging to the team, being one of the boys. The fact that his walking had reflected adversely on his team-mates could be smoothed over and apologised for but never escaped. A hero he was, to parents and children alike; for all of Steve Waugh's talk about 'legacy' and the 'example' this Australian cricket team would set for youngsters, Gilchrist was the one who would sacrifice his own interests in order to do the right thing – he was the one who, so to speak, walked the walk.

OPPOSITE: Gilchrist walks; cricket world about to erupt.

THE FINAL FRONTIER

Kandy, March 2004
Nagpur, October 2004

WHEN RICKY PONTING WAS A FOUR-YEAR-OLD CHILD, HIS GRANDMOTHER HAD DRESSED HIM IN A T-SHIRT SAYING: 'INSIDE THIS SHIRT IS AN AUSTRALIAN TEST CRICKETER.'

The peak of the Australian cycle, which started after the defeat by India in 2001, survived the captaincy transition with only the slightest tic. Ponting was captain-in-waiting for so long, and a World Cup winning leader by 2003, that there was no debate or vote or campaign to succeed Steve Waugh, just an orderly transfer of power. John Howard, for all his love of cricket, wasn't watching closely enough.

The last of Waugh's four tours of the West Indies was the most comfortably won. Without Warne, who had accepted a one-year ban for the drug offence, Australia played grinding rather than spectacular cricket on comatose pitches. In recognition of a number of factors – Gilchrist's skills with the bat, the unthreatening West Indian bowling, the wickets – Australia played the four Tests with five specialist batsmen and five bowlers, Gilchrist batting at number six. All of the top six averaged higher than 58, with Ponting the leader, scoring 523 runs at 130.7. MacGill (20) led the wicket-taking, but an even bowling performance saw Gillespie and McGrath both taking 17 and Bichel 11. Lara was again the lone tower for the home side, making 533 runs at 66.6, getting occasional support from

ONCE AGAIN, SOMETHING **OUT OF THE BOX** WAS NEEDED TO BEAT AUSTRALIA

Daren Ganga, Shiv Chanderpaul and Ramnaresh Sarwan. Their bowling was a sorry sight, only Jermaine Lawson taking wickets at an average of less than 44.

The West Indies did enjoy one spectacular highlight, making a world record 418 in the last innings to win the dead Fourth Test in Antigua. Lawson had taken 7/78 to dismantle Australia on the first day, but second-innings centuries from Langer and Hayden seemed to make the tourists' whitewash an inevitability. However, Sarwan and Chanderpaul – then at the start of a career second wind that would carry him to the top of the international batting rankings – scored hundreds, and on the last morning Vasbert Drakes and Omari Banks, names to conjure with, struck an untroubled forty-six for the eighth wicket to give the West Indians an extraordinary victory. Once again, something out of the box was needed to beat Australia. Once again, with McGrath in a provoked but spiteful altercation with Sarwan, Australia showed that they were faithful to their 'spirit of cricket' avowals only as long as things were going their way.

Their employer's chief executive, James Sutherland, said as much in a phone call to Waugh after McGrath offered Sarwan

LEFT: Last time: Steve Waugh acknowledges his fifty at Sydney.

an on-the-spot laryngectomy: 'It's all very well to be playing the game in the right spirit when things are going your way, but if things are not going your way, that's when the real test is on.'

Sutherland's was a good point, followed, however, by a thorough flogging with a wet lettuce leaf, the full wrath of the Australian Cricket Board. 'If you can't carry yourself in the true spirit of the game at those times,' thundered Sutherland, 'perhaps you need to have a good look at yourself.'

While Waugh went home and took a good look at himself, a seven-match series followed for the one-day team. This, on the back of a World Cup, which was on the back of an Ashes series: little wonder that some of the Australian players were resenting only having had five days at home to 'soak up' the afterglow of being World Cup champions for an unprecedented third time. Anyone seeking an explanation for their behaviour by the end of the West Indies tour didn't have too many dots to connect.

A mixture of obligation and greed had turned the Australian team into a golden goose, and in 2003–04 the scheduling was out of control. The West Indian tour involved some high-quality cricket, but its being played in the shadow of the World Cup de-valued both events. Then, after their return, the Australians had a few weeks off before playing two low-key Tests against Bangladesh in Darwin and Cairns – 'not the kind of Test cricket I'd grown up dreaming about', Gilchrist remarked wryly – which in turn was followed by two Tests at home against Zimbabwe, then a lengthy one-day tournament in India before shuttling home for four Tests against the Indians.

By now Waugh had announced his prospective retirement and the summer became a struggle for the physically tested and in-creasingly listless Australians. One moment they were planning a series of events to commemorate Waugh's summer-long lap of honour; the next, they were in a tooth-and-nail battle to protect their eleven-year unbeaten streak at home. On a spicy Gabba wicket, Sourav Ganguly hit a memorable 144 to secure a rain-marred draw, Greg Baum of the *Age* famously writing that the Indian captain 'came to Australia as a caricature but will leave as a character'. In Adelaide, Ponting's 242 in a first innings 556 was not enough to prevent defeat. The Laxman–Dravid show put on an encore 303 partnership in India's first innings, Ajit Agarkar rolled Australia on the fourth day, and Dravid, in sublime form, guided India home by four wickets.

Behind, at home, Australia almost panicked when Virender Sehwag clubbed his way to 195 during Boxing Day at the MCG; but after he mis-hit a Simon Katich full toss, the tide swung Australia's way, Ponting scoring 257 and Hayden 136, and the series-levelling win looked easier than it was. Sydney was the zenith of a batsmen's summer, Tendulkar redeeming a lean tour with 241 not out and Laxman caressing 178 in India's 705 before Langer and Katich did the heavy lifting in Australia's reply, soaking up enough time to make the draw the favourite. Ganguly declared late on the fourth afternoon 442 ahead, but this time he had mistimed his run. India could not sustain any kind of pressure on the last day, and the occasion of Waugh's last innings was sufficient motivation for the Australians to dig in.

For poetry, the final moments did not really do Waugh's career or captaincy justice. The match stuttered towards a draw, neither side quite game enough to go all-out for victory; a pity for Waugh, the captain whose teams came closest to rendering the dull draw a thing of the past. And he finished up with an agricultural swipe, a little unseemly for the ice-man.

But he did get to retire on his own terms, as had Taylor. Waugh's legacy as a captain was well established by 2003–04, and although debate will go on forever about the relative merits of Border, Taylor, Waugh and Ponting as captains, there are fair grounds to place Waugh on the highest step of the dais. When sportsmen say it is harder to stay on top than to get there, it is another of those cli-chés that also happens to be the truth. To keep a team motivated, to sustain its hunger, to stimulate its ambitions, and to teach it that merely winning is not quite enough, all require more thoughtful and imaginative captaincy than simply climbing to the summit. All too often, the struggle exhausts the victor. Few teams can cohere well enough to continue achieving goals after they have become the best. When Waugh inherited such a succesful team he was on a hiding to nothing, yet it was under his stewardship that the

Australian cricket team really did move beyond invincible. They also entertained, to an unprecedented degree. Twice they scored 400 in a day, and frequently more than 350. By 2003 they scored at 4.1 an over; the ferocity of their batting was as feared as the great West Indian team's bowling.

Waugh, as well as realising all these gains, invested for the future. He did not run down the team's savings of talent and desire, in the way Viv Richards had done with the West Indies. He left his successor with a team well prepared for the coming challenges. Waugh, like any good historian, had learnt the lessons of the past. From them he devised new plans, and with the help of his players he was able to execute them.

But life goes on, and it's also true to say that most of his team-mates were as relieved as he was to have his retirement behind them. They confessed to moments of annoyance with Waugh during the captain's swansong, feeling that it had sucked the oxygen out of the team's drive for victory against India. Certainly the 2003–04 series, while nailing India's shingle to the wall as a force to be taken seriously on Australian soil, was frustrating for the Australian players. They did not like how close they had come to losing. Nor did they enjoy missing the chance of avenging 2001. India, by drawing the series 1-1, were the moral victors, retaining the Border–Gavaskar Trophy, which had become by this stage the most relevant symbol of Test cricket supremacy.

The campaign to win the Border–Gavaskar would be, as Buchanan might say, a two-step process. The autumn tour of Sri Lanka would be the first step. Australia had not won a series there for a decade, and under the new leadership this tour was seen as the preliminary examination for India later in the year.

Judging by results, the Sri Lanka tour went like clockwork. A 3-1 victory in the one-day series was followed by 3-0 in the Tests. But Australia won each Test match courageously, fighting back after conceding first-innings leads. In the First Test, at Galle, the deficit was 161, but centuries from Hayden, Martyn and Lehmann built a second-innings of 512. Warne, returning from his suspension, was as frisky as a rabbit and delivered evidence backing his statements that the twelve-month break might be the best thing for his cricket. He took a match-winning 5/43 in the second innings, to go with five in the first, and declared that he had never bowled better. When Symonds caught Hashan Tillakaratne off a skied sweep at mid-wicket, Warne had 500 wickets. Fifteen years earlier, after batting against Warne in a Melbourne club cricket match, Rodney Hogg had written in the *Truth* that the blond St Kilda leggie would one day take 500 Test wick-

WARNE, RETURNING FROM SUSPENSION, WAS AS FRISKY AS A RABBIT

ets. Shortly afterwards, Hogg was sacked by the newspaper for a pattern of intemperate remarks showing that he did not know what he was talking about.

In many ways the series was a shoot-out between Warne and Muralidaran, who had just been through yet more official testing of his action. Warne eclipsed Murali in the race to 500 wickets, but Murali took 28 in the series, at 23.17, to Warne's 26 at 20.03. So who won the argument? Australia won every match. Lehmann and Martyn topped the aggregates and scored two centuries apiece, while Gilchrist played what he regarded as his best-ever Test innings, a fighting 144 in the Second Test at Kandy.

The hallmark of Australia's approach was its intelligence. Batsmen and bowlers exchanged ideas, turning team meetings into think tanks; the new physiotherapist, Alex Kountouris, a Melburnian who had been the Sri Lankan physio, provided valuable insights into the opponent and the conditions. The Australian unit was working together, very much in the style Steve Waugh had instilled, but with a new freshness. Like Border, Waugh had ended up as a gnarled presence, monumental and hard as rock but also as inflexible; like Border, he got out of the game just when he looked like getting in the way.

Kandy was Ponting's real statement of assumption of the captaincy. When Ricky Ponting was a four-year-old child, his grandmother had dressed him in a T-shirt saying: 'Inside this shirt is an Australian Test cricketer.' Since his rehabilitation and marriage he had seemed fated to the captaincy. Publicly disgraced over drunken incidents in Sydney and Kolkata in the late 1990s, Ponting had taken his time growing up; but grow up he had, and by the early 2000s his behaviour was exemplary and his ambition was unalloyed. Now was his time, and his batting would thrive on the responsibility. More than any of his recent captaincy predecessors, Ponting was able to blend his roles: one-day and Test, batsman and leader, fieldsman and field-setter. There was none of the divided identity that hobbled Taylor and Waugh in their later years. Ponting, wrote Gideon Haigh, 'personifies Australian cricket: busy, industrious, confident, aggressive, combative, sometimes truculent, always in the thick of the action ... [He] fields as close to the bat as circumstances permit, close enough for the batsman to feel his spiky aura.' None of the detached ruminations of a Taylor at first slip or a Waugh at gully. Ponting was leading from front and centre.

Kandy was an epic Test match in its own right. On the first day, seventeen wickets fell; on the second, five. The pitch didn't change much, but the attitude of the batsmen did. Australia wasted a won toss, surviving the first hour without losing a wicket, then lost four men in the second hour and six in the third. Langer made 3 in thirty-nine balls before Ponting, Martyn, Lehmann, Symonds and Gilchrist lasted forty-nine balls collectively. Hayden top-scored with 54 in Australia's 120, a mystifying collapse on a good wicket.

Kasprowicz, showing his taste for subcontinental strips, was the saviour in McGrath's absence. Soon, Sri Lanka were making Australia's innings look competitive, losing 7/92 by stumps; yet on the second day the Test's direction switched back on itself, Chaminda Vaas and Muralidaran, all eye and follow-through, swatting a national record 79 for the last wicket and taking the home side ninety-one runs into the lead.

Gilchrist, who had been in the first extended batting slump of his Test career, volunteered to go in at number three when Ponting pulled up with a slipped disc in his back. Buchanan and Ponting considered Martyn, but the number four liked it where he was and had a superstitious aversion to sudden changes of routine. Gilchrist's scores in the series had been 4, 0 and 0. He needed something to shake him up, and as stand-in captain was

ABOVE: Warne in Sri Lanka: back, and back to his best.

in a position to grasp it. He had been having trouble with Murali, and wanted to come in against the new ball, before the spin was taking hold and the catchers were closing in around the bat. He got his wish, coming in at 1/11 when Hayden was out, and was soon joined by Martyn at 2/26, deep in arrears.

Martyn nicked one to second slip before he had scored, but Mahela Jayawardene couldn't hold the chance. This seemed to ginger up Gilchrist's determination, and he proceeded to accumulate a measured (by his standards) 144, resisting the unending pressure of Murali, Vaas and left-armer Nuwan Zoysa. He eliminated the sweep from his repertoire, forcing himself to hit full balls down the ground rather than square. Martyn, following his plan, camped on his back foot, playing the turn off the wicket.

At the end of Australia's first innings Murali had taken his 500th Test wicket, that of Kasprowicz, who, Ponting observed, was the only batsman he knew who believed Murali could be cover-driven. The other was Glenn McGrath. But it would be many hours' bowling before Murali had his 501st. In two and a half sessions Gilchrist and Martyn accumulated 200 pressure-packed runs before Murali, who had resorted to bowling around the wicket to defensive fields, trapped Gilchrist. Martyn went on to make 161, also one of his best knocks. Having gone through 2003 without a Test century, he now had two in successive matches. While Murali was able to exploit the increasing turn against new batsmen, Australia scrambled to a lead of 351. Martyn was last out after a nine-hour vigil.

The lead seemed ample when Sri Lanka lost two cheap wickets, but Jayasuriya gave a reprise of past glories in smashing the Australians for 131 at nearly a run a ball. Suffering from cramp, he gave up on running. He didn't need to. He hit seventeen fours and two sixes before edging Gillespie to Gilchrist. Notwithstanding Jayasuriya's virtuosity, Australia had stopped Sri Lanka from forming any partnerships greater than seventy-six, and wickets fell steadily on the fourth afternoon. Still, with three wickets in hand and fifty to get on the last day, and Vaas not out 30 to follow his unbeaten 68 in the first innings, Australia could ill-afford to celebrate on the fourth night.

On the last morning, Ponting dropped the field deep to give Vaas a single. Vaas responded by trying to win the match in boundaries. He took ten off a Gillespie over, then clobbered Warne through deep mid-wicket. Two overs into the day, Sri Lanka had reduced their requirement from fifty-one to thirty-three.

Holding his nerve, Warne tossed one up to Vaas, who committed the crucial error, lifting a drive to the only man in the infield in front of point on the off side, the gifted catcher Symonds.

Symonds dropped it.

Two balls later, pumped taut by the belief that this was his lucky day, Vaas slog-swept Warne. The ball turned and caught a bit of under-edge; Vaas went through with his shot and dragged it towards deep square leg, where Langer was waiting, his fully bent midriff behind the ball. Four overs later, Australia had won by twenty-seven runs, reminiscent of their get-out-of-jail win over the same opponent on Warne's first tour, twelve years earlier. This was the first time since then that an Australian team had come to Sri Lanka and won. The achievement, winning in one of their unhappy hunting grounds, was a rehearsal of the challenge that would confront them six months later.

The golden goose was given another kicking through the winter, with a meaningless compromise tour to Zimbabwe (Test cricket was cancelled, but three one-dayers and plenty of golf were played by all except MacGill, who refused to tour on moral grounds); a forgettable two-match series against Sri Lanka in northern Australia; and the ICC Champions' Trophy in England, the 'mini-World Cup' that Australian teams were still having trouble treating with the utmost focus.

Minds were trained on September, and the tour to India. A lot of the team's energy went to blotting out the winter diversions and retaining the momentum and intelligence gained from the autumn tour of Sri Lanka.

All of this preparation was thrown out of kilter when Ponting broke a thumb batting against England in the Champions' Trophy. A reluctant Gilchrist – Oh no, he thought when Ponting gave him the news, I don't need this – was talked into accepting the interim captaincy by his wife. Another aspect of Gilchrist's refreshing and unusual honesty was his inability to feign ambition.

The planning for India continued. Now it would be a test of whether processes, and teamwork, could overcome the loss of the whole's most central part. And the Indian series in 2004 was indeed a triumph of planning. No stone would be left unturned. Hotel chefs would be given strict instructions. A yoga teacher would be employed. The players would be taught how to drink their water during play (sips, not gulps). Buchanan's laptop was in danger of blowing a diode.

The main innovations in the plan revolved around the bowling. Rather than follow India down the path of spin, Australia would play to its strong suit, selecting three pacemen plus Warne. The bowlers would aim at the Indian top order's stumps rather than the defensive outside-off line that evolved under pressure in 2001. Knowing that the Indian batsmen would want to whip them through the on side, Australia would stack the field between the lines of mid-on and fine leg, putting as many as five men in that sector. The previous tour's tactic had been to bowl outside off stump and try to get the batsmen caught in

BUCHANAN'S LAPTOP WAS IN DANGER OF BLOWING A DIODE

the cordon, while leaving vacancies in the on side to tempt the Indians to play injudiciously across the line. This time, Australia would try to frustrate Indian egos: give them their favourite leg-side shots but clog the field and deny them the pay-off in boundaries. It had been observed that many of the Indian batsmen grew jittery without a diet of fours. So the Australian attitude was starve them and win the game of patience.

In their batting, the Australians would embroider the theories they had worked on in Sri Lanka. Martyn, for instance, declared that he was going to play every ball from the spinners, barring a soft half-volley, off the back foot. Rather than leaping forward to smother the spin, he would wait and play late, watching the ball off the pitch and committing at the last moment. Lehmann preferred to dance laterally on the crease and prevent the bowlers from settling. Hayden and Langer used the sweep, but more selectively than in 2001. Gilchrist would hold faith with aggression.

At Bangalore in the First Test, it was the newcomer who had the best plan. Michael Clarke, from the western suburbs of Sydney, had been selected for the tour to gain experience but found himself replacing Ponting in the eleven, batting at six while Katich was bumped up to number three. Both starred in Bangalore. Katich employed the light feet and wrists of an Indian to score a ballast-like 81, while Clarke sparkled, cavorting fearlessly down the wicket to clip Kumble and Harbhajan into the deep. His 151 was one of those innings that really captured the imagination, not simply because it was on his debut but because it was on his debut in India. This was the place where Australia had developed phobic difficulties, where batsmen of the calibre of Ponting, Gilchrist and Blewett had ended previous series barely able to make a run, psychologically crushed; and this open-faced cricket nut skipped in, handled the spin like Allan Border, and put Australia in a winning position. Gilchrist, inspired by his junior partner, exorcised a few of his 2001 demons by scoring 104 off 109 balls. All of the bowlers contributed to keeping India below 250 in both innings, and Australia won by 217 runs.

One down. In the Second Test, in Chennai, the Australians braced for an Indian rebound. At first they countered India's renewed energy, with the top order constructing a platform of 2/189, but then Anil Kumble took seven wickets in an hour and a half, and Australia lost 8/46 to post a moderate 235. Kumble's record against Australia was superb, whether on dusty turners such as Delhi in 1996 and Chennai in 1998 or by his labours on the road of Adelaide in 2003/04. An unconventional leg-spinner, almost a medium-pacer whose stock ball was the in-dipping top-spinner, his courtly personality and gentle nature belied the awkward subtlety of his bowling. He rarely had a hair out of place, nor a loose ball. He was a bowler who embodied the batsman's saying of 'You're never in' – that is, no matter how confident or settled the batsman, Kumble was always capable of something dangerous.

Bolstered by 155 from Virender Sehwag, the Tendulkar-lookalike with a more tempestuous, belligerent game, India led by 141 on the first innings. Warne, incidentally, took 6/125, his only five-wicket haul in three tours to India. Australia faltered early in their second innings, with Gilchrist going in at number three and almost but not quite pulling off the desired miracle, scoring 49 yet being bowled around his legs by Kumble just before stumps. Then, though, Australia kicked again in the middle-order, Martyn (104) and nightwatchman Gillespie (26) batting together for four hours on the fourth day, adding 149 and giving the captain Gilchrist what he called his favourite day in ninety-six Test matches.

Set 229 to win, India were 0/19 at the start of what promised to be a spine-tingling fifth day. Instead, the only tingling sound was that of the monsoon on the metal roofing of the Chidambaram Stadium, and the anticipated epic finish was consigned to the closet of might-have-beens.

At one up with two to play, the Australian squad departed from routine again. Buchanan, Ponting, Gilchrist and the ACB had agreed that a scheduled mid-tour provincial match would do the players more harm than good. These matches, a political sop from the Indian board to one of its satellite members, were poorly attended, mostly involved a composite home selection rather than a true provincial team, and required an exhausting travel schedule. Almost without exception, they were boring draws on featherbed wickets. So this time, rather than drain their energies in such a match, the Australians were excused from their duties for five days. The announcement, mid-tour, led to great excitement. Warne wanted to go to England (but was turned down). Gilchrist ended up joining his family in Singapore, Hayden went fishing in Goa, some players relaxed in Mumbai, and they came together a week later with all the freshness and anticipation of a First Test at Brisbane. It sounds like a small thing, but in the minds of the touring players it felt like Christmas.

The Indians, meanwhile, were squabbling. Ganguly's batting had been shaky again, and he pressed the groundsman at the Vidarbha Cricket Association ground in Nagpur to shave the pitch bare for the Third Test. The groundsman did not like the cut of Ganguly's jib, however, and defied him. On the morning of the

Test, the English umpire David Shepherd said, 'Looks like home, doesn't it?' The strip was as green as Gloucester in May.

Gilchrist went out to toss, knowing that Tendulkar was returning from his chronic tennis-elbow injury. India would be at full strength then, as long as Ganguly ... but where was Ganguly? Gilchrist was met on the field by Rahul Dravid. He asked Dravid where Ganguly was. Dravid mumbled that he didn't have a clue. The Prince of Bengal had walked out in a huff. Then, it seemed, Harbhajan had come down with gastroenteritis. With the Indian team falling apart before their eyes, the Australians grew tense with excitement. Gilchrist told his men they were batting.

The first day yielded 362 runs for seven wickets, as India, crying out for a third seamer, could not take advantage of the green track. Ganguly might have regretted storming off when he saw how much hay the batsmen were making, Martyn scoring another century while Clarke got 91 and Lehmann 70. Australia's 398 turned out to be more than ample for a lead. On the second and third days India capitulated for 185, Gillespie taking five and McGrath, becoming the first Australian fast bowler to play 100 Test matches, three.

At lunch on the third day, then, Australia found itself in a familiar position: one Test up, more than 200 runs ahead on the first innings, India on its knees. Kolkata, anyone? This time, Gilchrist had no hesitation taking a more conservative line than Steve Waugh in 2001. He batted again. Hayden and Langer fell early but it was the new middle-order, each having a superlative series, who piled on the pain for Dravid and his increasingly desperate bowlers. Katich made 99, Martyn 97 and Clarke 73 as Australia moved to 5/329 before Gilchrist declared. This time, surely, India were gone. The target was 543. Australia had the best part of five sessions to get them out. There was no rain forecast between the Himalayas and the equator.

The fourth-day rout of India had a spirit of celebration – thirty-five years of steam being let off, but more particularly, all that pain from 2001 and, for those who were there, 1998. In his second over Gillespie bowled Akash Chopra, Sehwag's sidekick who had been a pebble in Australia's shoe in the 2003–04 series. In his next over

ABOVE: Gilchrist and company storming the mountain in Nagpur.

Gillespie bowled Dravid: no Kolkata today. McGrath didn't strike until his fifth over – but it was Tendulkar he got, caught by Martyn for 2. Ten minutes later, Laxman lifted a catch off Kasprowicz to McGrath. Kasprowicz was one of the 1998–2001 veterans. His Australian career had been intermittent, a disproportion of it played in India: he would send a message to the selectors, 'I can handle a cocktail in the West Indies, too, it's not just curries I like.' He had Mohammad Kaif nicking to Gilchrist in his next over, and India was 5/37. Sehwag banged out a lonely 58 like a let-down reporter on a late deadline before becoming Warne's first wicket of the day.

Relegated to a supporting role in this series, Warne did not mind. He had taken stick but restrained his ego, starting his spells with deep fielders and keeping to the holding pattern where it was needed. He, Kasprowicz and Lehmann were usually in a delirious state by the end of their Indian tours; this time it was the delirium of happiness.

The Indian tail gave a flutter, or perhaps a twitch of rigor mortis. The game was over late on the fourth afternoon when Zaheer Khan lofted a catch to the deep. The catcher was Martyn, the flat-track bully from Perth who had just proved himself the world's premier batsman on the low turners of Sri Lanka and India. The bowler was Warne, who had come to India in 1998 with the expectation of bringing the real thing to the home of spin, but was finishing now as a wiser, scarred, sunburnt stock bowler humbly following a team plan. And the captain, leaping around in his gloves and pads to give full voice to the long years of anguish, was a fellow whose dearest wish was to give the leadership back to its rightful holder.

This victory had only one parallel in the recent era: Sabina Park in 1995. Australia had won in India, at last. Allan Border was there, again, as a commentator, and Ponting was able to share in the celebration as a travelling squad member. But this time the players' thoughts extended, as Taylor's had to Border in Jamaica nine years previously, to the man who had been here four times and never been able to win. Steve Waugh was kept very busy on the phone that night.

'DO ANYTHING ... BUT DON'T LOSE TO THE POMS'

Edgbaston, August 2005

BEFORE THE SERIES, IAN CHAPPELL ASKED ROD MARSH, THEN ENGLAND'S ACADEMY HEAD COACH, IF ENGLAND WOULD DARE PICK PIETERSEN. 'THEY'D BETTER,' MARSH GROWLED, 'OR ELSE THEY WON'T WIN.'

In his 2008 novel *Netherland*, which features a cricket club in the boroughs of New York, the Irish writer Joseph O'Neill speaks of luck as a kind of haunting. One character tells another how 'when you're running for your life, you have this strong sense of luck. You don't feel lucky, that's not what I mean. What I mean is, you feel luck, good and bad, everywhere. The air is luck. Do you understand what I'm saying? I tell you, it's a horrible feeling.'

When the Australian Ashes tourists of 2005 arrived at Heathrow, their captain, Ricky Ponting, was informed that the British boxer Ricky Hatton had just knocked out the Australian champion Kostya Tszyu. Ponting's shoulders slumped, as if this were not the first straw but the last. 'Well,' he said, 'that's just what we need.'

From that moment, there seemed a haunting of luck around this group. The air was luck. They were looking for portents, and everywhere they found signs of doom and dread. Before the tour started, senior players and their employer, Cricket Australia (the ACB having updated its name in mid-2003), had clashed over the arrangements for travelling wives and children. The upshot was that the players had to make all their bookings

ANDREW SYMONDS HAD A DRINK **AND** COULDN'T STOP

themselves and find apartments near the team hotels, in which they were compelled to stay. Then, Cricket Australia had refused a request for another stopover at Gallipoli. The players were partially mollified by the promise of a day trip to Fromelles.

Evil things floated on the air. England, meanwhile, were hammering Bangladesh. England had been hammering everyone. When they first met, in a Twenty20 match in Southampton, England extinguished Australia's batting line-up for 79 runs, taking seven wickets for eight at one point. Australia had trained for four hours that morning, with Buchanan dismissing the Twenty20 fixture as a hit-and-giggle nonsense. Then Somerset chased down Australia's 342 in a one-dayer with three overs to spare. Bad, bad, bad.

It got worse. The young all-rounder Shane Watson was celebrating his birthday the night before a one-day international against Bangladesh in Cardiff. Andrew Symonds had a drink and couldn't stop. He arrived for breakfast in the team hotel still in his going-out clothes, then went to his room and fell so deeply asleep that Michael Clarke was unable to wake him. 'He was still drunk,' Gilchrist said, 'when the team bus left for the ground' on match morning. On the field, Symonds leaned

LEFT: Nightmare vision: Was this what the Australians had come all that way to see?

on a wheelie bin while stretching his legs, and fell over. He was dropped from the match, but Ponting and Buchanan didn't get their stories straight before giving conflicting explanations to the press. Symonds was injured. Symonds had flu. Ponting and Buchanan were caught dissembling; the team was caught with its pants down and lost the match. To Bangladesh. Symonds was fined and suspended, but some of the players who had been drinking with him on the night in question felt he'd been hard done by. Two factions of Australian cricketers travelled in the one bus to Bristol to play England. Their bus dropped them on the wrong side of the ground and they had to drag their kitbags through an honour guard of English mockery. They were an embarrassment. Then they lost. To England. Hayden and Gilchrist were the subject of a tabloid attack for allegedly shouting at a boy in the crowd. On 7 July, bombs went off in London. 'If this was Pakistan,' one of the Australians said, 'we'd be going home already.'

Bad, bad, bad.

How had it come to this? Unlike most twists of cricketing fate, this one came without either warning or tense build-up. Australia's springtime conquest of the final frontier had been followed by a majestic home summer: their roadkill was New Zealand at home 2-0, Pakistan at home 3-0, and New Zealand away 2-0. In eight Tests, one draw was caused by rain but otherwise the narrowest margin was nine wickets. Australia was as dominant as at any time during the run of 1999–2001. Desperate to give them a contest, the ICC was cobbling together an international all-stars team to tour Australia in late 2005.

So where had the haunting come from? Gilchrist gave a hint when he said that he had played each of his Ashes series 'with a kind of nervous dread. What if we were going to be the group that lost them? … I always felt I was playing to avoid the negative of losing the Ashes.' Avoiding a negative can be a dicey motivation. There was also the inevitable mental staleness caused by too easy a procession of victories. Teams, like muscles, become less adaptable after excessive repetition of the one action.

Beyond what was happening to the Australians were recent changes in the English team. Gone were the sufferers of 'recent trauma syndrome': Stewart, Hussain, Caddick, Gough, Butcher and company. Now they had three world-class fast bowlers in Harmison, Flintoff and Jones, with able back-up in Hoggard and Giles. They had two proven top-order batsmen in Vaughan and Trescothick. And they had one new player who was capable of inspiring genuine fear among the Australians. Kevin Pietersen had left South Africa because he feared the system of selecting national teams by racial quotas would work against him. For perhaps the only time in his life, he was overly pessimistic about his talents. As it turned out, no selection system could have worked against him. But he wasn't to know that when he had moved to England at the age (it can't be called a tender age, in Pietersen's case) of nineteen. As a new Englishman, he was regularly clubbing county attacks and international limited-overs teams. He smacked Australia for 91 not out in the one-dayer at Bristol. He had an earring, a Pepé Le Pew hairstyle and a love of the spotlight that he shared with his good mate and Hampshire colleague Warne. He spoke like a South African and played in English colours, but the feelings he aroused in the Australians were connected with India (Tendulkar) and the Caribbean (Lara). In Pietersen, England finally had one of those batsmen who could turn any game around. No match could be considered won till Pietersen was twice out. Not since David Gower, or Ian Botham at his peak, had England had a batsman capable of inciting these kinds of caveats.

Nonetheless, it was no certainty that Pietersen would be selected. Graham Thorpe, more than a decade older, had his supporters (among them, no doubt, Warne and Ponting, calling 'Pick him!' from the back of the room). For England to pick Pietersen over Thorpe would signal more than a judgement of talent: it would be a statement of intent. Before the series, Ian Chappell asked Rod Marsh, then England's academy head coach, if England would dare pick Pietersen. 'They'd better,' Marsh growled, 'or else they won't win.'

Beyond the pure talent, there was a singleness of purpose that had seldom attached itself to England teams in the previous two decades. Vaughan's men went around in the correct uniforms. They practised intensely and professionally. They enjoyed each other's company. They were men in their twenties, wholly committed to winning back the Ashes, unlike the Australians, who were mostly in their thirties and as likely to be thinking about when to make time for their children and their sponsors as about cricket.

All these things were in the English air, floating about with a fine early summer mist and a haunting of luck.

The Australians collected themselves and won the balance of their one-day encounters with England, but this was a summer when pure results and statistics told even less of the story than usual. England were the coming men; Australia were applying all their grit and gifts to hanging on.

In an odd way, even Australia's 239-run win in the First Test at Lord's seemed to bring them down a peg. The first morning was dominated by three balls from Harmison from the Pavilion End. None took a wicket, but that was not the point. His steeplers biffed Langer's arm, Hayden's helmet and Ponting's cheek. The memorable images of that first morning are of bloodied Australian batsmen consulting their medical staff while Harmison stood around with his teammates looking like a giant child who is still coming to know his own strength.

If first sessions had recently been telling overtures to Ashes series, England's at Lord's lacked subtlety. By tea, Australia was out for 190 and England was 0/10. Harmison was having a cup of tea, his name going on the Lord's honour board for his 5/43.

Australia, though, had not lost at the ground since 1934, and the Pavilion End, with the slope taking the ball into the bat, was McGrath's second home. In thirty-one balls he took five wickets; by the end of the first day seventeen batsmen were out. On days two and three Australia managed a lead of thirty-five and extended it by 384 runs in its second innings, Martyn, Clarke and Katich leading with half-centuries. McGrath did his thing again in the fourth innings, and business seemed, on the scorecard at least, to be proceeding as usual.

Yet in a summer of signs, there were indicators, if you looked closely enough, that this was not the typical English failure. Harmison, with eight wickets, generated the kind of pace and bounce in both innings that made it a certainty that he would run through the Australian batting at some stage during the series. England had a spearhead, a very sharp and fast-moving one. In their batting, although they made 155 and 180 they also unveiled a talisman. Pietersen hit McGrath for three fours in one over, and also lifted Warne out of the ground, during his first-innings 57. He was only dismissed in the game by Martyn's magnificent outfield catch; in the second innings he was undefeated on 64. Australia had beaten England, but they had not beaten Pietersen.

In defeat, Vaughan's captaincy had an air of confidence and certainty that Ponting's lacked. Australia appeared to be running its tactics by committee, and Ponting rarely took a decision without going into conference with Warne, Gilchrist and Hayden. Personally, Vaughan had the better of a brief sledging encounter with his counterpart. When Vaughan came out to bat in the first innings, Ponting remarked on how many England throws had been pegged close to the Australian batsmen. 'Yes, plenty,'

THERE WERE INDICATORS THAT THIS WAS NOT THE TYPICAL ENGLISH FAILURE

Vaughan replied. Mishearing him as saying, 'Yes, we meant it,' Ponting retorted, 'If you hang around here for a while you can expect your fair share flying around too.' To which Vaughan gave a smirk and said, 'You're no Steve Waugh. Get back to second slip.'

(Martyn, incidentally, came up with the best possible response to the throwing tactic in the second innings: when one ball was chucked at him, he clipped it off his toes to the boundary. No more throws came anywhere near him.)

As for the Australian bowling, although McGrath was McGrath and donned new boots marked '500' after taking his 500th Test wicket in the first innings, Gillespie, after a stellar three years free of injury, had lost pace and movement and was caned. Gilchrist had failed to influence the match with his batting, falling in both innings to Flintoff bowling around the wicket, an old trick teams had tried on Gilchrist ever since his first appearance. It's easy to say this in retrospect, but Australia's win, resting so heavily on the efforts of one bowler, was not quite as it looked.

The Australians sang their victory song in the England changing room. The only courtesy they showed was to wait until the English players had left. Hubris, complacency, over-confidence: Ponting's team was tempting all three. The truth was that they weren't all that confident. They were shaky deep inside, and were using bluff and bluster to reassure themselves. The question was whether they had England bluffed. After all these years, it was possible. David Graveney, the English chairman of selectors who had taken full responsibility for past defeats except in the sense of reconsidering either his position or his ideas, said England was still on track for the 2-1 series win he had predicted. The problem was, England was also on track for the 0-5 loss that Glenn McGrath had predicted.

One thing McGrath could not predict was the location of a cricket ball lying on the grass at Edgbaston while the Australians were warming up for the Second Test. As he ran about, full of beans in the hope of bowling on a pitch that had been underwater a few days earlier, McGrath stepped on the loose ball, his ankle ligaments went whang, and Australia's Ashes campaign went kerplunk. Many of McGrath's teammates, seeing him writhing on the turf, thought he was joking. Perhaps they refused to believe it. Perhaps Ponting, also, refused to believe that the series momentum had just taken a U-turn, because when he won the toss he went ahead with his preconceived decision to bowl. He would say that the pitch felt cold to the touch, indicating moisture beneath, and with the overcast day he expected the ball to swing and seam.

Others differed. When Vaughan indicated that England would be batting first, his coach Duncan Fletcher thought, Great toss to win, Vaughany. There would be newspaper reports that Warne confronted Ponting over the decision, and that they had a changing room dust-up. These speculations might have been speculative, giving concrete form to a logical idea: surely Warne, with all his experience, would not have made the same mistake. But if he thought so, he only expressed a mild preference for batting first and did not vociferously contest Ponting's decision. For all

ABOVE: Warne steps on his stumps; Flintoff finds it funny.

the apparent wisdom in W.G. Grace's dictum, 'When you win the toss, bat. If in doubt, think about it and then bat. If you have very big doubts, consult a colleague – and then bat', there were many recent precedents for successfully inserting opponents. Steve Waugh had done it in eleven Tests and Australia won every time.

Australia would have been happy to bowl England out within eighty overs on that first day, very happy indeed. But they could never have accounted for England scoring 407 runs in that time. Australia had not conceded 400 in the first day of a Test since 1938. Who could have expected it now? Not Ponting, who spent much of the day standing at second slip with his arms folded and a hand scratching his chin.

His first problem was that Gillespie's loss of form, out of the blue and without any obvious explanation, was total. His second problem was that the lion-hearted Kasprowicz had run out of steam. His third problem was that Lee, who had spent seventeen Tests out of the Australian team, was neither bowling at sufficient pace nor moving it in the air enough to trouble the England batsmen.

But here was Ponting's biggest problem: the liberated, free-wheeling Englishmen. With the ball not moving laterally, Trescothick's non-existent footwork was no handicap. He stood on his crease and swung everything around his off stump through the arc between point and mid-off. Twenty fours came in the first session, one every nine balls. He was desperately unlucky not to score a century, being caught behind off Kasprowicz for 90. Andrew Strauss contributed 48 and England went to lunch at 1/132. Vaughan made a brisk 24, but the hammer blow came after Vaughan was fourth out at 187, the day not even halfway old, and Pietersen was joined by Flintoff.

Here were another two cases of statistics' failure to tell the true story. Pietersen averaged 53 throughout the 2005 series; ask any Australian player, and they would swear he averaged close to 100. Flintoff's batting average in the series was 40, his bowling 27. Ask the Australians, and he scored 70 every time he batted and took 5/50 whenever he bowled. The fact was, Pietersen and Flintoff timed their contributions to marvellous perfection. On the first day at Edgbaston they added 103 for the fifth wicket, Pietersen scoring 71 and Flintoff 68. But the psychological effect was more like a 200-run partnership in a session. Flintoff had played forty-eight Tests and built up a reputation as large as his physique, but Lord's was his first Ashes Test and he had failed there. At Edgbaston he was streakiness personified, throwing his bat at everything, but also lucky; whatever he tried, it seemed, the ball ended up flying to or over the boundary. Pietersen was more measured in his brutality. After Flintoff was out, the hurricane leaving a trail of wrecked Australian nerves, the tail also had a happy fling. England knocked up six sixes and fifty-four fours in the day.

In *Wisden*, Andrew Miller wrote of a 'guilelessness' in England's first-day batting: 'Like a gang of pikey chancers, they couldn't believe their luck at sneaking into the warehouse behind the guard dog's back, but instead of making off with the goods in a calm and orderly fashion, they decided to whoop and yell and holler, and got themselves evicted anyway.'

Never can a score of 407, lacking a single century, have had such a demoralising effect on an Australian team. The bowlers came off looking cowed; Ponting chewed his lips. Hayden, relieved by rain from batting on the first evening, confirmed his iffy lead-up form by wafting his first ball on day two to cover. He hadn't made a Test duck for nearly three years. Piece by piece, Australia was coming apart. Langer, Ponting, Martyn, Clarke and Katich started like they meant business but could not finish the job on a 500-run wicket. Gilchrist seemed as if he was going to step in and save them, as he always did, but this time the tail-enders let him down and the last five wickets went for forty-six. Gillespie, the stalwart of the rear-end, was batting as badly as he was bowling. Gilchrist might have only needed another hour at the crease to reverse the tide of the series, but was stranded on 49. It would be his last innings of any threat or substance.

The Australian bowlers, two days after their humbling, were not quite done with. Gillespie and Kasprowicz were ineffectual again, but Warne stepped up to carry the attack, as he would for the next four Tests. The soap opera of his private life was turning into … a soap opera, with multiple domestic separations and reconciliations being documented for posterity in women's magazines. During 2005, his wife was divorcing him. Did it affect his performances? Without a doubt: the 2005 tour would turn out to be his most personally profitable Ashes series, with 40 wickets at less than 20 and 249 runs at nearly 30. Divorce must have cleared his mind. This was his series, more than any other Australian's or Englishman's. On the third day he was all over the English, bowling Strauss with a Gatting ball and removing Pietersen and Flintoff, though not before the latter had clubbed 73 off the pacemen. Lee built up real steam and took four wickets of his own. England collapsed like a nervous lot on the third morning, only increasing their ninety-nine-run first-innings lead by a further 131 when the ninth wicket went down. This was the Australian fightback. This was why they were the best.

But England had some fight in them too. Simon Jones hung around with Flintoff for fifty-one late but critical runs. They didn't take long. Kasprowicz and Lee went for thirty-eight in two overs. Lee, whom Ponting had intended to use as a strike bowler in four-over bursts, was needed for longer spells to make up for the

DIVORCE MUST HAVE CLEARED HIS MIND

bluntness of Kasprowicz and Gillespie, and was consequently tiring by the time Flintoff began hitting out. *Wisden* recorded that Graham Gooch had to fish one of Flintoff's sixes out of the television cables on the pavilion roof. Yet again, England was taking command of the symbolism, the iconic moments upon which each match turned.

Australia now needed 281 to win, a half-century more than they had been hoping to chase. But they were confident. Too confident? This would be the question raised by their batting. From the first session of this series, the Australian approach had been questionably aggressive. Of course, they had built their record on attacking cricket. But in the previous few months they had honed this aggression on the softness of New Zealand and Pakistan. England was a harder nut, and the Australians didn't seem to be taking account of their opponents' skills. They would crash through, or crash. As it turned out at Edgbaston, they crashed.

Langer and Hayden skittered away to forty-seven in twelve overs before Langer was bowled by Flintoff for a breezy 28. Flintoff followed with a memorable over of brutish in-duckers to Ponting before getting one to nip away and take the edge. Ponting rated it 'among the best sequence of deliveries I have ever received in any form of cricket.' This was the over, the moment; it called up memories of McGrath dismantling Brian Lara. The Australians watching in the changing room knew they were in strife.

With Ponting gone for a duck, Hayden continued the dumb cricket he would employ right up to the Fifth Test, 'dominating' with his body language but failing on the scoreboard. Martyn, Clarke, Katich – all made starts, but none could go on. Having started the series with such promise, the Australian middle-order would by the end be the scapegoats for defeat. Martyn received some poor decisions as the series went on, but over-confidence quickly flipped into no-confidence, and the trio of four, five and six seemed to infect each other. If at the beginning of the series they were batting well without being able to convert good starts into scores, by the end they were just batting badly.

Likewise Gilchrist, whose 49 not out in the first innings at Edgbaston must have been his first thought when he woke up in the middle of the night as the tour went on. His bogeyman Flintoff got him again in the second innings, this time with a catch off the spinner Giles – another Englishman who didn't take many wickets but popped up when needed. Terry Alderman had said that any batsman who got out in this series to Ashley Giles ought to hang himself. By the end of the series, ten Australians would have been swinging.

Gillespie, the nightwatchman's nightwatchman, went in above Warne but got a duck, lbw to Flintoff. With half an hour left on day three, Australia was 7/140. Vaughan thought he could win by stumps and pressed ahead, calling for the optional half-hour. But Warne possessed what might that summer have been called an English confidence: he slashed and swirled and knocked up a quick 35 with Clarke. At 7/175, Australia was still twitching. With Warne and Clarke restarting the next day, another 106 runs were beginning to hover into the realm of possibility.

Then, in the last over, Harmison thundered in and bowled

what looked to Clarke like a searing hip-high full-toss. Clarke, customarily nervy at the end of the day, stood on his crease, adjusting to the higher ball. But to his horror it was neither searing nor hip-high. It wasn't even a full-toss. It was a ballooning, giggling slower ball, a joke ball, a whoopee cushion of a ball. While all of Clarke's weight was moving back, the ball dropped in front of him, pitched perfectly on his crease, and bobbed through his late downward jam. Australia, 8/175, was surely gone now.

Some 15,000 spectators turned out to watch what could have been a two-ball fourth day. They came to celebrate; but they also came with that gruesome fascination the English had for Warne. A part of them wanted to see him lose and to dance on his grave; another part was riveted by the possibility of what he might do. In England, he was Merlin. The day before, he had become the first overseas bowler to take 100 career Test wickets on English soil. Not only that, but he was the only bowler from anywhere to take 100 wickets in a country that was not his own. Perhaps they also came to pay tribute.

He batted wonderfully that morning. Lee, with his floppy-wristed grip and big heart, got behind the ball at the other end while Warne employed, selectively, his back-foot artistry, as ever just a tick short of looking like an orthodox top-order batsman. England bowled too short, though it seemed to pay off at 8/220 when Warne, on 62, went back to swing a Flintoff lifter to deep square leg. Too far back, as it turned out: he had trodden on his stumps.

England now had sixty-one runs to defend. Australia's last pair was Kasprowicz and Lee. Now it was Lee to take over. He told Kasprowicz they might as well 'dig in and have some fun'. But this was not Allan Border and Jeff Thomson in 1982–83 at Melbourne. There was no 'senior' partner. Lee and Kasprowicz were genuine tail-enders, though neither was a genuine number ten or eleven. They were a bit better than that. With Harmison bowling too frequently into the ribs, both Australians were flinching as it hit them on the body but then smiling as they took the leg byes. They smacked three fours off a Giles over and dragged the required target down to thirty-three. As they edged and hoicked their way forward, England turned to water. The field fell silent. Vaughan didn't seem able to tell his pacemen to bowl a 'batsmen's' length; instead they kept trying to knock heads off.

England always had so much more to lose, by losing. It was written later that the very future of the game in England hinged on this result. That might be overstating it, but while Lee, Warne and Kasprowicz were whittling down both the target and English nerves on the fourth day, two sacred cows of broadcasting were put on hold: Channel 4 didn't show the day's horse races from Redcar, and BBC Radio didn't provide the shipping forecast. That much was at stake. Certainly defeat would have meant the end, for the time being, of hope.

Lee flat-batted Harmison square for four, and Australia needed fifteen to win. On the first ball of the next over, Flintoff dropped short and Kasprowicz upper-cut to third man; Simon Jones ran around, cupped his hands – and the ball burned through them. A single took the required runs to fourteen. Flintoff's next ball to Lee was a no-ball, and it ran to the fence for five. Nine to get. Now, it seemed, all the hauntings and all the omens had been wrong. Australia was Australia, England was England, and the Ashes were going nowhere. Well, the Ashes went nowhere anyway; but it started to look as if the status quo, on the field, was as permanent as the location of the urn. This was a win for the ages. These Australians were not the nervous nellies of the Border and Taylor years; they could chase down anything. Even with nothing left in the tank, even when beaten pillar to post for four days, they could still get up and throw the last punch to end the fight.

Lee took a single and Kasprowicz blocked out the rest of Harmison's next over, his seventeenth. Australia now needed five to win. Was Lee seizing up? He couldn't get a run off Flintoff's next five balls. Then, on the sixth, he got one. Perfect. Four to get, Lee back on strike.

On the first ball of Harmison's eighteenth over, the bowler made the error, giving Lee some width outside off. Lee squirted it to cover point, almost out of the screws. By a freak of luck, it went straight to the deep fielder. The batsmen took a single. Three to win. Vaughan would be asked why he had left a fieldsman out at deep cover point, of all places. He said that with the way Lee

ABOVE: In victory at Edgbaston, Flintoff didn't forget the beaten Lee.

swung at the ball, anything he hit perfectly would go to the rope; but if he mis-hit one just a little, it tended to go square on the off-side. It was smart captaincy which, in hindsight, took on an aura of genius.

Two balls later, Harmison and Vaughan would have cause to say they'd been right all along to bowl bouncers at the tail-enders' heads. Harmison dropped short, Kasprowicz half-ducked into it, half away from it, like the kid cornered against a wall in a school game of brandings. The ball hit his glove and popped up. Did it have enough pace to carry to keeper Geraint Jones? Would Jones, who had dropped most of what came his way that Test, be able to intercept it? Yes, and yes. Often the term 'eruption' exaggerates people's reactions; but this time, England did erupt into celebrations of what they would instantly call 'the Greatest Test'. There was a DVD out with that title before the next Test had even started.

Australia had lost by two runs, the closest margin in 125 years of Ashes cricket. Kasprowicz and Lee sank to their haunches, un-intentionally mirroring each other. Flintoff gave Lee a brief pat, preserved for eternity by the photographers, before racing off to his teammates. The ball hadn't hit Kasprowicz's glove while it was attached to his bat handle, but Billy Bowden gave a lot worse ver-dicts every day of his umpiring career, and even if he was mistaken here, nobody could argue that he'd done the wrong thing. More competent umpires than Bowden would have seen it the same way. Kasprowicz said he would be replaying that ball in his mind for the rest of his life. He wasn't prone to exaggeration, Kasprowicz. He may well be replaying it right now.

Australia had lost. But more significantly, from this point, the 2005 Australians were losers. This is not to ridicule them, but to characterise their state of mind. They grew intrigued by, and fear-ful of, the capacity of Flintoff and Jones to reverse-swing the old ball. They developed paranoid theories about the illegal use of mints and the English bowlers leaving the fields before starting their spells to grab a massage and a few cans of highly caffein-ated 'energy' drinks. The Australians were preoccupied with these tactics, envying the English, and cursing their own bad luck: they decided not to copy the English because they were certain they would be caught and condemned. All of the evil portents now seemed to be coming true. This was a tour born under a bad sign. Gilchrist 'sensed that we were spiralling out of control. Everyone seemed agitated and anxious, and not responding to each other.' There were mutinous words spoken about the coach, Buchanan, who had either run out of ideas or the ideas he presented had worn out. Either way, a significant faction of the team was not interested in what he had to say.

In Manchester, for the next Test match, eight of the Australians played with a defeated air about them. Stuart Clark, the New South Wales bowler brought in as cover for McGrath, observed how exhausted and disunited the Australian changing room seemed. Gilchrist, 'desperate to do something' to dispel 'the tension in the group', snatched at an edge from Vaughan on 41 on the first morning, and the English captain went on to make 166. Only the combined obduracy of Warne, the miraculously recovered McGrath and Ponting, batting throughout the fifth day until the second-last over, could stave off defeat.

At Trent Bridge, that burning core of Australian combativeness was never fully extinguished, but again it lingered in too few. Flintoff made another century, Warne bowled heroically in McGrath's absence, but the batsmen could not finish what they started. Australia followed on for the first time in a Test since Karachi in 1988. They batted better the second time around, but in the turning point Ponting was run out by a specialist fielding substitute, the well-named Gary Pratt. Ponting threw a tantrum in the direction of England's coach Fletcher, only underlining the fact that by now Australia were not only being outplayed, but outgeneralled. Yet again, Warne and Lee marshalled an improbable fightback on the last day, but England overcame the constrictions in their throats and squeaked home by three wickets.

Off the field, the Australians were suffering. Some of the bowlers were bickering about the batsmen: the team was cleaved into multiple factions now. There were unpleasantries among, of all people, the wives and girlfriends. These kinds of things are probably more an effect than a cause of on-field difficulties, but over time the causal order can reverse itself. Gilchrist, who confessed to

A decade later, the spine still tingles and the palms go moist. Edgbaston, World Cup semi-final, 1999.

He could keep wicket fairly well, too. Gilchrist with a reminder that he wasn't just a batsman who wore gloves, catching Sourav Ganguly, Adelaide, 1999.

McGrath's 300th: Lara caught by MacGill first ball, middle of a hat-trick, Perth, 2000. Perfect days were becoming routine.

RIGHT: Oh, for a bit of colour in the game. Australia's Test cricketer of the year, Colin Miller, celebrates another scalp against the West Indies, Sydney, 2001.

BELOW: Heavy-footed, unsubtle, too reliant on the sweep to succeed in India. Matthew Hayden, the boy least likely, relaunches his Test career with a century at Chennai, 2001.

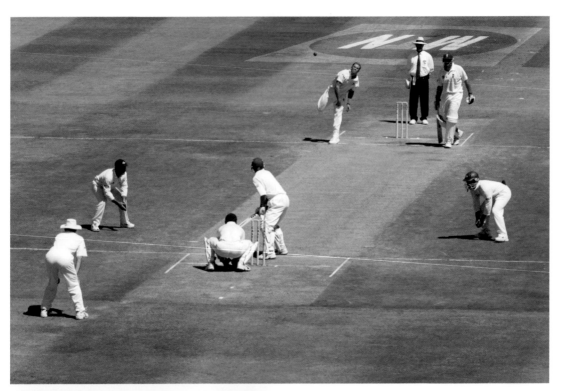

ABOVE: No Warne, no golden age. His hundredth Test, at Cape Town in 2002, was one of his greatest, with 70 overs out of a possible 81 in South Africa's second innings and six match-winning wickets. Gary Kirsten, facing here, was not one of them.

LEFT: 'Go. Walk.' Gilchrist sweeps de Silva onto his pad and the ball pops up, Port Elizabeth, World Cup semi-final, 2003. A moment later, the Australian would hear a voice in his head.

ABOVE: Tendulkar often had to carry India on his own. He can't manage it at Johannesburg, World Cup final, 2003. McGrath and friends watch the replay.

RIGHT: A seamless transition. Steve Waugh consulting with Ponting, who was still learning a captain's body language. Sydney, 2004.

A slog, a catch, and that's it after eighteen years. Steve Waugh farewells the SCG, 2004.

The final frontier conquered, and the unlikely name of Nagpur takes its place in Australian cricket history. Note the non-playing captain, Ponting, jubilant at the rear.

ABOVE: Three and out: Warne, McGrath and Langer survey their domain for the last time: the whitewashed English. Sydney, 2007.

LEFT: He always had a high grip … Gilchrist chooses the biggest stage to play one of the greatest one-day innings, Barbados, World Cup final, 2007.

feeling strained by competing familial and team obligations, said he felt so ashamed walking down the street in Manchester that he pulled his cap low over his eyes. It was twenty years since an Australian cricketer in England had felt the need to do that.

Behind in the series, as if needing a punch in the face to wake them up, Australia's batsmen knuckled down at The Oval. Gideon Haigh had observed something 'puzzling' in the Australians' approach all series: 'England's summer mission statement has been pretty clear and simple: "Win the Ashes." Australia's seems to have been more ambiguous: "Yeah yeah, let's retain the Ashes and all that. But let's become the Chicago Bulls too."' During Buchanan's six-year tenure, this had been the theme: to fend off any satisfaction at merely being the best, and to strive for something greater. Until now, it had worked. But now that it wasn't, they lacked the resources to adapt.

When they came to The Oval, all of that 'Chicago Bulls' aura had been blown away. Australia was not the best anymore. Australia was running second now. The Oval gave them a chance to square things up. Their challenge became pretty clear and simple now too: win the match. They did rise, competing with noticeable focus and vigour, but unfortunately for them, their last-ditch rally was doused by rain, bad light and Pietersen's fifth-day 158. There might have been a way out of this one if Australia had held one of the three catches Pietersen offered, but by the end of the game England, as David Graveney had forecast, had won the series 2-1. And deservingly. To the Australian players it felt more like 4-1. If Lee's shot at Edgbaston had gone a few yards to right or left, they might have ended up fulfilling McGrath's 5-0 boast. (In the 'McGrath Ashes', incidentally, the three matches he played, comprising the Tests at Lord's, Old Trafford and The Oval, Australia won 1-0.) But an Australian win would have been a victory of bluff over skill; in any case, it mattered little now. The Ashes were gone. The legacy of Border, Taylor and Waugh, it seemed in the immediate depression after The Oval, was gone. The empire that took fifteen, twenty years to build had crashed down in the space of a month. Or so it seemed.

By the end of the series, the statistics did give a fairly accurate version of the difference between the teams. England had three batsmen (Pietersen, Flintoff and Trescothick) scoring more than 400 runs at 40-plus averages, whereas Australia had none, their best being Langer's 394 at 43.8. The English scored five centuries and fourteen fifties compared with Australia's three centuries (two of them at The Oval) and nine fifties. England's bowling was an ensemble effort, with Jones taking 18, Flintoff 24, Hoggard 16 and Harmison 17. Australia relied too heavily on Warne's 40, while McGrath took 19 and Lee 20.

The fifth-day English fans at The Oval celebrated with dignity, rising to applaud Warne and McGrath as they returned to their fielding positions after another over. The Australian champions seemed taken aback by such warm tribute, which they accepted with humility. England's players, on the other hand, were soon celebrating as if they had won the right to hold the Ashes not for two years but sixteen. Flintoff and friends took the view that eating's cheating and even sleeping's cheating in the binge that followed The Oval. Perhaps there the seeds were sown. Perhaps the fall began at the moment of triumph. Simon Jones took 5/44 to rout the Australians in the first innings at Trent Bridge, becoming the most feared of England's reverse-swing battery, but broke down after four overs in the second innings and, at the time of writing, has not played another Test.

In Australia, Ponting came home and uttered an ill-judged comment about the series being a 'wake-up call'. It was wake up and good night as well. Ponting had earlier drawn criticism for 'taking the positives' out of each defeat. For their national captain, Australians were much more comfortable with the image of Allan Border hurling his worry ball at the floor. There were no positives to be taken from losing to England. None. No wake-up calls, no positives, no credit to the opponent. The Ashes were gone. As Ian Chappell advised Border when he became captain in 1984, 'You can do anything you like but just make sure you don't lose to the Poms.'

And yet, as is universally the case in the age of PR, Ponting's packaged platitudes bore little resemblance to the reality beneath. McGrath and Langer were filthy at losing. Warne was shattered. Gilchrist and Hayden were in a state of deep personal crisis. Gillespie was looking at the end of a career. Martyn, Clarke and Katich bore the stigma of being known as Australia's soft underbelly. It is no exaggeration to say the Australian players were traumatised, not only by the defeat but by the realignment of loyalties and allegiances within the team. Just as victory is a panacea, defeat is a merciless neon striplight, exposing every spot and blemish. Time would tell whether the trauma led to rejuvenation or dissolution.

Beyond Australia's pain, however, there was something transcendently wonderful about the 2005 Ashes. As Matthew Engel wrote in *Wisden*, the series had to be seen as a victory for cricket. The cliché, Engel said, 'is for once the simple truth'.

'This was the old game routing its enemies, including those inside the walls. The 2005 Ashes constituted cricket in its purest form. There was no artificial colouring, no artificial flavouring, no added sugar. Nothing had to be sexed up or dumbed down. Everything was already there ... Exhilarating contests just unfolded before our eyes. For 22 days of play one hardly dared fetch a beer, have a pee, or sometimes even blink, because the situation could turn on its head in an instant. It was a triumph for the real thing.'

ABOVE: Simon Jones: world's best swing bowler one minute, gone the next.

THE LAST HIGH

Adelaide, December 2006

THESE PLAYERS WERE ITCHING TO PLAY ENGLAND. THIS WAS WHAT THEY WERE WAITING FOR. THIS WAS WHAT KEPT THIS NUCLEUS OF MID-THIRTIES VETERANS MEAN AND ATTUNED.

The last thing anyone in the cricket world expected in September 2005 was that Ponting and Buchanan, with their outwardly phlegmatic reaction to losing the Ashes, might be proven right. 'Taking the positives'? Surely they were taking the piss. Both were widely predicted to be out of their jobs by 2006. England were parading the replica Ashes in Trafalgar Square and 10 Downing Street. England's players were on the right side of thirty, England were the coming men. Australia, meanwhile, were resting their (ageing, weary) bones for a couple of weeks before playing a pretend series, now rich in irony. The ICC Super XI, assembled to give Australia a decent match, was now on its way to Melbourne and Sydney to play the second-best team in the world.

Australia's earlier sequences of Test victories had been prompted by a common denominator: defeat. Losing in Sri Lanka in 1999 and India in 2001 had set off great poultices of winning. Yet few believed the 2005 Ashes would have the same effect. The Australians had been up for too long. They were too old. Ponting's captaincy was too stereotyped. Buchanan's ideas had withered into empty buzzwords.

BOTH WERE WIDELY PREDICTED **TO BE** OUT OF THEIR JOBS BY 2006

The Australian cricketers, however, started winning again. They beat the ICC team, its English members still looking hungover. Covering the bizarre Super Series, Gideon Haigh wrote, was 'like being sent to review Plan 9 From Outer Space'. The contest felt 'as fake as the Hitler Diaries', but the Australian players, on a program of rehabilitation from the Ashes, took it much more seriously than did their celebrity opponents. Then Australia beat the West Indies at home by 379 runs, nine wickets and seven wickets. The opposition was weak, but Hayden and Ponting used the series to regain form. Michael Hussey, the ultra-professional West Australian, failed in his overdue Test debut as an opener but swiftly became indispensable down the order. McGrath, Warne and Lee seemed if anything to have benefited from their hard English summer. So much for Dad's Army.

This new winning run continued, at home and away, against South Africa. Australia won 2-0 at home, crushingly in Melbourne and Sydney after having the better part of a draw in Perth. Almost by stealth, at a time when they were meant to be going into a steep fall, they were regenerating.

There was little of the expected personnel upheaval. Buchanan was given a new contract, with Ponting's backing.

LEFT: With that balance and those hands, Martyn couldn't remain a scapegoat for long.

THE GREATEST 353

Ponting's own position was not under serious threat. The top three endured. Martyn was dropped, then reinstated. Clarke was retained, then dropped, but would soon be reinstated again. Katich was left out for longer, but would come back in time. The selectors tried the Victorian Brad Hodge for a while, but not even a double century against South Africa in Perth could persuade them. He looked like a poor man's Martyn, and they liked the real Martyn more. Kasprowicz and Gillespie would be pensioned off, but not immediately. After being left out for the home summer, Kasprowicz was again invited for a hard foreign slog, in South Africa this time, and Gillespie would enjoy a spectacular encore in Bangladesh in 2006. New bowlers such as Nathan Bracken and Brad Williams were given a try before Australia found a long-term answer to the third seamer's vacancy in Stuart Clark. Stuart MacGill added some more Tests to his fitful career. The longer they went on, the more the Australians were showing that the old order, the established team nucleus, was the foundation not merely for the past but for the future.

Not only were they regrouping that summer, but they seemed, improbably, to be improving. In South Africa they were able to achieve what none of Taylor's or Waugh's teams had done: a 3-0 win, with some style, too, and without the injured McGrath. Clark, from McGrath's Sutherland club in Sydney, had a similar way of running through the crease rather than leaping up and flinging the ball down. He wasn't quite as tall or as fast or as awkward as McGrath, and could not be expected to go on for as long, but after taking 5/55 on the first day of his Test career in South Africa he was good enough. With 20 wickets at 15.8 he was the man of the series.

Hussey, with 257 runs at 64.2, answered all the questions about middle-order stabilisers and raised just one: why wasn't he selected a year earlier? But with a long and distinguished but not quite electrifying first-class career already behind him, this kind of performance at Test level was as much of a pleasant surprise as Clark's.

Australia's most thrilling match of the South Africa tour was the Third Test in Johannesburg. They conceded a thirty-three-run first-innings deficit after South Africa scored 303 and then Langer, in his hundredth Test, was sconed by Makhaya Ntini and retired hurt after a single ball. Only Hussey and Lee passed fifty as Ntini, another of the long line of Test cricketers who showed their best against countries other than Australia, found his line and took six wickets. South Africa looked to put the match beyond doubt with a big second innings, but Clark, Warne and Lee plugged away to stop the home side's lead short of 300. Chasing 294 in the fourth innings, and missing Langer, Hussey showed he could do anything at any time, opening the batting and making 89, sharing a 165-run third-wicket stand with Martyn. Australia needed another ninety-four when Hussey fell, and the match seemed won. But Symonds tried to hit the ball all the way to Brisbane and was out for 29, Gilchrist and Warne failed, and when Martyn was finally out for one of his finest Test innings, 101 in five hours, Australia still needed thirty-four. Clark bashed a quick 10, but top-edged a pull straight into the air. The target was now seventeen.

So: Lee and Kasprowicz, again. This time they weren't trying to stage a break-out from Colditz. This time they were trying to stop five days of good work being wasted by poor application in the middle-order. This time they only needed three overs, from Pollock and Ntini, and a few lusty swipes. In the changing rooms, Langer was inciting furious debate about his mental and physical health as he put on his pads. He wasn't needed:

NOT BAD FOR A TEAM THAT WAS SHATTERED

Australia had Lee and Kasprowicz. Finally Lee cut Pollock over point, a shot not dissimilar to the one he had crunched straight to the fieldsman at Edgbaston, but this time it went to the rope and closed out the match.

Since The Oval, then, Australia had played ten Tests, won nine and drawn one. Not bad for a team that was shattered and over the hill. Their taskmasters sent them off to Bangladesh for another two Tests, both of which they won, though not without a scare. In the First Test in Fatullah, it was impossible to imagine a team looking more beaten than Australia during the first innings. They were hot, bothered, exhausted, some carrying injuries, and to a man looked like they wanted to be doing anything but chasing the balls Shahriar Nafees kept belting to the boundary. Gilchrist's 144, his first century since Wellington thirteen months and seventeen long Tests earlier, saved Australia from a worse first-innings deficit than 158. Bangladesh hiccuped in the face of victory and Australia picked itself off the floor to chase 307 and salvage a three-wicket win, thanks to a second-innings century from Ponting that deserved the epithet of a 'captain's knock'. It was either him doing that or the team suffering an embarrassing defeat. As a comeback, that match deserves a place among the finer Australian wins of the period; the only thing that keeps it from that level is a suspicion that, with 427 on the board and Australia 6/93, the Bangladeshis suffered an attack of vertigo.

In Dhaka, Gillespie nudged and deflected his way to a vaudevillean 201 not out as nightwatchman in what turned out to be the signing-off to his Test career. He faced 425 balls – more, in fact, than he had bowled cumulatively in his ill-fated three Ashes Tests the previous year. But as remarkable as his double-century was, Gillespie's batting was not going to save his place in the team. With Clark's arrival in South Africa and McGrath's impending return, Gillespie, and Kasprowicz as well, had come to the end of the line.

The staggering (in both senses of the word) end to Australia's 2005–06 campaign showed two things. One, they were utterly spent after two years of constant cricket. They had barely had time to think about England, which might have been a good thing. The Englishmen, given more chance to soak up the significance of what they had achieved in 2005, set off on a different trajectory. After the Ashes series they lost 0-2 in Pakistan, grabbed a creditable 1-1 draw in India, were held at home by Sri Lanka, and then beat Pakistan 3-0 at home, helped by a controversial forfeit at The Oval. The official result was England being awarded the match because 'the opposition refused to play'. So deeply offended were the Pakistanis by Darrell Hair's suggestion that they had doctored the ball, Inzamam's team refused to come back onto the field and their administrators spent the next three years alternately arguing over the result and preventing Hair from umpiring. They succeeded only in dragging out the agony.

ABOVE: At Johannesburg, Martyn played another of his match-winning innings – overseas.

Still, it was clear by mid-2006 that England had not come up well after the Ashes. Vaughan, beset by a knee injury among other ailments, was hobbled just as he had reached his prime. So too Simon Jones, who hadn't been sighted since routing the Australians at Nottingham. Harmison showed himself to be a man for one season. Trescothick went the sad way of those whose personalities and temperaments were all too human, and had to suffer the nickname 'Loopy' among his teammates for the frequency of his retreats home from foreign tours in order to attend to private problems. Pietersen charged forward, and Flintoff's bowling maintained a high standard while his batting and captaincy did not. Strauss and Ian Bell retained their places through a mixture of everlasting promise and weak internal competition. Failing to learn the one key lesson from the 2005 Ashes – they only used twelve players in five Tests – England's selectors jumped back on the merry-go-round. It was astonishing that in the eighteen months after the Ashes, it was the losing team, Australia, who stuck with a stable playing group, while it was the winners, England, who blinked.

Australia's campaign to wrest back the Ashes probably started at The Oval in September 2005, when all of that public humility and avowals about the spirit of the game disguised a bitter and impatient appetite for vengeance. The twelve Tests Australia played in 2005–06 had the nature of a hiatus, a period in which they were readying for the series that really mattered to them. It was a fruitful hiatus, but a hiatus all the same. These players were itching to play England. It didn't matter how many runs or wickets they racked up against South Africa, the West Indies or Bangladesh; they would not be tested again until they met Harmison and Flintoff reverse-swinging the old ball under the pressure of a first-innings deficit. This was what they were waiting for. This was what kept this nucleus of mid-thirties veterans mean and attuned.

The campaign proper started in Bangladesh, when Buchanan announced a plan to take the squad on a special exercise in August 2006. This would be the well-documented 'boot camp' near Brisbane run by ex-military specialists. Stuart MacGill would come out of it with a career-crippling knee injury, Shane Warne would rely on his cigarettes as 'special medication' but make the supreme sacrifice of giving up his mobile phone for a week, and the rest of the team would embrace the regime as they had once embraced India: with what can be called a grimacing whole-heartedness. Much of what was said, if put into words, sounds like the patented Buchanan psychobabble; but it seems to have penetrated the heads of those who were there, and the squad emerged from it with fresh spirit and unity.

Three one-day tournaments interposed themselves between August and the 2006–07 Ashes. Chief among these was the ICC Champions Trophy on the subcontinent, which Australia won for the first time, but chief among the actual matches was their encounter with England at Jaipur on 21 October. Their first meeting since The Oval started ominously for Australia. Strauss and Bell cantered along for a bright eighty-three in eighteen overs, knocking Lee, Bracken and McGrath out of the attack. But Strauss and Bell were all England had, as it turned out. The Australian neophytes, Shane Watson and unorthodox left-armer Mitchell Johnson, ran through the top order and England made only 169. Martyn hit a glossy 78 as Australia won by seven wickets. The hauntings of ill-fortune now seemed to be following the English. Flintoff, who was not coping with the quadruple demands as batsman, slipper, bowler and captain, was on the drink and complaining a bit too vocally about his coach. The Australians sniffed opportunity.

Every Australian team, and probably most teams in most sports anywhere, are more comfortable being the hunter than the hunted. The strains of being a target for year after year had finally told on Australia in 2005. They had to break somewhere, and when they did they broke spectacularly. But losing cleansed the system; it put someone else at the head of the pack. Now the Australians could aim up rather than look worriedly over their shoulder.

Meanwhile, England's celebrations after 2005 had betrayed a brittleness, as if they'd better make the most of it. The subsequent hangover exposed disunity. Flintoff, a captain in the Botham mould, was always the wrong substitute for Vaughan; and Vaughan, knowing it, couldn't quite keep his nose out. After the selectorial chops and changes of 2006, Duncan Fletcher asserted his will to restore the 2005 squad by bringing back Geraint Jones and Ashley Giles for 2006–07. Both had contributed well in the earlier series, but were moderate cricketers for whom the chemistry of the 2005 team was a once-in-a-lifetime event. The missing keystone was Vaughan. Nor would Simon Jones be adequately replaced by a third seamer. Moreover, the former Tasmanian Troy Cooley's work with the English pacemen in 2005 had convinced Australia to finally recognise the need for a specialist bowling coach. So they poached Cooley, who had known Ponting since the Australian captain was a pubescent clubmate in Mowbray. Cooley's inclusion in the coaching staff was testament to Ponting's determination and Buchanan's recognition of his own shortcomings as a coach of cricketing skills.

As Harmison revved up to deliver the first ball of the 2006–07 series to Langer, in the Australian viewing box at the Gabba Cooley said, 'There's every chance this first ball can go to first or second slip.' And it did. Harmison sprayed it. Flintoff intercepted it between first and second slips. Not since Phil DeFreitas's half-tracker to Slater in 1994–95 did an England opening bowler start an Ashes series with such a clear statement of what was to follow. Langer smacked two fours in the over, another two in Harmison's next, and that was pretty much it for the England spearhead, removed from the attack after twelve balls and consigned thereafter to sheepish attempts to redeem himself.

Ponting would go to bed that night with 137 runs under his personal belt, his team 3/346, and front-running in the series. England did not show the same hopeless sloppiness as Hussain's team in 2002, Stewart's in 1998 or Atherton's in 1994 on the corresponding day, nor the same doomed sense of 'here we go again'; nonetheless, they had put in a poor day and were up against an Australian team armed with a motivation they hadn't had since 1989. The golden age had sputtered in 2005, but it would not die just yet.

Australia went on to pile up 602, and England replied, if that is the right word, with 157. Expecting to be sent in again, instead they had to go out and give centre-wicket practice to Langer, Hayden and Ponting for another three hours before Australia declared a mere 647 runs ahead. To their credit, Pietersen and Paul Collingwood found some form in the second innings, racking up nineties in a lost cause. Pietersen, patchy since 2005, remained the one man capable of inspiring fear in Australian hearts, and Warne showed his respect by engaging him in a nasty little slanging match. Collingwood was a plucky Scot with a short backlift and simple back-foot technique that might do well on Australian pitches, and the temperament to put up with the incessant sledging from Warne, who was appalled – in the name of imperial honour? – that Collingwood should have received an MBE for the 17 runs he contributed at The Oval as Simon Jones's replacement in 2005.

The Australians could have been more thorough in their work in Brisbane, because in Adelaide Pietersen and Collingwood dotted one and carried it over into the Second Test. This time a relieved Flintoff won the toss and batted on the usual Adelaide Oval road. Having lost by 277 runs less than a week before, his teammates were playing in hopes of arresting the slide, like a man grasping for a tuft of grass as he goes down the cliff face.

They got more than that. Collingwood came to the wicket in the twenty-first over and left it in the 146th. He batted for nearly nine hours and put on 310 for the fourth wicket with Pietersen. This was some batting. Of the thirty-two boundaries the pair scored, only seven were behind the wicket, six of them from Collingwood. Pietersen, perceived to be a leg-side player with a dominant bottom hand, dented the fences primarily on the off. He was so commanding that Warne had to resort to bowling well wide of his legs from around the wicket – the type of tactics you might expect from Ashley Giles, not Shane Warne. Warne and Ponting were widely criticised for this, but they might have responded that you can't have it both ways. The main cavil with Australia's tactics during the Lara–Adams partnership at Kingston in 1999 and the Dravid–Laxman stand at Kolkata in 2001 was that there was no plan B; that Australia attacked and kept attacking and didn't know how to switch to containment. This time they did just that: acknowledging the unlikelihood of dismissing Pietersen or Collingwood by conventional means, they switched to pure constraint. And they were lambasted for negative play. Damned if they did, damned if they didn't. But this is always the problem in cricket, in sport: when you are losing the fight, your tactics always appear to be too aggressive or not aggressive enough, not because of any inherent problem with the tactics, but because they are being interpreted in the light of their failure.

Ultimately, the negative bowling and field placements did yield a result, of sorts. England got to 6/551 before Flintoff declared, but had taken 168 overs to get there. Had this been Edgbaston 2005, England would have scored 900 in that many overs. But in Adelaide their scoring rate was kept to around three an over, and the fact that they were unable to reach 550 until the shadows were long on the second day

DAMNED IF THEY DID, DAMNED IF THEY DIDN'T

would have a critical impact on the shape of the match. Ponting had a second reason for hope: three years earlier, Australia had scored 556 in the first innings on this ground and lost.

Australia lost Langer before stumps, and Hayden and Martyn also failed early on the third morning. If 3/65 looked dire, 4/78 would have been truly calamitous, and that was what it looked like when Ponting, on 35, swung Hoggard straight to Giles at deep square leg. But Giles, in his last significant contribution to a Test match, juggled and dropped the chance, and Ponting wasn't to give another until he was 142.

Coming from so far behind, Ponting's fourth-wicket partnership with Hussey had epic qualities. There was the captain seeking personal redemption after 2005. And there was the aged novice, the man who had waited all those years, who was putting every minute of that waiting into his cricket. Hussey once asked Allan Border what was the best preparation for a six-hour Test innings. Border said, 'Bat for six hours in the nets', and that was what Hussey did. When it came to cricket, it was inadvisable to joke around with Mike Hussey. He took every aspect of the game and his preparation for it with the ultimate seriousness. Yet he was not a dour batsman to watch. Alongside Ponting at Adelaide, he could have dug in like Slasher Mackay, but instead he was the all-round professional, defending against the accurate Flintoff and Hoggard but making merry against the others.

Ponting and Hussey both fell to Hoggard late on the third day, and the balance was firmly in England's favour when Gilchrist joined Clarke at 5/286. It would still take some batting to avert the follow-on. Gilchrist, who had been in terrible form, survived until stumps and on the fourth morning hit out. When Flintoff came around the wicket, Gilchrist stepped inside the line of the ball and swung it to leg. Now everyone knew where they stood. Gilchrist seemed set for the big innings that would spring-clean his mental cupboard when, on 64, he clubbed Giles down Ian Bell's throat on the mid-wicket boundary.

Clarke, enjoying his most consistent season after being re-called for the injured Watson, wasn't finished, and Warne came in to help out with another 118 runs on top of the ninety-eight Clarke had added with Gilchrist. As Australia moved up through the four hundreds, England's fragility began to show. Flintoff was showing the pains of a sore ankle and frustrated plans, whereas Vaughan had always displayed a cool façade. The resistance of the Australian lower order was doing what England's tail had done to Australia in 2005: broken their hearts. It is immeasurable in cricket what an active tail-end can do. Once given away, these are runs that can never be got back. For the batting team, tail-end runs are cream on the cake. In this match, they would be the difference between probable Australian defeat and a microscopic chance of victory.

Clarke made 124, the best innings of his career to that point, and Warne 43 as Australia clawed their way to 513 late on the fourth day. The 165 overs they had batted, coming back from 3/65 against an England attack that had all the moving parts except a penetrating spinner, was one of the most worthy feats of deter-mination in the golden age. Ponting, Hussey and Clarke were its driving force; Gilchrist and Warne the necessary reinforcements.

When they went in for their second innings on day four, England were resigned to a dull draw. Clark got Cook, but Strauss and Bell batted out the day as if enjoying some practice time in the middle.

For England, a draw was disappointing after scoring 551, but they would have taken it after Brisbane. A draw would give them the toehold they needed. They could then look at counter-attacking in Perth and Melbourne, which would suit their pacemen. As Ashes holders, they only needed to square the series.

These thoughts were predictable and even understandable as the Adelaide match entered its fifth day. Most of the Australian players were having the same kinds of thoughts: play out the day and regroup in Perth. But not Warne. Warne arrived at the Adelaide Oval on the fifth day in the kind of mood he had taken to Edgbaston in the 1999 World Cup. Acting like the St Kilda football star he would dearly have loved to be, Warne ranted and raved about victory during the Australian warm-ups. 'We can do it, we can do it!' he kept saying. His bemused teammates humoured him by agreeing. Gilchrist said Warne 'was acting like he'd drunk about ten Red Bulls.' But Warne had a most unlikely bedfellow in Buchanan, who dropped his usual realist's reticence and also revved up the players, urging them in the direction of the miraculous. 'Don't deny,' he said, 'that someone can win this Test match.'

Two teams took to the Adelaide Oval on 5 December, and, as had been said seventy-four summers previously, only one was playing cricket. Strauss and Bell, who would retain their places for the full length of that summer against the evidence provided by their scores, scored ten runs off the first ten overs from Warne and Clark. Strauss's nerve began to crack in Warne's fifth over of the day, as he hared down the pitch at the first ball before bunting it away with his chest. Four balls later he came down the pitch again, tried to turn the ball to leg, missed it, and the Australians appealed for the catch off his pad. To general surprise, Steve Bucknor gave Strauss out and Warne was jubilant. He could control umpires' minds. He could work magic.

Things, English things, were starting to tremble. Collingwood came in and sparred at one outside off stump, doing everything but edging it. In Warne's next over, Bell prodded the ball into the covers and Collingwood ran. Bell disagreed, Collingwood kept coming, and Bell eventually sacrificed himself. England 3/70.

Something very odd was going on. Usually, when players have batted for seven or eight hours in the first innings, they come in for their second innings seeing the ball like a bean bag. But Collingwood and Pietersen were acting as though they were on a pair. To his third ball from Clark, Pietersen did everything but run himself out. Strange times.

'We had to get Pietersen out quickly,' Ponting would say later, 'or we couldn't win.' Perhaps it was Warne and another of his spells, the conjuring kind. With his next ball, he gave it a rip and curled it into Pietersen's blind spot. The former South African went down to sweep, in his customary half-bent way, and from the cloud of dust and gravel it emerged that Warne had done it again, bowled a right-hander around or through his legs, nobody could tell at first. For Ponting, it was 'an iconic moment in Ashes history'.

Now the belief began to radiate outwards. In twenty minutes England had gone from 1/69 to 4/73. There were still about eighty possible overs left in the day, and England led by 111, a number to make their feet itch.

Collingwood and Flintoff became deeply bogged. Unlike Strauss and Bell, this was not a matter of flawed tactics so much as inability to cope with Lee's reverse swing and Warne's bite and bounce.

NOW THE BELIEF BEGAN TO RADIATE OUTWARDS

Five overs passed, four runs were scored, and Flintoff, after a woeful few minutes of trying to give the Australian cordon a catch off Lee, eventually succeeded. 5/77. The crowd was growing through the day, the noise building, as office workers streamed down from the city: memories of Australia Day 1993.

Geraint Jones had been chosen, the word had it, for his batting. Few thought he could have been the first pick for his wicketkeeping. This, then, was his day. If he was to justify his place, he had to bat for a session with Collingwood. He lasted ten overs, stopping the rot but not decisively, then reached for a wide Lee half-volley and squeezed the catch to Hayden at gully. Giles came and went, another victim of Warne's, and the stubborn Hoggard also hung in but not quite long enough, dragging a rare Warne wrong'un back onto his stumps. Harmison came in and stayed in, seeing off Lee.

It was now the sixty-third over of the innings, the forty-fourth of the day. The battle of midway, literally. England, 8/115, led by 153. Another hour's batting and they would be safe. Ponting gave the ball to McGrath.

McGrath, who hadn't bowled a ball all day. McGrath, who had taken 0/107 in the first innings. McGrath, who looked all done, finished, washed up. McGrath, who never had that many strings to his bow anyway. McGrath, who'd taken nearly 600 wickets bowling lucky fast-mediums in the corridor, no outswinger, no inswinger, nothing much at all. The distinctly ordinary McGrath.

McGrath's first ball was almost a wide. It went through a surprised Gilchrist's legs and England took a bye. McGrath's second ball was a wide, a blooper to rival the one bowled at the Gabba by the batsman, Harmison, to start the series. McGrath's third ball was nearly another wide. He was bowling at a third set of stumps outside off. McGrath's fourth and fifth balls were more of the same. Poor old McGrath.

McGrath's sixth ball started down the same line. If it went away it might be another wide. Harmison looked to leave it. It didn't go away. It wobbled through the air, ducked in, bounced, cut in further, and hit Harmison a little high, but the Australians were all up and so was Rudi Koertzen's Hitchcockian digit.

Still, Jimmy Anderson could bat a bit. And he only had to last another ten or so overs, and that was it, England would have their draw.

Anderson lasted nine overs. Warne kept bowling spitters out of the rough, but couldn't break through. Again: McGrath. He was now actually bowling well, pushing the batsmen back before offering them something to nibble at around the top of the off stump. Anderson went across, McGrath hit him, and Koertzen's interminable finger gave another skyward point. McGrath, in the end, had done it. Warne had 4/49 off thirty-two overs, unchanged in two sessions on the last day. McGrath had 2/15 off nine – an afterthought, but he had done it.

The Australians' fate was now on their bat, in their hands. They had thirty-six overs to score 168 and take a two-Test lead

ABOVE: The iconic Ashes moment: Warne conquers Pietersen in Adelaide.

on a crumbling pitch. Flintoff was hobbled by his ankle, but would bowl. Hoggard had taken seven wickets in the first innings. Harmison and Anderson could always have their day, as Dean Headley had once had his. An England win was not out of the question.

Death or glory? Australia was confident enough this time to risk it. Langer pounded Hoggard's second ball from off stump through mid-wicket. It was clear now, and what a contrast to the scene at the start of the day. Australia wasn't afraid of losing. The top order would, at least, go for the win. If it came to putting up the shutters later, so be it. But Langer and Hayden were going to go at it as if this were a one-day chase with the Duckworth-Lewises sucked out of it.

Fourteen runs came off the first thirteen balls, but then Langer cut one to gully and was gone. Two overs later Hayden was out bashing too, for a quick 18, just that ambiguous kind of score that gave Australia enough hope but didn't steer them into comfortable territory.

On Ponting's orders, Hussey came in ahead of Martyn. Reprising their first innings, in the next hour Ponting and Hussey took the Ashes away from England with intelligent shot-making, picking off five runs an over like a comfortable chase in coloured clothes. Giles was no Warne, and England looked to Flintoff in vain. Ponting's confidence shot up when, after he popped a near-chance wide of slip off Giles, Flintoff eased the slip back to short third man. 'We've got them,' Ponting told Hussey.

Harmison seemed to have succumbed to his periodic home-sickness, and swapped some derogatory comments with Pietersen in the field. Anderson wasn't quite up to this level. Hoggard had lost his swing. It was beginning to look easy for the Australians until at 2/116, with fifty-two needed off fourteen overs, Ponting mistimed Giles to short cover. Game on? Perhaps. Martyn charged Flintoff and edged to slip.

Game on? Never. All series, Hussey and Clarke provided the rock-hard (and lucky) middle-order Australia had lacked in 2005. Hussey, having hidden in plain sight for the best part of a decade, was now averaging somewhere in that ancient rift valley between

George Headley and Don Bradman. Many lingered in that place for a while, but few lasted. Hussey, in total control, picked off most of the remaining runs and finally cover-drove Anderson to ring up the unlikeliest of wins, with eighteen balls to spare. How unlikely? The 1928–29 series was the last time the English had scored more than 500 in their first innings and lost a Test. It just wasn't done.

It had been done. The Australians went a little bit crazy, letting off all the tension stored up over the previous two years. This win didn't seal the Ashes, but it restored their belief that they could win anything from anywhere. In this respect it most resembled their win at Hobart in 1999. They were, once again, invincible.

And it was also an end, of sorts. Martyn, an increasingly morose figure over the previous weeks, was a lost boy in the riotous cele-brations, and later that night had a beery argument with Hayden before disappearing without a word. A walkout in victory; there was something new. But Martyn was that most enigmatic of humans: the cricketer of other-worldly talent, natural grace and a chip on the shoulder. In Martyn's case, the chip had a history. Blamed unfairly for the loss in Sydney in 1994, he had lost six years of a career. He had come back splendidly, winning Test matches for Australia on deadly turning pitches in Sri Lanka and India and convincing many English and South African fans that he was the most gifted Australian player of the entire era. For someone re-garded as a Perth specialist, that was quite something. But it also deepened his grievance, because, as his finest hours were played away from home, he did not feel that he received due recognition in Australia. He was right; he didn't. Ponting, with Martyn in India in 2006, commented on the difficulty of batting in Test matches on the subcontinent. Martyn surprised his captain by replying: 'It's better than playing in Australia. I'll play here any day of the week.'

Between 2001 and 2005, Martyn was as important a cog in that machine as any other player barring Warne and McGrath. But then, after the 2005 Ashes, he was scapegoated once more. It was plain to see, when he didn't make runs in the first two clashes of 2006–07, how deeply he dreaded the whole circus again. Being questioned, being dropped. He no longer had the stomach for it. He never exuded much personality on the field except through his perfectly stylish batting. Like many Test cricketers, he gave the impression that his dream match would take place in someone's back yard, with only a dog and a few mates for a crowd.

Amid the excitement, another hint of departure also went unnoticed. Warne told the world that when he looked back on his career, it would be Tests like Adelaide 2006 that he would remember most fondly. Looking back? Warne? Ah, but he was the boy who cried wolf. He had threatened retirement too often, going all the way back to 1994. In late 2006 he was bowling as if he could go on forever. He had just rolled the English, again, pulled off another of his tricks. Of course, Warne alluding to 'looking back' was just another ploy to grab attention, wasn't it? Adelaide was one of the greatest wins of all. Why would he want to end now?

OPPOSITE: Adelaide: one reasonably satisfied Australian captain.

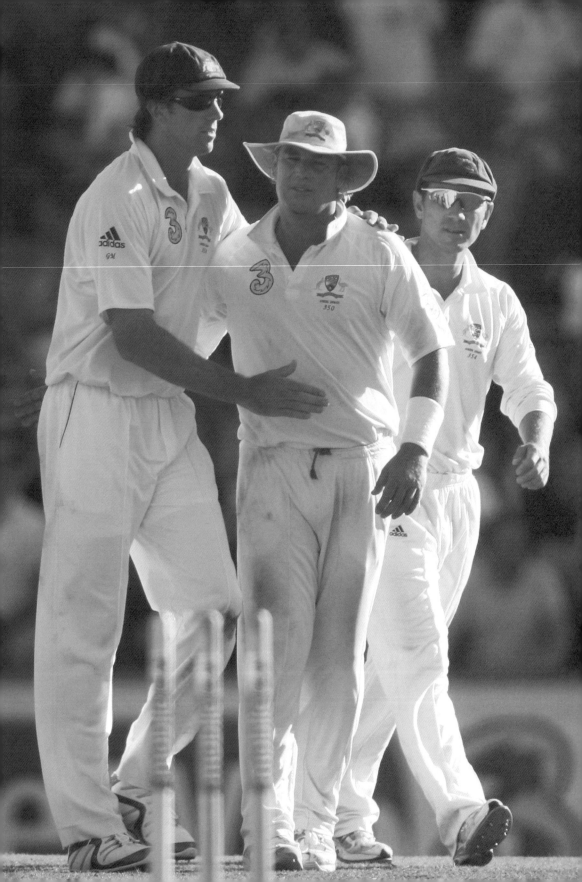

BACK TO THE PACK

Melbourne, December 2008

THE SECOND TEST, IN
SYDNEY, WAS ONE OF THE
MOST CONTROVERSIAL.
IT WAS A FITTING CODA
TO THE ERA: SUPERB
CRICKET, GRIPPING FINISH,
ATROCIOUS BEHAVIOUR.

The finale would roll out like a triumphant stage show, where each of the audience's favourites would come out and give one last flourish, accept the bouquets, and wave goodbye.

Martyn was the first, and Martyn did it the Martyn way: hoping for nobody to notice, mishandling it to the extent that the world came looking for him, wherever he was hiding.

Warne was next. Two weeks after his mysterious allusion in the Adelaide post-match interview, he announced that he would be retiring after the Sydney Test. Australia completed the series win in Perth, where Warne had wheeled in for another forty-eight overs. None of the Adelaide fireworks there; it was late-stage Warne, grinding and grinding until the opponent was a fine particulate matter blown away on the Fremantle Doctor. He gave his last twirl in Melbourne. Because of luck and circumstances he had rarely bowled on Boxing Day, the only day of the Test match calendar to simulate his unrealised dream of running out in a September Grand Final for St Kilda. He got everything he wanted and deserved: five wickets on the day, the 700th of his career, and Pietersen, second-last man out. Warne's final Test wicket would be Flintoff in Sydney, overbalancing

SO MCGRATH AND WARNE HAD PERSONALLY FINISHED OFF PIETERSEN AND FLINTOFF: **POETIC**

and stumped by Gilchrist. Well bowled, Shane, and thank you.

McGrath took his leave in Warne's shadow. That was apt. It was almost as if McGrath had been waiting for Warne to announce his retirement from stage right so that he, McGrath, could slip away unseen at stage left. McGrath was driven by simplicities: winning matches and hitting the off bail. Adulation was a necessary evil. His last Test wicket was Pietersen, caught by Gilchrist, in Sydney. So McGrath and Warne had personally finished off Pietersen and Flintoff: poetic. McGrath took a final bow in the 2007 World Cup in the Caribbean, where he was the best bowler in a tournament Australia won without serious challenge. The three World Cup-winning campaigns had got progressively easier. Now they would get harder again.

McGrath and Warne went off to India to play in the first season of the Twenty20 Indian Premier League, for the Delhi Daredevils and Rajasthan Royals respectively. The IPL was all about the new: new tactics, new stars, new shots, new balls. The best bowlers in that first season, by a country mile, were Glenn McGrath and Shane Warne. The shock of the old.

Langer retired from Test cricket in the same match as McGrath and Warne. When they were chaired off the SCG

LEFT: Age will weary him: Warne had had enough of cricket before cricket had had enough of him.

after the whitewash, Langer having scampered the winning run with his boon companion Hayden, the curtain closed. Of course, ages don't end just like that, and the winning didn't stop for Australia. But, to repeat, no Warne, no golden age. No Warne and McGrath, no inevitability of victory, no confidence that any trap can be sprung. Langer was the most dispensable of the three, but for much of his career he had similar figures to Ponting, and he did it at the top of the order. In England in 2005, when all others had failed, Langer was Australia's toughest nut.

Gilchrist went next. Since the Wellington Test in early 2005, when he had creamed the New Zealand bowlers so easily that he even scored a century after arriving at the Basin Reserve a few minutes before going out to bat, his batting form would start to fluctuate. Up to his sixty-eighth Test, he was averaging 55.6; in his last twenty-eight, he averaged 30.2, the productivity of a mortal keeper-batsman. Gone was the consistency, the regularity of the miracles. But he still had some highlights in his bag. His fifty-eight-ball century in the Third Test against England at Perth in 2006-07 was second only to Viv Richards' world speed record. For many fans, that was their favourite. Stress and a perception of failure had reduced him to tears the previous night, and he had decided to retire from the game immediately. Then he went out and scored the second-fastest century in 130 years of Test cricket. It took one innings to remind him how much he enjoyed this cricket business. Two months later, his 149 off 104 balls in the World Cup final in Barbados was as explosive a one-day innings as was ever played, and he chose the biggest limited-overs stage to do it. In his final season, 2007–08, he chose his last one-day international game in his adopted home town to raise three figures again, another layer of icing on that groaning cake. He was the last, after Warne and McGrath, of the indispensables. Once they were gone, so was the aura.

Australia won the 2007 World Cup in the Bajan darkness against Sri Lanka, a complicated end to a simple campaign. McGrath retired, and so did Buchanan, who, like Steve Waugh and Border before him, had succeeded by making himself surplus to requirements. 'I've been basically a passenger for the last three years or so,' he said. 'I get there [to practice], put the gear out and bring it back in again.'

It was left to Ponting, Hayden and Lee to shoulder what looked like becoming the burden of seniority. Tim Nielsen, the new coach, was a diffident background figure in the mould of Geoff Marsh to Ponting's Mark Taylor. Ponting now, for the first time, assumed the mantle of the team's longest-serving player. To the new players coming in, he was a hero they had admired on television. Leaders are always defined by the attitudes of their teammates. No current teammate had any memory of Ponting as the cocky little punk who couldn't handle his drink. To the new boys, he was almost an éminence grise.

Australia did not fall away drastically in the lee of the champions' retirement, as the West Indies had, and as Australia had too in 1984. There were still memorable Test and one-day matches, some won and some lost, as Ponting tried to dig new channels for the rivers of gold.

In Gilchrist's last summer, Australia managed to defeat India 2-1 at home. The series began in disappointment for neutral fans, with India's meek capitulation at the MCG signalling a tedious Australian dominance. But the Second Test, in Sydney, was one of the most controversial of the era, and it brought to the surface many half-buried enmities brought on by Australia's manner of play. It was a fitting coda to the era: superb cricket, gripping finish, atrocious behaviour.

Dismay at India's poor First Test grew when umpires Steve Bucknor and Mark Benson, on the first day in Sydney, gave a string of poor decisions mainly, if not exclusively, benefiting Australia. The chief beneficiary was Andrew Symonds, who knocked the cover off the ball when caught behind off the whippy newcomer Ishant Sharma, but was given not out. He went on to make a century, and admitted candidly in his press conference that he had hit it.

Such honesty, as Symonds should have learnt but never did, was not always the best policy, and he became a personal lightning rod for India's frustration. He had been in a running battle with Harbhajan Singh, who had called him a 'monkey' in a one-day series in India in late 2007, supposedly in response to some sledging from the Australian. Adjudicating whoever started it would be as fruitful as separating warring five-year-olds, and in retrospect the best action would have been to send both players to their rooms for, say, six months. But Harbhajan again used the term of abuse in the Sydney Test when the Indian spinner was staging a late stand with Tendulkar. Confronted by the Australians on the field, Harbhajan said he was sorry and would not do it again. He later denied this, and the Indians told a story wherein Harbhajan had called Symonds a Hindi term of abuse that sounded like 'monkey' but didn't have the same racial connotation. The ICC's arbitrators, with an eye on India's threat to walk out of the tour, accepted this tale and gave Harbhajan a weak slap for abusive Hindi.

Had either Australia or India taken the matter of racial abuse with sufficient seriousness, the matter would have ended differently. India, who knew all about racism in cricket circles, having been its victim for several decades, might have accepted Harbhajan's punishment rather than defending him and counter-alleging that the match referee, Mike Procter, had accepted 'a white man's word over a brown man's', as Sunil Gavaskar put it. Gavaskar's authority depended on short memories:

WAS SYMONDS REALLY HURT BY BEING CALLED A MONKEY?

he was the one who had taken his bat and ball and tried to go home after a bad decision in Melbourne in 1980–81. Racism was a convenient shield behind which any gripe could hide.

If India's authorities continued to squib holding Harbhajan to account, Australia's could have stood firm until justice was done. But nobody did take the issue of racial abuse seriously, and it was lost in the machinations of politics and process.

The incident brought out the worst in both cricketing nations, and that SCG Test would be remembered as one of the most bad-tempered. From India there was bellicose over-reaction, spoilt-brat threats to fly home and a suspicious change in the evidence given by the hitherto saintly Tendulkar. India reacted along the same lines as Arjuna Ranatunga at his most cynical: their grievance was real but their response was disproportionate. They had been subject to racial discrimination and condescension from England and Australia over the years, but in this case they picked too ethically muddied a battleground, and too compromised a character to defend. This was a fact recognised within India two months later, when Harbhajan was banned from the IPL for slapping a rival, the paceman Shanta Sreesanth. His banning met with widespread approval from Indian audiences.

From Australia's board there was craven appeasement of India's threats. Among Australia's players there was a disingenuous mock outrage at the racial slur. Was Symonds really hurt by being called a monkey? Highly unlikely. Rather, the players' reaction, typified by Hayden's response on the field to Harbhajan – 'You've got a witness now, you're gone, mate' – was that the Indian player had stepped into a trap laid by rules that nobody genuinely believed in. Racism itself was never the issue that it should have been. What was at issue was a secondary game between the players, a game not of physical skill but of how to work within codes of conduct and political correctness. The Australians' view was not that Symonds had been horribly wounded by racism; it was that Harbhajan had broken a rule of which some Australians over the years, most notably Darren Lehmann when he was suspended for referring to Sri Lankan players as 'black c—s', had fallen foul. Their view was that Harbhajan had slipped up and deserved to be punished. Then, when Cricket Australia declined to stand up to India's threats, the Australian players felt betrayed by their employer.

ABOVE: He Said, They Said: Forget the mouth, what counted with Harbhajan was the spinning fingers.

The racism row dovetailed with an ethical one. The Australians over-appealed and acted with a general surliness in the field, particularly on the last day of the Test. Ponting tried to umpire the match from his fielding position, catches were claimed unfairly, and the Australian players, no doubt hoping to replicate the tactical pressure they had undergone on last days in Kolkata and Chennai, lost their self-control. Gilchrist was criticised for claiming a catch off Dravid, when replays showed the batsman missed the ball. Having set such high standards by walking, Gilchrist's morality was now being used as a stick to beat him with. But, as he pointed out, the issues were different. When batting, he said, 'you know for sure you are out. The matter is in your hands.' Whereas appealing was 'my right as a keeper, and it's completely different from being the batsman and knowing you're either out or not out.' The baying crowd, however, wasn't listening to subtle delineations of morality. To many of their countrymen, the Australians were an uncouth lot who had been getting away with it for too long, and India were the poor helpless victims who could do no wrong. When India's captain Anil Kumble said, at the end of the match, that 'Australia do not play within the spirit of the game', the two separate issues – Australia's behaviour and Harbhajan's comment to Symonds – became hopelessly conflated, and critics of Australia's style seemed to think that the locals' perceived history of poor sportsmanship justified, or nullified, whatever the Indian spin bowler had said.

It was a terrible mess, and a situation that Australia's behaviour, or lack of it, throughout the fifteen years of its golden age had done much to foment. They were reaping what they had sown. Ponting was finding it hard to earn the widespread personal fealty in Australia that his predecessors had enjoyed. Perhaps there was some class snobbery in this. Even though Ponting's origins were not meaningfully lower than Waugh's, Taylor's or Border's, he carried the whiff of the greyhound track on him, and many Australian traditionalists saw uncomfortable traces of the working-class scrapper in Ponting's demeanour. He was admired for his batting, but the morass of the Indian Test at the SCG in 2008 gave his critics the opening they wanted to vent feelings that derived from an irrational dislike of his manner. It wasn't only the sniffy types. Peter Roebuck in *The Sydney Morning Herald* declared that Ponting must immediately be sacked and Hayden and Gilchrist should be pushed into retirement. These suggestions were never taken seriously, but they did indicate how much distaste for Australia's supposed win-at-all-costs approach had been pent up and was now finding its release. Ponting, whose joy at having won the series was smothered beneath the consequent referee's hearings and bad press, said that he felt 'let down, drained, a target'.

All this tended to conceal what was a great Sydney Test match, with Australia winning in the second-last over, as dramatic a game in its way as Adelaide a year earlier. Michael Clarke took three wickets in that over to seal the victory. Perhaps Sydney 2008, and not Sydney 2007, was the real end of the era. Australia would win none of its next five Tests against India, home or away, losing three. In the second half of the home 2007–08 series and the away series in 2008, Australia looked to have lost the Border–Gavaskar Trophy for an extended future.

Ponting's team lurched through India in 2008, missing a leg-spinner more than ever. They were beaten in a manner that seemed far more conclusive than the losses in 1998 and 2001. The age of spin was over. Perhaps the real end of the era came in the West Indies in early 2008, when MacGill succumbed to his injuries and announced his retirement. The man who had lived in Warne's shadow could not, finally, emerge from it. MacGill's misfortune, the body failing him just as the big chance finally arrived, left Australia without a Test-class spinner of either the wrist or finger variety.

This dearth, as much as anything, would signal, if not the end of success, a return to the pack. Consistent Test-match series wins around the world need a spinning option. Only the West Indies reached the top without spin, and Australia had not one Malcolm Marshall or Curtly Ambrose, let alone four or five of them.

In a more intangible realm, the era also finished with the retirements of the indispensables. Cricket offers great latitude for the expression of personality; indeed, personality is expressed through cricket whether the player likes it or not. With the departures of Warne, McGrath, Langer, Gilchrist and, in early 2009, Hayden, the Australian team suffered an extreme blood loss. These were cricketers whose individual styles had grown on the public, and there was as much magnetism in their faces, their tics, their stylistic signatures and their personal idiosyncrasies as in their achievements. It could be said that the Australian team went into a personality deficit after those retirements. Symonds, whose towering talent was matched only by his monumental immaturity, would eventually quit the scene saying he felt 'caged in' by a culture that relied on laptop analysis and sports science more than a beer and a song. The culture had been evolving in that direction steadily through the Taylor–Waugh–Ponting years, and was reflected in Ponting's personal journey from binge-drinking brawler into public speaker and fashion plate: he had become both role model and Rolex model. Like Warne before him, Symonds was stranded in an era that was not his own. Unlike Warne, he was unable to leave his inner disquiet off the field, and he never built up the immunity of a peerless playing record.

This cultural change was not, per se, to be mourned. We only have to think back to the preference Steve Waugh developed for trips to Gallipoli over trips to the Gallipoli Arms to realise that the shedding of alcohol-as-bonding-agent aided both the players and the way they played. But when we look at the products of cookie-cutter academies and formulaic high-performance coaching techniques, there is something to be mourned in the disappearance of more homemade types. As impressive as are Cricket Australia's many elite and community programs, the professionalisation of the game at all levels tends to cast a fixed template and leave less room for the spontaneous development of those who emerge out of nowhere. 'Nowhere', indeed, is a shrinking space. But such is the blank canvas that the game itself provides for individual artistry, we can hope that one day Peter Siddle will be regarded with the same fondness and familiarity as Glenn McGrath, Mitchell Johnson as compelling a performer as Merv Hughes, and Michael Clarke as aesthetically pleasing as Mark Waugh or Damien Martyn. Personality in cricket is not a product of manufactured exuberance, but of time.

The Australian era ended with that sequence of retirements and symbolic moments in 2006, 2007 and 2008. It ended on the scoresheet with the Boxing Day Test match of 2008. Up to that point, since Australia Day 1993, Australia had won forty-two of the fifty-five Test series it had played, drawing six and losing seven. The only team in history which compares is the West Indies between 1980 and 1995: it played twenty-nine series, winning twenty-one, drawing eight and losing – none. There is only one debate of 'greatest ever' to be had, and it is between these two eras.

Graeme Smith's South Africans had won the First Test of the 2008–09 series in Perth chasing 414 to win; they did it with four wickets down. Australia's lack of a spinner had always been a weakness on the WACA, but that Test revealed an overall thinness of bowling depth. That South Africa could win the match was one thing; that they could win the end-game had the more lasting significance.

The 2008–09 South Africans were a young and glamorous team of confident aggressive batsmen in Smith, A.B. de Villiers, Hashim Amla and J.P. Duminy, stout veterans in Jacques Kallis and Mark Boucher, and most importantly a penetrative attack with an authentic spearhead in Dale Steyn. At the end of 2008 they, like India had a few months earlier, looked quite simply to be better cricketers than the Australians. It was a long time since we had last said that.

The end, when it came, was meek, a very pale echo of Allan Border and his worry ball in 1993. As they had in Perth, Australia got the better of the opening sessions but then let South Africa off the hook. South Africa did an Australia on Australia. They came back from 7/184, chasing Australia's 394, and won the match. Brett Lee's heart got the better of his judgement and he played half-fit, letting his side down when Duminy and Steyn dug in for the ninth wicket. Steyn, who averaged just under 10 with the bat, came in at 8/251. Duminy was showing himself to be a good enough player to keep Ashwell Prince, by then one of the top batsmen in the world, in his tracksuit. Duminy, a compact left-hander with hints of Lara and Ganguly, had the impact of a Gilchrist. With Steyn he added 180 runs, then another twenty-eight with Ntini, to convert Australia's expected first-innings lead of around 200 into a deficit of sixty-five.

Ponting (99) and Johnson (43 not out) aside, Australia's second innings had a sad air of inevitability. Cricket matches, as Australia had shown so amply over the previous sixteen years, are won at the end, not the beginning. The manner of South Africa's win in Perth had shown that they were men who would time their run and wrest control of the 'big moments', in other words, the final stages when the climactic plot points arrive in the story. So it was again in Melbourne. Steyn's fluid approach and delivery were a delight to watch, as was Ntini's unflagging effort and Kallis's second life as a

ABOVE: The Superhuman Steyn: South Africa's new spearhead rampant in Melbourne, 2008.

swing-seam paceman. The South Africans were unusually likeable as a team: they were fresh and aggressive and tight-knit and always entertaining. They bristled with personality.

Australia was only able to set them 183 to win in the fourth innings, and South Africa never showed a hint of taking that old inhalation of gas. Smith blasted away all doubt with a rapid 75, and Neil McKenzie and Hashim Amla cruised home. Australia mounted no challenge, posed no threat of pulling off the mildly unpredictable, let alone the miraculous. They had no Test-class spinner. They had no McGrath. They went out with a whimper.

When he watched the fated McDermott–May stand in Adelaide on Australia Day 1993, Allan Border had been waiting thirteen years to beat the West Indies. The dynasty that would start two years later would reign for another thirteen years. It was a fair trade. But there was little drama or passion in Australia's last stand at Melbourne in 2008. They were just well beaten by a much better outfit.

And yet, their return to the pack promises engaging Test contests. Just when they had surrendered their sixteen-year unbeaten home record – the definitive closing parenthesis around their golden age – Ponting's Australians won their next three matches against the same opponent, taking the honours in the 2009 series on the veldt. They are not finished. There will be no 1984–85, one senses, no swift descent into defeat. But we won't see what we have just seen for a long time, possibly a lifetime, and that's because the years 1993–2008 provided a perfect storm of cricketing talent in this country.

The champions came in three waves: Steve Waugh, Healy, Taylor, Mark Waugh; then Warne, McGrath, Ponting, Langer, Slater and Gillespie; and finally Gilchrist, Hayden, Martyn, MacGill and Lee. With each wave, there were the bit-players, the Reiffels, Blewetts, Bevans, Kasprowiczes, Bichels, Lehmanns and Millers; and there are the leading men of the transition, Hussey, Clarke, Katich, Clark and Johnson. A three-wave set; no wonder it drowned those who tried to fight it.

The selectors never had to bite the bullet and 'rebuild', a euphemism for gambling on youth and asking for public tolerance for short-term failure. Indeed, the selectors seldom went for young players at all: Ponting, Clarke, Phillip Hughes and Shaun Tait were rare choices from the under-25 brigade. This was a departure from the Australian tradition, which had in the past been unafraid of youth. This is a cause for concern, but it was also a cause for concern ten years ago. The fact is that the age parameters have changed, and the mature-age success of players like Lehmann, Martyn and Hussey has created a perception that thirty is the new twenty.

It was not only the juniors who had to queue up and wait behind greatness. An era can also be measured by the quality of those who remained more or less permanently beneath the surface, their talent unfulfilled because of the fortunes of the age in which they played. Between them, Jamie Siddons, Stuart Law, Martin Love, Brad Hodge and Chris Rogers scored 84,000 first-class runs and 243 centuries up to late 2009. Yet they have played a combined 13 Test matches. At any other time, these batsmen would

THE YEARS 1993–2008 PROVIDED A PERFECT STORM OF CRICKETING TALENT

have had ten-year international careers. Under the glittering façade was an alternative era, a shadow team of very fine cricketers.

There has always been energetic theorising about how such success came to be. Of course, this discussion is not for idle academic interest, but to see if continuity can be maintained – a fourth wave, even. For policy-makers, such as administrators, coaches and selectors, the last admission they want to make is that the Australian ascendancy was simply a freak moment in which the maturity of many inimitable natural talents coincided. Luck! What policy-makers are looking for is some kind of system that can fertilise and nurture new talent and control the future. Hence, the Australian Cricket Academy, the evolution of high-performance programs, the talent-scouting, the development programs for ever-younger up and comers. If Australia can say it owes its success to a system rather than to freak individuals, then success can conceivably be perpetuated. We can avoid the fate of the West Indies, where the head was never supported by a healthy body, where the talent died barren.

There is no doubt that the systematisation of Australian cricket has helped turn good young players into better ones. No doubt at all. But as an explanation for what we saw between 1993 and 2008, 'structures' can only go so far. The Waughs, Taylor and Healy pre-dated such organisation of talent. Warne dropped out of the academy for misbehaviour. McGrath was not spotted until he was fully grown. Hayden was unwanted at the academy because Rod Marsh considered the institution's purpose was to develop only players capable of reaching first-class level or better. Many of the greats did go through the system, such as Ponting, Gilchrist, Martyn and Langer, but in the case of the first three of those names there was such a richness of natural ability that it is hard not to see them achieving greatness whether there was a cricket academy or not; and in the case of the last-named, his Test record was a function of maturity, innate courage and persistence, qualities which could not be taught and took many years to emerge.

As much as we like to credit the 'Australian way', be it in our professionalisation of sport or certain ineffable national values, we can't avoid Occam's razor. The first way to explain any fact is to seek the simplest reason. And the simplest, inarguable explanation for Australia's cricketing record from 1993 to 2008 is pure luck, that three waves of extraordinary talent and character arrived on top of the other. History, and fate, smiled upon us.

To every good story, if not every story per se, there are two sides. For full interest and relief in the canvas, every stroke of light needs a shadow. In the Australian teams of this era, there was plenty of shadow: sledging, betting, over-aggression, factionalism, gamesmanship, an undercurrent of charmlessness. Under Taylor, Waugh and Ponting, the Australian team was more admired than loved. There was little of, say, Frank Worrell's and Richie Benaud's 1960–61 spirit about them. This is not something to be judged or condemned. They could no more change the way they were than a lion can become a vegetarian. Their defence – that the aggression required to play entertaining, risky, winning cricket necessarily spawns an aggression that flows over into human relationships, and is not often attractive – is quite plausible. The rarity in all sports of personalities who play aggressively, win, and win well provides no kind of reason to expect that everyone should play that way. There was only one Adam Gilchrist in this era, and it is pie in the sky to expect the others simply to wake up to themselves and play like him. Character is not like that.

The real question is, what will last in our memories? The work, or the human frailty? It's easy to contrast artists with, say, political or business leaders in this light. There are few new books or discussions about John F. Kennedy's public policy contributions, but the fascination with and revelations about his personal life are endless. Yet just as a politician can become remembered more and more as a drug-addicted womaniser, an artist's reputation moves in the other direction. In a hundred years, Michael Jackson's music will still inspire while his 'eccentricities' will recede into the footnotes. With any artist, the work continues to touch people and the personal weaknesses and scandals lose their relevance.

Where do sportspeople lie on this continuum? The indications are that even though their work may not have the timeless qualities of great writing, music or painting, memories of their exploits on the field last a lot longer than does interest in their squabbles. The moment he retired, Shane Warne's reputation soared. Did the text messages or the boorish displays matter anymore? No; what mattered now was the wickets he had taken, the matches he won, even the individual balls he bowled. All was forgiven. During his career, a friend of Gideon Haigh's had summed up many Australians' ambivalence towards Warne: 'When he's not bowling, I simply can't stand him. But when he's bowling, I could watch him all day.' Now that he would never play again for Australia, in memories he would keep on bowling into eternity.

Likewise, when Glenn McGrath retired and no longer suffered from bouts of white-line fever, he emerged as the genial personality he had always been as a private citizen. His stoicism in the face of his wife's death not only consolidated the respect in which he was held, but erased any lingering memories of the spitting, cursing, snarling McGrath who used to arouse such mixed feelings among Australian fans. Likewise, Allan Border's grumpiness has been buried under his 11,000 runs and his courage in the face of defeathu. Mark Taylor's form slump was a blip, not a curse. Steve

Waugh's involvement in gamesmanship seems almost quaint, looking back on it, and fades in memory against the image of him driving Richard Dawson into the shadows of the Brewongle Stand on 3 January 2003. There was a dark side, there were controversies and there were legitimate reasons to pull away the pedestal upon which we had stood them. But with the benefit of time, it is the great days and nights of cricket that remain, and the rest is swiftly forgiven on the way to being forgotten.

STATISTICS

FOURTH TEST (Test 1211)
Australia v West Indies

At Adelaide Oval, Adelaide, January 23, 24, 25, 26, 1993. West Indies won by one run.
Toss: West Indies. **Player of the Match:** CEL Ambrose. **Umpires:** DB Hair and LJ King.
Close of play: First day, Australia (1) 1/2 (Boon 1, Langer 0); Second day, Aus (1) 3/100 (SR Waugh 35, Border 18); Third day, W.I (2) 146 all out

WEST INDIES

DL Haynes st Healy b May	45	c Healy b McDermott	11
PV Simmons c Hughes b SR Waugh	46	b McDermott	10
*RB Richardson lbw b Hughes	2	c Healy b Warne	72
BC Lara c Healy b McDermott	52	c SR Waugh b Hughes	7
KLT Arthurton c SR Waugh b May	0	c Healy b McDermott	0
CL Hooper c Healy b Hughes	2	c Hughes b May	25
+JR Murray not out	49	c ME Waugh b May	0
IR Bishop c ME Waugh b Hughes	13	c ME Waugh b May	6
CEL Ambrose c Healy b Hughes	0	st Healy b May	1
KCG Benjamin b ME Waugh	15	c Warne b May	0
CA Walsh lbw b Hughes	5	not out	0
L-b 11, n-b 12	23	L-b 2, n-b 12	14
(67.3 overs, 282 mins)	252	(41.5 overs, 179 mins)	146

Fall: 84 99 129 130 134 189 206 206 247 252   Fall: 14 49 63 65 124 137 145 146 146 146

Bowling: First Innings – McDermott 16-1-85-1; Hughes 21.3-3-64-5; SR Waugh 13-4-37-1; May 14-1-41-2; Warne 2-0-11-0; ME Waugh 1-0-3-1. Second Innings – McDermott 11-0-66-3; Hughes 13-1-43-1; SR Waugh 5-1-8-0; May 6.5-3-9-5; Warne 6-2-18-1.

AUSTRALIA

MA Taylor c Hooper b Bishop	1	(2) c Murray b Benjamin	7
DC Boon not out	39	(1) lbw b Ambrose	0
JL Langer c Murray b Benjamin	20	c Murray b Bishop	54
ME Waugh c Simmons b Ambrose	0	c Hooper b Walsh	26
SR Waugh c Murray b Ambrose	42	c Arthurton b Ambrose	4
*AR Border c Hooper b Ambrose	19	c Haynes b Ambrose	1
+IA Healy c Hooper b Ambrose	0	b Walsh	0
MG Hughes c Murray b Hooper	43	lbw b Ambrose	1
SK Warne lbw b Hooper	0	lbw b Bishop	9
TBA May c Murray b Ambrose	6	not out	42
CJ McDermott b Ambrose	14	c Murray b Walsh	18
B 7, l-b 3, n-b 19	29	B 1, l-b 8, n-b 13	22
(75.2 overs, 337 mins)	213	(79 overs, 361 mins)	184

Fall: 1 16 46 108 108 112 181 181 197 213   Fall: 5 16 54 64 72 73 74 102 144 184

Bowling: First Innings – Ambrose 28.2-6-74-6; Bishop 18-3-48-1; Benjamin 6-0-22-1; Walsh 10-3-34-0; Hooper 13-4-25-2. Second Innings – Ambrose 26-5-46-4; Bishop 17-3-41-2; Benjamin 12-2-32-1; Walsh 19-4-44-3; Hooper 5-1-12-0.

FIRST TEST (Test 1224)
England v Australia

At Old Trafford, Manchester, June 3, 4, 5, 6, 7, 1993. Australia won by 179 runs.
Toss: England. **Player of the Match:** SK Warne. **Umpires:** HD Bird and KE Palmer.
Close of play: First day, Australia (1) 5/242 (Border 9, Healy 6); Second day, Eng (1) 8/202 (Caddick 6, Such 9); Third day, Aus (2) 3/231 (Boon 85, Border 29); Fourth day, Eng (2) 2/133 (Gooch 82)

AUSTRALIA

MA Taylor c and b Such	124	(2) lbw b Such		9
MJ Slater c Stewart b DeFreitas	58	(1) c Caddick b Such		27
DC Boon c Lewis b Such	21	c Gatting b DeFreitas		93
ME Waugh c and b Tufnell	6	b Tufnell		64
*AR Border st Stewart b Such	17	c and b Caddick		31
SR Waugh b Such	3	not out		78
+IA Healy c Such b Tufnell	12	not out		102
BP Julian c Gatting b Such	0			
MG Hughes c DeFreitas b Such	2			
SK Warne not out	15			
CJ McDermott run out	8			
B 8, l-b 8, n-b 7	23	B 6, l-b 14, n-b 8		28
(112.3 overs, 439 mins)	289	(130 overs, 528 mins)	(5 wickets dec)	432

Fall: 128 183 221 225 232 260 264 266 267 289   Fall: 23 46 155 234 252

Bowling: First Innings – Caddick 15-4-38-0; DeFreitas 23-8-46-1; Lewis 13-2-44-0; Such 33.3-9-67-6; Tufnell 28-5-78-2. Second Innings – Caddick 20-3-79-1; DeFreitas 24-1-80-1; Such 31-6-78-2; Tufnell 37-4-112-1; Hick 9-1-20-0; Lewis 9-0-43-0.

ENGLAND

*GA Gooch c Julian b Warne	65	handled ball	133
MA Atherton c Healy b Hughes	19	c Taylor b Warne	25
MW Gatting b Warne	4	b Hughes	23
RA Smith c Taylor b Warne	4	b Warne	18
GA Hick c Border b Hughes	34	c Healy b Hughes	22
+AJ Stewart b Julian	27	c Healy b Warne	11
CC Lewis c Boon b Hughes	9	c Taylor b Warne	43
PAJ DeFreitas lbw b Julian	5	lbw b Julian	7
AR Caddick c Healy b Warne	7	c Warne b Hughes	25
PM Such not out	14	c Border b Hughes	9
PCR Tufnell c Healy b Hughes	1	not out	0
B 6, l-b 10, n-b 5	21	L-b 11, W 1, n-b 4	16
(74.5 overs, 306 mins)	210	(120.2 overs, 481 mins)	332

Fall: 71 80 84 123 148 168 178 183 203 210   Fall: 73 133 171 223 230 238 260 299 331 332

Bowling: First Innings – McDermott 18-2-50-0; Hughes 20.5-5-59-4; Julian 11-2-30-2; Warne 24-10-51-4; Border 1-0-4-0. Second Innings – McDermott 30-9-76-0; Hughes 27.2-4-92-4; Warne 49-26-86-4; Julian 14-1-67-1.

SECOND TEST (Test 1244)
Australia v South Africa

At Sydney Cricket Ground, Sydney, January 2, 3, 4, 5, 6, 1994. South Africa won by five runs.
Toss: South Africa. **Player of the Match:** PS De Villiers. **Umpires:** SG Randell and WP Sheahan.
Close of play: First day, Australia (1) 1/20 (Slater 5, Boon 7); Second day, Aus (1) 5/200 (Martyn 15, Healy 6); Third day, SAf (2) 2/94 (Cronje 37, Wessels 7); Fourth day, Aus (2) 4/63 (Waugh 4, Border 7)

SOUTH AFRICA

AC Hudson lbw b McGrath	0	c Healy b McDermott	1
G Kirsten st Healy b Warne	67	b McDermott	41
WJ Cronje c Waugh b McDermott	41	b McDermott	38
DJ Cullinan b Warne	9	(5) lbw b Warne	2
JN Rhodes lbw b Warne	4	(6) not out	76
*KC Wessels c and b Warne	3	(4) b Warne	18
+DJ Richardson c Taylor b Warne	4	lbw b McGrath	24
PL Symcox b Warne	7	c Healy b McDermott	4
CR Matthews c Taylor b Warne	0	c Waugh b Warne	4
PS De Villiers c Waugh b McDermott	18	lbw b Warne	2
AA Donald not out	0	c Healy b Warne	10
B 1, l-b 4, n-b 11	16	B 13, l-b 1, n-b 5	19
(74.1 overs, 301 mins)	169	(109 overs, 395 mins)	239

Fall: 1 91 110 133 134 141 142 142 152 169   Fall: 2 75 101 107 110 182 188 197 203 239

Bowling: First Innings – McDermott 18.1-2-42-2; McGrath 19-5-32-1; Warne 27-8-56-7; May 10-1-34-0. Second Innings – McDermott 28-9-62-4; McGrath 14-3-30-1; May 22-4-53-0; Warne 42-17-72-5; Border 3-1-8-0.

AUSTRALIA

MJ Slater b Donald	92	(2) b De Villiers	1
MA Taylor c Richardson b Donald	7	(1) c Richardson b De Villiers	27
DC Boon b De Villiers	19	c Kirsten b De Villiers	24
ME Waugh lbw b Symcox	7	(5) lbw b Donald	11
*AR Border c Richardson b De Villiers	49	(6) b Donald	7
DR Martyn c Richardson b De Villiers	59	(7) c Hudson b Donald	6
+IA Healy c Richardson b Donald	19	(8) b De Villiers	1
SK Warne c Rhodes b Symcox	11	(9) run out (Cronje)	1
CJ McDermott c Cronje b De Villiers	6	(10) not out	29
TBA May not out	8	(4) lbw b De Villiers	0
GD McGrath b Donald	9	c and b De Villiers	1
B 1, l-b 2, n-b 3	6	L-b 3	3
(141.2 overs, 596 mins)	292	(56.3 overs, 264 mins)	111

Fall: 10 58 75 179 179 229 250 266 281 292   Fall: 4 51 51 56 63 72 73 75 110 111

Bowling: First Innings – Donald 31.2-8-83-4; De Villiers 36-12-80-4; Matthews 28-11-44-0; Symcox 46-11-82-2. Second Innings – Donald 17-5-34-3; De Villiers 23.3-8-43-6; Matthews 6-5-9-0; Symcox 10-3-22-0.

FIRST TEST (Test 1253)
South Africa v Australia

At Wanderers Stadium, Johannesburg, March 4, 5, 6, 7, 8, 1994. South Africa won by 197 runs.
Toss: South Africa. **Player of the Match:** WJ Cronje. **Umpires:** SB Lambson and DR Shepherd.
Close of play: First day, Australia (1) 0/34 (Slater 26, Hayden 6); Second day, SAf (2) 0/42 (Hudson 22, G Kirsten 17); Third day, SAf (2) 5/335 (PN Kirsten 32, De Villiers 4); Fourth day, Aus (2) 2/123 (Boon 56, ME Waugh 16)

SOUTH AFRICA

AC Hudson c Healy b McDermott	17	b Warne	60
G Kirsten b Hughes	47	c Hughes b May	35
WJ Cronje c Border b SR Waugh	21	c SR Waugh b Hughes	122
*KC Wessels c Hayden b Hughes	18	c Border b Warne	50
PN Kirsten b May	12	c Boon b May	53
JN Rhodes c ME Waugh b McDermott	69	c Healy b SR Waugh	14
BM McMillan c Boon b May	0	(8) b Warne	24
+DJ Richardson lbw b Warne	31	(9) c Border b Warne	20
CR Matthews c Boon b Hughes	6	(10) not out	31
PS De Villiers b McDermott	16	(7) b McDermott	4
AA Donald not out	0	not out	15
B 1, l-b 10, n-b 3	14	B 13, l-b 4, n-b 5	22
(80.2 overs, 329 mins)	251	(159.5 overs, 606 mins) (9 wickets dec)	450

Fall: 21 70 103 116 126 126 194 203 249 251

Fall: 76 123 258 289 324 343 366 403 406

Bowling: First Innings – McDermott 15.2-3-63-3; Hughes 20-6-59-3; May 22-5-62-2; SR Waugh 9-2-14-1; Warne 14-4-42-1. Second Innings – McDermott 35-3-112-1; Hughes 25-5-86-1; May 39-11-107-2; SR Waugh 10-3-28-1; ME Waugh 6-2-14-0; Warne 44.5-14-86-4.

AUSTRALIA

MJ Slater c Hudson b De Villiers	26	(2) b De Villiers	41
ML Hayden c Richardson b Donald	15	(1) b De Villiers	5
DC Boon c De Villiers b Donald	17	b Matthews	83
ME Waugh run out (PN Kirsten/G Kirsten)	42	c Richardson b Donald	28
*AR Border run out (Rhodes/G Kirsten)	34	c G Kirsten b McMillan	14
SR Waugh not out	45	c Richardson b Matthews	0
+IA Healy b Matthews	11	c and b Donald	30
MG Hughes c G Kirsten b McMillan	7	not out	26
SK Warne lbw b Matthews	15	lbw b McMillan	1
CJ McDermott lbw b Donald	31	b McMillan	10
TBA May lbw b De Villiers	2	c G Kirsten b Cronje	11
B 1, l-b 1, n-b 1	3	L-b 5, n-b 2	7
(67.3 overs, 301 mins)	248	(96.3 overs, 417 mins)	256

Fall: 35 56 70 136 142 169 176 201 245 248

Fall: 18 95 136 164 164 191 219 225 235 256

Bowling: First Innings – Donald 19-0-86-3; De Villiers 19.3-1-74-2; McMillan 14-3-46-1; Matthews 15-4-40-2. Second Innings – Donald 23-3-71-2; De Villiers 30-11-70-2; McMillan 19-2-61-3; Matthews 20-6-42-2; G Kirsten 4-0-7-0; Cronje 0.3-0-0-1.

FOURTH TEST (Test 1298)
West Indies v Australia

At Sabina Park, Kingston, April 29, 30 May 1, 3, 1995. Australia won by an innings and 53 runs.
Toss: West Indies. **Player of the Match:** SR Waugh. **Umpires:** SA Bucknor and KE Liebenberg.
Close of play: First day, W.I (1) 265 all out; Second day, Aus (1) 4/321 (SR Waugh 110, Blewett 6); Third day, W.I (2) 3/63 (Adams 13, WKM Benjamin 1)

WEST INDIES

SC Williams c Blewett b Reiffel	0	b Reiffel	20
*RB Richardson lbw b Reiffel	100	c and b Reiffel	14
BC Lara c Healy b Warne	65	lbw b Reiffel	0
JC Adams c Slater b Julian	20	c SR Waugh b McGrath	18
CL Hooper c ME Waugh b Julian	23	(6) run out (Julian)	13
KLT Arthurton c Healy b McGrath	16	(7) lbw b Warne	14
+CO Browne c Boon b Warne	1	(8) not out	31
WKM Benjamin lbw b SR Waugh	7	(5) lbw b Reiffel	51
CEL Ambrose not out	6	st Healy b Warne	5
CA Walsh c Boon b SR Waugh	2	c Blewett b Warne	14
KCG Benjamin c Healy b Reiffel	5	c Taylor b Warne	6
B 1, l-b 9, w 1, n-b 9	20	B 13, l-b 8, n-b 6	27
(85.4 overs, 374 mins)	265	(69.4 overs, 305 mins)	213

Fall: 0 103 131 188 220 243 250 251 254 265

Fall: 37 37 46 98 134 140 166 172 204 213

Bowling: First Innings – Reiffel 13.4-2-48-3; Julian 12-3-31-2; McGrath 20-4-79-1; Warne 25-6-72-2; SR Waugh 11-5-14-2; ME Waugh 4-1-11-0. Second Innings – Reiffel 18-5-47-4; Julian 10-2-37-0; Warne 23.4-8-70-4; ME Waugh 1-0-1-0; McGrath 13-2-28-1; SR Waugh 4-0-9-0.

AUSTRALIA

*MA Taylor c Adams b Walsh	8
MJ Slater c Lara b Walsh	27
DC Boon c Browne b Ambrose	17
ME Waugh c Adams b Hooper	126
SR Waugh c Lara b KCG Benjamin	200
GS Blewett c WKM Benjamin b Arthurton	69
+IA Healy c Lara b WKM Benjamin	6
BP Julian c Adams b Walsh	8
PR Reiffel b KCG Benjamin	23
SK Warne c Lara b KCG Benjamin	0
GD McGrath not out	3
B 11, l-b 6, w 1, n-b 26	44
(160.5 overs, 659 mins)	531

Fall: 17 50 73 304 417 433 449 522 522 531

Bowling: First Innings – Ambrose 21-4-76-1; Walsh 33-6-103-3; KCG Benjamin 23.5-0-106-3; WKM Benjamin 24-3-80-1; Hooper 43-9-94-1; Adams 11-0-38-0; Arthurton 5-1-17-1.

AUSTRALIA v SRI LANKA (World Cup Final)

At Lahore (Gaddafi) Stadium, Lahore, March 17, 1996 Day/night game. Sri Lanka won by seven wickets.
Toss: Sri Lanka. **Player of the Match:** PA De Silva. **Umpires:** SA Bucknor and DR Shepherd.

AUSTRALIA

*MA Taylor c Jayasuriya b De Silva	74	(84)
ME Waugh c Jayasuriya b Vaas	12	(15)
RT Ponting b De Silva	45	(77)
SR Waugh c De Silva b Dharmasena	13	(25)
SK Warne st Kaluwitharana b Muralidaran	2	(6)
SG Law c De Silva b Jayasuriya	22	(30)
MG Bevan not out	36	(50)
+IA Healy b De Silva	2	(3)
PR Reiffel not out	13	(18)
DW Fleming		
GD McGrath		
L-b 10, w 11, n-b 1	22	
(50 overs, 206 mins)	(7 wkts) 241	

Fall: 36 137 152 156 170 202 205

Bowling: Wickramasinghe 7-0-38-0; Vaas 6-1-30-1; Muralidaran 10-0-31-1; Dharmasena 10-0-47-1; Jayasuriya 8-0-43-1; De Silva 9-0-42-3.

SRI LANKA

ST Jayasuriya run out (McGrath/Healy)	9	(7)
+RS Kaluwitharana c Bevan b Fleming	6	(15)
AP Gurusinha b Reiffel	65	(99)
PA De Silva not out	107	(127)
*A Ranatunga not out	47	(37)
HP Tillakaratne		
RS Mahanama		
WPUJC Vaas		
M Muralidaran		
HDPK Dharmasena		
GP Wickramasinghe		
B 1, l-b 4, w 5, n-b 1	11	
(46.2 overs, 206 mins)	(3 wkts) 245	

Fall: 12 23 148

Bowling: McGrath 8.2-1-28-0; Fleming 6-0-43-1; Warne 10-0-58-0; Reiffel 10-0-49-1; ME Waugh 6-0-35-0; SR Waugh 3-0-15-0; Bevan 3-0-12-0.

SECOND TEST (Test 1361)
South Africa v Australia

At St George's Park, Port Elizabeth, March 14, 15, 16, 17, 1997. **Australia won by two wickets.**
Toss: Australia. **Player of the Match:** ME Waugh. **Umpires:** RE Koertzen and S Venkataraghavan.
Close of play: First day, Australia (1) 1-10 (Taylor 7, Elliott 1); Second day, SAf (1) 0-83 (Kirsten 41, Bacher 38); Third day, Aus (2) 3-145 (ME Waugh 54, SR Waugh 11)

SOUTH AFRICA

G Kirsten c Hayden b Gillespie	0	b Gillespie	43
AM Bacher c Elliott b McGrath	11	c McGrath b Gillespie	49
JH Kallis c Blewett b Gillespie	0	run out (Blewett)	2
DJ Cullinan c Warne b Gillespie	34	lbw b Gillespie	2
*WJ Cronje b McGrath	0	c Healy b Bevan	27
HH Gibbs b Gillespie	31	c ME Waugh b McGrath	7
BM McMillan c SR Waugh b Warne	55	lbw b Bevan	2
SM Pollock lbw b Gillespie	0	lbw b Warne	17
+DJ Richardson c McGrath b Warne	47	not out	3
AA Donald c and b Warne	9	c Warne b Bevan	7
PR Adams not out	5	c Taylor b Warne	1
B 8, l-b 8, w 1	17	B 1, l-b 5, n-b 2	8
(74.4 overs, 323 mins)	209	(73.4 overs, 296 mins)	168

Fall: 13 17 21 22 70 95 95 180 204 209   Fall: 87 98 99 100 122 137 152 156 167 168

Bowling: First Innings – McGrath 22-7-66-2; Gillespie 23-10-54-5; Warne 23.4-5-62-3; Blewett 4-2-3-0; Bevan 2-0-8-0. Second Innings – McGrath 13-3-43-1; Gillespie 18-4-49-3; SR Waugh 4.3-0-16-0; Blewett 7.3-3-16-0; Warne 17.4-7-20-2; Bevan 13-3-18-3.

AUSTRALIA

ML Hayden c Cullinan b Pollock	0	(2) run out (Cronje)	14
*MA Taylor c Richardson b Pollock	8	(1) lbw b McMillan	13
MTG Elliott run out (Cronje/Bacher)	23	c and b Adams	44
ME Waugh lbw b Cronje	20	b Kallis	116
SR Waugh c Richardson b McMillan	8	c Cronje b Kallis	18
GS Blewett b Donald	13	b Adams	7
MG Bevan c Richardson b McMillan	0	c Cullinan b Cronje	24
+IA Healy c Bacher b Cronje	5	not out	10
SK Warne lbw b Adams	18	lbw b Kallis	3
JN Gillespie not out	1	not out	0
GD McGrath c Richardson b Kallis	0		
B 1, l-b 7, w 2, n-b 2	12	B 11, l-b 8, W 3	22
(70.4 overs, 309 mins)	108	(93.3 overs, 412 mins) (8 wickets)	271

Fall: 1 13 48 64 66 70 85 86 106 108   Fall: 23 30 113 167 192 258 258 265

Bowling: First Innings – Donald 23-13-18-1; Pollock 6-3-6-2; Adams 4-0-5-1; McMillan 14-2-32-2; Cronje 14-7-21-2; Kallis 9.4-2-18-1. Second Innings – Donald 26-6-75-0; McMillan 21-5-46-1; Cronje 9.3-1-36-1; Kallis 16-7-29-3; Adams 21-4-66-2.

THIRD TEST (Test 1373)
England v Australia

At Old Trafford, Manchester, July 3, 4, 5, 6, 7, 1997. Australia won by 268 runs.
Toss: Australia. **Player of the Match:** SR Waugh. **Umpires:** G Sharp and S Venkataraghavan.
Close of play: First day, Australia (1) 7-224 (SR Waugh 102, Reiffel 26); Second day, Eng (1) 8-161 (Ealham 23, Caddick 15); Third day, Aus (2) 6-262 (SR Waugh 82, SK Warne 32); Fourth day, Eng (2) 5-130 (Crawley 53, Ealham 5).

AUSTRALIA

*MA Taylor c Thorpe b Headley	2	(2) c Butcher b Headley	1
MTG Elliott c Stewart b Headley	40	(1) c Butcher b Headley	11
GS Blewett b Gough	8	c Hussain b Croft	19
ME Waugh c Stewart b Ealham	12	b Ealham	55
SR Waugh b Gough	108	c Stewart b Headley	116
MG Bevan c Stewart b Headley	7	c Atherton b Headley	0
+IA Healy c Stewart b Caddick	9	c Butcher b Croft	47
SK Warne c Stewart b Ealham	3	c Stewart b Caddick	53
PR Reiffel b Gough	31	not out	45
JN Gillespie c Stewart b Headley	0	not out	28
GD McGrath not out	0		
B 8, l-b 4, n-b 3	15	B 1, l-b 13, n-b 6	20
(77.3 overs, 326 mins)	235	(122 overs, 509 mins) (8 wickets dec)	395

Fall: 9 22 42 85 113 150 160 230 235 235   Fall: 5 33 39 131 132 210 298 333

Bowling: First Innings – Gough 21-7-52-3; Headley 27.3-4-72-4; Caddick 14-2-52-1; Ealham 11-2-34-2; Croft 4-0-13-0. Second Innings – Gough 20-3-62-0; Headley 29-4-104-4; Croft 39-12-105-2; Ealham 13-3-41-1; Caddick 21-0-69-1.

ENGLAND

MA Butcher st Healy b Bevan	51	c McGrath b Gillespie	28
*MA Atherton c Healy b McGrath	5	lbw b Gillespie	21
+AJ Stewart c Taylor b Warne	30	b Warne	1
N Hussain c Healy b Warne	13	lbw b Gillespie	1
GP Thorpe c Taylor b Warne	3	c Healy b Warne	7
JP Crawley c Healy b Warne	4	hit wicket b McGrath	83
MA Ealham not out	24	c Healy b McGrath	9
RDB Croft c SR Waugh b McGrath	7	c Reiffel b McGrath	7
D Gough lbw b Warne	1	b McGrath	6
AR Caddick c ME Waugh b Warne	15	c Gillespie b Warne	17
DW Headley b McGrath	0	not out	0
B 4, l-b 3, n-b 2	9	B 14, l-b 4, W 1, n-b 1	20
(84.4 overs, 339 mins)	162	(73.4 overs, 299 mins)	200

Fall: 8 74 94 101 110 111 122 123 161 162   Fall: 44 45 50 55 84 158 170 177 188 200

Bowling: First Innings – McGrath 23.4-9-40-3; Reiffel 9-3-14-0; Warne 30-14-48-6; Gillespie 14-3-39-0; Bevan 8-3-14-1. Second Innings – McGrath 21-4-46-4; Gillespie 12-4-31-3; Reiffel 2-0-8-0; Warne 30.4-8-63-3; Bevan 8-2-34-0.

THIRD TEST (Test 1398)
Australia v South Africa

At Adelaide Oval, Adelaide, January 30, 31, February 1, 2, 3, 1998. Match drawn.
Toss: South Africa. **Player of the Match:** SM Pollock. **Umpires:** DB Cowie and SG Randell.
Close of play: First day, SAf (1) 4-269 (Cronje 70, Richardson 0); Second day, Aus (1) 1-71 (Taylor 26, Blewett 31); Third day, Aus (1) 9-327 (Taylor 157, MacGill 2); Fourth day, Aus (2) 2-32 (Blewett 9, ME Waugh 11)

SOUTH AFRICA

AM Bacher c Warne b Bichel	64	(2) c MacGill b Warne		41
G Kirsten c Warne b Kasprowicz	77	(1) not out		108
JH Kallis lbw b MacGill	15	b Kasprowicz		15
*WJ Cronje b Warne	73	c Warne b Kasprowicz		5
HH Gibbs c Healy b Blewett	37	(7) st Healy b MacGill		2
+DJ Richardson c Taylor b Warne	15			
JN Rhodes c Bichel b Kasprowicz	6-	(8) not out		19
BM McMillan not out	87			
SM Pollock c Blewett b Kasprowicz	40			
L Klusener c Warne b MacGill	38	(5) b MacGill		0
PL Symcox lbw b SR Waugh	54	(6) c Healy b MacGill		2
L-b 8, w 2, n-b 1	11	N-b 1		1
(166 overs, 628 mins)	517	(58 overs, 235 mins)	(6 wkts dec)	193

Fall: 140 148 160 269 275 286 305 374 443 515   Fall: 80 133 155 155 157 165

Bowling: First Innings – Kasprowicz 39-7-125-3; Bichel 35-10-103-1; Warne 33-6-95-2; MacGill 29-7-112-2; ME Waugh 6-1-21-0; Blewett 14-5-26-1; SR Waugh 10-3-27-1. Second Innings – Kasprowicz 18-5-55-2; Bichel 14-2-51-0; SR Waugh 4-1-13-0; Warne 15-2-52-1; MacGill 7-1-22-3.

AUSTRALIA

*MA Taylor not out	169	(2) b Klusener		6
MTG Elliott c Kallis b Pollock	8	(1) c Richardson b Pollock		4
GS Blewett c Bacher b Pollock	31	b Pollock		16
ME Waugh c Gibbs b Pollock	63	not out		115
SR Waugh c Richardson b Pollock	6	c Richardson b Klusener		34
RT Ponting b Klusener	26	c Symcox b Klusener		23
+IA Healy c and b Pollock	1	c Richardson b Kallis		10
AJ Bichel c Symcox b Pollock	0	lbw b Klusener		7
SK Warne c Richardson b Pollock	0	not out		4
MS Kasprowicz c Symcox b Kallis	17			
SCG MacGill b Symcox	10			
B 2, l-b 12, n-b 5	19	B 2, n-b 6		8
(122.5 overs, 524 mins)	350	(108.4 overs, 444 mins)	(7 wkts)	227

Fall: 15 71 197 207 263 273 279 279 317 350   Fall: 6 17 54 112 185 202 215

Bowling: First Innings – Pollock 41-11-87-7; McMillan 23-5-60-0; Kallis 18-5-45-1; Klusener 27-6-104-1; Symcox 13.5-3-40-1. Second Innings – Pollock 30.4-12-61-2; Klusener 30-10-67-4; Kallis 16-10-20-1; Symcox 18-2-42-0; McMillan 13-2-33-0; Cronje 1-0-2-0.

FIRST TEST (Test 1406)
India v Australia

At MA Chidambaram Stadium, Chennai, March 6, 7, 8, 9, 10, 1998. India won by 169 runs.
Toss: India. **Player of the Match:** SR Tendulkar. **Umpires:** G Sharp and S Venkataraghavan.
Close of play: First day, Ind (1) 5-232 (Dravid 42, Kumble 19); Second day, Aus (1) 7-193 (Healy 31, Warne 13); Third day, Ind (2) 1-100 (Sidhu 55, Dravid 18); Fourth day, Aus (2) 3-31 (Reiffel 0).

INDIA

+NR Mongia c Healy b Kasprowicz	58	lbw b Blewett	18
NS Sidhu run out (ME Waugh)	62	c Ponting b Robertson	64
RS Dravid c Robertson b Warne	52	c Healy b Warne	56
SR Tendulkar c Taylor b Warne	4	not out	155
*M Azharuddin c Reiffel b Warne	26	c SR Waugh b ME Waugh	64
SC Ganguly lbw b Robertson	3	not out	30
AR Kumble c SR Waugh b Robertson	30		
J Srinath c Taylor b Warne	1		
RK Chauhan c Healy b Robertson	3		
Harvinder Singh not out	0		
SL Venkatapathy Raju b Robertson	0		
B 8, l-b 6, n-b 4	18	B 18, l-b 6, n-b 7	31
(104.2 overs, 428 mins)	257	(107 overs, 458 mins) (4 wkts dec)	418

Fall: 122 126 130 186 195 247 248 253 257 257   Fall: 43 115 228 355

Bowling: First Innings – Kasprowicz 21-8-44-1; Reiffel 15-4-27-0; Warne 35-11-85-4; Robertson 28.2-4-72-4; ME Waugh 1-0-4-0; SR Waugh 4-1-11-0. Second Innings – Kasprowicz 14-6-42-0; Reiffel 9-1-32-0; Robertson 27-4-92-1; Warne 30-7-122-1; Blewett 10-2-35-1; ME Waugh 9-0-44-1; SR Waugh 8-0-27-0.

AUSTRALIA

*MA Taylor c Mongia b Harvinder Singh	12	(2) c Srinath b Kumble	13
MJ Slater c Dravid b Kumble	11	(1) b Srinath	13
ME Waugh c Ganguly b Venkatapathy Raju	66	(5) c Dravid b Kumble	18
SR Waugh b Kumble	12	(6) c Dravid b Venkatapathy Raju	27
RT Ponting c Mongia b Venkatapathy Raju	18	(7) lbw b Venkatapathy Raju	2
GS Blewett lbw b Chauhan	9	(3) c Dravid b Kumble	5
+IA Healy c Ganguly b Venkatapathy Raju	90	(8) not out	32
PR Reiffel c Dravid b Kumble	15	(4) c Azharuddin b Venkatapathy Raju	8
SK Warne c Tendulkar b Kumble	17	c Kumble b Chauhan	35
GR Robertson c Mongia b Srinath	57	b Chauhan	0
MS Kasprowicz not out	11	c Srinath b Kumble	4
B 1, l-b 6, n-b 3	10	B 4, l-b 3, n-b 4	11
(130.3 overs, 517 mins)	328	(67.5 overs, 260 mins)	168

Fall: 16 44 57 95 119 137 173 201 297 328   Fall: 18 30 31 54 79 91 96 153 153 168

Bowling: First Innings – Srinath 17.3-3-46-1; Harvinder Singh 11-4-28-1; Kumble 45-10-103-4; Chauhan 25-3-90-1; Venkatapathy Raju 32-8-54-3. Second Innings – Srinath 6-4-9-1; Harvinder Singh 2-0-9-0; Chauhan 22-7-66-2; Kumble 22.5-7-46-4; Venkatapathy Raju 15-3-31-3.

SECOND TEST (Test 1427)
Pakistan v Australia

At Arbab Niaz Stadium, Peshawar, October 15, 16, 17, 18, 19, 1998. Match drawn.
Toss: Australia. **Player of the Match:** MA Taylor. **Umpires:** SA Bucknor and Mohammad Nazir jr.
Close of play: First day, Australia (1) 1-224 (Taylor 112, Langer 97); Second day, Aus (1) 4-599 (Taylor 334, Ponting 76); Third day, Pak (1) 2-329 (Ijaz Ahmed 125, Inzaman-ul-Haq 31); Fourth day, Aus (2) 0-21 (Slater 7, Taylor 13).

AUSTRALIA

*MA Taylor not out		334	(2) b Aamir Sohail		92
MJ Slater c Azhar Mahmood b Shoaib Akhtar		2	(1) lbw b Mushtaq Ahmed		21
JL Langer c Moin Khan b Azhar Mahmood		116	c Mohammad b Mushtaq Ahmed		14
ME Waugh c Salim Malik b Aamir Sohail		42	b Shoaib Akhtar		43
SR Waugh c Moin Khan b Shoaib Akhtar		1	not out		49
RT Ponting not out		76	lbw b Ijaz Ahmed		43
+IA Healy	not out	14			
DW Fleming					
CR Miller					
SCG MacGill					
GD McGrath (did not bat).					
L-b 9, w 3, n-b 16		28	L-b 4, n-b 9		13
(174 overs, 720 mins)	(4 wickets dec)	599	(88 overs, 348 mins)	(5 wickets dec)	289

Fall: 16 295 418 431   Fall: 39 67 170 179 269

Bowling: First Innings – Shoaib Akhtar 31-6-107-2; Mohammad Zahid 16-0-74-0; Mushtaq Ahmed 46-3-153-0; Azhar Mahmood 23-2-82-1; Aamir Sohail 42-8-111-1; Salim Malik 16-0-63-0. Second Innings – Shoaib Akhtar 16-2-68-1; Azhar Mahmood 3-0-18-0; Mushtaq Ahmed 20-1-59-2; Mohammad Zahid 10-2-42-0; Aamir Sohail 10-1-35-1; Salim Malik 15-1-30-0; Ijaz Ahmed 14-1-33-1.

PAKISTAN

Saeed Anwar c Healy b Miller	126
*Aamir Sohail c Fleming b McGrath	31
Ijaz Ahmed c Healy b MacGill	155
Inzamam-ul-Haq c Healy b SR Waugh	97
Salim Malik c Taylor b McGrath	49
Mohammad Yousuf c SR Waugh b MacGill	28
+Moin Khan c Healy b Ponting	0
Azhar Mahmood c Langer b McGrath	26
Mushtaq Ahmed not out	48
Mohammad Zahid lbw b Fleming	1
Shoaib Akhtar (did not bat).	
B 5, l-b 9, w 1, n-b 4	19
(172.1 overs, 702 mins) (9 wickets dec)	580

Fall: 45 256 371 454 500 501 521 571 580

Bowling: First Innings – McGrath 36-8-131-3; Fleming 35.1-6-103-1; MacGill 42-5-169-2; Miller 38-12-99-1; ME Waugh 8-0-32-0; SR Waugh 8-1-19-1; Ponting 5-1-13-1.

SECOND TEST (Test 1452)
West Indies v Australia

At Sabina Park, Kingston, March 13, 14, 15, 16, 1999. West Indies won by ten wickets.
Toss: Australia. **Player of the Match:** BC Lara. **Umpires:** SA Bucknor and P Willey.
Close of play: First day, West Indies (1) 4-37 (Lara 7, Collins 1); Second day, West Indies (1) 4-377 (Lara 212, Adams 88); Third day, Australia (2) 8-157 (Gillespie 7).

AUSTRALIA

MJ Slater c Jacobs b Walsh	22	(2) b Walsh	0
MTG Elliott c Lara b Walsh	0	(1) lbw b Perry	16
JL Langer c Jacobs b Walsh	8	c Jacobs b Perry	24
ME Waugh b Perry	67	c Walsh b Ambrose	21
*SR Waugh c Joseph b Collins	100	c Jacobs b Perry	9
GS Blewett lbw b Walsh	5	c Lara b Perry	30
+IA Healy run out (Joseph/Perry)	6	run out (Collins/Jacobs)	10
SK Warne c Joseph b Collins	24	c Joseph b Walsh	23
JN Gillespie b Ambrose	1	c Jacobs b Walsh	7
SCG MacGill c Joseph b Collins	0	c Joseph b Perry	7
GD McGrath not out	2	not out	11
B 1, l-b 3, n-b 17	21	L-b 3, n-b 16	19
(71.3 overs, 332 mins)	256	(66 overs, 287 mins)	177

Fall: 8 28 46 158 171 179 227 242 248 256   Fall: 4 36 51 63 86 107 137 157 159 177

Bowling: First Innings – Ambrose 17-9-33-1; Walsh 20-6-55-4; Collins 16.3-2-79-3; Perry 17-1-79-1; Adams 1-0-6-0. Second Innings – Ambrose 14-4-28-1; Walsh 18-3-52-3; Perry 26-8-70-5; Collins 8-0-24-0.

WEST INDIES

SL Campbell b McGrath	12	not out	1
S Ragoonath lbw b Gillespie	0	not out	2
LA Roberts c Warne b McGrath	0		
*BC Lara c Healy b McGrath	213		
DRE Joseph c Blewett b McGrath	14		
PT Collins c ME Waugh b MacGill	13		
JC Adams c Elliott b McGrath	94		
+RD Jacobs c Gillespie b Warne	25		
NO Perry not out	15		
CEL Ambrose b MacGill	3		
CA Walsh lbw b MacGill	0		
B 12, l-b 8, n-b 22	42	0	
(132.3 overs, 604 mins)	431	(0.3 overs, 2 mins)	(0 wkt) 3

Fall: 4 5 17 34 378 398 420 427 431 431   Fall:

Bowling: First Innings – McGrath 35-11-93-5; Gillespie 33-7-79-1; Warne 30-8-94-1; MacGill 22.3-3-84-3; Blewett 10-1-48-0; ME Waugh 2-0-13-0. Second Innings – McGrath 0.3-0-3-0.

THIRD TEST (Test 1454)
West Indies v Australia

At Kensington Oval, Bridgetown, March 26, 27, 28, 29, 30, 1999. West Indies won by one wicket.
Toss: Australia. **Player of the Match:** BC Lara. **Umpires:** EA Nicholls and DL Orchard.
Close of play: First day, Australia (1) 4-322 (SR Waugh 141, Ponting 65); Second day, West Indies (1) 4-80 (Campbell 23, Hooper, 13); Third day, Australia (2) 2-18 (Slater 14, Gillespie 1); Fourth day, West Indies (2) 3-85 (Griffith 35, Lara 2)

AUSTRALIA

MJ Slater c Lara b Ambrose	23	(2) run out (Campbell)	26
MTG Elliott c Jacobs b Walsh	9	(1) c Jacobs b Walsh	0
JL Langer b Hooper	51	lbw b Ambrose	1
ME Waugh b Ambrose	0	(5) lbw b Walsh	3
*SR Waugh lbw b Perry	199	(6) b Collins	11
RT Ponting c Hooper b Perry	104	(7) c Griffith b Walsh	22
+IA Healy lbw b Walsh	0	(8) c Jacobs b Collins	3
SK Warne c Lara b Perry	13	(9) lbw b Walsh	32
JN Gillespie not out	23	(4) b Ambrose	14
SCG MacGill run out (Ambrose)	17	c Campbell b Walsh	1
GD McGrath c Joseph b Hooper	3	not out	8
B 4, l-b 10, n-b 34	48	L-b 5, w 1, n-b 19	25
(153.4 overs, 647 mins)	490	(50.1 overs, 251 mins)	146

Fall: 31 36 36 144 425 427 429 446 483 490   Fall: 0 12 35 46 48 73 81 134 137 146

Bowling: First Innings – Ambrose 31.3-7-93-2; Walsh 38-8-121-2; Perry 33-5-102-3; Collins 35.3-7-110-0; Hooper 15.4-4-50-2. Second Innings – Walsh 17.1-3-39-5; Ambrose 20-2-60-2; Collins 9-0-31-2; Perry 4-0-11-0.

WEST INDIES

SL Campbell c SR Waugh b Gillespie	105	lbw b McGrath	33
AFG Griffith run out (Ponting)	0	lbw b Gillespie	35
DRE Joseph lbw b McGrath	26	lbw b MacGill	1
PT Collins lbw b McGrath	0	lbw b McGrath	0
*BC Lara c Healy b Gillespie	8	not out	153
CL Hooper c Warne b McGrath	25	c Healy b Gillespie	6
JC Adams c ME Waugh b McGrath	0	b McGrath	38
+RD Jacobs c ME Waugh b Ponting	68	lbw b McGrath	5
NO Perry lbw b Gillespie	24	lbw b McGrath	0
CEL Ambrose not out	28	c Elliott b Gillespie	12
CA Walsh c Slater b Warne	12	not out	0
B 10, l-b 3, n-b 20	33	B 8, l-b 13, W 2, n-b 5	28
(103.5 overs, 439 mins)	329	(120.1 overs, 523 mins)	(9 wkts) 311

Fall: 1 50 50 64 98 98 251 265 291 329   Fall: 72 77 78 91 105 238 248 248 302

Bowling: First Innings – McGrath 33-5-128-4; Gillespie 28-14-48-3; Warne 15.5-2-70-1; MacGill 20-5-47-0; Ponting 4-1-12-1; ME Waugh 3-0-11-0. Second Innings – McGrath 44-13-92-5; Gillespie 26.1-8-62-3; Warne 24-4-69-0; MacGill 21-6-48-1; SR Waugh 5-0-19-0.

AUSTRALIA v SOUTH AFRICA (World Cup Semifinal)

At Edgbaston, Birmingham, June 17, 1999. Match tied.
Toss: South Africa. **Player of the Match:** SK Warne. **Umpires:** DR Shepherd and S Venkataraghavan.

AUSTRALIA

+AC Gilchrist c Donald b Kallis	20	(39)
ME Waugh c Boucher b Pollock	0	(4)
RT Ponting c Kirsten b Donald	37	(48)
DS Lehmann c Boucher b Donald	1	(4)
*SR Waugh c Boucher b Pollock	56	(76)
MG Bevan c Boucher b Pollock	65	(101)
TM Moody lbw b Pollock	0	(3)
SK Warne c Cronje b Pollock	18	(24)
PR Reiffel b Donald	0	(1)
DW Fleming b Donald	0	(2)
GD McGrath not out	0	(1)
B 1, l-b 6, w 3, n-b 6	16	
(49.2 overs)	213	

Fall: 3 54 58 68 158 158 207 207 207 213

Bowling: Pollock 9.2-1-36-5; Elworthy 10-0-59-0; Kallis 10-2-27-1; Donald 10-1-32-4; Klusener 9-1-50-0; Cronje 1-0-2-0.

SOUTH AFRICA

G Kirsten b Warne	18	(42)
HH Gibbs b Warne	30	(36)
DJ Cullinan run out (Bevan)	6	(30)
*WJ Cronje c ME Waugh b Warne	0	(2)
JH Kallis c SR Waugh b Warne	53	(92)
JN Rhodes c Bevan b Reiffel	43	(55)
SM Pollock b Fleming	20	(14)
L Klusener not out	31	(16)
+MV Boucher b McGrath	5	(10)
S Elworthy run out (Reiffel/McGrath)	1	(1)
AA Donald run out (ME Waugh/Fleming/G'ist)	0	(0)
L-b 1, w 5	6	
(49.4 overs)	213	

Fall: 48 53 53 61 145 175 183 196 198 213

Bowling: McGrath 10-0-51-1; Fleming 8.4-1-40-1; Reiffel 8-0-28-1; Warne 10-4-29-4; ME Waugh 8-0-37-0; Moody 5-0-27-0.

SECOND TEST (Test 1470)
Australia v Pakistan

At Bellerive Oval, Hobart, November 18, 19, 20, 21, 22, 1999. Australia won by four wickets.
Toss: Australia. **Player of the Match:** JL Langer. **Umpires:** PD Parker and P Willey.
Close of play: First day, Australia (1) 0/29 (Slater 16, Blewett 9); Second day, Pakistan (2) 1/61 (Saeed Anwar 36, Saqlain Mushtaq 0); Third day, Pakistan (2) 7/351 (Inzamam-ul-Haq 116, Wasim Akram 1); Fourth day, Australia (2) 5/188 (Langer 52, Gilchrist 45)

PAKISTAN

Saeed Anwar c Warne b McGrath	0	b Warne	78
Mohammad Wasim c Gilchrist b Muller	91	c McGrath b Muller	20
Ijaz Ahmed c Slater b McGrath	6	(4) c SR Waugh b McGrath	82
Inzamam-ul-Haq b Muller	12	(5) c ME Waugh b Warne	118
Mohammad Yousuf c ME Waugh b Fleming	17	(6) c Ponting b Fleming	2
Azhar Mahmood b Warne	27	(7) lbw b Warne	28
+Moin Khan c McGrath b Muller	1	(8) c Gilchrist b Fleming	6
*Wasim Akram c Gilchrist b Warne	29	(9) c Blewett b Warne	31
Saqlain Mushtaq lbw b Warne	3	(3) lbw b Warne	8
Waqar Younis not out	12	run out (Gilchrist)	0
Shoaib Akhtar c Gilchrist b Fleming	5	not out	5
B 10, l-b 6, w 3	19	L-b 6, w 1, n-b 7	14
(72.5 overs, 283 mins)	222	(128.4 overs, 521 mins)	392

Fall: 4 18 71 120 148 153 188 198 217 222   Fall: 50 100 122 258 263 320 345 357 358 392

Bowling: First Innings – McGrath 18-8-34-2; Fleming 24.5-7-54-2; Muller 12-0-68-3; Warne 16-6-45-3; Blewett 2-1-5-0. Second Innings – McGrath 27-8-87-1; Fleming 29-5-89-2; Warne 45.4-11-110-5; Muller 17-3-63-1; SR Waugh 4-1-19-0; ME Waugh 2-0-6-0; Ponting 2-1-7-0; Blewett 2-0-5-0.

AUSTRALIA

MJ Slater c Ijaz Ahmed b Saqlain Mushtaq	97	(2) c Azhar Mahmood b Shoaib Akhtar	27
GS Blewett c Moin Khan b Azhar Mahmood	35	(1) c Moin Khan b Azhar Mahmood	29
JL Langer c Mohammad Wasim b Saqlain Mushtaq	59	c Inzamam-ul-Haq b Saqlain Mushtaq	127
ME Waugh lbw b Waqar Younis	5	lbw b Azhar Mahmood	0
*SR Waugh c Ijaz Ahmed b Wasim Akram	24	c and b Saqlain Mushtaq	28
RT Ponting b Waqar Younis	0	lbw b Wasim Akram	0
+AC Gilchrist st Moin Khan b Saqlain Mushtaq	6	not out	149
SK Warne b Saqlain Mushtaq	0	not out	0
DW Fleming lbw b Saqlain Mushtaq	0		
GD McGrath st Moin Khan b Saqlain Mushtaq	7		
SA Muller not out	0		
B 2, l-b 6, n-b 5	13	B 1, l-b 4, n-b 4	9
(80 overs, 355 mins)	246	(113.5 overs, 503 mins) (6 wickets)	369

Fall: 76 191 206 206 213 236 236 236 246 246   Fall: 39 81 81 125 126 364

Bowling: First Innings – Wasim Akram 20-4-51-1; Shoaib Akhtar 17-2-69-0; Waqar Younis 12-1-42-2; Saqlain Mushtaq 24-8-46-6; Azhar Mahmood 7-1-30-1. Second Innings – Wasim Akram 18-1-68-1; Waqar Younis 11-2-38-0; Shoaib Akhtar 23-5-85-1; Saqlain Mushtaq 44.5-9-130-2; Azhar Mahmood 17-3-43-2.

SECOND TEST (Test 1536)
India v Australia

At Eden Gardens, Kolkata, March 11, 12, 13, 14, 15, 2001. **India won by 171 runs.**
Toss: Australia. **Player of the Match:** VVS Laxman. **Umpires:** SK Bansal and P Willey.
Close of play: First day, Australia (1) 8-291 (SR Waugh 29, Gillespie 6); Second day, India (1) 8-128 (Laxman 26, Raju 3); Third day, India (2) 4-254 (Laxman 109, Dravid 7); Fourth day, India (2) 4-589 (Laxman 275, Dravid 165)

AUSTRALIA

MJ Slater c Mongia b Zaheer Khan	42		(2) c Ganguly b Harbhajan Singh	43
ML Hayden c (sub) Badani b Harbhajan Singh	97		(1) lbw b Tendulkar	67
JL Langer c Mongia b Zaheer Khan	58		c Ramesh b Harbhajan Singh	28
ME Waugh c Mongia b Harbhajan Singh	22		lbw b Venkatapathy Raju	0
*SR Waugh lbw b Harbhajan Singh	110		c (sub) HK Badani b Harbhajan Singh	24
RT Ponting lbw b Harbhajan Singh	6		c Das b Harbhajan Singh	0
+AC Gilchrist lbw b Harbhajan Singh	0		lbw b Tendulkar	0
SK Warne c Ramesh b Harbhajan Singh	0		(9) lbw b Tendulkar	0
MS Kasprowicz lbw b Ganguly	7		(10) not out	13
JN Gillespie c Ramesh b Harbhajan Singh	46		(8) c Das b Harbhajan Singh	6
GD McGrath not out	21		lbw b Harbhajan Singh	12
B 19, l-b 10, n-b 7	36		B 6, n-b 8	19
(131.5 overs, 575 mins)	445		(68.3 overs, 272 mins)	212

Fall: 103 193 214 236 252 252 252 269 402 445   Fall: 74 106 116 166 166 167 173 174 191 212

Bowling: First Innings – Zaheer Khan 28.4-6-89-2; Venkatesh Prasad 30-5-95-0; Ganguly 13.2-3-44-1; Venkatapathy Raju 20-2-58-0; Harbhajan Singh 37.5-7-123-7; Tendulkar 2-0-7-0. Second Innings – Zaheer Khan 8-4-30-0; Venkatesh Prasad 3-1-7-0; Harbhajan Singh 30.3-8-73-6; Venkatapathy Raju 15-3-58-1; Tendulkar 11-3-31-3; Ganguly 1-0-2-0.

INDIA

SS Das c Gilchrist b McGrath	20		hit wicket b Gillespie	39
S Ramesh c Ponting b Gillespie	0		c ME Waugh b Warne	30
RS Dravid b Warne	25		(6) run out (SR Waugh/Kasprowicz)	180
SR Tendulkar lbw b McGrath	10		c Gilchrist b Gillespie	10
*SC Ganguly c SR Waugh b Kasprowicz	23		c Gilchrist b McGrath	48
VVS Laxman c Hayden b Warne	59		(3) c Ponting b McGrath	281
+NR Mongia c Gilchrist b Kasprowicz	2		b McGrath	4
Harbhajan Singh c Ponting b Gillespie	4		(9) not out	8
Zaheer Khan b McGrath	3		(8) not out	23
SL Venkatapathy Raju lbw b McGrath	4			
BK Venkatesh Prasad not out	7			
L-b 2, n-b 12	14		B 4, l-b 14, W 2, n-b 14	34
(58.1 overs, 258 mins)	171		(178 overs, 737 mins) (7 wickets dec)	657

Fall: 0 34 48 88 88 92 97 113 129 171   Fall: 52 97 115 232 608 624 629

Bowling: First Innings – McGrath 14-8-18-4; Gillespie 11-0-47-2; Kasprowicz 13-2-39-2; Warne 20.1-3-65-2. Second Innings – McGrath 39-12-103-3; Gillespie 31-6-115-2; Warne 34-3-152-1; ME Waugh 18-1-58-0; Kasprowicz 35-6-139-0; Ponting 12-1-41-0; Hayden 6-0-24-0; Slater 2-1-4-0; Langer 1-0-3-0.

FIFTH TEST (Test 1559)
England v Australia

At Kennington Oval, The Oval, August 23, 24, 25, 26, 27, 2001. Australia won by an innings and 25 runs.
Toss: Australia. **Player of the Match:** SK Warne. **Umpires:** RE Koertzen and P Willey.
Close of play: First day, Australia (1) 2-324 (ME Waugh 48, SR Waugh 12); Second day, England (1) 1-80 (Trescothick 55, Butcher 10); Third day, England (1) 8-409 (Ramprakash 124, Gough 17); Fourth day, England (2) 1-40 (Trescothick 20, Butcher 11)

AUSTRALIA

ML Hayden c Trescothick b Tufnell	68
JL Langer retired hurt	102
RT Ponting c Atherton b Ormond	62
ME Waugh b Gough	120
*SR Waugh not out	157
+AC Gilchrist c Ramprakash b Afzaal	25
DR Martyn not out	64
B Lee	
SK Warne	
JN Gillespie	
GD McGrath (did not bat).	
B 10, l-b 13, w 1, n-b 19	43
(152 overs, 628 mins) (4 wickets dec)	641

Fall: 158 292 489 534

Bowling: First Innings – Gough 29-4-113-1; Caddick 36-9-146-0; Ormond 34-4-115-1; Tufnell 39-2-174-1; Butcher 1-0-2-0; Ramprakash 4-0-19-0; Afzaal 9-0-49-1.

ENGLAND

MA Atherton b Warne	13	c Warne b McGrath	9
ME Trescothick b Warne	55	c and b McGrath	24
MA Butcher c Langer b Warne	25	c SR Waugh b Warne	14
*N Hussain b ME Waugh	52	lbw b Warne	2
MR Ramprakash c Gilchrist b McGrath	133	c Hayden b Warne	19
U Afzaal c Gillespie b McGrath	54	c Ponting b McGrath	5
+AJ Stewart c Gilchrist b Warne	29	b Warne	34
AR Caddick lbw b Warne	0	b Lee	17
J Ormond b Warne	18	c Gilchrist b McGrath	17
D Gough st Gilchrist b Warne	24	not out	39
PCR Tufnell not out	7	c Warne b McGrath	0
B 3, l-b 13, w 1, n-b 5	22	L-b 2, n-b 2	4
(118.2 overs, 514 mins)	432	(68.3 overs, 283 mins)	184

Fall: 58 85 104 166 255 313 313 350 424 432   Fall: 17 46 48 50 55 95 126 126 184 184

Bowling: First Innings – McGrath 30-11-67-2; Gillespie 20-3-96-0; Warne 44.2-7-165-7; Lee 14-1-43-0; Ponting 2-0-5-0; ME Waugh 8-0-40-1. Second Innings – Lee 10-3-30-1; McGrath 15.3-6-43-5; Warne 28-8-64-4; Ponting 2-0-3-0; Gillespie 12-5-38-0; ME Waugh 1-0-4-0.

SECOND TEST (Test 1594)
South Africa v Australia

At Newlands, Cape Town, March 8, 9, 10, 11, 12, 2002. Australia won by four wickets.
Toss: South Africa. **Player of the Match:** SK Warne. **Umpires:** SA Bucknor and RE Koertzen.
Close of play: First day, Australia (1) 0-46 (Langer 28, Hayden 17); Second day, South Africa (2) 0-7 (Gibbs 5, Kirsten 2); Third day, South Africa (2) 4-307 (McKenzie 28, Prince 5); Fourth day, Australia (2) 1-131 (Hayden 50, Ponting 17)

SOUTH AFRICA

HH Gibbs c ME Waugh b Gillespie	12	c Ponting b Warne	39
G Kirsten c ME Waugh b Lee	7	lbw b Lee	87
GC Smith c Ponting b McGrath	3	c Gilchrist b Warne	68
JH Kallis c Gilchrist b McGrath	23	lbw b Warne	73
ND McKenzie b Warne	20	run out (Martyn)	99
AG Prince c Gilchrist b McGrath	10	c Ponting b Warne	20
*+MV Boucher c Gilchrist b Lee	26	lbw b Gillespie	37
AJ Hall c Gilchrist b Gillespie	70	run out (Lee/Gillespie)	0
PR Adams c Warne b Gillespie	35	not out	23
M Ntini c ME Waugh b Warne	14	c Langer b Warne	11
D Pretorius not out	5	c ME Waugh b Warne	0
B 4, l-b 5, n-b 5	14	B 8, l-b 3, w 2, n-b 3	16
(80 overs, 355 mins)	239	(162 overs, 683 mins)	473

Fall: 15 18 25 70 73 92 147 216 229 239   Fall: 84 183 254 284 350 431 433 440 464 473

Bowling: First Innings – McGrath 20-4-42-3; Gillespie 15-4-52-3; Lee 16-1-65-2; Warne 28-10-70-2; ME Waugh 1-0-1-0. Second Innings – McGrath 25-7-56-0; Gillespie 29-10-81-1; Warne 70-15-161-6; Lee 22-3-99-1; ME Waugh 9-3-34-0; Martyn 4-0-15-0; SR Waugh 3-0-16-0.

AUSTRALIA

JL Langer b Ntini	37	b Pretorius	58
ML Hayden c Hall b Kallis	63	c Boucher b Kallis	96
RT Ponting c Boucher b Adams	47	not out	100
ME Waugh c Gibbs b Ntini	25	c Boucher b Ntini	16
*SR Waugh b Adams	0	b Adams	14
DR Martyn c Boucher b Ntini	2	lbw b Adams	0
+AC Gilchrist not out	138	c McKenzie b Kallis	24
SK Warne c Kallis b Adams	63	not out	15
B Lee c Prince b Kallis	0		
JN Gillespie c Kallis b Adams	0		
GD McGrath lbw b Ntini	2		
B 2, l-b 1, w 2	5	L-b 6, n-b 5	11
(80.5 overs, 369 mins)	382	(79.1 overs, 366 mins) (6 wickets)	334

Fall: 67 130 162 168 176 185 317 338 343 382   Fall: 102 201 251 268 268 305

Bowling: First Innings – Ntini 22.5-5-93-4; Pretorius 11-1-72-0; Kallis 16-2-65-2; Hall 11-1-47-0; Adams 20-1-102-4. Second Innings – Ntini 24-4-90-1; Pretorius 14-5-60-1; Adams 21.1-0-104-2; Hall 3-0-6-0; Kallis 17-2-68-2.

FIFTH TEST (Test 1637)
Australia v England

At Sydney Cricket Ground, Sydney, January 2, 3, 4, 5, 6, 2003. England won by 225 runs.
Toss: England. **Player of the Match:** MP Vaughan. **Umpires:** DL Orchard and RB Tiffin.
Close of play: First day, England (1) 5-264 (Crawley 5, Stewart 20); Second day, Australia (1) 5-237 (Waugh 102, Gilchrist 45); Third day, England (2) 2-218 (Vaughan 113, Hussain 34); Fourth day, Australia (2) 3-91 (Bichel 49, Martyn 19)

ENGLAND

ME Trescothick c Gilchrist b Bichel	19	b Lee		22
MP Vaughan c Gilchrist b Lee	0	lbw b Bichel		183
MA Butcher b Lee	124	c Hayden b MacGill		34
*N Hussain c Gilchrist b Gillespie	75	c Gilchrist b Lee		72
RWT Key lbw b Waugh	3	c Hayden b Lee		14
JP Crawley not out	35	lbw b Gillespie		8
+AJ Stewart b Bichel	71	not out		38
RKJ Dawson c Gilchrist b Bichel	2	c and b Bichel		12
AR Caddick b MacGill	7	c Langer b MacGill		8
MJ Hoggard st Gilchrist b MacGill	0	b MacGill		0
SJ Harmison run out (Langer/MacGill)	4	not out		20
B 6, l-b 3, n-b 13	22	B 9, l-b 20, w 2, n-b 10		41
(127 overs, 530 mins)	362	(125.3 overs, 530 mins)	(9 wickets dec)	452

Fall: 4 32 198 210 240 332 337 348 350 362   Fall: 37 124 313 344 345 356 378 407 409

Bowling: First Innings – Gillespie 27-10-62-1; Lee 31-9-97-2; Bichel 21-5-86-3; MacGill 44-8-106-2; Waugh 4-3-2-1. Second Innings – Gillespie 18.3-4-70-1; Lee 31.3-5-132-3; MacGill 41-8-120-3; Bichel 25.3-3-82-2; Martyn 3-1-14-0; Waugh 6-2-5-0.

AUSTRALIA

JL Langer c Hoggard b Caddick	25	lbw b Caddick	3
ML Hayden lbw b Caddick	15	lbw b Hoggard	2
RT Ponting c Stewart b Caddick	7	(4) lbw b Caddick	11
DR Martyn c Caddick b Harmison	26	(5) c Stewart b Dawson	21
*SR Waugh c Butcher b Hoggard	102	(6) b Caddick	6
ML Love c Trescothick b Harmison	0	(7) b Harmison	27
+AC Gilchrist c Stewart b Harmison	133	(8) c Butcher b Caddick	37
AJ Bichel c Crawley b Hoggard	4	(3) lbw b Caddick	49
B Lee c Stewart b Hoggard	0	c Stewart b Caddick	46
JN Gillespie not out	31	not out	3
SCG MacGill c Hussain b Hoggard	1	b Caddick	1
B 2, l-b 6, w 2, n-b 9	19	B 6, l-b 8, W 3, n-b 3	20
(80.3 overs, 367 mins)	363	(54 overs, 240 mins)	226

Fall: 36 45 56 146 150 241 267 267 349 363   Fall: 5 5 25 93 99 109 139 181 224 226

Bowling: First Innings – Hoggard 21.3-4-92-4; Caddick 23-3-121-3; Harmison 20-4-70-3; Dawson 16-0-72-0. Second Innings – Hoggard 13-3-35-1; Caddick 22-5-94-7; Harmison 9-1-42-1; Dawson 10-2-41-1.

AUSTRALIA v SRI LANKA (World Cup Semifinal)

At St George's Park, Port Elizabeth, March 18, 2003. **Australia won by 48 runs.**
Toss: Australia. **Player of the Match:** A Symonds. **Umpires:** RE Koertzen and DR Shepherd.

AUSTRALIA

+AC Gilchrist c Sangakkara b De Silva	22	(20)
ML Hayden c Tillakaratne b Vaas	20	(38)
*RT Ponting c Jayasuriya b Vaas	2	(8)
DS Lehmann b Jayasuriya	36	(66)
A Symonds not out	91	(118)
MG Bevan c Sangakkara b Jayasuriya	0	(1)
GB Hogg st Sangakkara b De Silva	8	(19)
IJ Harvey c Sangakkara b Vaas	7	(10)
AJ Bichel not out	19	(21)
B Lee		
GD McGrath		
L-b 3, w 3, n-b 1	7	
(50 overs, 199 mins)	(7 wkts) 212	

Fall: 34 37 51 144 144 158 175

Bowling: Vaas 10-1-34-3; Gunaratne 8-0-60-0; De Silva 10-0-36-2; Muralidaran 10-0-29-0; Jayasuriya 10-0-42-2; Arnold 2-0-8-0.

SRI LANKA

MS Atapattu b Lee	14	(17)
*ST Jayasuriya c Symonds b McGrath	17	(24)
HP Tillakaratne c Gilchrist b Lee	3	(15)
DA Gunawardene c Ponting b Lee	1	(4)
PA De Silva run out (Bichel)	11	(16)
+KC Sangakkara not out	39	(70)
DPM Jayawardene c Gilchrist b Hogg	5	(8)
RP Arnold c Lee b Hogg	3	(27)
WPUJC Vaas not out	21	(50)
M Muralidaran		
PW Gunaratne		
B 4, l-b 1, w 2, n-b 2	9	
(38.1 overs, 167 mins)	(7 wkts) 123	

Fall: 21 37 37 43 51 60 76

Bowling: McGrath 7-1-20-1; Lee 8-0-35-3; Bichel 10-4-18-0; Hogg 10-1-30-2; Harvey 2.1-0-11-0; Lehmann 1-0-4-0.

THIRD TEST (Test 1719)
India v Australia

At Vidarbha CA Ground, Nagpur, October 26, 27, 28, 29, 2004. **Australia won by 342 runs.**
Toss: Australia. **Player of the Match:** DR Martyn. **Umpires:** Aleem Dar and DR Shepherd.
Close of play: First day, Australia (1) 7-362 (Clarke 73, Gillespie 4); Second day, India (1) 5-146 (Kaif 47, Patel 20); Third day, Australia (2) 3-202 (Martyn 41, Clarke 10)

AUSTRALIA

JL Langer c Dravid b Zaheer Khan	44	c Laxman b Kartik	30
ML Hayden c Patel b Zaheer Khan	23	b Zaheer Khan	9
SM Katich c Chopra b Kumble	4	lbw b Kartik	99
DR Martyn c Agarkar b Kumble	114	c Patel b Zaheer Khan	97
DS Lehmann c Dravid b Kartik	70		
MJ Clarke c Patel b Zaheer Khan	91	(5) c Kaif b Kumble	73
*+AC Gilchrist c and b Kartik	2	(6) not out	3
SK Warne st Patel b Kartik	2		
JN Gillespie lbw b Zaheer Khan	9		
MS Kasprowicz c Patel b Agarkar	0		
GD McGrath not out	11		
B 6, l-b 13, w 1, n-b 8	28	B 1, l-b 15, w 2	18
(100.2 overs, 436 mins)	398	(98.1 overs, 410 mins) (5 wickets dec)	329

Fall: 67 79 86 234 314 323 337 376 377 398   Fall: 19 99 171 319 329

Bowling: First Innings – Agarkar 23-2-99-1; Zaheer Khan 26.2-6-95-4; Kumble 25-6-99-2; Kartik 20-1-57-3; Tendulkar 6-1-29-0. Second Innings – Zaheer Khan 21.1-5-64-2; Agarkar 21-7-68-0; Kumble 21-1-89-1; Tendulkar 8-1-12-0; Kartik 26-5-74-2; Sehwag 1-0-6-0.

INDIA

A Chopra c Warne b Gillespie	9	b Gillespie	1
V Sehwag c Gilchrist b McGrath	22	c Clarke b Warne	58
*RS Dravid c Warne b McGrath	21	b Gillespie	2
SR Tendulkar lbw b Gillespie	8	c Martyn b McGrath	2
VVS Laxman c Clarke b Warne	13	c McGrath b Kasprowicz	2
M Kaif c Warne b McGrath	55	c Gilchrist b Kasprowicz	7
+PA Patel c Hayden b Warne	20	c Gilchrist b Gillespie	32
AB Agarkar c Clarke b Gillespie	15	not out	44
AR Kumble not out	7	b Gillespie	2
M Kartik c Clarke b Gillespie	3	c Gilchrist b McGrath	22
Zaheer Khan b Gillespie	0	c Martyn b Warne	25
L-b 10, w 1, n-b 1	12	L-b 2, n-b 1	3
(91.5 overs, 379 mins)	185	(53.3 overs, 237 mins)	200

Fall: 31 34 49 75 103 150 173 178 181 185   Fall: 1 9 20 29 37 102 114 122 148 200

Bowling: First Innings – McGrath 25-13-27-3; Gillespie 22.5-8-56-5; Kasprowicz 21-4-45-0; Warne 23-8-47-2. Second Innings – McGrath 16-1-79-2; Gillespie 16-7-24-4; Kasprowicz 7-1-39-2; Warne 14.3-2-56-2.

SECOND TEST (Test 1759)
England v Australia

At Edgbaston, Birmingham, August 4, 5, 6, 7, 2005. **England won by two runs.**
Toss: Australia. **Player of the Match:** A Flintoff. **Umpires:** BF Bowden and RE Koertzen.
Close of play: First day, England all out 407; Second day, England (2) 1-25 (Trescothick, 19, Hoggard 0);
Third day, Australia (2) 8-175 (Warne 20)

ENGLAND

ME Trescothick c Gilchrist b Kasprowicz	90	c Gilchrist b Lee	21
AJ Strauss b Warne	48	b Warne	6
*MP Vaughan c Lee b Gillespie	24	(4) b Lee	1
IR Bell c Gilchrist b Kasprowicz	6	(5) c Gilchrist b Warne	21
KP Pietersen c Katich b Lee	71	(6) c Gilchrist b Warne	20
A Flintoff c Gilchrist b Gillespie	68	(7) b Warne	73
+GO Jones c Gilchrist b Kasprowicz	1	(8) c Ponting b Lee	9
AF Giles lbw b Warne	23	(9) c Hayden b Warne	8
MJ Hoggard lbw b Warne	16	(3) c Hayden b Lee	1
SJ Harmison b Warne	17	c Ponting b Warne	0
SP. Jones not out	19	not out	12
L-b 9, w 1, n-b 14	24	L-b 1, n-b 9	10
(79.2 overs, 357 mins)	407	(52.1 overs, 249 mins)	182

Fall: 112 164 170 187 290 293 342 348 375 407   Fall: 25 27 29 31 72 75 101 131 131 182

Bowling: First Innings – Lee 17-1-111-1; Gillespie 22-3-91-2; Kasprowicz 15-3-80-3; Warne 25.2-4-116-4.
Second Innings – Lee 18-1-82-4; Gillespie 8-0-24-0; Kasprowicz 3-0-29-0; Warne 23.1-7-46-6.

AUSTRALIA

JL Langer lbw b SP. Jones	82	b Flintoff	28
ML Hayden c Strauss b Hoggard	0	c Trescothick b SP. Jones	31
*RT Ponting c Vaughan b Giles	61	c GO Jones b Flintoff	0
DR Martyn run out (Vaughan)	20	c Bell b Hoggard	28
MJ Clarke c GO Jones b Giles	40	b Harmison	30
SM Katich c GO Jones b Flintoff	4	c Trescothick b Giles	16
+AC Gilchrist not out	49	c Flintoff b Giles	1
SK Warne b Giles	8	(9) hit wicket b Flintoff	42
B Lee c Flintoff b SP. Jones	6	(10) not out	43
JN Gillespie lbw b Flintoff	7	(8) lbw b Flintoff	0
MS Kasprowicz lbw b Flintoff	0	c GO Jones b Harmison	20
B 13, l-b 7, w 1, n-b 10	31	B 13, l-b 8, W 1, n-b 18	40
(76 overs, 344 mins)	308	(64.3 overs, 301 mins)	279

Fall: 0 88 114 194 208 262 273 282 308 308   Fall: 47 48 82 107 134 136 137 175 220 279

Bowling: First Innings – Harmison 11-1-48-0; Hoggard 8-0-41-1; SP. Jones 16-2-69-2; Flintoff 15-1-52-3;
Giles 26-2-78-3. Second Innings – Harmison 17.3-3-62-2; Hoggard 5-0-26-1; Giles 15-3-68-2; Flintoff 22-3-79-4;
SP. Jones 5-1-23-1.

SECOND TEST (Test 1820)
Australia v England

At Adelaide Oval, Adelaide, December 1, 2, 3, 4, 5, 2006. Australia won by six wickets.
Toss: England. **Player of the Match:** RT Ponting. **Umpires:** SA Bucknor and RE Koertzen.
Close of play: First day, England (1) 3-266 (Collingwood 98, Pietersen 60); Second day, Australia (1) 1-28 (Hayden 12, Ponting 11); Third day, Australia (1) 5-312 (Clarke 30, Gilchrist 13); Fourth day, England (2) 1-59 (Strauss 31, Bell 18)

ENGLAND

AJ Strauss c Martyn b Clark	14	c Hussey b Warne		34
AN Cook c Gilchrist b Clark	27	c Gilchrist b Clark		9
IR Bell c and b Lee	60	run out (Clarke/Warne)		26
PD Collingwood c Gilchrist b Clark	206	not out		22
KP Pietersen run out (Ponting)	158	b Warne		2
*A Flintoff not out	38	c Gilchrist b Lee		2
+GO Jones c Martyn b Warne	1	c Hayden b Lee		10
AF Giles not out	27	c Hayden b Warne		0
MJ Hoggard	b Warne	4		
SJ Harmison	lbw b McGrath	8		
JM Anderson (did not bat).	lbw b McGrath	1		
L-b 10, w 2, n-b 8	20	B 3, l-b 5, w 1, n-b 2		11
(168 overs, 707 mins)	(6 wickets dec) 551	(73 overs, 323 mins)		129

Fall: 32 45 158 468 489 491   Fall: 31 69 70 73 77 94 97 105 119 129

Bowling: First Innings – Lee 34-1-139-1; McGrath 30-5-107-0; Clark 34-6-75-3; Warne 53-9-167-1; Clarke 17-2-53-0. Second Innings – Lee 18-3-35-2; McGrath 10-6-15-2; Warne 32-12-49-4; Clark 13-4-22-1.

AUSTRALIA

JL Langer c Pietersen b Flintoff	4	c Bell b Hoggard		7
ML Hayden c Jones b Hoggard	12	c Collingwood b Flintoff		18
*RT Ponting c Jones b Hoggard	142	c Strauss b Giles		49
DR Martyn c Bell b Hoggard	11	(5) c Strauss b Flintoff		5
MEK Hussey b Hoggard	91	(4) not out		61
MJ Clarke c Giles b Hoggard	124	not out		21
+AC Gilchrist c Bell b Giles	64			
SK Warne lbw b Hoggard	43			
B Lee not out	7			
SR Clark b Hoggard	0			
GD McGrath c Jones b Anderson	1			
B 4, l-b 2, w 1, n-b 7	14	B 2, l-b 2, W 1, n-b 2		7
(165.3 overs, 719 mins)	513	(32.5 overs, 161 mins)	(4 wickets) 168	

Fall: 8 35 65 257 286 384 502 505 507 513   Fall: 14 33 116 121

Bowling: First Innings – Hoggard 42-6-109-7; Flintoff 26-5-82-1; Harmison 25-5-96-0; Anderson 21.3-3-85-1; Giles 42-7-103-1; Pietersen 9-0-32-0. Second Innings – Hoggard 4-0-29-1; Flintoff 9-0-44-2; Giles 10-0-46-1; Harmison 4-0-15-0; Anderson 3.5-0-23-0; Pietersen 2-0-7-0.

FIFTH TEST (Test 1827)
Australia v England

At Sydney Cricket Ground, Sydney, January 2, 3, 4, 5, 2007. Australia won by ten wickets.
Toss: England. Player of the Match: SR Clark. Umpires: Aleem Dar and BF Bowden.
Close of play: First day, England (1) 4-234 (Collingwood 25, Flintoff 42); Second day, Australia (1) 4-188 (Hussey 37, Symonds 22); Third day, England (2) 5-114 (Pietersen 29, Panesar 0)

ENGLAND

AJ Strauss c Gilchrist b Lee	29	lbw b Clark	24
AN Cook c Gilchrist b Clark	20	c Gilchrist b Lee	4
IR Bell b McGrath	71	c Gilchrist b Lee	28
KP Pietersen c Hussey b McGrath	41	c Gilchrist b McGrath	29
PD Collingwood c Gilchrist b McGrath	27	c Hayden b Clark	17
*A Flintoff c Gilchrist b Clark	89	st Gilchrist b Warne	7
+CMW Read c Gilchrist b Lee	2	(8) c Ponting b Lee	4
SI Mahmood c Hayden b Lee	0	(9) b McGrath	4
SJ Harmison lbw b Clark	2	(10) not out	16
MS Panesar lbw b Warne	0	(7) run out (Symonds)	0
JM Anderson not out	0	c Hussey b McGrath	5
L-b 5, w 3, n-b 2	10	B 2, l-b 3, w 1, n-b 3	9
(103.4 overs, 462 mins)	291	(58 overs, 278 mins)	147

Fall: 45 58 166 167 245 258 258 282 291 291   Fall: 5 55 64 98 113 114 114 122 123 147

Bowling: First Innings – McGrath 29-8-67-3; Lee 22-5-75-3; Clark 24-6-62-3; Warne 22.4-1-69-1; Symonds 6-2-13-0. Second Innings – Lee 14-5-39-3; McGrath 21-11-38-3; Clark 12-4-29-2; Warne 6-1-23-1; Symonds 5-2-13-0.

AUSTRALIA

JL Langer c Read b Anderson	26	not out	20
ML Hayden c Collingwood b Harmison	33	not out	23
*RT Ponting run out (Anderson)	45		
MEK Hussey c Read b Anderson	37		
MJ Clarke c Read b Harmison	11		
A Symonds b Panesar	48		
+AC Gilchrist c Read b Anderson	62		
SK Warne st Read b Panesar	71		
B Lee c Read b Flintoff	5		
SR Clark c Pietersen b Mahmood	35		
GD McGrath not out	0		
L-b 10, w 4, n-b 6	20	L-b 3	3
(96.3 overs, 432 mins)	393	(10.5 overs, 44 mins)	(0 wkt) 46

Fall: 34 100 118 155 190 260 318 325 393 393   Fall:

Bowling: First Innings – Flintoff 17-2-56-1; Anderson 26-8-98-3; Harmison 23-5-80-2; Mahmood 11-1-59-1; Panesar 19.3-0-90-2. Second Innings – Anderson 4-0-12-0; Harmison 5-1-13-0; Mahmood 1.5-0-18-0.

SECOND TEST (Test 1890)
India v Australia

At Punjab Cricket Association Ground, Mohali, October 17, 18, 19, 20, 21, 2008. India won by 320 runs.
Toss: India. **Player of the Match:** MS Dhoni. **Umpires:** Asad Rauf and RE Koetzen.
Close of play: First day, India (1) 5-311 (Ganguly 54, Sharma 2); Second day, Australia (1) 4-102 (Hussey 37); Third day, India (2) 0-100 (Gambhir 45, Sehwag 53); Fourth day, Australia (2) 5-141 (Clarke 42, Haddin 37)

INDIA

G Gambhir c Haddin b Johnson	67	c Hussey b White	104
V Sehwag c Haddin b Johnson	35	c Haddin b Siddle	90
RS Dravid b Lee	39		
SR Tendulkar c Hayden b Siddle	88	(5) not out	10
VVS Laxman c Haddin b Johnson	12		
SC Ganguly c Lee b White	102	(4) c Clarke b Lee	27
I Sharma c Katich b Siddle	9		
*+MS Dhoni lbw b Siddle	92	(3) not out	68
Harbhajan Singh b White	1		
Zaheer Khan run out (Lee/Haddin)	2		
A Mishra not out	0		
B 4, l-b 10, w 5, n-b 3	22	B 3, l-b 4, w 5, n-b 3	15
(129 overs, 592 mins)	469	(65 overs, 291 mins) (3 wickets dec)	314

Fall: 70 146 146 163 305 326 435 442 469 469   Fall: 182 224 290

Bowling: First Innings – Lee 24-5-86-1; Siddle 28-5-114-3; Johnson 27-4-85-3; Watson 24-3-71-0; Clarke 7-0-28-0; White 19-0-71-2. Second Innings – Lee 14-0-61-1; Siddle 15-1-62-1; Johnson 14-0-72-0; White 8-0-48-1; Watson 5-0-20-0; Hussey 8-0-38-0; Clarke 1-0-6-0.

AUSTRALIA

ML Hayden b Zaheer Khan	0	lbw b Harbhajan Singh	29
SM Katich b Mishra	33	c Tendulkar b Harbhajan Singh	20
*RT Ponting lbw b Sharma	5	b Sharma	2
MEK Hussey c Dhoni b Sharma	54	lbw b Harbhajan Singh	1
MJ Clarke lbw b Mishra	23	c Sehwag b Mishra	69
SR Watson lbw b Mishra	78	lbw b Sharma	2
+BJ Haddin b Harbhajan Singh	9	b Zaheer Khan	37
CL White b Mishra	5	c Dhoni b Zaheer Khan	1
B Lee c Dravid b Harbhajan Singh	35	b Zaheer Khan	0
MG Johnson not out	9	c and b Mishra	26
PM Siddle st Dhoni b Mishra	0	not out	0
L-b 13, n-b 4	17	B 4, n-b 4	8
(101.4 overs, 455 mins)	268	(64.4 overs, 286 mins)	195

Fall: 0 17 62 102 130 146 167 240 262 268   Fall: 49 50 52 52 58 142 144 144 194 195

Bowling: First Innings – Zaheer Khan 25-7-56-1; Sharma 21-5-68-2; Harbhajan Singh 29-9-60-2; Mishra 26.4-8-71-5. Second Innings – Zaheer Khan 15-3-71-3; Sharma 13-4-42-2; Harbhajan Singh 20-3-36-3; Mishra 11.4-2-35-2; Sehwag 5-2-7-0.

SECOND TEST (Test 1903)
Australia v South Africa

At Melbourne Cricket Ground, Melbourne, December 26, 27, 28, 29, 30, 2008. South Africa won by nine wickets.
Toss: Australia. **Player of the Match:** DW Steyn. **Umpires:** Aleem Dar and BR Doctrove.
Close of play: First day, Australia (1) 6-280 (Clarke 35, Lee 0); Second day, South Africa (1) 7-198 (Duminy 34, Harris 8); Third day, Australia (2) 0-4 (Hayden 1, Katich 2); Fourth day, South Africa (2) 0-30 (Smith 25, McKenzie 3).

AUSTRALIA

ML Hayden c Duminy b Ntini	8	c Duminy b Steyn	23
SM Katich b Steyn	54	c Boucher b Steyn	15
*RT Ponting c Amla b Harris	101	c Smith b Morkel	99
MEK Hussey c Boucher b Steyn	0	c Amla b Morkel	2
MJ Clarke not out	88	c McKenzie b Steyn	29
A Symonds c Kallis b Morkel	27	c Kallis b Steyn	0
+BJ Haddin c Smith b Ntini	40	c Kallis b Ntini	10
B Lee c Kallis b Steyn	21	b Kallis	8
MG Johnson b Steyn	0	not out	43
NM Hauritz c Smith b Steyn	12	b Kallis	3
PM Siddle c De Villiers b Kallis	19	c Boucher b Steyn	6
B 5, l-b 12, n-b 7	24	B 1, l-b 3, n-b 5	9
(113.4 overs, 505 mins)	394	(84.2 overs, 366 mins)	247

Fall: 21 128 143 184 223 277 322 326 352 394   Fall: 37 40 49 145 145 165 180 212 231 247

Bowling: First Innings – Steyn 29-6-87-5; Ntini 27-7-108-2; Kallis 18.4-4-55-1; Morkel 22-3-89-1; Harris 17-3-38-1. Second Innings – Steyn 20.2-3-67-5; Ntini 14-1-26-1; Morkel 15-2-46-2; Harris 21-1-47-0; Kallis 14-1-57-2.

SOUTH AFRICA

*GC Smith c Haddin b Siddle	62	lbw b Hauritz	75
ND McKenzie b Siddle	0	not out	59
HM Amla c Symonds b Johnson	19	not out	30
JH Kallis c Haddin b Hauritz	26		
AB De Villiers b Siddle	7		
JP Duminy c Siddle b Hauritz	166		
+MV Boucher c Hussey b Hauritz	3		
M Morkel b Johnson	21		
PL Harris c Johnson b Hussey	39		
DW Steyn b Siddle	76		
M Ntini not out	2		
B 5, l-b 13, n-b 15	38	L-b 9, W 2, n-b 8	19
(153 overs, 616 mins)	459	(48 overs, 204 mins)	(1 wkt) 183

Fall: 1 39 102 126 132 141 184 251 431 459   Fall: 121

Bowling: First Innings – Lee 13-2-68-0; Siddle 34-9-81-4; Johnson 39-6-127-2; Hauritz 43-13-98-3; Clarke 8-0-26-0; Hussey 5-0-22-1; Symonds 11-3-14-0. Second Innings – Lee 10-0-49-0; Siddle 14-5-34-0; Johnson 11-1-36-0; Hauritz 10-0-41-1; Clarke 3-0-14-0.

STATISTICS

(Qualification: November 27, 1992 to January 7, 2009)

RESULTS

Team	Tests	Won	Lost	Drawn	% Won
Australia	189	117	37	35	61.90
South Africa	166	81	41	44	48.80
Pakistan	133	54	44	35	40.60
Sri Lanka	142	54	47	41	38.03
India	151	54	41	56	35.76
England	193	66	69	58	34.20
New Zealand	135	36	54	45	26.67
West Indies	159	39	76	44	24.53
Zimbabwe	80	8	48	24	10.00
Bangladesh	59	1	52	6	1.69
World XI	1	-	1	-	0.00
Total	704	510	510	194	

AUSTRALIAN RESULTS

Opponent	Tests	Won	Lost	Drawn	% Won
Bangladesh	4	4	-	-	100.00
World XI	1	1	-	-	100.00
Zimbabwe	3	3	-	-	100.00
Sri Lanka	13	9	1	3	69.23
Pakistan	18	12	2	4	66.67
England	42	27	9	6	64.29
West Indies	33	21	8	4	63.64
New Zealand	22	14	1	7	63.64
South Africa	27	16	6	5	59.26
India	26	10	10	6	38.46
Total	189	117	37	35	

AUSTRALIAN TEST MATCHES

Venue	Toss	Australia 1st	Australia 2nd	Opponent	Opponent 1st	Opponent 2nd	Result	Captain
1992–93 in Australia								
Brisbane	Aus	293*	308	West Indies	371	8-133	Drawn	AR Border
Melbourne	Aus	395*	196	West Indies	233	219	Aus by 139 runs	AR Border
Sydney	Aus	9d-503*	0-117	West Indies	606	-	Drawn	AR Border
Adelaide	WI	213	184	West Indies	252*	146	WI by 1 run	AR Border
Perth	Aus	119*	178	West Indies	322	-	WI by an inns & 25 runs	AR Border
1992–93 in New Zealand								
Christchurch	NZ	485*	-	New Zealand	182	243	Aus by an inns & 60 runs	AR Border
Wellington	Aus	298	-	New Zealand	329*	7-210	Drawn	AR Border
Auckland	Aus	139*	285	New Zealand	224	5-201	NZ by 5 wickets	AR Border
1993 in England								
Manchester	Eng	289*	5d-432	England	210	332	Aus by 179 runs	AR Border
Lord's	Aus	4d-632*	-	England	205	365	Aus by an inns & 62 runs	AR Border
Nottingham	Eng	373	6-202	England	321*	6d-422	Drawn	AR Border
Leeds	Aus	4d-653*	-	England	200	305	Aus by an inns & 148 runs	AR Border
Birmingham	Eng	408	2-120	England	276*	251	Aus by 8 wickets	AR Border
The Oval	Eng	303	229	England	380*	313	Eng by 161 runs	AR Border

Venue	Toss	Australia 1st	Australia 2nd	Opponent	Opponent 1st	Opponent 2nd	Result	Captain

1993–94 in Australia

Venue	Toss	Australia 1st	Australia 2nd	Opponent	Opponent 1st	Opponent 2nd	Result	Captain
Perth	NZ	398*	1d-323	New Zealand	9d-419	4-166	Drawn	AR Border
Hobart	Aus	6d-544*	-	New Zealand	161	161	Aus by an inns & 222 runs	AR Border
Brisbane	NZ	6d-607	-	New Zealand	233*	278	Aus by an inns & 96 runs	AR Border
Melbourne	Aus	7d-342*	-	South Africa	3-258	-	Drawn	AR Border
Sydney	SAf	292	111	South Africa	169*	239	SAf by 5 runs	AR Border
Adelaide	Aus	7d-469*	6d-124	South Africa	273	129	Aus by 191 runs	AR Border

1993–94 in South Africa

Venue	Toss	Australia 1st	Australia 2nd	Opponent	Opponent 1st	Opponent 2nd	Result	Captain
Johannesburg	SAf	248	256	South Africa	251*	9d-450	SAf by 197 runs	AR Border
Cape Town	SAf	435	1-92	South Africa	361*	164	Aus by 9 wickets	AR Border
Durban	SAf	269*	4-297	South Africa	422	-	Drawn	AR Border

1994–95 in Pakistan

Venue	Toss	Australia 1st	Australia 2nd	Opponent	Opponent 1st	Opponent 2nd	Result	Captain
Karachi	Aus	337*	232	Pakistan	256	9-315	Pak by 1 wkt	MA Taylor
Rawalpindi	Pak	9d-521*	1-14	Pakistan	260	537	Drawn	MA Taylor
Lahore	Pak	455	-	Pakistan	373*	404	Drawn	MA Taylor

1994–95 in Australia

Venue	Toss	Australia 1st	Australia 2nd	Opponent	Opponent 1st	Opponent 2nd	Result	Captain
Brisbane	Aus	426*	8d-248	England	167	323	Aus by 184 runs	MA Taylor
Melbourne	Eng	279*	7d-320	England	212	92	Aus by 295 runs	MA Taylor
Sydney	Eng	116	7-344	England	309*	2d-255	Drawn	MA Taylor
Adelaide	Eng	419	156	England	353*	328	Eng by 106 runs	MA Taylor
Perth	Aus	402*	8d-345	England	295	123	Aus by 329 runs	MA Taylor

1994–95 in West Indies

Venue	Toss	Australia 1st	Australia 2nd	Opponent	Opponent 1st	Opponent 2nd	Result	Captain
Bridgetown	WI	346	0-39	West Indies	195*	189	Aus by 10 wickets	MA Taylor
Antigua	WI	216*	7d-300	West Indies	260	2-80	Drawn	MA Taylor
Port-of-Spain	WI	128*	105	West Indies	136	1-98	WI by 9 wickets	MA Taylor
Kingston	WI	531	-	West Indies	265*	213	Aus by an inns & 53 runs	MA Taylor

1995–96 in Australia

Venue	Toss	Australia 1st	Australia 2nd	Opponent	Opponent 1st	Opponent 2nd	Result	Captain
Brisbane	Aus	463*	-	Pakistan	9-97	240	Aus by an inns & 126 runs	MA Taylor
Hobart	Aus	267*	9d-306	Pakistan	198	220	Aus by 155 runs	MA Taylor
Sydney	Pak	257	172	Pakistan	299*	204	Pak by 74 runs	MA Taylor
Perth	SL	5d-617	-	Sri Lanka	251*	330	Aus by an inns & 36 runs	MA Taylor
Melbourne	SL	6d-500*	0-41	Sri Lanka	233	307	Aus by 10 wickets	MA Taylor
Adelaide	Aus	9d-502*	6d-205	Sri Lanka	317	252	Aus by 148 runs	MA Taylor

1996–97 in India

Venue	Toss	Australia 1st	Australia 2nd	Opponent	Opponent 1st	Opponent 2nd	Result	Captain
Delhi	Aus	182*	234	India	361	3-58	Ind by 7 wickets	MA Taylor

1996–97 in Australia

Venue	Toss	Australia 1st	Australia 2nd	Opponent	Opponent 1st	Opponent 2nd	Result	Captain
Brisbane	WI	479*	6d-217	West Indies	277	296	Aus by 123 runs	MA Taylor
Sydney	Aus	331*	4d-312	West Indies	304	215	Aus by 124 runs	MA Taylor
Melbourne	Aus	219*	122	West Indies	255	4-87	WI by 6 wickets	MA Taylor
Adelaide	WI	130*	204	West Indies	517	-	Aus by an inns & 183 runs	MA Taylor
Perth	Aus	243*	194	West Indies	384	0-57	WI by 10 wickets	MA Taylor

1996–97 in South Africa

Venue	Toss	Australia 1st	Australia 2nd	Opponent	Opponent 1st	Opponent 2nd	Result	Captain
Johannesburg	SAf	8d-628	-	South Africa	302*	130	Aus by an inns & 196 runs	MA Taylor
Port Elizabeth	Aus	108	8-271	South Africa	209*	168	Aus by 2 wickets	MA Taylor
Centurion	SAf	227*	185	South Africa	384	2-32	SAf by 8 wickets	MA Taylor

Venue	Toss	Australia 1st	Australia 2nd	Opponent	Opponent 1st	Opponent 2nd	Result	Captain

1997 in England

Venue	Toss	Australia 1st	Australia 2nd	Opponent	Opponent 1st	Opponent 2nd	Result	Captain
Birmingham	Aus	118*	477	England 9d-478		1-119	Eng by 9 wickets	MA Taylor
Lord's	Aus	7d-213	-	England	77*	4-266	Drawn	MA Taylor
Manchester	Aus	235*	8d-395	England	162	200	Aus by 268 runs	MA Taylor
Leeds	Aus	9d-501	-	England	172*	268	Aus by an inns & 61 runs	MA Taylor
Nottingham	Aus	427*	336	England	313	186	Aus by 264 runs	MA Taylor
The Oval	Eng	220	104	England	180*	163	Eng by 19 runs	MA Taylor

1997–98 in Australia

Venue	Toss	Australia 1st	Australia 2nd	Opponent	Opponent 1st	Opponent 2nd	Result	Captain
Brisbane	NZ	373*	6d-294	New Zealand	349	132	Aus by 186 runs	MA Taylor
Perth	NZ	461	-	New Zealand	217*	174	Aus by an inns & 70 runs	MA Taylor
Hobart	Aus	400*	2d-138	New Zealand 6d-251		9-223	Drawn	MA Taylor
Melbourne	Aus	309*	257	South Africa	186	7-273	Drawn	MA Taylor
Sydney	SAf	421	-	South Africa	287*	113	Aus by an inns & 21 runs	MA Taylor
Adelaide	SAf	350	7-227	South Africa	517*	6d-193	Drawn	MA Taylor

1997–98 in India

Venue	Toss	Australia 1st	Australia 2nd	Opponent	Opponent 1st	Opponent 2nd	Result	Captain
Chennai	Ind	328	168	India	257*	4d-418	Ind by 179 runs	MA Taylor
Kolkata	Aus	233*	181	India 5d-633		-	Ind by an inns & 219 runs	MA Taylor
Bangalore	Ind	400	2-195	India	424*	169	Aus by 8 wickets	MA Taylor

1998–99 in Pakistan

Venue	Toss	Australia 1st	Australia 2nd	Opponent	Opponent 1st	Opponent 2nd	Result	Captain
Rawalpindi	Pak	513	-	Pakistan	269*	145	Aus by an inns & 99 runs	MA Taylor
Peshawar	Aus	4d-599*	5d-289	Pakistan 9d-580		-	Drawn	MA Taylor
Karachi	Aus	280*	390	Pakistan	252	5-262	Drawn	MA Taylor

1998–99 in Australia

Venue	Toss	Australia 1st	Australia 2nd	Opponent	Opponent 1st	Opponent 2nd	Result	Captain
Brisbane	Aus	485*	3d-237	England	375	6-179	Drawn	MA Taylor
Perth	Aus	240	3-64	England	112*	191	Aus by 7 wickets	MA Taylor
Adelaide	Aus	391*	5d-278	England	227	237	Aus by 205 runs	MA Taylor
Melbourne	Aus	340	162	England	270*	244	Eng by 12 runs	MA Taylor
Sydney	Aus	322*	184	England	220	188	Aus by 98 runs	MA Taylor

1998–99 in West Indies

Venue	Toss	Australia 1st	Australia 2nd	Opponent	Opponent 1st	Opponent 2nd	Result	Captain
Port-of-Spain	Aus	269*	261	West Indies	167	51	Aus by 312 runs	SR Waugh
Kingston	Aus	256*	177	West Indies	431	0-3	WI by 10 wickets	SR Waugh
Bridgetown	Aus	490*	146	West Indies	329	9-311	WI by 1 wkt	SR Waugh
Antigua	Aus	303*	306	West Indies	222	211	Aus by 176 runs	SR Waugh

1999–2000 in Sri Lanka

Venue	Toss	Australia 1st	Australia 2nd	Opponent	Opponent 1st	Opponent 2nd	Result	Captain
Kandy	Aus	188*	8d-140	Sri Lanka	234	4-95	SL won by 6 wickets	SR Waugh
Galle	SL	228	-	Sri Lanka	296*	0-55	Drawn	SR Waugh
Colombo SSC	Aus	342*	-	Sri Lanka	4-61	-	Drawn	SR Waugh

1999–2000 in Zimbabwe

Venue	Toss	Australia 1st	Australia 2nd	Opponent	Opponent 1st	Opponent 2nd	Result	Captain
Harare	Zim	422	0-5	Zimbabwe	194*	232	Aus by 10 wickets	SR Waugh

1999–2000 in Australia

Venue	Toss	Australia 1st	Australia 2nd	Opponent	Opponent 1st	Opponent 2nd	Result	Captain
Brisbane	Aus	575	0-74	Pakistan	367*	281	Aus by 10 wickets	SR Waugh
Hobart	Aus	246	6-369	Pakistan	222*	392	Aus by 4 wickets	SR Waugh
Perth	Pak	451	-	Pakistan	155*	276	Aus by an inns & 20 runs	SR Waugh
Adelaide	Aus	441*	8d-239	India	285	110	Aus by 285 runs	SR Waugh
Melbourne	Ind	405	5d-208	India	238	9d-195	Aus by 180 runs	SR Waugh
Sydney	Ind	5d-552	-	India	150*	9d-261	Aus by an inns & 141 runs	SR Waugh

Venue	Toss	Australia 1st	Australia 2nd	Opponent	Opponent 1st	Opponent 2nd	Result	Captain

1999–2000 in New Zealand

Venue	Toss	Aus 1st	Aus 2nd	Opponent	Opp 1st	Opp 2nd	Result	Captain
Auckland	Aus	214*	229	New Zealand	163	218	Aus by 62 runs	SR Waugh
Wellington	NZ	419	4-177	New Zealand	298*	294	Aus by 6 wickets	SR Waugh
Hamilton	Aus	252	4-212	New Zealand	232*	229	Aus by 6 wickets	SR Waugh

2000–01 in Australia

Venue	Toss	Aus 1st	Aus 2nd	Opponent	Opp 1st	Opp 2nd	Result	Captain
Brisbane	Aus	332	-	West Indies	82*	124	Aus by an inns & 126 runs	SR Waugh
Perth	Aus	396	-	West Indies	196*	173	Aus by an inns & 27 runs	SR Waugh
Adelaide	WI	403	5-130	West Indies	391*	141	Aus by 5 wickets	AC Gilchrist
Melbourne	WI	364*	5d-262	West Indies	165	109	Aus by 352 runs	SR Waugh
Sydney	WI	452	4-174	West Indies	272*	352	Aus by 6 wickets	SR Waugh

2000–01 in India

Venue	Toss	Aus 1st	Aus 2nd	Opponent	Opp 1st	Opp 2nd	Result	Captain
Mumbai	Aus	349	0-47	India	176*	219	Aus by 10 wickets	SR Waugh
Kolkata	Aus	445*	212	India	171	7d-657	Ind by 171 runs	SR Waugh
Chennai	Aus	391*	264	India	501	8-155	Ind by 2 wickets	SR Waugh

2001 in England

Venue	Toss	Aus 1st	Aus 2nd	Opponent	Opp 1st	Opp 2nd	Result	Captain
Birmingham	Aus	576	-	England	294*	9d-164	Aus by an inns & 126 runs	SR Waugh
Lord's	Aus	401	2-14	England	187*	267	Aus by 8 wickets	SR Waugh
Nottingham	Eng	190	3-158	England	185*	162	Aus by 7 wickets	SR Waugh
Leeds	Aus	447*	4d-176	England	309	4-315	Eng by 6 wickets	AC Gilchrist
The Oval	Aus	4d-641*	-	England	432	184	Aus by an inns & 25 runs	SR Waugh

2001–02 in Australia

Venue	Toss	Aus 1st	Aus 2nd	Opponent	Opp 1st	Opp 2nd	Result	Captain
Brisbane	NZ	9d-486*	2-84	New Zealand	8d-287	6-274	Drawn	SR Waugh
Hobart	NZ	8d-558*	-	New Zealand	7-243	-	Drawn	SR Waugh
Perth	NZ	351	7-381	New Zealand	9d-534*	9d-256	Drawn	SR Waugh
Adelaide	Aus	439*	7d-309	South Africa	374	128	Aus by 246 runs	SR Waugh
Melbourne	Aus	487	1-10	South Africa	277*	219	Aus by 9 wickets	SR Waugh
Sydney	Aus	554*	0-54	South Africa	154	452	Aus by 10 wickets	SR Waugh

2001–02 in South Africa

Venue	Toss	Aus 1st	Aus 2nd	Opponent	Opp 1st	Opp 2nd	Result	Captain
Johannesburg	Aus	7d-652*	-	South Africa	159	133	Aus by an inns & 360 runs	SR Waugh
Cape Town	SAf	382	6-334	South Africa	239*	473	Aus by 4 wickets	SR Waugh
Durban	SAf	315	167	South Africa	167*	5-340	SAf by 5 wickets	SR Waugh

2002–03 in Sri Lanka and United Arab Emirates

Venue	Toss	Aus 1st	Aus 2nd	Opponent	Opp 1st	Opp 2nd	Result	Captain
Colombo	Aus	467*	127	Pakistan	279	274	Aus by 41 runs	SR Waugh
Sharjah	Pak	310	-	Pakistan	59	9d-53	Aus by an inns & 198 runs	SR Waugh
Sharjah	Aus	444*	-	Pakistan	221	203	Aus by an inns & 20 runs	SR Waugh

2002–03 in Australia

Venue	Toss	Aus 1st	Aus 2nd	Opponent	Opp 1st	Opp 2nd	Result	Captain
Brisbane	Eng	492*	5d-296	England	9d-325	9d-79	Aus by 384 runs	SR Waugh
Adelaide	Eng	9d-552	-	England	342*	159	Aus by an inns & 51 runs	SR Waugh
Perth	Eng	456	-	England	185*	8d-223	Aus by an inns & 48 runs	SR Waugh
Melbourne	Aus	6d-551*	5-107	England	270	387	Aus by 5 wickets	SR Waugh
Sydney	Eng	363	226	England	362*	9d-452	Eng by 225 runs	SR Waugh

2002–03 in West Indies

Venue	Toss	Aus 1st	Aus 2nd	Opponent	Opp 1st	Opp 2nd	Result	Captain
Georgetown	WI	489	1-147	West Indies	237*	398	Aus by 9 wickets	SR Waugh
Port-of-Spain	Aus	4d-576*	3d-238	West Indies	408	288	Aus by 118 runs	SR Waugh
Bridgetown	WI	9d-605*	1-8	West Indies	328	284	Aus by 9 wickets	SR Waugh
St John's	Aus	240*	417	West Indies	240	7-418	WI by 3 wickets	SR Waugh

		Australia			Opponent			
Venue	Toss	1st	2nd	Opponent	1st	2nd	Result	Captain
2003–04 in Australia								
Darwin	Aus	7d-407	-	Bangladesh	97*	178	Aus by inns & 132 runs	SR Waugh
Cairns	Aus	4d-556	-	Bangladesh	295*	163	Aus by inns & 98 runs	SR Waugh
Perth	Zim	6d-735*	-	Zimbabwe	239	321	Aus by inns & 175 runs	SR Waugh
Sydney	Zim	403	1-172	Zimbabwe	308*	266	Aus by 9 wickets	SR Waugh
Brisbane	Ind	323*	3d-284	India	409	2-73	Drawn	SR Waugh
Adelaide	Aus	556*	196	India	523	6-233	Ind by 4 wickets	SR Waugh
Melbourne	Ind	558	1-97	India	366*	286	Aus by 9 wickets	SR Waugh
Sydney	Ind	474	6-357	India	7d-705*	6-357	Drawn	SR Waugh
2003–04 in Sri Lanka								
Galle	Aus	220*	8d-512	Sri Lanka	381	154	Aus by 197 runs	RT Ponting
Kandy	Aus	120*	442	Sri Lanka	211	324	Aus by 27 runs	RT Ponting
Colombo SSC	Aus	401*	375	Sri Lanka	407	248	Aus by 121 runs	RT Ponting
2004–05 in Australia								
Darwin	SL	207*	201	Sri Lanka	97	162	Aus by 149 runs	AC Gilchrist
Cairns	SL	517*	9d-292	Sri Lanka	455	183	Drawn	RT Ponting
2004–05 in India								
Bangalore	Aus	474*	228	India	246	239	Aus by 217 runs	AC Gilchrist
Chennai	Aus	235*	369	India	376	0-19	Drawn	AC Gilchrist
Nagpur	Aus	398*	5d-329	India	185	200	Aus by 342 runs	AC Gilchrist
Mumbai	Ind	203	93	India	104*	205	Ind by 13 runs	RT Ponting
2004–05 in Australia								
Brisbane	NZ	585	-	New Zealand	353*	76	Aus by inns & 156 runs	RT Ponting
Adelaide	Aus	8d-575*	2-139	New Zealand	251	250	Aus by 213 runs	RT Ponting
Perth	Pak	381*	5d-361	Pakistan	179	72	Aus by 491 runs	RT Ponting
Melbourne	Pak	379	1-127	Pakistan	341*	163	Aus by 9 wickets	RT Ponting
Sydney	Pak	568	1-62	Pakistan	304*	325	Aus by 9 wickets	RT Ponting
2004–05 in New Zealand								
Christchurch	Aus	432	1-135	New Zealand	433*	131	Aus by 9 wickets	RT Ponting
Wellington	NZ	8d-570*	-	New Zealand	244	3-48	Drawn	RT Ponting
Auckland	NZ	383	1-166	New Zealand	292*	254	Aus by 9 wickets	RT Ponting
2005 in England								
Lord's	Aus	190	384	England	155*	180	Aus by 239 runs	RT Ponting
Birmingham	Aus	308	279	England	407*	182	Eng by 2 wickets	RT Ponting
Manchester	Eng	302	9-371	England	444*	6d-280	Drawn	RT Ponting
Nottingham	Eng	218	218	England	477*	7-129	Eng by 3 wickets	RT Ponting
The Oval	Eng	367	0-0	England	373*	335	Drawn	RT Ponting
2005–06 in Australia								
Sydney	Aus	345*	199	World XI	190	144	Aus by 210 runs	RT Ponting
Brisbane	WI	435*	2d-283	West Indies	210	129	Aus by 379 runs	RT Ponting
Hobart	WI	406	1-78	West Indies	149*	334	Aus by 9 wickets	RT Ponting
Adelaide	WI	428	3-182	West Indies	405*	204	Aus by 7 wickets	RT Ponting
Perth	Aus	258*	8d-528	South Africa	296	5-287	Drawn	RT Ponting
Melbourne	Aus	355*	7-321	South Africa	311	181	Aus by 184 runs	RT Ponting
Sydney	SAf	359	2-288	South Africa	9d-451*	6d-194	Aus by 8 wickets	RT Ponting

Venue	Toss	Australia 1st	Australia 2nd	Opponent	Opponent 1st	Opponent 2nd	Result	Captain
2005–06 in South Africa								
Cape Town	SAf	308	3-95	South Africa	205*	197	Aus by 7 wickets	RT Ponting
Durban	Aus	369*4d-307		South Africa	267	297	Aus by 112 runs	RT Ponting
Johannesburg	SAf	9d-270	8-294	South Africa	303*	270	Aus by 2 wickets	RT Ponting
2005–06 in Bangladesh								
Fatullah	Ban	269	7-307	Bangladesh	427*	148	Aus by 3 wickets	RT Ponting
Chittagong	Ban	4d-581	-	Bangladesh	197*	304	Aus by inns & 80 runs	RT Ponting
2006–07 in Australia								
Brisbane	Aus	9d-602*	1d-202	England	157	370	Aus by 277 runs	RT Ponting
Adelaide	Eng	513	4-168	England	6d-551*	129	Aus by 6 wickets	RT Ponting
Perth	Aus	244*	5d-527	England	215	350	Aus by 206 runs	RT Ponting
Melbourne	Eng	419	-	England	159*	161	Aus by an inns & 99 runs	RT Ponting
Sydney	Eng	393	0-46	England	291*	147	Aus by 10 wickets	RT Ponting
2007–08 in Australia								
Brisbane	SL	4d-551*	-	Sri Lanka	211	300	Aus by an inns & 40 runs	RT Ponting
Hobart	Aus	5d-542*	2d-210	Sri Lanka	246	410	Aus by 96 runs	RT Ponting
Melbourne	Aus	343*	7d-351	India	196	161	Aus by 337 runs	RT Ponting
Sydney	Aus	463*	7d-401	India	532	210	Aus by 122 runs	RT Ponting
Perth	Ind	212	340	India	330*	294	Ind by 72 runs	RT Ponting
Adelaide	Ind	563	-	India	526*	7d-269	Drawn	RT Ponting
2007–08 in West Indies								
Kingston	Aus	431*	167	West Indies	312	191	Aus by 95 runs	RT Ponting
North Sound	Aus	7d-479*	6d-244	West Indies	352	5-266	Drawn	RT Ponting
Bridgetown	WI	251*	5d-439	West Indies	216	387	Aus by 87 runs	RT Ponting
2008–08 in India								
Bangalore	Aus	430*	6d-228	India	360	4-177	Drawn	RT Ponting
Chandigarh	Ind	268	195	India	469*	3d-314	Ind by 320 runs	RT Ponting
Delhi	Ind	577	0-31	India	7d-613*	5d-208	Drawn	RT Ponting
Nagpur	Ind	355	209	India	441*	295	Ind by 173 runs	RT Ponting
2008–09 in Australia								
Brisbane	NZ	214*	268	New Zealand	156	177	Aus by 149 runs	RT Ponting
Adelaide	NZ	535	-	New Zealand	270*	203	Aus by an inns & 62 runs	RT Ponting
Perth	SAf	375*	319	South Africa	281	4-414	SAf by 6 wickets	RT Ponting
Melbourne	Aus	394*	247	South Africa	459	1-183	SAf by 9 wickets	RT Ponting
Sydney	Aus	445*	4d-257	South Africa	9d-327	272	Aus by 103 runs	RT Ponting

(* denotes team batting first)

MOST RUNS AGAINST AUSTRALIA

Batsman	M	Inn	NO	Runs	Best	50	100	Avrge	Stk/Rt
BC Lara (WI)	30	56	2	2798	277	10	9	51.81	61.67
SR Tendulkar (Ind)	24	46	5	2380	241*	11	8	58.05	60.47
VVS Laxman (Ind)	24	44	4	2204	281	10	6	55.10	54.98
RS Dravid (Ind)	27	50	5	1860	233	11	2	41.33	39.30
MA Butcher (Eng)	20	40	1	1287	173*	4	3	33.00	46.55
AJ Stewart (Eng)	28	55	6	1586	107	11	1	32.37	57.15
N Hussain (Eng)	23	45	4	1581	207	11	2	38.56	42.58

Batsman	M	Inn	NO	Runs	Best	50	100	Avrge	Stk/Rt
MA Atherton (Eng)	26	52	1	1548	99	14	0	30.35	39.36
V Sehwag (Ind)	15	30	1	1483	195	7	3	51.14	74.75
SC Ganguly (Ind)	24	44	4	1403	144	7	2	35.08	52.57
JH Kallis (SAf)	21	40	4	1375	114	7	3	38.19	42.60
GP Thorpe (Eng)	16	31	4	1235	138	8	3	45.74	49.11
S Chanderpaul (WI)	15	29	4	1210	118	7	4	48.40	45.37
G Kirsten (SAf)	18	34	1	1134	153	5	2	34.36	39.94
ME Trescothick (Eng)	15	30	1013	-	90	7	-	33.77	59.38

HIGHEST AVERAGE AGAINST AUSTRALIA

Batsman	M	Inn	NO	Runs	Best	50	100	Avrge	Stk/Rt
Saeed Anwar (Pak)	8	15	-	886	145	5	3	59.07	54.36
SR Tendulkar (Ind)	24	46	5	2380	241*	11	8	58.05	60.47
Salim Malik (Pak)	8	14	1	749	237	2	2	57.62	50.10
Ijaz Ahmed (Pak)	8	15	2	733	155	1	4	56.38	49.29
VVS Laxman (Ind)	24	44	4	2204	281	10	6	55.10	54.98
KP Pietersen (Eng)	10	20	2	963	158	6	2	53.50	57.56
BC Lara (WI)	30	56	2	2798	277	10	9	51.81	61.67
V Sehwag (Ind)	15	30	1	1483	195	7	3	51.14	74.75
KR Rutherford (NZ)	6	12	1	548	102	4	1	49.82	52.44
S Chanderpaul (WI)	15	29	4	1210	118	7	4	48.40	45.37

(Qualification: 10 innings)

AUSTRALIAN BATSMEN

Batsman	M	Inn	NO	Runs	Best	50	100	Avrge	Stk/Rt
RT Ponting	128	215	26	10750	257	44	37	56.88	59.02
SR Waugh	124	193	35	8830	200	37	29	55.89	48.43
ML Hayden	103	184	14	8625	380	29	30	50.74	60.12
JL Langer	105	182	12	7696	250	30	23	45.27	54.24
ME Waugh	114	186	15	7331	153*	44	18	42.87	52.27
AC Gilchrist	96	137	20	5570	204*	26	17	47.61	81.97
MJ Slater	74	131	7	5312	219	21	14	42.84	53.36
MA Taylor	71	124	9	4683	334*	23	11	40.72	41.74
DR Martyn	67	109	14	4406	165	23	13	46.38	51.47
IA Healy	80	124	19	3138	161*	16	4	29.89	51.38
MJ Clarke	44	70	8	3063	151	12	10	49.40	52.74
SK Warne	141	192	16	3060	99	12	-	17.39	58.98
MEK Hussey	34	58	9	2909	182	13	9	59.37	49.17
DC Boon	41	69	8	2723	164*	12	8	44.64	40.94
GS Blewett	46	79	4	2552	214	15	4	34.03	41.26
SM Katich	35	60	5	2389	157	13	6	43.44	49.76
DS Lehmann	27	42	2	1798	177	10	5	44.95	61.85
A Symonds	26	41	5	1462	162*	10	2	40.61	64.80
B Lee	76	90	18	1451	64	5	-	20.15	52.96
AR Border	23	35	2	1399	200*	7	3	42.39	39.45
JN Gillespie	71	93	28	1218	201*	2	1	18.74	31.94
MTG Elliott	21	36	1	1172	199	4	3	33.49	44.29
PR Reiffel	34	49	14	946	79*	6	-	27.03	47.11
PA Jaques	11	19	-	902	150	6	3	47.47	54.24
MG Bevan	18	30	3	785	91	6	-	29.07	39.79
BJ Haddin	12	21	2	736	169	1	1	38.74	51.43

Batsman	M	Inn	NO	Runs	Best	50	100	Avrge	Stk/Rt
GD McGrath	124	138	51	641	61	1	-	7.37	40.64
BJ Hodge	6	11	2	503	203*	2	1	55.89	52.12
MS Kasprowicz	38	54	12	445	25	-	-	10.60	45.88
MG Johnson	18	23	6	439	64	2	-	25.82	54.67
CJ McDermott	32	36	8	358	35	-	-	12.79	69.11
AJ Bichel	19	22	1	355	71	1	-	16.90	64.08
SCG MacGill	44	47	11	349	43	-	-	9.69	48.81
MG Hughes	16	21	3	344	45	-	-	19.11	47.65
DW Fleming	20	19	3	305	71*	2	-	19.06	52.32
SR Watson	8	13	-	257	78	1	-	19.77	41.99
ML Love	5	8	3	233	100*	1	1	46.60	48.95
SR Clark	22	23	7	210	39	-	-	13.13	65.00
GB Hogg	7	10	3	186	79	1	-	26.57	49.60
CR Miller	18	24	3	174	43	-	-	8.29	56.68
CL White	4	7	2	146	46	-	-	29.20	44.24
GR Robertson	4	7	-	140	57	1	-	20.00	33.73
TBA May	17	18	8	135	42*	-	-	13.50	25.96
BP Julian	7	9	1	128	56*	1	-	16.00	47.58
GRJ Matthews	2	3	-	109	79	1	-	36.33	36.45
PM Siddle	4	7	2	75	23	-	-	15.00	44.91
NM Hauritz	4	6	-	72	41	-	-	12.00	56.25
JJ Krejza	2	4	1	71	32	-	-	23.67	48.63
NW Bracken	5	6	2	70	37	-	-	17.50	62.50
SG Law	1	1	1	54	54*	1	-	-	45.76
J Angel	4	7	1	35	11	-	-	5.83	28.69
BA Williams	4	6	3	23	10*	-	-	7.67	56.10
PE McIntyre	2	4	1	22	16	-	-	7.33	23.66
SW Tait	3	5	2	20	8	-	-	6.67	43.48
CJL Rogers	1	2	-	19	15	-	-	9.50	70.37
AB McDonald	1	1	-	15	15	-	-	15.00	27.78
MJ Nicholson	1	2	-	14	9	-	-	7.00	29.79
MR Whitney	1	2	-	13	13	-	-	6.50	48.15
B Casson	1	1	-	10	10	-	-	10.00	22.73
PA Emery	1	1	1	8	8*	-	-	-	30.77
SA Muller	2	2	2	6	6*	-	-	-	33.15
AC Dale	2	3	-	6	5	-	-	2.00	31.58
S Young	1	2	1	4	4*	-	-	4.00	14.81
SH Cook	2	2	2	3	3*	-	-	-	16.67
BA Reid	1	2	1	2	1*	-	-	2.00	10.00
DE Bollinger	1	1	1	0	0*	-	-	-	0.00
P Wilson	1	2	2	0	0*	-	-	-	0.00
DJ Cullen	1	-	-	-	-	-	-	-	-

DOUBLE CENTURIES AGAINST AUSTRALIA

281	VVS Laxman (Ind)	Kolkata	2000–01
277	BC Lara (WI)	Sydney	1992–93
241*	SR Tendulkar (Ind)	Sydney	2003–04
237	Salim Malik (Pak)	Rawalpindi	1994–95
233	RS Dravid (Ind)	Adelaide	2003–04
226	BC Lara (WI)	Adelaide	2005–06
213	BC Lara (WI)	Kingston	1998–99
207	N Hussain (Eng)	Birmingham	1997

206	PD Collingwood (Eng)	Adelaide	2006–07
206	G Gambhir (Ind)	Delhi	2008–09
200*	VVS Laxman (Ind)	Delhi	2008–09

AUSTRALIAN DOUBLE CENTURIES

380	ML Hayden	v Zimbabwe at Perth, 2003–04
334*	MA Taylor	v Pakistan at Peshawar, 1998–99
257	RT Ponting	v India at Melbourne, 2003–04
250	JL Langer	v England at Melbourne, 2002–03
242	RT Ponting	v India at Adelaide, 2003–04
223	JL Langer	v India at Sydney, 1999–2000
219	MJ Slater	v Sri Lanka at Perth, 1995–96
215	JL Langer	v New Zealand at Adelaide, 2004–05
214	GS Blewett	v South Africa at Johannesburg, 1996–97
207	RT Ponting	v Pakistan at Sydney, 2004–05
206	RT Ponting	v West Indies at Port-of-Spain, 2002–03
204*	AC Gilchrist	v South Africa at Johannesburg, 2001–02
203	ML Hayden	v India at Chennai, 2000–01
203*	BJ Hodge	v South Africa at Perth, 2005–06
200*	AR Border	v England at Leeds, 1993
201*	JN Gillespie	v Bangladesh at Chittagong, 2005–06
200	SR Waugh	v West Indies at Kingston, 1994–95

MOST WICKETS AGAINST AUSTRALIA

Bowler	M	Overs	Mdns	Runs	Wkts	Avrge	5Wi	10wm	Best	RPO
AR Kumble (Ind)	20	1086	180	3366	111	30.32	10	2	8-141	3.10
CA Walsh (WI)	22	899.1	189	2448	86	28.47	4	-	6-54	2.72
Harbhajan Singh (Ind)	14	747.4	131	2277	79	28.82	7	3	8-84	3.05
CEL Ambrose (WI)	16	644.4	174	1548	77	20.10	6	1	7-25	2.40
D Gough (Eng)	17	651.3	124	2280	74	30.81	4	-	6-49	3.50
AR Caddick (Eng)	18	681.3	107	2560	64	40.00	4	1	7-94	3.76
DL Vettori (NZ)	16	687.1	141	2014	57	35.33	6	1	7-87	2.93
M Muralidaran (SL)	11	612.2	88	1903	55	34.60	5	1	6-59	3.11
AA Donald (SAf)	14	544.2	116	1647	53	31.08	2	-	6-59	3.03
M Ntini (SAf)	12	465	82	1675	48	34.90	2	1	6-100	3.60

BEST BOWLING AVERAGE AGAINST AUSTRALIA

Bowler	M	Overs	Mdns	Runs	Wkts	Avrge	5Wi	10wm	Best	RPO
CEL Ambrose (WI)	16	644.4	174	1548	77	20.10	6	1	7/25	2.40
IR Bishop (WI)	9	322.3	60	881	39	22.59	1	-	6/40	2.73
DW Headley (Eng)	6	252.5	40	867	35	24.77	1	-	6/60	3.43
CA Walsh (WI)	22	899.1	189	2448	86	28.47	4	-	6/54	2.72
Harbhajan Singh (Ind)	14	747.4	131	2277	79	28.82	7	3	8/84	3.05
Wasim Akram (Pak)	10	362.4	65	970	33	29.39	1	-	5/63	2.67
A Flintoff (Eng)	11	365	55	1243	42	29.60	1	-	5/78	3.41
AR Kumble (Ind)	20	1086	180	3366	111	30.32	10	2	8/141	3.10
D Gough (Eng)	17	651.3	124	2280	74	30.81	4	-	6/49	3.50
AA Donald (SAf)	14	544.2	116	1647	53	31.08	2	-	6/59	3.03

(Qualification: 30 wickets)

AUSTRALIAN BOWLERS

Bowler	M	Overs	Mdns	Runs	Wkts	Avrge	5Wi	10wm	Best	RPO
SK Warne	141	6677.5	1744	17609	704	25.01	37	10	8-71	2.64
GD McGrath	124	4874.4	1471	12186	563	21.64	29	3	8-24	2.50
B Lee	76	2755.1	547	9554	310	30.82	10	-	5-30	3.47
JN Gillespie	71	2372.2	629	6770	259	26.14	8	-	7-37	2.85
SCG MacGill	44	1872.5	366	6038	208	29.03	12	2	8-108	3.22
CJ McDermott	32	1247.4	291	3661	124	29.52	5	-	6-38	2.93
MS Kasprowicz	38	1190	245	3716	113	32.88	4	-	7-36	3.12
PR Reiffel	34	1039.1	273	2724	102	26.71	5	-	6-71	2.62
SR Clark	22	810.4	218	2067	90	22.97	2	-	5-32	2.55
MG Johnson	18	746.2	145	2233	78	28.63	2	1	8-61	2.99
DW Fleming	20	688.1	153	1942	75	25.89	3	-	5-30	2.82
CR Miller	18	681.5	163	1805	69	26.16	3	1	5-32	2.65
MG Hughes	16	644	159	1863	68	27.40	2	-	5-64	2.89
AJ Bichel	19	556.1	112	1870	58	32.24	1	-	5-60	3.36
TBA May	17	763.2	234	1711	50	34.22	3	-	5-9	2.24
SR Waugh	124	621.3	172	1465	48	30.52	1	-	5-28	2.36
ME Waugh	114	677.5	140	2037	48	42.44	1	-	5-40	3.01
MG Bevan	18	214.1	30	703	29	24.24	1	1	6-82	3.28
A Symonds	26	349	81	896	24	37.33	-	-	3-50	2.57
MJ Clarke	44	236.4	40	680	18	37.78	1	-	6-9	2.87
PM Siddle	4	188.4	50	532	17	31.29	1	-	5-59	2.82
GB Hogg	7	254	40	933	17	54.88	-	-	2-40	3.67
DS Lehmann	27	162.2	36	412	15	27.47	-	-	3-42	2.54
BP Julian	7	183	43	599	15	39.93	-	-	4-36	3.27
NM Hauritz	4	168	44	452	14	32.29	-	-	3-16	2.69
SR Watson	8	161.4	28	498	14	35.57	-	-	4-42	3.08
GS Blewett	46	239.2	60	720	14	51.43	-	-	2-9	3.01
SM Katich	35	128.5	13	479	13	36.85	1	-	6-65	3.72
GR Robertson	4	149.4	20	515	13	39.62	-	-	4-72	3.44
JJ Krejza	2	123.5	8	562	13	43.23	1	1	8-215	4.54
NW Bracken	5	185	53	505	12	42.08	-	-	4-48	2.73
J Angel	4	124.4	22	463	10	46.30	-	-	3-54	3.71
BA Williams	4	142	43	406	9	45.11	-	-	4-53	2.86
SH Cook	2	37.2	10	142	7	20.29	1	-	5-39	3.80
BA Reid	1	53	9	151	7	21.57	1	-	5-112	2.85
SA Muller	2	58	8	258	7	36.86	-	-	3-68	4.45
AC Dale	2	58	19	187	6	31.17	-	-	3-71	3.22
PE McIntyre	2	65.3	10	194	5	38.80	-	-	3-103	2.96
RT Ponting	128	89.5	23	242	5	48.40	-	-	1-0	2.69
SW Tait	3	69	6	302	5	60.40	-	-	3-97	4.38
CL White	4	93	8	342	5	68.40	-	-	2-71	3.68
MJ Nicholson	1	25	4	115	4	28.75	-	-	3-56	4.60
GRJ Matthews	2	99	28	228	4	57.00	-	-	2-169	2.30
AB McDonald	1	35	14	73	3	24.33	-	-	2-32	2.09
B Casson	1	32	4	129	3	43.00	-	-	3-86	4.03
MR Whitney	1	23	6	59	2	29.50	-	-	1-27	2.57
DE Bollinger	1	44	9	131	2	65.50	-	-	2-53	2.98
DR Martyn	67	58	16	168	2	84.00	-	-	1-0	2.90
MJ Slater	74	4.1	1	10	1	10.00	-	-	1-4	2.40
MA Taylor	71	7	3	26	1	26.00	-	-	1-11	3.71
DJ Cullen	1	14	-	54	1	54.00	-	-	1-25	3.86

Bowler	M	Overs	Mdns	Runs	Wkts	Avrge	5Wi	10wm	Best	RPO
MEK Hussey	34	28	4	100	1	100.00	-	-	1-22	3.57
AR Border	23	78	30	135	1	135.00	-	-	1-16	1.73
P Wilson	1	12	2	50	0	-	-	-	-	4.17
ML Hayden	103	9	-	40	0	-	-	-	-	4.44
S Young	1	8	3	13	0	-	-	-	-	1.63
SG Law	1	3	1	9	0	-	-	-	-	3.00
DC Boon	41	4	2	9	0	-	-	-	-	2.25
BJ Hodge	6	2	-	8	0	-	-	-	-	4.00
MTG Elliott	21	2	1	4	0	-	-	-	-	2.00
JL Langer	105	1	-	3	0	-	-	-	-	3.00

BEST BOWLING IN AN INNINGS AGAINST AUSTRALIA

8-84	Harbhajan Singh (Ind)	Chennai	2000–01
8-141	AR Kumble (Ind)	Sydney	2003–04
7-25	CEL Ambrose (WI)	Perth	1992–93
7-48	AR Kumble (Ind)	Chennai	2004–05
7-66	PCR Tufnell (Eng)	The Oval	1997
7-78	JJC Lawson (WI)	St John's	2002–03
7-87	SM Pollock (SAf)	Adelaide	1997–98
7-87	DL Vettori (NZ)	Auckland	1999–2000
7-89	DK Morrison (NZ)	Wellington	1992–93
7-94	AR Caddick (Eng)	Sydney	2002–03

BEST BOWLING IN AN INNINGS BY AUSTRALIA

8-24	GD McGrath	v Pakistan at Perth, 2004–05
8-38	GD McGrath	v England at Lord's, 1997
8-61	MG Johnson	v South Africa at Perth, 2008–09
8-71	SK Warne	v England at Brisbane, 1994–95
8-108	SCG MacGill	v Bangladesh at Fatullah, 2005–06
8-215	JJ Krejza	v India at Nagpur, 2008–09
7-23	SK Warne	v Pakistan at Brisbane, 1995–96
7-36	MS Kasprowicz	v England at The Oval, 1997
7-37	JN Gillespie	v England at Leeds, 1997
7-39	MS Kasprowicz	v Sri Lanka at Darwin, 2003–04

BEST BOWLING IN A TEST AGAINST AUSTRALIA

15-217	Harbhajan Singh (Ind)	Chennai	2000–01
13-181	AR Kumble (Ind)	Chennai	2004–05
13-196	Harbhajan Singh (Ind)	Kolkata	2000–01
12-149	DL Vettori (NZ)	Auckland	1999–2000
12-279	AR Kumble (Ind)	Sydney	2003–04
11-93	PCR Tufnell (Eng)	The Oval	1997
11-212	M Muralidaran (SL)	Galle	2003–04
11-224	Harbhajan Singh (Ind)	Bangalore	2004–05
10-120	CEL Ambrose (WI)	Adelaide	1992–93
10-123	PS De Villiers (SAf)	Sydney	1993–94

BEST BOWLING IN A TEST FOR AUSTRALIA

12-107	SCG MacGill	v England at Sydney, 1998–99
12-128	SK Warne	v South Africa at Sydney, 1993–94
12-246	SK Warne	v England at The Oval, 2005
12-358	JJ Krejza	v India at Nagpur, 2008–09

11-77	SK Warne	v Pakistan at Brisbane, 1995–96
11-109	SK Warne	v South Africa at Sydney, 1997–98
11-110	SK Warne	v England at Brisbane, 1994–95
11-159	MG Johnson	v South Africa at Perth, 2008–09
11-188	SK Warne	v Pakistan at Colombo, 2002–03
11-229	SK Warne	v England at The Oval, 2001

MOST CONSECUTIVE WINS

16	Australia	(Harare 1999–2000 to Mumbai 2000–01)
12	Australia	(Melbourne 2005–06 to Sydney 2006–07)
11	West Indies	(Bridgetown 1983–84 to Adelaide 1984–85)
9	Sri Lanka	(Colombo 2001–02 to Lahore 2001–02)
9	South Africa	(Durban 2001–02 to Dhaka 2002–03)
8	Australia	(Sydney 1920–21 to Leeds 1921)
8	England	(Lord's 2004 to Port Elizabeth 2004–05)

MOST CONSECUTIVE TESTS WITHOUT DEFEAT

27	West Indies	(Sydney 1981–82 to Melbourne 1984–85)
26	England	(Lord's 1968 to Manchester 1971)
25	Australia	(Wellington 1945–46 to Adelaide 1950–51)
18	England	(Christchurch 1958–59 to Birmingham 2000–01)
18	Australia	(Galle 1999–2000 to Mumbai 2000–01)
17	Australia	(Madras 1956–57 to Delhi 1959–60)
17	India	(Kandy 1985–86 to Ahmedabad 1986–87)
17	Australia	(Melbourne 2005–06 to Sydney 2006–07)

1948 AUSTRALIAN INVINCIBLES

Batsman	M	Inn	NO	Runs	Best	50	100	Avrge
AR Morris	5	9	1	696	196	3	3	87.00
DG Bradman	5	9	2	508	173*	1	2	72.57
SG Barnes	4	6	2	329	141	3	1	82.25
AL Hassett	5	8	1	310	137	-	1	44.29
RN Harvey	2	3	1	133	112	-	1	66.50
SJE Loxton	3	3	-	144	93	1	-	48.00
RR Lindwall	5	6	-	191	77	1	-	31.83
KR Miller	5	7	-	184	74	2	-	26.29
D Tallon	4	4	-	112	53	1	-	28.00
WA Brown	2	3	-	73	32	-	-	24.33
ERH Toshack	4	4	3	51	20*	-	-	51.00
WA Johnston	5	5	2	62	29	-	-	20.67
IWG Johnson	4	6	1	51	21	-	-	10.20
DT Ring	1	1	-	9	9	-	-	9.00
RA Saggers	1	1	-	5	5	-	-	5.00

Bowler	M	Overs	Mdns	Runs	Wkts	Avrge	5Wi	10wm	Best	RPO
RR Lindwall	5	222.5	57	530	27	19.63	2	-	6-20	2.38
WA Johnston	5	309.2	91	630	27	23.33	1	-	5-36	2.04
KR Miller	5	138.1	43	301	13	23.15	-	-	4-125	2.18
ERH Toshack	4	173.1	70	364	11	33.09	1	-	5-40	2.10
IWG Johnson	4	183	60	427	7	61.00	-	-	3-72	2.33
SJE Loxton	3	63	11	148	3	49.33	-	-	3-55	2.35
DT Ring	1	28	13	44	1	44.00	-	-	1-44	1.57
SG Barnes	4	5	2	11	0	-	-	-	-	2.20
AR Morris	5	8	1	24	0	-	-	-	-	3.00

WEST INDIES
(Qualification: 1973 in England to 1994–95 in New Zealand)

Batsman	M	Inn	NO	Runs	Best	50	100	Avrge
IVA Richards	121	182	12	8540	291	45	24	50.24
CG Greenidge	108	185	15	7558	226	34	19	44.46
DL Haynes	116	202	25	7487	184	39	18	42.30
CH Lloyd	82	123	10	5698	242*	30	15	50.42
RB Richardson	76	130	11	5445	194	25	15	45.76
AI Kallicharran	59	97	8	3886	187	18	10	43.66
PJL Dujon	81	115	11	3322	139	16	5	31.94
HA Gomes	60	91	11	3171	143	13	9	39.64
RC Fredericks	35	62	5	2699	169	16	7	47.35
AL Logie	52	78	9	2470	130	16	2	35.80
CL Hooper	43	73	6	2094	178*	10	4	31.25
BC Lara	21	34	-	1975	375	10	4	58.09
MD Marshall	81	107	11	1810	92	10	0	18.85
DL Murray	48	72	6	1614	91	10	0	24.45
LG Rowe	23	39	1	1532	302	5	5	40.32
JC Adams	14	21	6	1296	174*	6	4	86.40
KLT Arthurton	25	39	5	1149	157*	7	2	33.79

Bowler	M	Overs	Mdns	Runs	Wkts	Avrge	5Wi	10wm	Best	RPO
MD Marshall	81	2930.4	615	7876	376	20.95	22	4	7-22	2.69
J Garner	58	2195.5	576	5433	259	20.98	7	-	6-56	2.47
CA Walsh	70	2409.1	511	6317	255	24.77	9	2	7-37	2.62
MA Holding	60	2113.2	459	5898	249	23.69	13	2	8-92	2.79
CEL Ambrose	50	2026.1	527	4730	224	21.12	11	3	8-45	2.33
AME Roberts	47	1855.5	382	5174	202	25.61	11	2	7-54	2.79
CEH Croft	27	1027.3	211	2913	125	23.30	3	-	8-29	2.84
BP Patterson	28	804.5	109	2874	93	30.90	5	-	5-24	3.57
IR Bishop	18	652	151	1698	83	20.46	5	-	6-40	2.60
VA Holder	27	1002.4	207	2540	78	32.56	3	-	6-28	2.53
WKM Benjamin	17	518.2	120	1357	52	26.10	0	-	4-46	2.62
BD Julien	24	757	192	1868	50	37.36	1	-	5-57	2.47

BIBLIOGRAPHY

Baum G, *The Waugh Era: The making of a cricket empire 1999–2004*, ABC Books, 2004.

Boon D, *Under the Southern Cross: The autobiography of David Boon*, HarperSports, 1996.

Border A, *Beyond Ten Thousand: My life story*, Swan Publishing, 1993.

Chappell, I, *A Golden Age: Australian cricket's two decades at the top*, Pan Macmillan, 2006.

Coward M, *Cricket Beyond the Bazaar*, Allen & Unwin, 1990.

Gilchrist A, *Walking to Victory: A personal story of the Ashes and World Cup campaigns 2002–03*, Pan Macmillan, 2003.

——, *True Colours: My life*, Pan Macmillan, 2008.

Haigh G, *The Border Years*, Text, 1994.

——, *One Summer, Every Summer*, Text, 1995.

——, *The Summer Game*, Text, 1997.

—— (ed), *Endless Summer: 140 years of Australian cricket in Wisden*, Hardie Grant Books, 2002.

——, *A Fair Field and No Favour: The Ashes 2005*, Scribe, 2005.

——, *The Green & Golden Age: Writings on Australian cricket today*, Black Inc, 2007.

Hair D, *Decision Maker: An umpire's story*, Random House, 1998.

Healy I, *Hands & Heals: The autobiography*, HarperSports, 2000.

Knight J, *Mark Waugh: The biography*, HarperSports, 2002.

Knox M, *Taylor & Beyond*, ABC Books, 2000.

Langer J, *Power of Passion: The Justin Langer story*, Swan Sport, 2002.

—, *Seeing the Sunrise*, Allen & Unwin, 2008.

Lara B, *Beating the Field: My own story*, Patridge Press, 1995.

Maxwell J, *Stumps*, Hardie Grant Books, 2001.

McDermott C, *McDermott: Strike bowler*, ABC Books, 1992.

Miller A (ed), *Allan's Cricket Annual*, Allan Miller, 1996–99.

Nowra L, *Warne's World*, Duffy & Snellgrove, 2002.

Piesse K, *The Taylor Years*, Viking, 1999.

Ponting R and Murgatroyd B, *Ricky Ponting's World Cup Diary*, HarperSports, 2003.

—, *A Captain's Diary: My first year*, HarperSports, 2004.

—, *Ashes Diary 2005*, HarperSports, 2005.

Ponting, R, *Captain's Diary 2007*, HarperSports, 2007.

—, *Captain's Diary 2008*, HarperSports, 2008.

Ray M, *Border & Beyond*, ABC Books, 1995.

—, *Cricket Masala*, ABC Books, 2002.

Reiffel P and Baum G, *Reiffel: Inside out*, HarperSports, 1999.

Roebuck P, *Sometimes I Forgot to Laugh*, Allen & Unwin, 2004.

Ryan C, *Golden Boy: Kim Hughes and the bad old days of Australian cricket*, Allen & Unwin, 2009.

Simpson B, *The Reasons Why: A decade of coaching, a lifetime of cricket*, HarperSports, 1996.

Slater M, *Slats: The Michael Slater story*, Random House, 2005.

Symonds A and Gray S, *Roy: Going for broke*, Hardie Grant Books, 2006.

Taylor M, *Mark Taylor: A captain's year*, Ironbark Press, 1997.

—, *Time to Declare: An autobiography*, Ironbark Press, 1999.

The Wisden Cricketer, *Story of the Ashes: Cricket's greatest rivalry by the writers who were there*, Wisden Cricketer Publishing, 2009.

Warne S, *Shane Warne: My own story*, Swan Publishing, 1997.

—, *My Autobiography*, Hodder & Stoughton, 2001.

Waugh S, *West Indies Tour Diary*, HarperSports, 1995.

——, *World Cup Diary*, HarperSports, 1996.

——, *No Regrets: A captain's diary*, HarperSports, 1999.

——, *Never Satisfied*, HarperSports, 2000.

——, *Ashes Diary 2001*, HarperSports, 2001.

——, *Captain's Diary 2002*, HarperSports, 2002.

——, *Never Say Die*, HarperSports, 2003.

——, *Out of My Comfort Zone: The autobiography*, Viking, 2005.

Wisden Cricketers' Almanack, John Wisden & Sons, 1992–2008.

Wisden Cricketers' Almanack Australia, Hardie Grant Books, 1998–2005.

ACKNOWLEDGEMENTS

Big thanks to the team of people, all of them essential, who helped put this book together: Sandy Grant, Lyn Tranter, Emma Schwarcz, Megan Taylor, Warwick Franks, Chris Ryan, Ross Dundas, Luke Causby, Josh Durham, Lynne Hamilton, Jane Winning and Keiran Rogers.

Also to the colleagues, both on tour and in various offices, who turned up the brightness on the business of writing about cricket. Among many others, special thanks to Greg Baum, Martin Blake, Ken Casellas, Ben Coady, Malcolm Conn, Robert Craddock, Peter Deeley, Michael Donaldson, Michael Koslowski, Tim Lane, Jim Maxwell, Steve Meacham, Fazeer Mohammed, Mark Ray, Peter Roebuck, Chris Ryan (again), Will Swanton, Phil Wilkins and most of all Mike Coward.

The line referring to Allan Border and his cape on page 83 is gratefully adapted from Les Carlyon.

INDEX

White, Craig 306
Williams, Brad 354
Williams, Stuart 74, 79, 83
Wilson, Paul 150, 152, 158
Woolmer, Bob 111, 115, 139–40, 199, 203
World Cup
    1996 v Sri Lanka (Lahore) 97–101
    1999 v South Africa (Edgbaston) 200–9
    2003 v India (Port Elizabeth) 309–12

Yousuf Youhana 166, 218, 219
Zaheer Abbas 55
Zaheer Khan 246, 255, 329
Zimbabwe 232, 324
Zoehrer, Tim 22, 139, 217, 293
Zoysa, Nuwan 323